TONICS

Also by Robert A. Barnett

The Guilt-Free Comfort Food Cookbook
The American Health Food Book

TONICS

MORE THAN 100 RECIPES THAT IMPROVE THE BODY AND THE MIND

ROBERT A. BARNETT

HarperPerennial
A Division of HarperCollins*Publishers*

This is a book of journalism, not medicine. It is intended for education, not treatment. The information and recipes are provided to edify and to entertain, and to encourage the adoption of a more healthful lifestyle. If you have a medical concern, bring it to a qualified health care practitioner. If you believe some of the information and recipes in this book may be helpful for your condition, bring that to the attention of your practitioner and begin a dialogue.

HarperCollins books may be purchased for educational, business, or sales promotional use. For information please write: Special Markets Department, HarperCollins Publishers, Inc., 10 East 53rd Street, New York, NY 10022.

FIRST EDITION

Designed by Joseph Rutt

Library of Congress Cataloging-in-Publication Data

Barnett, Robert A.
    Tonics : more than 100 recipes that improve the body and the mind / Robert A. Barnett. — 1st ed.
        p.   cm.
    Includes index.
    ISBN 0-06-095111-7
    1. Tonics (Medicinal preparations). 2. Diet therapy.   I. Title.
RM217.B37   1997
615'.321—dc20   96-38357

---

97 98 99 00 01 ❖/HC 10 9 8 7 6 5 4 3

To Chris, my tonic

CONTENTS

ACKNOWLEDGMENTS

First thanks go to Stephana Bottom, who helped develop the recipes. Every other Saturday or so, for more than a year, Stephana and I would meet in the Starbucks at 102nd Street and Broadway, drink hot cider, and share ideas and food.

I would bring books and notes, and sometimes ingredients; she would bring not only notes but soups, liqueurs, drinks, and dishes for me to take home and taste. When we first went together to Chinese grocery stores on Canal Street that sold herbs such as ginseng and astragalus, they were exotic; through her work, they became delicious. She was unfailing in her enthusiasm, her willingness to explore ingredients no matter how strange, and her focus on what real people might actually want to make and consume. When a recipe wasn't working, she was dogged in her determination to experiment until it did. When an ingredient, exotic or common, revealed a new taste possibility, she was infectious in her enthusiasm. She is that rare combination, creative and careful. (Stephana, in turn, extends her sincere thanks to her "unparalleled" teacher, Barbara Kafka, her fellow food editor, Susan Sugarman, and her husband, Duncan Webb, the "real bread maker," for putting up with a "kitchen strewn with Chinese herbs and flax seeds.")

I am deeply thankful for the generosity of the experts and healers who helped me learn about herbal medicine: acupuncturist Harriet Beinfield, L.Ac., herbalist Christopher Hobbs, and Chinese herbalist Jacqueline Sa each took valuable time to talk to me about the meaning of tonics, generally and specifically. Importer Ron Teeguarden gave me recipe ideas and hard-to-find contacts; importer Alan Lau dug through his huge warehouse to find a menu from his now-defunct Chinese herbal restaurant Imperial Palace. Herb industry spokesperson Mark Blumenthal gave me many contacts. Researcher Daniel Mowrey, Ph.D., spent hours with me on the phone; so did researcher Rob McCaleb, Ph.D., who always found a way to return my calls wherever he was. Andrew Weil, M.D., helped me separate the wheat from the chaff. Paul Stamets, Ph.D., set me right on "kombucha" and shared his knowledge of reishi and shiitake mushrooms. Writer Michael Castleman was generous in helping a fellow writer find contacts in San Francisco.

Botanist James Duke, Ph.D., a pioneer in the study of plant-based therapeutic compounds, gave me hours of his time on the phone and in his office, and on one occasion, put me up on his farm; he helped me see many connections, and see through hype. Natural drugs expert Varro Tyler, Ph.D., was always generous with his time in interviews, sharing his practical reading of the scientific literature. Daniel Bensky, D.O., walked me through the use of several Chinese tonic herbs and explained their use in traditional Chinese medicine. And when it came down to cooking these things in the kitchen, Nam Singh, an expert in Chinese food cures, gave me hours of his time in his kitchen plus a crucial recipe.

I would also like to thank the many researchers who were patient in explaining their work: Terry Leighton, Ph.D., on quercetin; Herb Benson, M.D., on meditation; Irwin Ziment, M.D., on chili peppers and garlic; Anthony Sebastian, M.D., on calcium; Michael Baker, M.D., on licorice; David Bailey, M.D., on grapefruit; Eric Block, Ph.D., Yu-Yan Yeh, Ph.D., Robert Lin, Ph.D., and John Pinto, M.D., on garlic; Jerry Avorn, M.D., on cranberries; Paul Talalay, M.D., on broccoli; Blair Justice, Ph.D., on friends; Artemis Simopoulos, M.D., and William E. Connors, M.D., on tuna, tofu, walnuts, and other sources of omega-3 fatty acids; Joseph Martarano, M.D., and Nicholas Bazan, M.D., on ginkgo; Alvin R. Loosli, M.D., on iron; Christina Benishim, Ph.D., and Edwin McClesky, Ph.D., on ginseng; Mark Messina, Ph.D., on tofu; Edward Giovannucci, M.D., on tomatoes; Allan H. Conney, Ph.D., on rosemary; Dennis Savaiano, Ph.D., and Barry Goldin, M.D., on yogurt.

For helping me understand the lovely epidemiological complexities of the Mediterranean and Asian diets, let me thank Marion Nestle, Ph.D., who opened her files; Walter C. Willett, M.D., for several interviews; Lawrence Kushi, Ph.D., for showing me the connections between what people eat in Iowa and in China; Anna Ferro-Lutzi, Ph.D., for giving me an Italian view of things; Serge Renaud, M.D., for a French view; Martti Karvonen, M.D., for a Finnish view; and Ancel Keys, Ph.D., and his wife, Margaret, for giving me several days in their sun-drenched home in Italy, serving up history, science, and wonderful tastes. And thanks to Greg Drescher, K. Dun Gifford, Sara Baer-Sinnott, and Nancy Harmon Jenkins, for helping me taste such foods firsthand.

A special thanks go to cookbook author Barbara Kafka, who introduced me to Stephana Bottom, who was then in her employ, and let me work with her. Restaurateur and author Barbara Tropp gave me her views of Chinese taste, encouraged me, and gave me contacts. Historian William Wos Weaver gave me his learned ideas about punch. John Martin Taylor taught me how to fry oysters.

I am grateful to my editor, Susan Friedland, who saw the promise in this idea from a little one-paragraph postscript in a long memo and encouraged me to develop it into a book proposal; to Kathy Martin, whose editorial acumen led me back from my wanderings to my core ideas, while retaining my words; to

Nancy Palmer Jones, whose copy-editing helped me avoid mistakes and clarify meanings; to Jennifer Griffin, for her patience in guiding me through deadlines. As for my trusted agent, Alice Martell, I want to thank her not only for helping me develop this project, but for her support over the years.

A personal thanks goes out to Margie Cohen, for letting me use her files on Lydia Pinkham, and for sharing her work; and to Janet Basu, for giving me her husband's mother's Indian tea recipe.

Finally, let me thank my wife, Chris, for seeing me through the writing of this book, putting up with lost days and nights, and helping ensure that in writing a book on health, I kept mine.

Many, named and unnamed, have helped me develop the ideas and recipes that have become this book. Any faults, of course, are mine alone.

PREFACE

"Where a cure can be obtained by diet, use no drugs, and avoid complex remedies where simple ones will suffice."

One might expect such a statement from a contemporary practitioner of alternative medicine, or perhaps from a physician who believes in prevention. It is older, however. Ar-Razi, an Arab Muslim physician, wrote this down about a thousand years ago. He was following an even older tradition—that of Hippocrates, the ancient Greek "father of medicine" (460–377 B.C.). Hippocrates is famous for many statements, including these two: "Let your food be your medicine," and "First, do no harm."

In *Green Pharmacy: The History and Evolution of Herbal Western Medicine*, historian Barbara Griggs contrasts the Hippocratic approach to healing with that of Galen. Hippocrates came first. "Like the great medical traditions of ancient China, India and Egypt," she writes, "Hippocratic medicine had stressed the idea of balance—mental, emotional and physical—as essential to health: disease was a disturbance of this balance, which it was the duty of the physician to restore, assisted by the patient's own natural powers of recuperation." Hippocratic medicine emphasizes a wholesome diet, exercise, fresh air, good climate, and the careful use of botanical medicines integrated into a healing plan.

Galen (A.D. 129–199), a surgeon to gladiators who eventually became personal physician to the emperor Marcus Aurelius, codified Hippocratic practice. What had begun as a democratic, patient-centered, holistic approach became rigid, imperial, and physician-centered. Galenic theory became the basis for medieval and early modern European medicine, creating "an elaborate and rigid system of medicine, which effectively paralysed European medical thinking for the next 1500 years," writes Griggs. Galenic medicine emphasized professionally trained physicians over amateur healers and herbalists. It was male, urban, professional, expensive, complex; most significantly, it focused on the doctor's drugs rather than on the patient's natural ability to heal. The amateur healer, writes Griggs, "expected his plants to do their work gently and thoroughly, but not necessarily quickly; every countryman knows that you cannot hurry nature. The professional doctor, on the other hand, confident in his superior knowledge, was also confident that he could hurry nature as much as he wished to."

Today, one sees both Galenic and Hippocratic influences in the healing arts. Where they pop up is not always predictable. Conventional medicine, with its specialization, obscurity, and expense, its emphasis on intervention rather than lifestyle, is often Galenic. Yet the individual physician who emphasizes that good health begins with healthful habits—not smoking, drinking only in moderation, engaging in physical activities for thirty minutes a day, consuming a diet low in saturated fat and high in fiber—is acting squarely in the tradition of Hippocrates.

Conversely, the "alternative" practitioner who diagnoses obscure ailments and prescribes expensive nostrums without helping the patient make healthful lifestyle changes may be more Galenic than he or she at first appears. The impetus to turn the simple into the complex, the common into the rare, and the sensible into the mysterious is not confined to conventional medicine.

Galen stalks the health food store as well. It was a revelation to me, as I wrote this book, to realize that nearly every commercial "tonic" I investigated had its origins in a food context—as a whole food simmered in a tea or broth or stew, even steeped in spirits or wine. It's not just garlic (see page 135) that tastes better and is probably better for you on the plate than in a pill. When tonic herbs flavor a chicken soup, they enhance an already restorative broth. In the Qingping market in the Chinese city of Guangzhou (Canton), one finds ginseng (page 161), astragalus (page 24), dioscorea (page 105), and other traditional tonic herbs right next to the dates, mushrooms, and beans and not far from the fresh greens, handmade noodles, and live fish. When one understands the traditions of tonic soups, the proximity of ginseng bundles and squirming carp in the marketplace becomes less surprising: they go into the same pot.

In her small shop called Roots and Legends, in Mill Valley, just north of San Francisco, Vietnam-born Chinese herbalist Jacqueline Sa sells small bags, each tied with a ribbon, that contain tonic herbs out of which to make soup. When I interviewed her, she served green tea. "The tradition of tonics comes from Taoism," she explained. "There is no extreme good or bad to anything. Everything is part of nature, a balance of yin and yang, day and night, light and darkness. When one's nature is cool, one eats hot foods. When one's nature is hot, one eats cool foods. The point is to stay in balance."

This book is my attempt to apply a Hippocratic approach to the study of foods and botanicals that may improve health. We now know enough about the pharmacology and nutritional impact of many foods and herbs to be able to connect contemporary scientific research to traditional use. Now we need to integrate this new information about specific substances into the broader context of nutrition, disease prevention, and a healthful lifestyle.

Tradition is an ally in this search. In societies where traditional medicine holds sway, there is an attempt to match the symptom to the person, the imbalance to the life, what one eats and drinks to how one feels. I believe many chronic health conditions can be substantially improved by the adoption of a wholesome diet, exercise both gentle and vigorous, an open heart, a willingness to make changes in one's priorities, a sense of optimism, and appropriate therapeutic consultation and intervention.

If I were sick, I would begin the process of healing by looking at the way I ate, moved, relaxed, enjoyed myself, thought, and felt. If I smoked, I would admit that making another effort to overcome this addiction was the best single thing I could do. If I had a problem with alcohol or drugs, I would attend to it and, if need be, seek help. If I were sedentary, I would take a walk every day for starters (see "Walking," page 289). I would look at my emotional life and pay attention to whether I had someone in my life whom I could trust and in whom I could confide (see "Friend," page 133). I would take time to sit quietly and breathe deeply, letting my thoughts come and go as they will (see "Breath," page 34).

Well before I started brewing special teas and taking supplements, I would pay attention to my diet. I would listen to Percy Bysshe Shelley, who wrote in the preface to *Queen Mab,* "There is no disease, bodily or mental, which adoption of a vegetable diet and pure water has not infallibly mitigated, wherever the experiment has been fairly tried."

Then I would seek out a health care practitioner with Hippocratic leanings and, working together, use what I had learned about the powers of fresh, whole foods and their extracts to restore health.

Tonics may help lead us back toward balance, but there are no magic bullets.

It is the whole that heals.

WHAT IS A TONIC?

A tonic is something—a food, an herb, a thought—that improves your well-being. It *tones*—hence the name. It helps restore balance to the body. It nourishes.

Rather than rectifying a specific problem, as a remedy does, a tonic supports health in many interrelated ways. It doesn't make you feel bad in the process of making you feel better.

There are many definitions of a tonic. In traditional Chinese medicine, a tonic supports normal functioning and often enhances immunity, while more specific herbs attack the root cause of a medical problem. In India's tradition of Ayurvedic medicine, the approach is similar: first purify, then tonify—that is, one eliminates the root cause of the illness, then strengthens the patient.

In the European tradition, tonics are quite different. They generally stimulate digestion; they are bitters. Bitter substances stimulate the liver to produce more bile acid salts, which help the body digest fats. Bitters also stimulate saliva and other digestive "juices." By improving the efficiency of the digestive process, European bitters or tonics often do improve one's energy and sense of well-being. (Our Spring Tonic, page 101, is in this tradition.)

Then there are more contemporary definitions. One influential one was crafted by Daniel B. Mowrey, who did pioneering work at Brigham Young University on the efficacy of ginger in treating motion sickness and who now runs the American Phytotherapy Laboratory. (Phytotherapy is the use of plants to improve health.) In his book *Herbal Tonic Therapies,* Dr. Mowrey defines a tonic as a substance that can help the body restore balance—in either direction. Ginseng, for example, can raise blood pressure in people with low blood pressure yet lower it in people with high blood pressure; it does so, perhaps, because it contains different compounds that have opposite effects. "A tonic is any substance that balances the biochemical and physiological events that comprise body systems," Dr. Mowrey writes. He outlines specific "tonics" for the immune system, the cardiovascular system, the nervous system, the digestive system, the musculoskeletal system, and the female and male reproductive systems, and takes a stab at "the concept of a whole body tonic."

Finally, there is common usage. Perhaps the word *tonic* makes you think of a drink. After all, there is the gin and tonic—which, containing quinine, did protect many of the English against malaria in India. There is Dr. Brown's Cel-Ray Tonic, a popular New York soda. (We propose our own celery "tonic" in the chapter on celery, page 60.) There is the hoary tradition of patent medicines, including the most famous of them all, Lydia Pinkham's Vegetable Compound. (We provide a recipe for an alcohol-based tonic with a nod toward Lydia in the chapter on fenugreek, page 118.) A tonic in this folk tradition is just about anything you take by mouth that makes you feel better and improves your health.

I have my own ideas about what constitutes a tonic, especially as it relates to nutrition and food, my main interests. I'll get to these in a moment. But I'm a journalist, not a health care professional, so rather than impose my concepts on you, I'd like to explore the many foods and herbs that have reputations as tonics in whatever tradition and see if I can understand, in terms of science, nutrition, history, and common sense, why they have this reputation.

One of the joys of the emerging era of complementary medicine—the use of traditional and alternative therapies as a complement to conventional medicine—is the opportunity to illuminate the use of a food or herb from ancient medical systems or folk traditions in terms of contemporary science. In a few places, I touch on remedies, but only when the resulting recipe is something that can be healthful in itself. I find it fascinating that onion juice has been used in many cultures to treat asthma and allergies, for example, and that modern research reveals that quercetin, an antioxidant found especially in yellow onions, "down regulates" the immune system, reducing the likelihood of allergic reactions that can trigger asthma attacks. Our Pink Onion Juice (page 216), though, is not only useful if you have allergies or asthma but is a delicious, bracing, cleansing, health-enhancing drink for anyone—a tonic.

Some of the recipes in this book are for traditional Chinese tonics, which have become increasingly popular in America. I look to biomedical research to help explain what they do and to traditional use (especially to their use as foods rather than as pills or supplements) to guide you in using them. If you want to learn to use Chinese herbs to treat a specific health condition, however, this book is an adjunct to your search, not the main text. The first thing you need to do is to find a health care professional trained in traditional Chinese herbal medicine (see "Sources," page 321); many acupuncturists are, for example. When I am sick, I see a doctor; if after years of research I don't trust myself to self-medicate, perhaps you shouldn't either.

But I'm mainly interested in tonic herbs that have a tradition of use *outside* the clinical setting. The herbs I have chosen to profile are part of a tradition of "kitchen medicine." In southern China and in those parts of the world to which Chinese people and ideas have migrated, there is a rich food tradition of herbal broths, soups, and stews. If we want to learn how to use these promising tonic herbs, the least we can do is to follow the tradition.

That is my guiding principle with these particular herbs. Each one is safe in the amounts suggested—and that's another criteria. I provide as much information as I can to help you distinguish situations in which it might be appropriate to cook up a batch of, say, "immune-boosting" Vegetarian Wei Qi Soup (page 27) or Energy-Boosting Asian Fish Stew (page 85), as well as situations in which it would be best to discuss their use with your health practitioner first.

A tonic in traditional herbal medicine is the closest a therapeutic herb comes to being a food. Some herbs are closer to drugs; they are used in specific medical circumstances and may have toxic side effects. Tonic herbs are closer to foods—their effects are subtle and mild, and they have few if any side effects. Many *are* foods: jujube, for example, is the Chinese red date, and it is rich in vitamins A and C. Tonic herbs do not predominate in a formula to kill bacteria, make you sweat, or act as a laxative—these are all "purifying" functions—rather, they are used to help your body get strong and return to normal. Tonics are the most nutritious of therapeutic herbs.

On the other hand, we are beginning to appreciate that many foods also have pharmaceutical-like actions. They contain "phytochemicals"—a fancy word for plant chemicals—that are being closely studied because they hold the promise of helping to prevent, and in some cases treat, major illnesses, including heart disease and cancer. Garlic (page 135), for example, is most definitely a food, but it may also prevent blood clots, lower elevated blood cholesterol, and lower blood pressure—functions for which we typically turn to drugs.

My own definition of a tonic begins with these traditions and applies them to the emerging discoveries of the new nutrition, which looks beyond conventional nutritional categories (preventing scurvy, for example) to public health (preventing heart disease) and functional issues (preventing depression, urinary tract infections, alcohol cravings).

We are at the beginning of a new era. The buzzwords include functional foods (foods that serve a function beyond nutrition—such as improving mood or stimulating immunity), phytochemicals, nutraceuticals (a cross between a nutrient and a pharmaceutical), designer foods (foods fortified with specific phytochemicals for specific purposes). As with anything new that promises to improve health, the commercial interests are out there gunning for you. They want to sell you new pills for new ills, grapefruit juice laced with garlic, potato chips fortified with vegetable compounds, and other monstrosities.

In order not to be misled and exploited, we need to understand how to use this new knowledge about the usefulness of plants; we need to connect it with the traditional medicinal uses of foods and herbs and to integrate our ideas into what we already know about how diet can sustain and improve health. Herbal medicine is a natural extension of a whole-foods approach to health. By understanding the properties of everyday foods and nutrients—rosemary (page 231), turmeric (page 279), vitamin E (page 285)—we can begin to appreciate the lost connections between what we eat to sustain health and what we eat to restore it, between treatment and prevention, between drug and food.

This seems to me a fruitful way to look at some of the most exciting developments in contemporary nutrition. In "Tuna" (page 275) and again in "Walnut" (page 292), for example, we look at recent work on omega-3 fatty acids, a class of highly polyunsaturated fatty acids found in fish and certain plants. A generation ago, scientists thought that all fats were simply sources of energy. But now we are beginning to appreciate and document the multitude of ways in which omega-3 fatty acids can help balance body systems. They affect immunity, autoimmune diseases, blood clotting, inflammation, the risk of cancer and heart disease, and even the ability of our children to see clearly and think well. Fish is indeed brain food. Eating fish once, twice, or three times a week—or eating plant sources of these fatty acids such as walnuts and tofu—helps the body stay in balance. These foods and herbs are contemporary tonics.

In a few places, just for fun, I stretch the definition. "Walking" (page 289), "Friend" (page 133), "Breath" (page 34), and "Fasting" (page 108) are each, in their own way, tonics. They support, nourish, balance.

This is a cookbook as well as a book of essays. Each herb, ingredient, or nutrient is translated into real food. Each chapter ends with one or more recipes. My goal is to reconnect our use of tonic herbs with the food context from which they arise and to put everyday foods and herbs in a preventive context.

If we want to stay healthy, or get healthy, the cornerstone is a plant-based diet, with plenty of fresh vegetables, legumes, fruits, herbs, and spices (see "How to Eat," page 11). There is no other way. It is the whole that heals. It is not enough to eat a low-fat diet and then take vitamin supplements. It won't work to eat on the run and pop into the health food store for an herbal pick-me-up to protect you from your own lifestyle. There is no substitute for green, orange, red, and yellow fruits and vegetables—for whole foods, every day.

Herbal nutrition begins with whole foods. The Chinese herbs we pick off the shelf in antiseptic tinctures are used even today in rich, aromatic, nourishing soups. The soup may be as responsible for their effectiveness as the herbs. Similarly, if you want the benefits of garlic, you can take a pill—and if you don't like garlic and have risk factors for heart disease such as elevated blood cholesterol, this is a good idea. But the people who consume plenty of garlic and onions and have low rates of heart disease and other chronic conditions in Italy, as in China, don't swallow pills. They eat it in all its pungent, aromatic glory.

Humankind has been looking to plants to nourish, soothe, stimulate, modulate, protect, and cure for a long, long time. Indeed, animals may pick and choose certain plants when they feel sick, recent studies find. As human culture arose, the interactions of plants and human beings were observed, recorded, codified. It is a rich tradition. To be sure, some of the putative powers of individual plant foods may be wrong; humans are human, after all. But as we search for new preventive drugs, we would do well to remember that the empirical traditions of herbal medicine may offer clues.

These traditions also offer a way to use the new findings of phytochemical nutrition. In Chinese medicine, for example, close attention is paid to an individual's temperature. This includes actual temperature, both internal and external—that is, the weather—but also extends into biochemical metaphor. A person who is overweight and has high blood pressure, for example, may be considered overheated. Someone who is "cold" may not only feel cold but may also suffer from listlessness and weakness. Foods also have temperatures. Part of this is literal: well-cooked foods are good for people with cool dispositions, while raw vegetables may help "cool" someone who is overheated. Spices such as ginger and hot chili peppers are heating, while celery and chrysanthemum are cooling, in both the literal and metaphorical sense. I am still a new student of these categories, but I have noted the connections where appropriate.

Seasonality is another link between traditional medicine and food. One eats foods appropriate to the season. This relates to temperature, of course. In Chinese medicine, there is no separation between an individual's internal milieu and the season. When the weather is cold, one needs heating foods. When it is hot, one needs cooling foods.

The final connection between traditional medicine and contemporary nutrition relates to taste. Traditional tonics—indeed, all therapeutic herbs—in Chinese, Ayurvedic, ancient Greek, and European medicine are characterized by their taste. The taste of a food, this tradition holds, is a key to its function, or "energetics." Sour foods are held to be astringent, contracting; salty foods, condensing, concentrating; spicy or pungent foods, stimulating and dispersing. Bitters—which, as we've noted, Europeans use as digestive tonics—tend to stimulate the production of saliva and bile acids. Many Chinese tonics are at least partly sweet, which is a clue to their nourishing aspect. Wherever appropriate, I have explored the connection between the taste of a food and its function.

How refreshing these connections are! We are besieged daily with subtle propaganda from the food industry that reinforces the idea that if a food tastes good, it can't be good for us, and if it is good for us, it can't taste good. This is diametrically wrong—a mirror image of the truth. Consider the American diet, sometimes called the standard American diet, or SAD. It is an odd combination of bland taste, partially compensated for by high levels of fat, salt, and sugar, so low in nutrients that it can lead simultaneously to obesity and malnutrition.

Fat carries flavor, to be sure. But the idea that the taste experience will lead us into temptation and that one needs special foods both to withstand the temptations and to avoid the putative poisons in our diets is an invention. The notion the food industry pushes—that healthful food lacks flavor, while processed foods are rich in flavor—is not only self-serving but provides another approach to marketing: newly engineered foods with natural or artificial substitutes for fat (salt, sugar) now promise that they have, by magic as it were, solved the age-old problem and delivered "good-for-you food that actually tastes good" or some other variation of that pitch.

"A high-fat diet is a developed taste," Anna Ferro-Lutzi told me a few years ago. I was sitting in her sunny office outside Rome, where she directs the Italian National Institute of Nutrition. "It only suits the food industry, which develops a taste for sweet and fatty things. These are not really good, it's just a question of having your palate twisted so that you like that, you become addicted to that. So there is a misrepresentation. Today, the food tastes of nothing. A salad of tomatoes tastes of nothing, because the tomatoes are grown to make them easily accessible. It is not a question of health but a disaster from the point of view of good-tasting foods."

One of the joys of discovering traditional cuisines from every continent is the realization that a low-fat or moderate-fat, high-fiber, largely plant-based cuisine can provide extraordinary tastes. But consider an additional possibility: that the loss of taste is in fact a disaster from the standpoint of health. Perhaps the flavors that make real food so good also make it healthful. Let your mind savor the memory of the flavors of apples, yogurt, licorice, cinnamon, ginger, rosemary, thyme, garlic, onions, tomatoes, spinach, shiitake mushrooms, oysters, red wine. Their flavors not only make them attractive but offer clues to their function, their ability to keep our bodies healthy, balanced, and toned.

Each of us, in our striving for a healthier, happier life, is looking for a little extra help these days. If we look carefully, it is all around us. Every food, herb, or activity in this book, if used appropriately, can promote health in a fundamental way.

Each is a tonic. Some may actually be, in different amounts and when used with appropriate supervision, medicine. The better we understand the ways in which plant foods and herbs can promote health in a healthy person, the more able we will be to use them to restore balance when it has gone awry.

HOW TO EAT

In the chapters ahead, you'll read about foods that protect against heart disease and cancer, help the body rid itself of toxins, improve your mood, and do other good things. You'll also encounter a lot of references to a "plant-based" diet. Let me explain.

"Plant based" has become nutritional shorthand for the kind of eating pattern that best supports health. It's not necessarily a vegetarian diet, although vegetarian diets are, of course, plant based. Rather, it's a diet in which most of the calories come from grains—rice in China, for instance, or pasta and bread in Italy—followed by a tremendous variety and amount of vegetables, legumes, fruits, nuts, and seeds. These foods comprise 70, 80, even 90 percent of the calories people consume in parts of the world where the chronic diseases of modern society—heart disease, cancer, diabetes—are rare. It's an approach worth emulating.

To this plant base, one may add animal foods. It can be a shock for a nutritionally aware American to travel to, say, Italy and see how happy the famously plant-based eaters there are to have pork or beef. Part of this is modernity. But part of it is also tradition. In many rural areas, people eat a mostly vegetarian diet during the week out of necessity and a meat meal on Sunday as a special occasion. Dairy products, often fermented as yogurt or cheese, are consumed, too, often daily. A similar pattern exists in India, China, and other Asian countries (minus the dairy). Some anthropologists have suggested that the natural human diet is centered on starchy staples supplemented by vegetables, fermented foods, and animal products.

You may think you know much of this already. But the sheer amount of plant foods consumed in cultures with low rates of chronic disease can be staggering to Americans. In contemporary China, for example, an average person in a rural setting eats a pound of cereals (mostly rice), two-thirds of a pound of vegetables, and three ounces of root vegetables every day. In Greece in 1960—before the diet became industrialized, Americanized, and more meat centered—the average consumption of vegetables was almost half a pound a day, plus a pound of fruit, six ounces of potatoes, and about an ounce of beans. In southern Italy, it was about half a pound of vegetables and legumes, half a pound of fruit. At the same time, animal flesh—red meat but also chicken and fish—might average only a couple of ounces a day. In Italy in 1960, for example, the average person ate only one pound of red meat, poultry, and fish combined per week. Red meat consumption itself was only about a pound per month.

When nutritionists and journalists talk about a plant-based diet, this is what they have in mind. There is no substitute for real fruits and vegetables; nonfat frozen yogurt and fat-free cakes, rich in sugars, may get you through the day, but they do not promote health.

Ancel Keys, who more than any other scientist established the link between diet and cardiovascular health and the benefits of the so-called Mediterranean diet, offered this advice in *Eat Well and Stay Well,* a book he wrote with his wife, Margaret, in 1959:

- Do not get fat; if you are fat, reduce.

- Restrict saturated fats—the fats in beef, pork, lamb, sausages, margarine, solid shortenings, and dairy products.

- Prefer vegetable oils to solid fats, but keep total fat under 30 percent of your diet calories.

- Favor fresh vegetables, fruits, and nonfat milk products.

- Avoid heavy use of salt and refined sugar.

- Good diets do not depend on drugs and fancy preparations.

- Get plenty of exercise and outdoor recreation.

- Be sensible about cigarettes, alcohol, excitement, business strain.

- See your doctor regularly and do not worry.

Today, we know that it is not possible to be "sensible" about the highly addictive, carcinogenic drug-delivery system known as cigarettes. But everything else Ancel Keys suggested remains germane. I would personally prefer olive oil to polyunsaturated vegetable oils (see "Olive Oil," page 208); put some emphasis on grains, especially whole grains, and starchy root vegetables; emphasize legumes for everyone but especially vegetarians; and encourage a greater shift away from animal products. But the rudiments of healthful eating were there nearly forty years ago. Now all we have to do is follow them.

A NOTE ON KITCHEN EQUIPMENT

We have attempted to make this book accessible without the purchase of a long list of expensive equipment. However, there are a few items that are essential for the recipes in the book, and a few more that are needed for specific recipes.

Blender. For all those tonic drinks!

Canning jars. We pickle ginger, garlic, onions, and other foods.

Cheesecloth. To make Yogurt Cheese, page 316.

Flame tamer. These are simple, inexpensive metal discs with holes in them that sit on top of a gas burner. They allow for very low temperatures, useful for long-simmering broths and teas.

Food mill. For grinding ingredients larger than spices.

Food processor. This really comes in handy in many of the recipes.

Ice cream maker. Donvier makes a good, relatively inexpensive one.

Ice cube trays. Get extra ones, for freezing stock in small amounts.

Juicer. An inexpensive one will do fine.

Kitchen scale, in ounces and grams.

Labels. Get the stick-on kind, for foods stored in the refrigerator or freezer.

Japanese mandoline. Several recipes use this for slicing vegetables thinly, and it is a handy tool but not absolutely necessary.

Muslin bags. We use these to make lavender pillows (page 198), but they also come in handy for Chinese herbs that need to be removed before serving a soup or tea.

Pharmaceutical-grade scale, in fractions of grams. This is necessary to make the Trikatu, page 206.

Pressure cooker (or crock pot). For the long-cooked rice congees in several chapters.

Spice grinder. To grind spices; you can use a coffee grinder, but use a separate one to grind coffee.

Steamer insert or other steamer. The inexpensive folding metal kind works fine.

Storage containers (plastic). For freezing all those delicious soups!

Timer. Every kitchen should have one.

Tongs (metal). Another useful, inexpensive item, especially for moving canning jars in and out of boiling water, removing muslin bags filled with herbs, etc.

APPLE

"Malus the Appyll tree is a tree yt bereth apples and is a grete tree," wrote Englishman Wynken de Worde in the fifteenth century.

He was translating *De Proprietatibus Rerum* ("The Property of Things"), written in Latin by Bartholomaeus Anglicus around 1250. As was the custom then, de Worde added a few thoughts of his own about the properties of things, including apples:

"[It] makyth shadowe wyth thycke bowes and braunches: and fayr with dyuers blossomes, and floures of swetnesse and lykynge: with good fruyte and noble. Some beryth sourysh fruit and harde and some ryght soure and some ryght swete, with a good savoure and mery." In sum, he wrote, the apple is "gracious in syght and in taste, and vertuous in medecyne."

Virtuous in medicine, indeed: few fruits garner such a healthful reputation—an apple a day and all that. Give your teacher an apple, and you are right as rain. (Give her a juicy pomegranate or luscious strawberries, and you might be suspected of having a crush or perhaps even sexual designs.) The manifest virtuousness of the apple has always seemed at odds with the biblical story of temptation in the Garden of Eden. In the end, it may have been a mistranslation: the "apple" that so tempted Eve with its sweet mortal knowledge was probably a close cousin to the peach—an altogether more voluptuous fruit.

Yet even the apple's virtuous reputation seems a mystery. How can an apple a day keep the doctor away when it is so low in the nutrients commonly considered important? A medium apple, eaten with the skin, has 138 calories, according to our own sacred text, *Bowes and Church's Food Values of Portions Commonly Used* by Jean A.T. Pennington. For that, you get only eight milligrams of vitamin C (a daily minimum is 60 milligrams) and hardly any carotenoids, calcium, or other standard nutrient worth noting.

To find the source of the apple's salutary reputation, we'll have to look beyond conventional nutrition. But not too far. One candidate is the kind of fiber most abundant in apples: pectin. Pectin is water soluble, like the fiber abundant in oats, barley, beans, and psyllium. And like other water-soluble fiber, pectin can lower blood cholesterol in people with high levels. (For more on soluble fiber, see "Psyllium," page 224.)

Our medium apple, that statistical artifact, has three grams of dietary fiber, half of it pectin. Apples are among the best dietary sources of pectin; a half-cup serving of brussels sprouts or spinach or a medium sweet potato contains about one gram. Citrus fruits, especially the white "albedo" or pith on the inside of their skin, are another rich source. The average American (another statistical artifact!) takes in only about ten grams of dietary fiber a day and should aim for 25 to 35. So snacking on a mere three apples a day—nine grams of fiber, four and a half grams of it as pectin—would nearly double daily fiber intake for most people.

Most likely it would also lower cholesterol. In one study, 33 people of varying ages who had elevated blood cholesterol levels were given a drink containing apple-derived pectin plus guar gum, another water-soluble fiber. In those who took the least amount—eight and a half grams a day, the equivalent of the pectin in six apples—total cholesterol dropped an average of 10 percent. LDL cholesterol, closely linked with heart attack risk, dropped 14.4 percent. (Taking more helped but not dramatically: those who consumed 64 grams of pectin a day—oh, say, 43 apples' worth—reduced their total cholesterol 15.7 percent, their LDL 19.1 percent.)

Ten percent may not seem a lot compared with cholesterol-lowering drugs, but then, even six apples don't have significant side effects, are cheaper, and taste better. One study reports that daily apple consumption—my abstract doesn't say how many—can drop cholesterol 16 percent; perhaps the apple is greater than the sum of its pectin. In pigs with very high cholesterol, those given pectin (from grapefruit) as 3 percent of their daily diet for nine months had significantly less clogging of coronary arteries.

"Most of the human studies find that about nine grams of pectin a day lowers blood cholesterol about 10 percent in people with elevated levels," says Jon Story, a professor in the department of foods and nutrition at Purdue University in West Lafayette, Indiana. His own research has determined that pectin lowers cholesterol because its viscosity inhibits the tendency of bile acids to be reabsorbed into the bloodstream. Bile acids are made from cholesterol. When they aren't reabsorbed in the small intestine, they get excreted, and the liver has to make more, drawing on cholesterol in the bloodstream. (Artichokes stimulate bile-acid synthesis by a different method; see page 20.)

Pectin, like other soluble fibers, also slows the rate at which food moves through the stomach, increasing one's sense of fullness. That's why eating an apple as an afternoon snack is a good way to stave off hunger. Pectin also lowers blood sugar in healthy volunteers, a generally good thing. Pectin, which absorbs water, is a remedy for diarrhea, and because it is fermented by gut bacteria, it acts as a "probiotic," stimulating "good bacteria" and reducing the ability of diarrhea-causing bacteria such as *Clostridium difficile* to multiply. An apple a day, indeed.

Whether pectin affects our chances of getting cancer is unclear. In some animal studies, large amounts of pectin actually promote tumor growth, but other studies have found that when as much as 20 percent of the diet is apple pectin, both the number and size of chemically induced tumors are reduced. One special kind of pectin, simplified in the lab so that it is less branched and more easily absorbed, prevents prostate cancer from spreading in rats. It is a reasonable but unproved possibility that natural pectin is similarly "cleaved" by stomach acid so that it resembles this modified pectin, notes researcher Avraham Raz of Wayne State University School of Medicine in Detroit. "The body's enzymes might cleave pectin so that it can be absorbed," says Dr. Raz. "The PH of the stomach is very acid, so it could happen, but we really have no idea."

What's nice about eating apples for health is that you really don't have to have any idea. An apple is fiber balanced; half is soluble, half is insoluble. Insoluble fiber is strongly cancer protective in animal studies. Says Dr. Story, "That's why it's better to eat foods that are rich in pectin, rather than get hung up on supplements. The pectin in an apple will help lower elevated cholesterol. But the rest of that apple has other kinds of fiber, and that's good."

Then again, perhaps it's not just the pectin that makes apples so healthful. Apples, particularly apples eaten with their skins, are rich in particular kinds of dietary antioxidants called flavonoids. In a 1993 Dutch study of 693 men with no history of heart disease, those who consumed the most dietary flavonoid were one-third less likely to suffer a fatal heart attack than those who consumed few flavonoid-rich foods. Good sources of flavonoids? Tea, red wine, onions, and—you guessed it—apples. (For more on flavonoids, see "Tea," page 252.)

Perusing the list of foods rich in pectin or flavonoids—spinach, brussels sprouts, onions, tea—the apple is the only one I would eat out of hand, on a whim, after a meal, at my desk, walking down the street, or driving in my car. A good, crisp apple in autumn is a tart wake-up call with sweet tones, almost a thirst quencher.

I know a doctor in New York City who periodically goes on an apple weight-loss regimen, eating apples all day long, a half dozen or more—in part to keep himself from more caloric fare, but also, I must assume, because he likes apples. Perhaps he even finds their "savoure" merry.

BAKED LICORICE APPLES

The idea for this recipe came from a *Wall Street Journal* article that mentioned that apples baked in wine are a traditional French dish. In a 1961 edition of Julia Child's *Mastering the Art of French Cooking,* we found a recipe calling for six apples, lemon juice, butter, sugar, dry white wine, cognac, oranges, currant jelly, and more cognac. The authors suggest serving it over canapés of white bread sautéed in clarified butter, with two cups of heavy cream poured over it. I'm sure it's delicious, but I wouldn't recommend it for those who wish to benefit from the apple's cholesterol-lowering effects.

Our adaptation uses whole apples (organic if you can get them, so you can feel good about eating the peels) and oranges peeled to include the pith—another good source of pectin. If you have crystallized ginger, throw some in.

The licorice adds its own healthful qualities (see page 199). This isn't licorice candy but actual licorice sticks, which look like twigs. You can buy them in Chinese markets, some health food stores, or by mail order (see "Sources," page 321).

YIELD: 4 SERVINGS

4 baking apples (preferably organic), unpeeled
1 lemon (preferably organic)
2 oranges (preferably organic)
4 teaspoons dark brown sugar
1 tablespoon ground cinnamon
4 licorice sticks
½ cup apple cider
¼ cup raspberry, apple, or quince jelly
2 to 3 tablespoons cognac (optional)

Wash and dry the apples, lemon, and oranges.

Slice the peels of the lemon and oranges into long thin strips, leaving as much white pith attached as possible. Juice the fruit, keeping the lemon and orange juices separate.

Adjust the oven rack so that it's in the center, and heat the oven to 350 degrees.

Core the apples, leaving the bottoms intact, and set them in a baking dish.

Put 1 teaspoon brown sugar in the hollow of each apple. Divide the lemon zest, lemon juice, and cinnamon among the apples, sprinkling it into the hollows. Insert a licorice stick into each one.

Pour the cider into the baking dish, and cover it with foil. Bake for 30 to 50 minutes, until the apples are tender when pierced with the tip of a knife but are not bursting. (The timing will vary with the type and freshness of the apples.)

While the apples are baking, blanch the orange peel in a small pan of boiling water for about 15 minutes, until tender. Drain and rinse under cold water.

When the apples are done, transfer them to a serving platter, and cover them again with the foil.

Pour the baking liquid into a small saucepan, and stir in the jelly and orange juice. Cook over high heat, stirring occasionally, for 10 to 20 minutes, until the liquid is thick enough to coat the back of a spoon.

Stir in the orange peel and, if desired, the cognac. Reduce the heat to low and cook for 3 to 4 minutes more.

Spoon the sauce over the apples, and serve immediately.

ARTICHOKE
(*Cynara scolymus*)

Traveling by train through verdant Provence into Italy, one sees field upon field of artichokes looking like tiny forests. In Mediterranean countries, the artichoke is grown in every variety from minuscule to large, green but often tinged in purple, so that a visitor to, say, the central market in Florence in April or May might be able to choose from a half-dozen kinds.

I was lucky enough once to visit Ancel and Margaret Keys, coauthors of the revolutionary 1959 American book *Eat Well and Stay Well,* at their home in Pioppi, Italy, south of Naples. Ancel Keys is a legendary figure in nutrition circles. He did more than anyone else to establish the link between diet and heart disease, and he more or less discovered the heart-protective benefits of what came to be called the Mediterranean diet.

Margaret, whose contribution to those discoveries remains hidden in modesty, served a lovely salad of romaine lettuce, tomatoes, and thin-sliced fennel and black olives with crusty bread and a bowl of baby artichokes from her garden. She had boiled the artichokes, then tossed them in olive oil with freshly squeezed lemon juice, sliced garlic, and capers. I wish I were eating them now, warmed by the sun on the portico, drinking wine, drinking water, watching the light blue sky and the wine-dark sea.

The artichoke is revered both for taste and health; at a bookstore in Avignon, I saw the artichoke mentioned in two or three books on Provençal folk cures. A medium-sized artichoke, boiled, has only 60 calories and provides 12 milligrams of vitamin C, about a fifth of the daily minimum, and 61 micrograms of folic acid, about one-seventh the amount a pregnant woman should take in daily to prevent birth defects. Not bad—but not enough to create a cultural reputation for healthfulness.

What makes artichokes unique is a bitter substance, cynaropicrin. Like many bitter-tasting compounds, it stimulates the liver to produce bile, which is stored in the gallbladder. Bile acids, and particularly the bile salts they contain, help in the digestion of fats. Artichokes stimulate the production of both. Foods and botanicals that stimulate bile production are known as cholagogues. According to researcher Daniel B. Mowrey, author of *Herbal Tonic Therapies,* the artichoke acts not only as a cholagogue but as a choleretic, an agent that increases the flow of bile from the gallbladder, and a cholekinetic, a stimulant to bile-duct contraction. The artichoke's balanced effect on digestion "helps to account for its popularity among European physicians," writes Mowrey.

Cholagogues often lower blood cholesterol, too. That's because bile is largely made of cholesterol. So when the liver makes more bile, it often draws on the cholesterol circulating in the bloodstream. Cynarin, an extract derived from artichoke leaves, is patented as a medicine in France and is used to treat liver disease and elevated blood cholesterol levels. Its effectiveness has been established in several human studies. For example, in a placebo-controlled study of 60 patients with high blood cholesterol published in the German medical journal *Arzneimittelforschung* in 1975, those who took 500 milligrams of cynarin for 50 days significantly lowered their blood cholesterol levels. Cynarin has also been shown to protect the liver, prevent the circulation of toxins, and stimulate liver-cell regeneration. In this regard, artichoke extract acts similarly to milk thistle (page 23), to which it is botanically related. In fact, milk thistle is sometimes called wild artichoke.

If you have high cholesterol levels, eating artichokes may help a little, though it's not likely to be a miracle cure. In one study, even cynarin wasn't useful for the kind of high cholesterol that runs in families, which tends to resist dietary intervention. But artichokes are more health promoting than their naked nutrient composition would suggest. If you like them, eat them often. Serve them at the beginning of the meal, and your guests' livers will be well primed to digest whatever comes afterward.

STEAMED BABY ARTICHOKES WITH VINAIGRETTE

Choose artichokes that are same size (about two ounces each) so they cook evenly. Baby artichokes haven't yet developed hairy chokes and are entirely edible.

If there is a hard core or "germ" in the center of your garlic, remove it; it is bitter, especially raw, as in this vinaigrette.

YIELD: 2 TO 4 SERVINGS

1 pound baby artichokes (about 7)
2 tablespoons fresh lemon juice
1 tablespoon capers
1 large garlic clove, peeled and sliced lengthwise very thinly
Kosher salt
Freshly ground pepper
5 tablespoons extra-virgin olive oil

Bring water to boil in a vegetable steamer or a large pan fitted with a steamer insert; the water should reach just below the perforated basket. Meanwhile, trim the stems from the artichokes and remove any brown leaves.

Steam the artichokes, pan lid slightly ajar, until the bottoms are easily pierced with the tip of a knife, about 20 minutes. Set them aside.

Combine the lemon juice, capers, garlic, salt, and pepper to taste in a small bowl. Gradually whisk in the olive oil.

When the artichokes are cool enough to handle, cut each in half lengthwise. Arrange the halves on a platter, and drizzle with vinaigrette. Serve warm or at room temperature. (If not eating right away, rub the vinaigrette over the cut surfaces and turn the artichokes cut-side down to keep them from discoloring.)

ARTICHOKE AND MILK THISTLE LIQUEUR

The various artichoke-flavored liqueurs popular in Europe are the inspiration for this little tonic, my favorite liqueur in this book. Although both artichoke and milk thistle are good for the liver, vodka is not; if you have a liver condition, see your doctor, and don't drink this. If you do drink alcohol, however, this liqueur is a kind of cardiovascular tonic. The alcohol, combined with the artichoke essence, should help lower blood cholesterol and "thin" the blood. The rosemary (see page 231) provides antioxidants, which help prevent LDL cholesterol from turning into arterial plaque. Milk thistle adds a little extra liver protection (see page 23). Tonic liqueurs are meant to be sipped, not gulped; try one-half to one ounce of this in the evening.

YIELD: ABOUT 2 CUPS

1 pound fresh artichokes (about 2 large)
1 ounce milk thistle tincture (available at health food stores)
2 large sprigs fresh rosemary
1 lemon, zested and juiced
1 cup vodka

Peel all the leaves from the artichokes and place them in a large, nonreactive pot. With a sharp paring knife, cut around the chokes and remove the hairy thistle in the center of each. Discard all hairy and prickly bits. Cut each heart into 4 pieces, and add to pot.

Add 6 cups water, cover, and bring to a boil. Reduce the heat to a simmer. Place a heat-proof plate or dish on top of the artichoke leaves to keep them at least partially submerged. Cook for about 1 hour and 15 minutes, until the liquid has reduced to about 1 cup—about ½ inch of liquid in the bottom of a 10-inch pot.

Meanwhile, sterilize a 1-pint canning jar and lid with boiling water, and set them aside to dry on a clean kitchen towel.

When the artichokes are done, set the leaves and hearts aside, and strain the liquid through a very fine sieve. Working in batches, place the leaves and hearts in the sieve and press firmly with the back of a wooden spoon to extract all the juices. Discard the solids, and wash the sieve well.

Line the sieve with a piece of slightly dampened cheesecloth. Strain the liquid again to remove any remaining hairy bits and solids. The liquid should measure about 1 cup.

Pour the artichoke essence into the sterilized jar, and stir in the milk thistle tincture. Poke the rosemary down into the jar, and add the lemon zest and juice. Add the vodka, and stir gently. Close the lid tightly, and shake the jar once or twice to distribute the ingredients.

Label and date the jar, and leave it in a cool, dark place to steep for 2 weeks. (Unless you have a cold room or basement for storage, keep it in the refrigerator.)

Strain again through a dampened cheesecloth. (You can also use a thin coffee filter such as a Melitta.) The liqueur will keep for several months in the refrigerator.

MILK THISTLE
(Silybum marianum)

Milk thistle, a botanical cousin of the artichoke (they are both in the daisy family), is among the most effective natural liver-protecting agents ever studied. Because it is not really a food and has no history of food use that I am aware of, it doesn't belong anywhere else in this book. It is generally available in alcoholic tinctures in health food stores. You put a few drops in water, so the alcohol content is very small; if you use boiling water, the alcohol will evaporate.

In Europe, milk thistle is well studied. It contains various substances, together referred to as silymarin, that protect both healthy and damaged liver cells so that toxins cannot attack them. It also stimulates protein synthesis, which in turn stimulates the regeneration of liver cells. In his excellent book *The Honest Herbal,* plant medicines expert Varro Tyler of Purdue University writes, "Studies in small animals have shown that silymarin exerts a liver protective effect against a variety of toxins including the phallotoxins of the deadly amanita [a lethal mushroom]. Human trials have also been encouraging for conditions including hepatitis and cirrhosis of various organs. The results of numerous studies suggest that silymarin has considerable therapeutic potential."

Silymarin is not particularly water soluble, so milk thistle tea is probably not very effective. That's why alcohol-based tinctures are most often used. You can also buy capsules containing 200 milligrams of milk thistle (about 140 milligrams of silymarin). If you are recovering from alcoholism or have a liver condition, this may be a prudent thing to do. It is very safe. If you have a serious condition such as hepatitis, you need to be under the care of a qualified health professional and should ask yours about milk thistle.

ASTRAGALUS
(Astragalus membranaceous)

Astragalus, the root of the yellow vetch plant, is sold in thin slices that look like tongue depressors. It has the kind of creamy yellow color one might pick for the walls of a bedroom. Unlike some Chinese tonic herbs, it tastes good. Herbalist Michael Tierra, in *Planetary Herbology*, describes it as "sweet, slightly warm." He calls it a "chi tonic" (chi or "qi" means energy) and writes:

> It strengthens digestion, raises metabolism, strengthens the immune system, and promotes the healing of wounds and injuries. It treats chronic weakness of the lungs with shortness of breath, collapse of energy, prolapse of internal organs, spontaneous sweating, chronic lesions, and deficiency edema. It is very effective in cases of nephritis [kidney inflammation] that do not respond to diuretics.

In *Prince Wen Hui's Cook: Chinese Dietary Therapy*, Bob Flaws and Honora Lee Wolfe discuss astragalus in the section on Wei Qi deficiency. *Qi* is "chi"— that is, vital energy. *Wei* is usually translated as "defensive." Another term for "defensive energy" might be immune system. Astragalus is the main herbal remedy for nourishing the Wei Qi, write Flaws and Wolfe. It is often used in tonifying meat broths, sometimes in combination with ginger and ginseng. Like most Chinese tonics, it is given after the acute or treatment phase of an illness in order to support and maintain health.

It is most definitely not a cold remedy. In traditional Chinese medicine, there is a distinction between serious internal conditions and relatively unimportant "surface" ailments. A cold is no big thing; it is a wind at the surface of the body. If one took astragalus for such a minor illness, the theory goes, the infection might be driven inward. As Flaws and Wolfe write, "tonification of the Wei Qi at such a point, closing tight the surface, would lock the pathogen inside the body like a thief in a house, and would lead to a definitely more dangerous situation."

They and other teachers of traditional Chinese medicine recommend astragalus as a "deep immune tonic," best used to restore an immune system that is chronically, rather than acutely, stressed. It is for people who get one cold or flu after another, who feel their "defenses are down." Astragalus, as part of other herbal therapies, has been used clinically with cancer patients undergoing chemotherapy and experimentally with those suffering from HIV infection and AIDS.

Astragalus is also believed to enter the "lung" channel. A lung chi deficiency manifests in a prolonged recovery from illness; it may include a weak, chronic cough, shortness of breath, fatigue, and excessive perspiration. Astragalus, a chi tonic that enters the lung channel, combined with codonopsis (page 83), a chi tonic that enters both the spleen and lung channels, would be expected to improve one's resistance—or as the Chinese say, one's defensive energy, Wei Qi.

In his *Handbook for Herbal Healing,* Christopher Hobbs writes that astragalus is a "deep immune tonic that increases the 'bone marrow reserve,' increasing the body's ability to produce more immune effector cells (such as T cells), protecting us from 'pathogens,' which the Chinese call 'pernicious influences.' Astragalus is a popular remedy in China, used as a daily tonic . . . if the constitution is weak."

Scientific research confirms that astragalus may have beneficial effects. The Chinese use it to treat heart disease. One 1995 Chinese study of 92 patients with angina pectoris, the severe chest pain that can accompany heart disease, found that after getting astragalus, patients "were remarkably relieved" of pain. Animal studies confirm that astragalus is a vasodilator—that is, it dilates the blood vessels and arteries, allowing blood to flow more freely, especially through partially clogged arteries. Yet another study of heart patients found that astragalus improved the ability of the heart to pump blood. In animals, it has been found to lower blood pressure.

It is the potential of astragalus to boost immunity, however, that has attracted the most attention in the United States, at least in the herbalist community. There are many small-animal studies demonstrating these effects but, unfortunately, few human studies. In a Japanese study, mice were forced to run to exhaustion five times a week for twelve weeks. That kind of thing can run anyone—or any mouse—down. Those that got astragalus had better phagocytic function, meaning the ability of their immune cells to engulf invaders. "The administration of astragalus," the study concluded, "enhanced immune function." In a Chinese study published in 1992, researchers took blood samples from 28 patients with lupus, an autoimmune disease. The blood showed decreased levels of natural killer cells; when treated with astragalus, it had more natural killer cells.

In a 1988 study at the M. D. Anderson Hospital and Tumor Institute at the University of Texas System Cancer Center in Houston, astragalus extract "was found to possess a potent immunorestorative activity in vitro," meaning in the test tube. In that study, animal cells were grafted with foreign cells. Those that were then given astragalus were better able to reject them, which is a sign of immunological competence. Other mouse studies at M. D. Anderson suggested that astragalus can increase the level of interleukin-2, an immune compound that has been used with limited success in the treatment of human cancers. "Success with interleukin-2 immunotherapy of human cancer appears to depend on the administration of high doses, which are frequently associated with excessive toxicity," wrote the authors in 1988. They found that in the lab, putting astragalus together with interleukin-2 increased its ability to kill tumor cells by a factor of ten—that's 1,000 percent.

In 1994, researchers at Loma Linda University in southern California paired astragalus with the herb *Ligustrum lucidum* (see page 29) in a study of mice in which tumor cells had been transplanted. When the tumor load was modest, the mice that got the herbs had a cure rate of 100 percent. With a larger tumor load, the cure rate was 57 percent. The astragalus-ligustrum combination, the researchers suggested, combated tumors primarily by stimulating the phagocytic, or invader-engulfing, activity of the immune system. We await human studies.

One 1995 Chinese study is worth noting. It's not about cancer, but it is about immunity. It comes from the traditional Chinese medicine hospital in Hangzhou in Zhejiang province. Patients with viral myocarditis, a life-threatening viral infection of the heart muscle, were given routine cardiac drug therapy. In these patients, T lymphocyte cells, which are important in immunity at the cellular level, were lower than in healthy controls. Those who were also given astragalus had much higher T cell counts.

Astragalus is "a very safe herb," Dan Bensky and Andrew Gamble write in *Chinese Herbal Medicine: Materia Medica*. In small animals, doses as high as 100 grams per kilogram (1,000 grams) of body weight have been given "without untoward effects." That is a huge amount, given to test toxicity. A normal dose, they note, is 9 to 30 grams per person per day.

Astragalus appears to have great potential for anyone suffering from a temporary or chronic lowering of immunity, such as cancer patients undergoing chemotherapy. It is used for that purpose in China and by Chinese herbalists in the United States. At the Oriental Healing Arts Institute in Long Beach, California, Qingcai Zhang, a medical doctor also trained in traditional Chinese medicine, uses a formula for AIDS patients that includes astragalus, viola (*Viola yedoensis*), *lonicera* (see the discussion of honeysuckle, page 76), ligustrum (see page 29), and ganoderma (see "Reishi," page 228).

Until more scientific studies are conducted, the use of astragalus in medicine in this country will remain on the margins. You and I, however, can rely on cultural uses. Astragalus is often added to tonic Chinese soups. We use it in the Vegetarian Wei Qi Soup that follows and in several other traditional Chinese tonic recipes: Inner-Strength Poached Chicken (page 170), Blood-Building Lamb Stew (page 75), and Energy-Boosting Asian Fish Stew (page 85).

ASTRAGALUS TEA

You can buy astragalus in Chinese markets, some health food stores, or via mail order (see "Sources," page 321). Look for sticks that are long and thick, firm but pliable, with few streaks (striations) and a slightly sweet taste.

YIELD: 4 CUPS

5 sticks astragalus
4 pieces Honey-Roasted Licorice Sticks (page 203)
1 2-inch piece fresh ginger, peeled and thinly sliced

Put the astragalus, licorice, and ginger in a medium-size saucepan. Add 5 cups water, cover, and bring to a boil over high heat. Remove the cover, reduce the heat to medium, and cook for 20 minutes.

Remove the tea from the heat, and let it steep, covered, for 10 minutes. It will take on a beautiful golden hue. Strain and drink warm. For the full flavor and benefit, chew the licorice sticks before discarding.

VEGETARIAN WEI QI SOUP

Wei Qi is the inner defensive chi. In the West, we call it immunity. Herbalist Christopher Hobbs got us started on this soup. His recipe calls for astragalus, reishi mushrooms (see page 228), ligustrum fruit, shiitake mushrooms (see page 240), plus "assorted vegetables" (carrots, beets, potatoes, yams, parsley, celery) cooked in water. He also suggests adding barley. In *Between Heaven and Earth: A Guide to Chinese Medicine*, Harriet Beinfield and Efrem Korngold, who practice acupuncture and Chinese herbology in San Francisco, give a recipe for Wei Qi soup that calls for astragalus, dioscorea (page 105), lotus seeds, codonopsis (page 83), Chinese red dates (see "Jujube," page 186), fresh ginger, vegetable or chicken stock, turnip, yams, and parsley. Our version follows Hobbs's, more or less. It is simpler. Red dates might improve it, as would home-made stock. Feel free to experiment, but keep the seasonings simple and not overly stimulating; tonic soups don't contain garlic or hot peppers.

Try to eat simply and become calm for a day or two before taking any tonic soup. Have two or three cups a day for one or two days, as often as once a week for a few weeks, if you feel run down or are recovering from illness. If you are under treatment for a medical condition, ask your practitioner about including this soup in your regimen.

YIELD: **12 CUPS**

2 medium beets with green tops
3 tablespoons olive oil
6 to 8 sticks astragalus
1 or 2 medium reishi mushrooms (¼ ounce)
¼ cup ligustrum fruit
1 medium onion, peeled and finely chopped
2 medium carrots, peeled and cut into ¼-inch slices
1 baking potato, peeled and cut into ¼-inch cubes
1 pound napa or green cabbage, thinly sliced
2 teaspoons sugar
¾ cup quinoa
2 tablespoons red wine vinegar
Kosher salt
Freshly ground pepper

Heat the oven to 450 degrees.

Trim the beet tops to 1½ inches. Wash the beets well, and cut them in half. Coat them with 1 tablespoon of the oil, wrap individually in foil, sealing tightly. Roast for 35 to 60 minutes, until the beets are easily pierced with the tip of a knife.

Meanwhile, put the astragalus, reishi, and ligustrum in a large soup pot with 6 cups water. Cover and bring to a boil. Reduce the heat to a simmer and cook for 45 minutes to 1 hour, uncovered, until the liquid has reduced to 2 cups. Pass the liquid through a fine strainer and discard the solids.

When the roasted beets are cool enough to handle, peel them and cut into ¼-inch cubes. Reserve.

Heat the remaining 2 tablespoons of oil in the soup pot over medium heat. Sauté the onion and carrots, stirring occasionally, until softened, about 7 minutes. Stir in the potato and cabbage, and cook for about 15 minutes, until the cabbage softens. Add the sugar and 6 cups fresh water. Cover and bring to a boil. Reduce the heat to a high simmer and cook, uncovered, until the potatoes are tender, 15 to 20 minutes.

While the vegetables are cooking, prepare the quinoa according to package directions. When the potatoes are tender, add the cooked quinoa, reserved beets, vinegar, and astragalus broth. Stir well, and cook another 5 minutes for flavors to combine. Season to taste with salt and pepper, and serve warm. The soup will keep in the refrigerator for up to 4 days. It doesn't freeze well.

LIGUSTRUM
(Ligustrum lucidum)

In many of the studies that show an immune-enhancing effect from astragalus, the herb is paired with ligustrum, also known as privet fruit or Japanese wax privet. (The active ingredient is in the seeds inside the fruit.) Astragalus is a "yang" chi tonic; ligustrum is a "yin" tonic. If yang is male, bright, and hot, yin is female, cool, and dark. In traditional Chinese medicine, ligustrum is used to nourish, tone, and augment the liver and kidneys. Together, the two herbs tonify both yin and yang.

Scientific studies of ligustrum by itself are few. Many focus on its cardiovascular effects. In rabbits with high blood cholesterol and heart disease, *Ligustrum japonicum,* a related species, lowered blood cholesterol and prevented the buildup of artery-clogging plaque. (But one rabbit study does not a cardiovascular tonic make, to be sure.) In mice, it lowers blood sugar. It is also diuretic (increases urine flow).

Astragalus, while a very safe herb, is contraindicated in cases of "damp obstruction" (that is, fluid retention and/or swelling that affects circulation), as well as for "yin deficiency with heat signs" (meaning a chronic illness that involves an acute fever). Ligustrum is also a very safe herb but is contraindicated in cases of "yang deficiency," which is characterized by coldness and fatigue. Combined, the two perform a balancing act. If I were to speculate, I might say that when the immune system is actively fighting an infection, it creates plenty of waste products, which a diuretic may help the body clear. I do know that if the Chinese have been combining ligustrum and astragalus in immune-enhancing formulas for centuries, I want to follow their example. That's why it's in our soup.

ATRACTYLODES
(Atractylodes macrocephala)

Atractylodes (pronounced uh-*tract*-ill-oh-dees) is a rhizome, as is ginger. Many of the "roots" we eat are actually rhizomes; these are the nodules on roots that produce the nutrients a plant needs. One of the most famous in agriculture is the pea rhizome, which adds nitrogen back into the soil. Rhizomes are often full of the most amazing biologically active chemicals.

Atractylodes is a bitter herb that the Chinese consider to have a warm energy. It is often added to tonic herbal broths, congees (long-cooked rice porridges), and decoctions (long-simmered herbal teas). In *Chinese Herbal Medicine: Materia Medica,* the best reference book on the subject in English, Dan Bensky and Andrew Gamble write that atractylodes "tonifies the Spleen and augments the qi."

What does this mean? When traditional Chinese medicine refers to an organ, it is usually referring more to a function or group of functions that the organ represents than to the physical organ itself. We are using a similar language when we say that something is "good for the heart" when what we really mean is it is good for the entire cardiovascular system. In Chinese medicine, the spleen governs digestion. Qi, which we Anglicize in this book as chi, is the central concept in Chinese medicine, often translated as "vital energy." So atractylodes improves the vital energy of the digestive process. It tones digestion. It is particularly useful, Bensky and Gamble write, "in the treatment of digestive disorders due to the failure of Spleen yang to rise." When spleen yang is not up to its job, they write, it loses its ability to transform food into energy, and "dampness" can build up. Next, Bensky and Gamble tell us that atractylodes "dries dampness." It is recommended for water retention (edema) and scanty urine. So, it is a diuretic—a substance that promotes the flow of urine.

In animals, atractylodes is indeed an effective diuretic. Animal studies also reveal that it improves the ability of the body to assimilate glucose; thus, it lowers blood sugar. Insulin resistance is a common occurrence in which the body becomes less sensitive to insulin (a hormone that regulates blood sugar) and has trouble handling a large meal. It is associated with aging and obesity and may eventually lead to diabetes. Insulin resistence might be interpreted as a "failure of Spleen qi to rise." Atractylodes, if we are to believe the tradition and the animal studies, might help a sluggish pancreas become more efficient.

Then there are the claims about performance. Here's where I get skeptical.

It's not the tradition I doubt—if the Chinese use atractylodes to tonify the chi, I am inclined to believe there is a reason—it's the science. Specifically, it's the famous mouse-swim test. Mice are given a substance, then forced to swim. How long they can swim before fatigue drops them is considered an indication of their endurance. When mice were given atractylodes in amounts of six grams per kilogram of body weight, they gained weight and swam longer. It sounds impressive until one considers the dose. A kilogram is about 2.2 pounds. So six grams per 2.2 pounds is about 420 grams for a 154-pound man. That's almost 14.8 ounces. So our mice are eating the human equivalent of nearly a pound of atractylodes, an intensely bioactive rhizome, while they are starved of other sustenance. Under such circumstances, even natural sugar, present in almost all roots and rhizomes, would give the mice more chi for their swimming. It could be simple nutrition, not fancy tonic effects.

A spleen chi tonic, one that improves the body's ability to handle sugar while acting as a mild diuretic, is good enough for me. The dosage that Bensky and Gamble cite, using classic Chinese texts, is four and a half to nine grams. This is safe. As with any Chinese herb, however, it is best to get guidance from a practitioner trained in traditional Chinese medicine, especially if you have a specific health problem.

Atractylodes, used wisely, is a "gentleman." In fact, it is one of the Four Gentlemen, the most famous digestive tonic in the Chinese canon. A more complete title would be the Four Gentlemen of Good Digestion. As a spleen chi tonic, atractylodes is a natural for a soup meant to improve digestion. It's not a soup like *pasta e fagioli,* to be sure, but a tonic to take once in a while—or more often under supervision—to improve a sluggish digestive constitution.

The other three "gentlemen" are ginseng (page 161), poria (another diuretic, page 34), and licorice (a stomach protector and harmonizer, page 199). Ginger (a circulatory and digestive stimulant, page 146) and jujube fruit (page 186) are sometimes added to the soup as well.

"In traditional Chinese culture it was common to refer to four important things that were harmonious as a group and not given to extremes as the 'four gentlemen' or the 'four noblemen' after the Confucian term for a person who exhibits ideal behavior," write Bensky and Randall Barolet in *Chinese Herbal Medicine: Formulas and Strategies.* "The four herbs in this formula are mild in nature and blend well together in tonifying the qi. They are therefore called the 'four gentlemen' of herbal medicine."

A person with spleen chi deficiency may have a pallid complexion, a reduced appetite, loose stools, a pale tongue, a low and soft voice, and weakness in the limbs. "This is the classic presentation of deficient Spleen qi," Bensky and

Barolet write, "usually caused by improper eating habits, excessive deliberation, or overworking."

Ginseng, the Chief or lead herb in Four-Gentlemen Soup, is "a powerful tonic for Spleen qi," they write. (In contemporary formulas, two or three times the amount of codonopsis or *dang shen*—see page 83—is usually substituted for ginseng; it is cheaper and milder.) Atractylodes is the Deputy, used to strengthen the spleen and dry dampness. Poria is the Assistant herb, which "leaches out dampness." Honey-roasted licorice is the Envoy, which warms and also regulates the "Middle Burner"—that is, the fire of digestion. Poria's diuretic effect balances licorice's water-retaining properties, while licorice, a sweet digestive herb, protects the entire gastrointestinal track and improves the taste of the soup.

Four-Gentlemen Soup "is distinguished by its relatively harmonious and moderate nature, unlike many of the other qi-tonifyng formulas that are quite warm and drying," Bensky and Barolet write. "It may be used in treating any disorder for which deficient Spleen qi is considered to be the root." In clinical practice, they note, the soup can play a role in treating chronic gastritis, peptic ulcer, irritable bowel syndrome, diabetes, and uterine fibroids and to aid recovery from gastric surgery. If you have one of these conditions, you might ask your health care practitioner about using this soup to augment your diet. If you don't, then a little soup might tonify your digestion long before you need medical help.

The Chinese use therapeutic herbs in food, but they also recognize that food is itself medicine. If you do have a spleen deficiency, a common suggestion would be to eat few cold and cooling foods—raw vegetables, salad, citrus fruit, undercooked foods, too much salt or sweet—which require extra energy from your Middle Burner to digest. You want to give your digestion a head start with foods that are already warm and warming. In *Prince Wen Hui's Cookbook: Chinese Dietary Therapy,* Bob Flaws and Honora Lee Wolfe suggest foods to restore deficient spleen energy and tonify the Middle Burner: cooked squash, sweet potato, yam, rutabaga, turnip, leek, onion, pumpkin, rice, oats; small amounts of poultry, lamb, or beef, particularly in broths or soups; cooked fruits; warm spices such as cardamom, ginger, cinnamon, nutmeg, and pepper; kudzu root; moderate amounts of sweeteners such as honey, maple syrup, or sugar.

This makes sense to me. Warm, well-seasoned, well-cooked foods are easier to digest than cold, raw foods. Whether or not warm foods, or Four Gentlemen, or atractylodes will improve your swimming endurance, we'll have to leave open.

FOUR-GENTLEMEN SOUP

As with any traditional Chinese tonic, Four-Gentlemen Soup is meant to be taken when one is recovering from, not acutely experiencing, an imbalance. It is not a good idea to take this somewhat warming soup when you have a high fever, or "a combination of irritability, thirst, and constipation," note Bensky and Barolet. If you drink more soup than you need, you may get thirsty and feel a little overstimulated from the ginseng. But if you are run down, pale, have a poor appetite, or are otherwise experiencing a deficiency in your "Spleen qi," this might be the soup for you. If you have access to a healer trained in traditional Chinese medicine, you may want to go in for a diagnosis. But nearly anyone can benefit from a tonic soup now and again to improve digestion. Take a cup a day for up to four days. (To learn more about these soups, see "Tonic Soup," page 268.) The optional soba noodles and tofu turn the tonic broth into a more nourishing soup. You can purchase the tonic herbs in herb shops or herb grocery stores in Chinese neighborhoods, in some health food stores, or by mail order (see "Sources," page 321).

YIELD: **5 1-CUP SERVINGS**

15 grams dried white ginseng (about ½ ounce)
30 grams atractylodes root (about 1 ounce)
30 grams poria (about 1 ounce)
15 grams Honey-Roasted Licorice Sticks (about ½ ounce) (see page 203)
5 grams fresh ginger, unpeeled, coarsely chopped (about 1 heaping
     teaspoon; optional)
1 jujube fruit (optional)
4 ounces soba noodles or ½ pound silken tofu, cubed
Thinly sliced scallions for garnish (optional)
Grated ginger for garnish (optional)

Combine the ginseng, atractylodes, poria, licorice, and chopped ginger in a saucepan with 6 cups water. Squeeze the jujube with a pair of pliers or kitchen shears so that the inner nut cracks, and add it to the pan.

Cover and bring to a boil over high heat. Reduce the heat to a high simmer and cook, with cover ajar, for about 45 minutes, until reduced to about 4 cups.

Strain the soup through a fine sieve, pressing down on the solids to extract all the juices. Discard the solids. This classic Four-Gentlemen Soup may be served immediately or refrigerated for up to a day. If there is extra, it can be frozen for 2 to 3 months. (*continued*)

For a more nourishing soup, add 1 cup of water to the strained broth. Combine it with the noodles or tofu in a clean saucepan, and bring it to a simmer. Cook the noodles until tender or the tofu until heated through, 3 to 4 minutes. Serve garnished with scallions and grated ginger.

PORIA
(Poria cocos)

Poria, one of the Four Gentlemen in our soup, is a mushroom, the fruiting body of a fungus. It is sometimes called tuckahoe.

In traditional Chinese medicine, a dose of 9 to 15 grams a day is recommended to "drain dampness." Unlike other diuretics, which can rob the body of potassium, poria is actually rich in potassium.

It may have other benefits. In animals, poria treats nephritis, or kidney inflammation. It contains a potentially cancer-protective compound, a polysaccharide. Finally, poria has a tranquilizing effect in animals, and this finding is in keeping with one of its traditional uses: to "calm the spirit."

BREATH

When John Lennon met Yoko Ono in 1966, she handed him a card that read simply, "Breathe."

We forget.

Not entirely, of course. Much of the time, though, we breathe shallowly, starving our lungs of the air they need to send oxygen to every cell. In particular, when we are anxious, we breathe shallowly. Conversely, breathing deeply, oxygenating the system, can sometimes help us relax.

Breathing well is a form of nutrition—ethereal nutrition, if you will: bathing cells in the oxygen they need for many purposes. Meditation, a technique for eliciting a state of calm awareness, often begins with attention to breath. As Bettina Vitell writes in *A Taste of Heaven and Earth,* "every tradition speaks reverently of the breath. Our word *spirit* comes from the Latin word for breath. The Greeks honored *pneuma,* the Indians *prajna,* the Chinese *chi,* and the Japanese *ki.* All these words mean 'breath.'"

The Beatles learned about breathing and meditation in 1967 when they trekked to India to study with the Maharishi Mahesh Yogi. The maharishi, adept at self-promotion, adapted classic yoga techniques to a form he called transcendental meditation (TM). In the fall of that year, some time after the Beatles had returned from India, Professor Herbert Benson, M.D., was studying high blood pressure in monkeys at Harvard Medical School. Some of his students, enthralled with TM, said, "Why don't you study us?" So he did.

Dr. Benson found that transcendental meditation invoked a wakeful "hypometabolic" state. In such a state, you are quite alert, but your heart and breathing rates are lower than normal. Benson then traveled to the East, where he tested yogic meditation masters. They had remarkably low metabolic rates, including low blood pressure. Perhaps transcendental meditation could be useful in the treatment of high blood pressure, he hypothesized.

Over the next few years, Dr. Benson discovered that the same state of alert calm could be elicited by many, many things, including prayer, running, even knitting. There was nothing unique about TM. The key was the repetition of a meaningful word or phrase (such as a mantra) and the perception of, then the disregarding of, any thoughts that came to mind.

He dubbed the resulting state the "relaxation response." It was the title of a book he wrote in 1975, which became a bestseller.

Later studies revealed that repeating a personally meaningful word is a particularly effective way of evoking the relaxation response. In religious terms, this is a prayer; in New Age terms, an affirmation. "TM does bring about beneficial health changes," says Dr. Benson, now president of the Mind/Body Institute, a nonprofit affiliate of Deaconess Hospital in Boston, "but Western prayer elicits the same response."

The relaxation response, he explains, is not a technique but a physiological state. It is the opposite of the "flight-or-fight" response to danger, real or perceived, which sets "stress hormones" such as epinephrine (once called adrenaline) surging. This hormonal surge raises blood pressure, heart rate, and breathing rate, restricts blood flow, and is often accompanied by feelings of anxiety, depression, anger, and hostility. If you have heart disease, a single bout of anger can precipitate a heart attack.

The relaxation response lowers blood pressure, heart rate, and anxiety.

Practiced daily for months, Dr. Benson found, any technique that elicits it makes the body less sensitive to stress hormones. One breathes more slowly, but because blood is flowing more quickly through wider vessels, the tissues of the body are bathed in more oxygen and can more efficiently shed waste products such as carbon dioxide.

Clinical studies have established that training in techniques that elicit the relaxation response can be useful in the treatment of mild hypertension, pain management (headaches, backaches, chronic pain), cardiovascular disorders such as arrhythmias, nausea, severe PMS, infertility, asthma, insomnia, panic attacks, and depression. "To the extent that a disorder is caused or made worse by stress, the relaxation response is useful," Dr. Benson says.

There are two basic steps. The first is the repetition of a word, sound, prayer, or muscular activity. It can be "love" or "peace" or "the Lord is my shepherd" or "shalom" or "Hail Mary, full of grace." Or it can be jogging, swimming, walking, bicycling—or knitting. The most popular classes in many health clubs have people working out on stationary bicycles while an instructor leads them in relaxation techniques.

"The second step," says Dr. Benson, "is passively to disregard everyday thoughts when they come to mind, and come back to the repetition."

Dr. Benson's work is profoundly democratic. You don't have to trek to India. You don't even have to get special training. All you need to do is to sit quietly. A chair is fine; you don't have to sit on the floor, though that's okay, too. Close your eyes. Let a word come to mind and repeat it quietly in your mind, from time to time. As Mary Roach wrote in an article on meditation in *Health* magazine, this word or phrase "should come easily, as though you're hearing it rather than thinking it." You'll hear noises, think of things you should have said at work, remember things to worry about, think of dinner. That's fine. Meditation doesn't mean you don't have distracting thoughts. Just let them come in and out, like your breath.

A still more democratic approach to relaxation is simply to sit still. In several studies, people who sit quietly without doing anything but also without consciously meditating experience the same physiological benefits as people who meditate. Dr. Benson notes, however, that if you are stressed and anxious, it might not be so easy to sit in a chair without television, radio, food, or conversation for 20 or 30 minutes. Learning techniques to concentrate the mind and handle distracting thoughts, he says, can improve your ability to elicit relaxation.

If sitting quietly elicits the relaxation response, you can go one step further: napping. A short nap can have many benefits. It, too, lowers stress levels. One study of Greek men several years ago found that those who participated in the siesta tradition in the afternoon had lower rates of heart attacks than men who had succumbed to the modern non-napping lifestyle. As a society, we are chronically sleep deprived, a state that may depress immunity.

In *Spontaneous Healing*, Andrew Weil, M.D., offers a few tips on using breathing to elicit relaxation. One is to "observe the breath." You simply sit quietly and pay attention to your breathing without trying to influence it in any way. Another is to "start with exhalation." Again, you pay attention to breath without trying to influence it. But instead of thinking of inhalation as the beginning of a new breath, you think of exhalation as the beginning of each cycle. Then, consciously exhale more deeply, squeezing out air from the lungs, and let the air come back in during inhalation. Dr. Weil's third tip is to "let yourself be breathed." This is best done lying on your back. With every inhalation, imagine the universe is blowing breath into you and, with each exhalation, withdrawing it. "As the universe breathes into you," he writes, "let yourself feel the breath penetrating to every part of the body, even to the tips of your fingers and toes. Try to hold this perception for ten cycles of exhalation and inhalation."

Breathing fully, the simplest thing, is often a victim of our anxious lives. If you begin to choke on food, simply concentrating on your breathing—making sure you breathe—stops the choking. Studies of people who experience panic attacks find that as their breathing is affected, their panic accelerates.

Meditative breathing may also help with insomnia. A 1995 study conducted at the University of Massachusetts Medical Center in Worcester, published in *Medical Hypotheses,* compared a group of women who meditated with a group who didn't. Those who meditated had nearly double the levels of a marker chemical for melatonin, a hormone secreted by the pineal gland that elicits sleep.

As the Beatles once sang, "turn off your mind, relax, and float downstream."

BREATHING

YIELD: OXYGENATED BLOOD, A FEELING OF CALM, LOWER BLOOD PRESSURE

20 minutes
A quiet place
Loose clothing
A chair

Put on comfortable clothes. Turn down the lights, turn off the television, the radio, the computer. Sit quietly in a chair.

Listen to your breath. Observe it as it comes into your body and leaves. Imagine that energy is coming in with each inhalation and that tension and anxiety are leaving with each exhalation.

Imagine yourself in a beautiful, relaxing setting.

Let a word that is meaningful to you come to mind. Let it repeat itself. As distracting thoughts arise, let them come and go. Even if you don't feel that you have successfully meditated, simply sitting still for 20 minutes or more may be beneficial.

BROCCOLI

Now broccoli, that strong, age-old green, leaps from its lowly pot to the Ritz's copper saucepan.
—M. F. K. Fisher, *Serve It Forth,* 1937

"I feel like I'm at a garage sale and everyone is pulling at the same sweater."

So Lisa Cork told me. It was late March 1992. Her company, Apio Produce, packs about 50 million broccoli bunches a year. She's such a big promoter that when then-president George Bush told the press he hated broccoli, she arranged for ten tons of it to be dumped on the White House lawn. It was a good press event. Barbara Bush met with her, and the broccoli was donated to charity.

But this was too much. The Great Broccoli Run was on. The *New York Times* had just run a front-page story reporting that scientists at Johns Hopkins University School of Medicine in Baltimore had found that a chemical in broccoli "is perhaps the most powerful cancer-protecting substance ever discovered."

Broccoli disappeared from supermarkets. Within two days, wholesale broccoli prices in California, a major producing state, rose 28 percent.

Maine farmer Andrew Ayer, who grows the SAGA broccoli variety that was found to contain the highest amount of the putative cancer protector, sulforaphane, told me, "I'm tickled to death to be part of this."

Recent studies have confirmed and extended the early enthusiasm. The class of compounds that includes sulforaphane, called isothiocyanates, has been shown to block the production of tumors by many different carcinogens in many different cancers. Broadly speaking, they are sulfur compounds. Garlic (see page 135) has cancer-protective sulfur compounds but different ones. In recent studies, when sulforaphane was added to the diets of rats given chemicals that cause breast cancer, the number of tumors they developed, their size, and the rate at which they grew were all inhibited. Paul Talalay, M.D., author of the 1992 Johns Hopkins study, reported in 1994 that not only sulforaphane but three synthetic analogues (equivalents) block breast cancer in rats. The race is on for the creation of a synthetic drug that can be patented by drug companies and eventually sold to people who are at increased risk of getting cancer—a chemo-preventive drug.

But let us not forget broccoli, that strong, age-old vegetable.

Broccoli is a member of a large class known as cruciferous vegetables, so named because their flowers have four petals that form a cross. (One might say they die for our sins.) Cruciferous vegetables include all types of cabbages, brussels sprouts, cauliflower, collard greens, horseradish, kale, kohlrabi, mustard seeds and greens, radish, rutabaga, turnip greens, watercress, garden cress, arugula, and bok choy.

They are extraordinarily nutritious. Most are excellent sources of fiber, vitamin C, beta-carotene and many other carotenoids (see page 000 for information on collard greens), and, in many cases, calcium. A cup of boiled broccoli, for example, has only 45 calories, yet it provides four grams of dietary fiber, about 20 percent of daily vitamin A needs, and 116 milligrams of vitamin C—nearly twice the RDA of 60 milligrams and more than half of the 200 milligrams that is probably optimal for human health. Although heat can destroy some vitamin C, quick boiling, steaming, or microwave cooking has minimal effects, and one study has found that vitamin C in cooked broccoli is more available to the body. That same cup of broccoli also provides 72 milligrams of calcium, nearly 10 percent of the U.S. RDA of 800 milligrams. (Turnip greens, collard greens, and bok choy are also rich in calcium.)

This is not what the excitement is about, of course. But each of these nutritional benefits—dietary fiber, vitamin C, mixed carotenoids, and calcium—has some cancer-protective potential. If a synthetic, chemo-preventive, sulforaphane analogue is developed, it would not include them.

As farmer Andy Ayer says, "Bottom line, if you eat more fruits and vegetables, it's gonna make a difference in your life."

Sulforaphane and other aromatic sulfur compounds in these vegetables protect against cancer in several ways. Two are particularly important. They affect the P-450, or phase I, enzymes, which are the liver's first defense against toxins. When some of these P-450 enzymes break down toxins, they create new kinds of toxins. In many cases, potential carcinogens don't became actual carcinogens until P-450 enzymes start to act on them. That's when phase II enzymes come into play. They break down the toxic by-products of phase I enzymes, making them harmless and water soluble. Out they go in the urine. Isothiocyanates inhibit the tendency of phase I enzymes to form carcinogens. They also stimulate the production of phase II enzymes, which detoxify many potential carcinogens. Sulforaphane is the most powerful phase II–stimulating isothiocyanate found so far. "Our strategy is to boost selectively the activity of Phase II detoxification enzymes," says Johns Hopkins's Dr. Talalay, who has been studying this approach to cancer protection for 15 years.

One contribution he has made to science is a rapid-measurement technology for determining the ability of vegetables to induce phase II enzymes. Sulforaphane is only one of the compounds that can do this; some exist in noncruciferous vegetables as well. He compared vegetables on a dry-weight basis to discount for different percentages of water. Each unit refers to the ability of one gram of dry-weight vegetable material to double the activity of the protective enzymes. Andy Ayer's SAGA-type broccoli, sown relatively late in the season, rated highest: 33. Another kind of broccoli, Effie May, rated 17. Green onions rated 22; kale (Winterbor variety, late sowing), 17; red cabbage (Lasso Red), 13; brussels sprouts, 11; cauliflower florets (Andes), 6; green cabbage, 6; ginger, 4; bok choy, 3; red leaf lettuce, 3; leeks, 3; broccoli (Winchester), 2; celery, 2; kohlrabi (Kolpak, late sowing), 2; spinach, 1; carrots, 1; beets, 1.

One interesting thing about the list is that broccoli is at the top, in the middle, and at the bottom. As Dr. Talalay, now head of the Brassica Chemoprotection Laboratory at Johns Hopkins, says, "commercial-stage vegetables, at the point they are purchased by consumers, vary enormously. There's no point in saying, 'Eat broccoli.' You have to know how it was grown, how it was stored, what variety it is, and what part of the plant you are eating."

It's worth thinking about as we play god with the genes in our food crops. Consider the celebrated Mediterranean diet. We know that the people in southern Italy, the Greek island of Crete, and a few other places who ate a traditional diet in 1960 had very low rates of heart disease and, later studies have found, of cancer as well. They ate plenty of vegetables. The ancient Romans ate broccoli; indeed, its name comes from the Latin word for "arm" or "branch." Since it was introduced into the United States by an Italian immigrant in the 1920s, it has become a different vegetable. How is our broccoli different from theirs? Does dark green, slightly bitter broccoli rabe have the same properties as our blander, paler broccoli? How much sulforaphane is there in broccoli rabe (the variety that predominates in Italy) or, say, Chinese broccoli? Our knowledge of the potentially protective compounds in plant foods is in its infancy. Yet we do know that many of those compounds vary widely in the "same" foods. Quercetin, a remarkable antioxidant (see "Onion," page 211), is rich in yellow onions but nonexistent in white onions.

One thing Andy Ayer does know about his SAGA broccoli. It's organic. Never been sprayed. Says Andy, "We're way up in northern Maine—the very top of the state. Lots of caribou. We're near the Canadian border. If you got in a car in Boston and drove the seven hours, exceeding the legal speed limit, you'd get to us. We don't get a lot of pests up here."

Sulforaphane is heat stable. Cooking doesn't affect it. Of course, overcooking any cruciferous vegetable will bring out the odoriferous side of sulfur. But cook it quickly, and it's delicious. I am particularly curious about the many ways one can cook three ingredients: broccoli rabe, olive oil, and garlic. You can bring the olive oil to a very high temperature, cook the sliced garlic until it is crispy, remove it, then quickly sauté well-chopped broccoli rabe until crisp-tender, turn off the heat, and add the garlic back in. Or you can sauté garlic over moderate heat, add large pieces of broccoli, cook for a few minutes, reduce the heat, and cover, allowing it to steam a little in its own moisture.

M. F. K. Fisher wrote about another sulfur-containing cruciferous vegetable that is often overcooked: cabbage. Her friend couldn't believe she ate it voluntarily. "In our homes," Fisher explained, "we cook it, and eat it, too, not for health, not for pretense. We like it."

BROCCOLI RABE SAUTÉ

For a richer dish, you can add a quarter cup of lightly toasted pine nuts along with the garlic. For a spicier dish, add a half teaspoon hot pepper flakes to the cooked garlic before adding the broccoli. In parts of southern Italy, this is traditionally served with white beans. That recipe follows.

YIELD: 4 SERVINGS AS A SIDE DISH

3 tablespoons olive oil
4 garlic cloves, smashed, peeled, and finely chopped
1 bunch (about a pound) broccoli rabe, stem ends trimmed, cut into 1½
   inch pieces
Kosher salt and pepper

Heat the oil in a large skillet or wok over medium-low heat. Add the garlic and cook, stirring, until it has softened, 1 or 2 minutes.

Add the broccoli rabe, increase the heat to medium high, and cook, uncovered, until the broccoli is cooked through but still firm when pierced with a knife, 8 to 10 minutes. Turn the broccoli a few times with tongs during cooking. Add salt and pepper to taste. Serve warm.

WHITE BEANS WITH GARLIC AND SAGE

YIELD: 4 SERVINGS

2 cups (12 ounces) dried cannellini or Great Northern beans
1 bay leaf
6 fresh sage leaves, coarsely chopped
4 garlic cloves, peeled
2 whole peppercorns
1½ teaspoons kosher salt or to taste
3 or more tablespoons olive oil

Pick through the beans, discarding any small stones or withered beans, and rinse in a colander. Put the beans in a large pot, cover them with 4 inches of water, and let them soak overnight.(Or use a quicker method: bring the beans and 6 cups water to boil in a large pot. Let them boil for 1 minute. Remove them from the heat and let them sit, covered, for 1 hour.)

Drain the beans, and return them to the pot with enough water to cover them by 2 inches. Add the bay leaf, sage, garlic, and peppercorns.

Cover and bring to a boil; reduce the heat to a simmer. Cook, with the lid ajar, until the beans are tender but not mushy, 45 to 60 minutes. (Timing will vary depending on the age of the beans.) Add salt and cook for 5 minutes more.

Drain the beans and discard the bay leaf and peppercorns. Mash the beans lightly, gradually adding the olive oil. Season to taste with salt. Transfer the beans to a serving dish, and drizzle a little olive oil over the top.

CABBAGE

A couple of millennia ago in Rome, Cato the Elder noted the detoxification powers of cabbage. "The cabbage surpasses all other vegetables," he wrote. "If, at a banquet, you wish to dine extravagantly and enjoy your dinner, then eat as much cabbage as you wish, seasoned with vinegar, before dinner, and likewise after dinner eat some half-dozen leaves. It will make you feel as if you had not eaten, and you can drink as much as you like."

The cabbage, a cruciferous vegetable, stimulates the production of phase II enzymes in the liver. In scientific studies, people who eat cruciferous vegetables break down "xenobiotic" (foreign) compounds, including drugs such as acetaminophen, faster than people who eat noncruciferous vegetables. More important, these enzymes safely break down a wide range of toxins, including many carcinogens. That's why cruciferous vegetables are on most lists of cancer-protective foods (see "Broccoli," page 38).

In particular, cruciferous vegetables, including cabbage, stimulate the production of the phase II detoxification enzyme glutathione-S-transferase. This is a very important enzyme. Among other things, scientists have recently discovered, it helps the body break down toxic by-products of alcohol.

There are healthier uses for cabbage, though, than reducing the side effects of Roman drinking orgies. In 1557, a Dutch physician named Dodens wrote, "The juice of cabbage soothes the abdomen and relieves constipation, cleans and heals old ulcers both internal and external."

Contemporary alternative health books continue to praise cabbage juice's "stomach-cooling" properties; "cooling" here is used in the traditional medicine sense of countering inflammation, burning, and "overheated" conditions. In *Kitchen Pharmacy,* British authors Rose Elliot and Carlo de Paoli write that "cabbage cools the digestive system, and is therefore effective for indigestion where there is not only swelling and flatulence but also acidity, burning and inflammation, as in gastritis and ulcers." In *Healing with Whole Foods: Oriental Traditions and Modern Nutrition,* Paul Pitchford writes that cabbage "moistens the intestines, benefits the stomach, improves digestion, and is used in many cultures to beautify the skin." For ulcers, either duodenal or stomach, he suggests drinking "one-half cupful of freshly made cabbage juice two or three times a day between meals."

Between the ancient and the New Age, there is also some science. A 1965 issue of the *Medical Gazette of France* trumpeted "a new therapy of peptic ulcer: 'the anti-ulcer factor of cabbage' (vitamin U)." The French, it turns out, were repeating studies made in the 1950s by Garnett Cheney, a professor of medicine at Stanford University. Dr. Cheney demonstrated, first in animals and later in humans, that large amounts of fresh cabbage juice—about a quart a day—could greatly hasten the healing of ulcers. Later research in India revealed that cabbage contains compounds that stimulate the stomach and other parts of the gastrointestinal system to produce mucus, which helps heal ulcers.

So we have provided here a lovely, cooling recipe for Sweet Cabbage Juice.

But don't use it just yet; if you think you have an ulcer, get to the cause first. The vast majority of ulcers in the United States are due to one of two factors: bacteria or prescription drugs. The bacteria, *H. pylori,* has been shown—conclusively, in the eyes of the American medical establishment—to cause about 60 percent of all ulcers. If you have an ulcer, your physician can most likely cure it with a combination of anti-ulcer drugs and antibiotics. (If you do take antibiotics, be sure to eat yogurt—see page 310—to help replenish the beneficial bacteria they kill. Onion juice—see page 211—may also kill *H. pylori.*)

And while the old theory that stress causes ulcers appears to have been vanquished by these new scientific findings, don't forget lifestyle. In the old days—say, ten years ago—the classic recommendation for a person with an ulcer was to learn to handle stress better. This may still be sage advice. After all, many people harbor *H. pylori* bacteria but never get ulcers. What causes one person to succumb while another remains immune? Could chronic stress, which is known to lower immune response, make one more susceptible? It seems likely.

The other major contributor to ulcers in this country is self-inflicted: nonsteroidal anti-inflammatory drugs (NSAIDs)—aspirin, ibuprofen, and many prescription varieties—taken in high doses, usually to treat osteoarthritis. Remember, if you are taking these for osteoarthritis, they are not improving your condition; they are just relieving the pain. Try acetaminophen first. Experiment with other alternatives, such as a topical cream that contains capsaicin (see "Chili Pepper," page 61). And by all means, protect your stomach.

Sweet Cabbage Juice is a good way to begin. (Licorice tea made from whole roots—page 204—is another.) The nice thing about whole-food approaches to health concerns is that they can improve health in many ways at once. This drink may ease indigestion, heartburn, and ulcers. It may also help lower blood pressure, thanks to the celery (page 57). And it provides the cancer-protective compounds found in cabbage, as a cruciferous vegetable.

It's also rich in vitamin C, which helps in just about any kind of healing. Besides, it is simply a delicious, refreshing drink. Cool!

SWEET CABBAGE JUICE

Spring and summer cabbages make the best juice. Look for fresh young heads, not big dark green ones.

YIELD: 1½ CUPS

10 ounces green cabbage (about ¼ small head)
2 stalks celery with leafy tops
1 medium red bell pepper, seeded and cored
3 tablespoons fresh lemon juice

Core the cabbage, and discard the hard white center. Cut the cabbage, celery, and bell pepper into medium chunks. Process them in the juicer. Stir in the lemon juice and drink immediately. Don't wait even 15 minutes, or the juice will separate.

CALCIUM

It's not how high you make it; it's how you make it high.
—Anthony Sebastian, professor of medicine at the
University of California, San Francisco

Calcium, a silvery white mineral, travels in nice company. It is linked with prevention and perhaps treatment of osteoporosis, colon cancer, high blood pressure, and menstrual pain. The U.S. RDA for calcium for adults over age 25 is 800 milligrams. A cup of skim milk supplies 300 milligrams; three ounces of salmon eaten with the bones, 200 milligrams; a cup of navy beans, 128 milligrams; a cup of steamed kale, 100 milligrams; a half cup of tofu, 120 milligrams; a cup of chopped, raw leeks, 60 milligrams; three ounces of shrimp, 44 milligrams; and three ounces of clams, 40 milligrams.

We humans once consumed more calcium. Studies of Paleolithic diets reveal that intakes of 1,500 milligrams a day were not uncommon. But milk? Not Stone Agers; nary a cow among them. Their calcium supply came from wild plants, nuts, and seeds. Maybe some fish with the bones, too.

Not that milk is a bad thing. Whole, 2 percent, and even 1 percent milk, as well as butter, ice cream, and sour cream, supply saturated fat, which increases the risk of coronary heart disease. But skim milk is free of saturated fat. (Skim-milk yogurt—see page 310—may have additional health advantages.)

Does that make skim milk a tonic? I don't drink a lot of milk by itself—except, sometimes, with cookies. But more mornings than not, I pour a cup or so of skim milk on my high-fiber cereal. Turns out this is a smart idea. Excess bile acids that flood the colon may lead to colon cancer, and both calcium and bran bind bile acids so that they are harmlessly excreted.

At the University of Arizona, researchers studied 95 people with a kind of benign colon polyp (adenomatous) that often becomes cancerous. Some ate a daily high-fiber cereal (it had 13.5 grams of dietary fiber, about what you'd get in two-thirds of a cup of All-Bran). Others took 1,500 milligrams of calcium a day. Some did both. Others did neither. The cereal eaters had a 52 percent lower level of bile acids and the calcium takers a 32 percent lower level than the control group. Those who took both excreted even fewer unbound bile acids. So adding calcium-rich milk to high-fiber cereal is a good thing to do.

Other studies suggest that people who consume low amounts of calcium are at higher risk of colon cancer. (Vitamin D is important, too.) A 1993 study of 35,000 women in Iowa found that those who consumed the most calcium were 32 percent less likely to develop colon cancer, though the link wasn't statistically strong. Other human studies have also found that calcium protects against this kind of cancer, while a few have found no effect.

If I had an adenomatous polyp, I might take a calcium supplement. As it is, I'll continue to pour skim milk on my Grape Nuts, though the five grams of dietary fiber in a half cup of the cereal is probably doing me the most good in terms of preventing colon cancer. The most effective way to reduce your risk is to eat a lot of fiber-rich whole grains, fruits, and vegetables, and little red meat and saturated fat. The rate of colon cancer goes up dramatically with the consumption of red meat. Folic acid, found in leafy green vegetables, lowers risk (see page 130). The calcium in skim milk may help a bit, but I wouldn't bet the farm on it.

Calcium does help regulate blood pressure. If you have a low calcium intake, your risk of developing high blood pressure is higher. This has led some researchers to hypothesize that giving calcium to people who already have high blood pressure will help normalize it. Calcium hasn't been a flashy success in these studies, but it does appear to work in some people. One study says it works better in blacks than whites; another, that it works better in whites than blacks.

An analysis of 33 studies over 30 years, conducted at McMaster University in Hamilton, Ontario, and published in the *Journal of the American Medical Association* in 1996, found that calcium supplementation was only mildly useful for most people but was helpful in populations that consume inadequate dietary calcium. That is, getting too little calcium may hurt, getting enough may help, and getting more than that may not do any more good.

The Canadian researchers did find that calcium supplementation significantly reduced pregnancy-induced high blood pressure. This makes sense, because pregnancy greatly increases the body's calcium needs—and therefore the chances of a deficiency. If I were pregnant (an exceedingly unlikely eventuality), I would pay close attention to the calcium in my diet and consider, with my doctor, a calcium supplement.

If I developed high blood pressure, I would also consider a calcium supplement. Hey, sometimes it works, and there are no adverse effects. On the other hand, as with colon cancer, the most effective way to lower blood pressure is to eat more fruits, vegetables, fish, and perhaps garlic and fewer highly salted, processed foods; to lose a few pounds; to walk more. Drinking more skim milk or taking a calcium pill is a modest contributor to an antihypertensive campaign, at best.

If someone asks you about calcium, the first thing you're likely to think of is bones. It's drilled into our heads from elementary school on that calcium, and therefore dairy products, are important for building strong bones and preventing osteoporosis. It's true that an adequate supply of calcium throughout life is associated with reduced risk of developing osteoporosis. In some women after menopause, when the loss of calcium from bones accelerates, supplementation with calcium (often with vitamin D) can slow the loss. This is especially true for women with very low levels of calcium in their diets to begin with. Some osteoporosis researchers have been pushing to make the RDA 1,000 or even 1,500 milligrams for high-risk groups. The research, however, doesn't support this approach.

You've heard of the French paradox, in which the French eat as much fat as Americans yet have much less heart disease. Here's an American paradox: we consume more high-calcium dairy foods than most of the rest of the world, yet we have one of the highest rates of osteoporosis. Says Harvard School of Public Health epidemiologist Walter C. Willett, M.D., "This idea of increasing calcium intake to 1,500 milligrams—do we really need this much? Much of the world, including Mediterranean and Asian countries, takes in much less calcium and has less osteoporosis." Curiouser and curiouser, Alice.

More than 50 years ago, public-health nutrition pioneer Mark Hegsted put prisoners in Peru on a very low calcium diet, only 300 milligrams a day. Yet after a while, they were in calcium "balance"—that is, they weren't losing calcium. Their bodies had become more efficient at absorbing calcium from foods and holding on to it. "These men were adapted to a low-calcium diet," Dr. Hegsted observed. "We who drink a lot of milk are also adapted, otherwise we would absorb so much we would become blocks of calcium phosphorus. Fractures are higher in populations that consume more calcium. One has to ask, 'Is a high-calcium, high-dairy diet causal for osteoporosis?'

"Man developed on a vegetarian diet," Dr. Hegsted said. "We have mechanisms to get calcium from a vegetable-based diet, and when we don't use them, they may atrophy."

He quoted Thoreau: "One farmer says to me, 'You cannot live on vegetable food solely, for it furnishes nothing to make bones with,' and so he religiously devotes a part of his day to improving his system with the raw materials of bones, walking behind his oxen."

Oxen are, after all, vegetarian. Somehow, implies Thoreau, *they* make bones from vegetable food.

The nutrition research community, which receives money from the dairy and supplement industries, has largely ignored the implications of Dr. Hegsted's work. But medicine is starting to pay attention. The key to preventing osteoporosis may turn not on how much calcium we pump into our systems but on how our diets affect our bodies' ability to retain calcium. A meat-based diet with too few fruits and vegetables produces so much sulfuric acid that the body is forced to release calcium from the bones continually to keep the acidity of the blood within bounds. You can throw more calcium at that imbalanced system, but it may not be as effective as rectifying the imbalance.

At the University of California, San Francisco, Anthony Sebastian, M.D., recently tried a simple experiment. He gave 18 postmenopausal women potassium bicarbonate. It's an antacid, but you can't find it in your drugstore—yet. Within weeks, the women stopped losing calcium and started rebuilding bones.

"Acidosis could be causing osteoporosis," says Dr. Sebastian. Fruits and vegetables are the best source of potassium bicarbonate; it is the main "base" chemical in plants—a base that neutralizes the sulfuric acid we produce when we metabolize animal protein.

Large amounts of animal protein, whether red meat, chicken, or fish, not only produce acid but these foods also contain little or no potassium or calcium. Fish with the bones and some shellfish, such as shrimp, do have calcium. Milk, a good source of protein, is also, of course, rich in calcium. Better yet are vegetable sources of calcium such as kale, collard greens, bok choy, legumes of all kinds, and tofu. Says Dr. Sebastian, "Drink your milk, reduce animal protein consumption, and increase fruits and vegetables."

Walking, or any weight-bearing exercise, is also essential for preventing osteoporosis. So is quitting smoking, if you smoke. There's nothing wrong with a glass of skim milk or even, under the right circumstances, a modest calcium supplement, such as 500 milligrams of calcium carbonate. But if you really want to improve your health, you'll change your diet. There's no quick fix.

In Mediterranean countries that have low rates of heart disease, various cancers, and osteoporosis, people consume a largely plant-based diet with small amounts of animal flesh, plus yogurt and cheese. It doesn't add up to 1,500 milligrams, but it keeps them healthy.

Adequate calcium may even keep many of the women feeling better. Several studies have found that adequate calcium may reduce symptoms of menstrual pain. In one, published in the *American Journal of Obstetrics and Gynecology,* ten women, in a carefully controlled metabolic ward, consumed either 587 milligrams of calcium or, with a supplement, 1,336 milligrams. When they took more, they reported better moods during their periods, less water retention, and less pain. Manganese helped, too. A population study in Oregon found that women who drank more milk reported less menstrual pain. Studies at Baylor College of Medicine in Houston, Texas, have found that supplements as small as 500 milligrams reduce PMS symptoms.

So, is a glass of skim milk or a calcium supplement a tonic? It depends on the rest of your diet. The key is balance. That's what we've sought to achieve in our High-Calcium Seafood Chowder. It combines high-calcium sources of animal protein (salmon with the bones, shrimp, clams), vegetable protein (beans), vegetables (leek), and low-fat dairy (skim milk). If you want to strengthen your bones, reduce your risk of colon cancer, regulate blood pressure, or reduce your susceptibility to menstrual pain, this chowder might be the place to start. It also tastes real good.

HIGH-CALCIUM SEAFOOD CHOWDER

To simplify preparation, cook the fish-bone broth a day ahead and refrigerate. You can substitute ½ cup store-bought roasted red peppers, drained, for the bell pepper.

YIELD: 8 TO 10 SERVINGS (3 QUARTS)

1 pound Idaho or other floury potatoes
2 medium leeks
2 celery stalks
1 medium red bell pepper
8 ounces or more salmon bones (ask your fishmonger)
1 pound fresh medium shrimp, peeled, deveined, and shells reserved
2 tablespoons unsalted butter
1 tablespoon dried thyme
1 tablespoon dried oregano
1 teaspoon cayenne
¼ cup dry sherry or chicken stock
1 bay leaf
4 cups skim milk
3 cups canned cannellini or other white beans, drained
8 ounces fresh salmon fillet
16 ounces fresh clams, cleaned, with their juice (optional)
Kosher salt
Freshly ground pepper
Grated Gruyère cheese for garnish (optional)

Peel the potatoes and cut them into ½-inch pieces. Trim the leeks, quarter lengthwise, wash well, and cut into ¼-inch slices. Reserve the celery leaves; cut the stalks in thirds lengthwise, and cut into ¼-inch pieces. Roast the bell pepper over a gas flame or under the broiler; peel, seed, and chop.

Put the salmon bones and shrimp shells in a soup pot, and add water to cover by 4 inches. Cover, bring to a boil, reduce the heat to high simmer, and cook uncovered for about 1½ hours, skimming occasionally, until the bones are falling apart. Strain the liquid through a very fine sieve and reserve.

About an hour before the broth is done, bring the potatoes and 6 cups water to a boil in a large saucepan. Reduce the heat to a high simmer and cook, uncovered, until the potatoes are tender, 20 to 25 minutes. Remove the potatoes with a slotted spoon and reserve. Continue cooking the potato water over medium-high heat until it is reduced to about 3 cups; this takes about 20 minutes.

Melt the butter in the soup pot over medium heat. Sauté the leeks and celery until softened, about 8 minutes. Stir in the thyme, oregano, and cayenne, and cook for 1 minute more. Stir in the sherry or chicken stock and cook for another 2 minutes.

Add the bay leaf, roasted pepper, milk, reserved potatoes and potato water, fish broth, and drained beans. Cover and bring to a high simmer. Cook 15 to 25 minutes for flavors to combine. (If you like a thick chowder, puree about half the potatoes and beans with 2 cups of soup liquid, and return it to the pot.)

Add the salmon, shrimp, celery leaves, and clams with their juice if using, and cook just until tender, about 5 minutes. Season to taste with salt and pepper, and remove the bay leaf. Serve warm, sprinkled with Gruyère cheese if you like.

CARROT

The more I read, the more I suspect that carrots, by virtue of their vitamins A, C, and E, pectin, fiber, and sitosterol content, might indeed be cancer preventive.
—James Duke, *Ginseng: A Concise Handbook*

Let us revere roots close to home: carrots. But first, let us consider the untoward fate of the nutrient to which it lends its name: beta-carotene. In 1981, Richard Peto, a famous British epidemiologist, asked in an influential medical journal, "Can beta-carotene materially reduce the rate of cancer?" That got everyone's attention.

Throughout the 1980s, beta-carotene, an antioxidant (at least under most circumstances), gained in reputation. An antioxidant is a substance that protects cells from the damaging effects of oxidation—cars rust and so do people. At a Produce Marketing Association meeting in Chicago in the mid-1980s, a down-home type who represented South Carolina's sweet-potato industry whispered to me almost conspiratorially, "Do you know about beta-carotene?" It was then that I knew it was going mainstream. In 1991, a *U.S. News & World Report* cover story told us that "oat bran is out; beta-carotene and garlic are in."

Oat bran, though out, still lowers elevated cholesterol reliably. Garlic (page 135), I'm all for. But does beta-carotene prevent cancer?

Probably not. At least not by itself in a pill.

Epidemiological studies have consistently shown that people who eat plenty of fruits and vegetables, including carrots, have a lower risk of many cancers. A 1986 study from Italy is a good illustration. The National Institute for the Study and Cure of Tumors at the Epidemiology Service in Milan compared 417 people with lung cancer to 849 healthy people in the Lombardy region. People who smoked and did not consume carrots were 300 percent more likely to have developed lung cancer than smokers who ate carrots more than once a week. Other studies find that people with low blood levels of beta-carotene, especially if they smoke, are at high risk of developing lung cancer. Some epidemiological studies have also found that people with *high* levels of beta-carotene in their bloodstream are *less* likely to get certain cancers.

So it seemed only a small jump from the "let's eat carrots" conclusion to the "let's give people a pill that will boost blood levels of beta-carotene" school of cancer prevention. In our society, we trust pills more than carrots. Because the effects of eating carrots—and other rich sources of carotenoids, including dark green leafy vegetables that mask their carotenoids with chlorophyll—are so good, it seemed reasonable to try to achieve those effects more directly. The Peto thesis was so exciting that major universities, supported by the federal government, spent millions of dollars on well-designed, large-scale studies to determine if taking a beta-carotene pill could prevent cancer.

It hasn't worked out well.

In January 1996, the National Institutes of Health announced that it was stopping a study of beta-carotene supplementation in 18,314 men and women at high risk of lung cancer 21 months early. The reason was that those who had taken the supplements for at least four years had a 28 percent increase in lung cancer and a 17 percent increase in deaths compared to those who took a placebo.

We could engage in scholastic biochemical arguments over the results of this and other studies. It is possible under certain circumstances that beta-carotene can act as an oxidant rather than an antioxidant. It may act differently in smokers than nonsmokers. But it is clear that beta-carotene is no magic bullet. There is no substitute for eating plenty of vegetables—including, if you like them, carrots.

It is the whole that heals. James Duke, a botanist who has spent more than 25 years compiling an international database on foods and health, writes, "For liver derangements, the French serve carrots at every meal, apparently with good results." Duke also notes that carrots show up in cancer treatments in folk traditions in Belgium, Chile, England, Germany, India, Russia, California, Connecticut, Ohio, Oregon, and Washington. Duke wrote a verse comparing carrots and ginseng:

> Some claim that ginseng is the best
> The miracle begetter
> But carrots cost a whole lot less
> And taste a wee bit better.

A medium carrot, about two and a half ounces, supplies 31 calories, about 7 milligrams or a little over 10 percent of the U.S. RDA of vitamin C, and 2.3 grams of dietary fiber, which is quite a lot. Most Americans consume a little over 10 grams of dietary fiber a day, whereas a level of 25 to 35 grams is recommended to prevent colon and other cancers. So if I were an average American, eating two carrots a day would boost my fiber intake by almost 50 percent.

Whole carrots may also lower blood sugar. Fiber is part of the reason. In a study from Lund University in Dalby, Sweden, published in the *European Journal of Clinical Nutrition* in 1994, researchers gave ten healthy men cooked carrots with their meals. They lunched on 3.5 ounces, 7 ounces, or 11 ounces of carrots. The more carrots they ate, the lower their blood sugar, the less insulin (a sugar-regulating hormone) they needed to produce, and the fuller they felt. It took about 7 ounces—about three medium carrots—to have significant effects. The authors concluded, "The addition of generous amounts of vegetables to a mixed meal improves the metabolic response." A 1995 study by the same group reported that the effects were even better with raw carrots.

The fiber in carrots is soluble, and soluble fibers are known to lower cholesterol. In 1987, a U.S. Department of Agriculture study found that a specific soluble fiber in carrots, calcium pectate, binds with bile acids, which the researchers speculated would lower blood cholesterol. A 1994 German study of women who were fed a pound or two of carrots a day for three weeks, however, showed no effects on either bile-acid secretion or blood cholesterol. (All that carrot fiber did increase their bowel movements, though.)

Beta-carotene has been reported to reduce the risk of coronary heart disease, probably because of its antioxidant capacity, but whole foods may be at least as effective. At the Heart Research Laboratory at the Medical Hospital in Moradabad, India, researchers gave carrots—along with plenty of fruits, other vegetables, legumes, and crushed almonds and walnuts mixed with skim milk (see "Walnut," page 292)—to men who had had heart attacks. Result: blood fats were much less likely to become oxidized, theoretically reducing the risk of a second heart attack.

A medium carrot supplies 20,253 international units (IUs) of vitamin A—about twice the U.S. RDA—in the form of, you guessed it, beta-carotene. But carrots have other carotenoids as well, and those may be more significant than we yet know. In the October 1995 issue of the *Journal of Nutrition*, researchers in the Department of Pediatrics at the University of Minnesota School of Medicine in Minneapolis reported on a carotenoid called astaxanthin. Though it has no vitamin A activity, it enhances immunity by boosting T helper cells, which help orchestrate immune responses. Some carotenoids, including astaxanthin, may help maintain certain immune responses at optimal levels. But if you took a beta-carotene pill, you wouldn't be getting them.

A recent report on the Western Electric Study, begun in 1958, illustrates the kind of evidence that seduced cancer researchers into believing they could bypass whole foods. In the December 1995 *American Journal of Epidemiology,* researchers reported that in the nearly 40 years of the study, 522 of the 1,556 men in the original group had died, 231 from coronary heart disease, 155 from cancer. Using an index for beta-carotene and vitamin C from foods, the researchers found that those with a low dietary score were 30 percent more likely to die from heart disease, 40 percent more likely to die from cancer. They concluded, "These results support the hypothesis that consumption of foods rich in vitamin C and beta-carotene reduces the risk of death in middle-aged men."

Notice the conclusion: foods.

So eat carrots. They do more good than beta-carotene pills, and they do no harm. They prevent constipation, lower blood sugar, protect the liver, help prevent many cancers, protect LDL cholesterol from becoming oxidized and thus may help prevent heart disease. It's possible they lower blood cholesterol. They are cheaper than pills, and they taste much better.

If you smoke, quit, then eat carrots. Don't be surprised, though, if you start munching carrots with the same ferocity that you once puffed cigarettes. A 1992 report—a tiny, scientifically unreliable, but fascinating report—in the British *Journal of the Addictions* suggested that carrots may be addictive. In it, three former smokers who had just quit reported that they were irritable and nervous when they weren't consuming carotenoids. The title of the paper: "Can Carrots Be Addictive? An Extraordinary Form of Drug Dependence." This particular addiction, if it exists, may have to do with a disorder in enzymes that affect immunity, the researchers wrote. It is not likely to occur in anyone who hasn't just quit smoking.

If it did, though, it wouldn't be such a bad thing.

CARROT ADDICTION SALAD

This lovely salad will keep in the refrigerator for a couple of days. Just knowing it's there makes us carrot addicts less nervous.

YIELD: 8 1-CUP SERVINGS

2 pounds carrots, trimmed and peeled
8 or 9 radishes, trimmed, halved, and thinly sliced (about 1 cup)
¼ cup sesame seeds, lightly toasted
2 tablespoons chopped fresh cilantro or mint
3 tablespoons fresh lime juice
1 tablespoon Dijon mustard
1½ teaspoons kosher salt
½ teaspoon freshly ground pepper
1 teaspoon ground cumin
1 teaspoon ground coriander
7 tablespoons virgin olive oil

Grate the carrots, and transfer them to a large bowl. Add the radishes, sesame seeds, and cilantro.

Combine the lime juice, mustard, salt, pepper, cumin, and coriander in a medium bowl. Gradually whisk in the oil.

Drizzle the dressing over the vegetables and toss gently. Serve chilled or at room temperature.

GINGERY CARROT-APPLE JUICE

YIELD: 1⅔ CUPS

1 1-inch piece fresh ginger, peeled and cut into 4 or 5 pieces
1 pound apples (3 medium), peeled and cored
12 ounces carrots (4 or 5 medium), trimmed and peeled

Put the ginger, apples, and carrots through a juicer, one at a time. Stir the juices together, and serve immediately.

BUGS BUNNY MEETS VIRGIN MARY

The sweetness of carrot juice is a nice foil for the tartness of tomato juice. Use the jalapeño sparingly; remember, the peppers vary in strength, and you can always add more.

YIELD: 3½ CUPS

4 sprigs fresh rosemary, needles only (discard stems)
½ fresh jalapeño or more to taste, seeded
2 garlic cloves, peeled
1 pound carrots (6 or 7 medium), trimmed
4 stalks celery with leaves
1½ pounds fresh tomatoes
¼ teaspoon freshly ground pepper
½ teaspoon kosher salt
¼ teaspoon sweet paprika
8 to 10 fresh basil leaves, thinly sliced
Juice of 1 lemon

Put the rosemary, jalapeño, and garlic through a juicer. Follow with the carrots, celery, and tomatoes. Transfer juice to a pitcher. Stir in the pepper, salt, paprika, basil, and lemon juice. Serve cool.

Variations

FOR A COLD SOUP: Add ¾ cup low-fat yogurt, more basil, and cubed cucumbers, and chill.

FOR A HOT SOUP: Double the amount of tomatoes. Proceed as directed, reserving the basil and lemon juice. Transfer the seasoned juice to a saucepan, and heat over medium heat until warmed through, about 5 minutes. Stir in the basil and lemon juice, and serve with toasted bread.

CELERY

If you are diagnosed with high blood pressure, chances are your doctor will hand you a list of high-sodium foods to avoid. There's a good possibility celery will be on it. A single stalk of celery, weighing 40 grams (a little over an ounce), has 35 milligrams of sodium. For a vegetable, that's quite high; the same amount of carrot has only about 20 milligrams.

Nevertheless, it's a ludicrous suggestion on many levels. To begin with, there is the question of sodium restriction. For a certain percentage of people with high blood pressure—so-called salt-sensitive hypertensives—cutting back radically on sodium intake can lower blood pressure. But in the regulation of blood pressure, it is equally important to balance sodium intake with potassium, as well as calcium, magnesium, and boron. Along with the 35 milligrams of sodium, a stalk of celery has 115 milligrams of potassium—a good balance. If your diet has too much sodium and too little potassium, eating more celery will improve that balance.

A greater ludicrousness lies in the idea that an unprocessed vegetable is a significant source of sodium. In the American diet, 85 percent of the sodium comes from processed foods, which also tend to be low in potassium, not to mention high in fat and low in fiber. So if you want to improve your sodium-potassium balance, cut back on processed and fast foods.

This puts celery in the "pretty good" category. But it gets better: celery may actually lower blood pressure. It has been a folk treatment for centuries. In *Healing with Whole Foods: Oriental Traditions and Modern Nutrition,* Paul Pitchford writes that celery has a "cooling" nature, "calms an aggravated liver," and is used for "heat excesses." Both the stalks and roots, he writes, "are used in the East and West to treat high blood pressure and are a safe remedy for high blood pressure during pregnancy."

Recent investigations have revealed that celery is a rich source of phthalides, natural compounds that contribute to celery's aroma. One in particular, 3-n-butyl phthalide, is a natural tranquilizer. It is an antispasmodic. And it lowers blood pressure.

When a graduate student at the University of Chicago reported that her 62-year-old father dropped his blood pressure from high (158/96) to almost normal (118/92) by eating two stalks of celery a day for a week, her supervisor, William J. Elliott, undertook a study of celery in animals and isolated the specific phthalide. Chinese researchers have also reported that three ounces of celery, about three stalks, lowered blood pressure in 14 out of 16 patients.

There may be more to celery's blood-pressure-lowering effect than 3-n-butyl phthalide. At the College of Medicine in the National Taiwan University in Taipei in 1991, researchers reported that another chemical in celery, apigenin, relaxed arteries. It may act similarly to calcium channel blockers, drugs that lower blood pressure. In 1995, at the National University of Singapore, researchers reported an even more curious fact: in animals, celery juice ("aqueous celery extract") reduced total cholesterol and LDL cholesterol. But celery juice doesn't contain 3-n-butyl phthalides; the phthalides are in the vegetable's oils, which are in the stalk and seeds and aren't expressed in the juice.

Whole is better than part, and whole foods often contain compounds that act in a similar fashion, creating a synergistic effect. If I had high blood pressure, I would eat two to four whole stalks of celery a day, raw or made into soup. I would drink celery juice as an option, and add celery seeds to dishes. However, I wouldn't consume huge amounts; celery can cause allergic reactions in some people. Too much can even make your skin hypersensitive to the sun. The beauty of celery is that a normal amount consumed as food may be beneficial. More is not necessarily better.

Celery's calming, "cooling" phthalides may have other beneficial effects. Researchers at LKT Laboratories in Minneapolis report that in animals, they protect against carcinogens. They stimulate the liver to produce more of the detoxifying enzyme glutathione S-transferase. When rats were given carcinogens plus 3-n-butyl phthalide, tumor incidence fell from 68 to 30 percent. In China, researchers report that 3-n-butyl phthalide can improve learning and memory and protect brain cells in animals. Does it work in humans? Someday we may know.

COOLING STEAMING SOUP

This soup cools in the Chinese sense of calming and lowering blood pressure. It steams in the literal sense. Garlic (page 135) also lowers blood pressure. So does a vegetarian diet. For a heartier soup, add fresh or frozen peas or lima beans.

YIELD: 4 OR 5 SERVINGS

1 tablespoon olive or canola oil
3 medium celery stalks, diced (about 1 cup)
5 garlic cloves, smashed, peeled, and minced
1 large onion, peeled, diced (about 1 cup)
2 medium turnips, peeled and diced (about 1½ cups)
2 medium parsnips, peeled and diced (about 1 cup)
1 teaspoon ground turmeric
2 teaspoons whole caraway seeds
1 teaspoon celery or dill seeds
3 tablespoons red wine vinegar
¼ cup fresh orange juice
Juice of 1 lemon
Kosher salt
Freshly ground pepper
½ cup chopped fresh parsley

Heat the oil in a soup pot over medium heat. Sauté the celery, garlic, and onion until the onion has softened, about 5 minutes.

Stir in the turnips and parsnips, reduce the heat to medium low, and cook 15 to 20 minutes, until the vegetables are soft. Stir in the turmeric and caraway and celery seeds, and cook 5 minutes. Add the vinegar, and stir to loosen any browned bits from the bottom of the pot.

Add 4 cups water. Cover and bring to a boil, reduce to a simmer, and cook, covered, for 30 minutes.

Add the orange juice and cook for 10 minutes. Add the lemon juice, salt and pepper to taste, and the parsley. Cook 5 minutes more, and serve. The soup can be refrigerated in a tightly covered container for a day or two, or frozen for a week or two; add fresh lemon juice before serving.

CELERY TONIC

In Jewish delicatessens in New York, one can still find Dr. Brown's Cel-Ray Tonic. Our homemade version has no connection to the company; why would they reveal their recipe? To my taste, ours is less sweet, with a nice ginger tingle. Made with a good sparkling mineral water, it contains calcium and magnesium, which do a heart good. Serve this pistachio-green tonic in a tall glass with a thin stalk of celery for stirring.

YIELD: 4 CUPS

1 1-inch piece fresh ginger, peeled and cut into 4 pieces
20 ounces celery (about 8 stalks with leaves), washed
2 teaspoons celery seeds
2 tablespoons honey
2 cups sparkling mineral water

Put the ginger and celery through a juicer. Transfer juice to a pitcher, and whisk in the celery seeds and honey. Add mineral water, mix well, and serve.

BRAISED FENNEL WITH CELERY JUICE

This quick, unusual side dish is particularly good paired with potatoes or rice to mop up the broth. The walnuts add a more complex flavor, but you can leave them out. Fennel (page 113), like celery, is antispasmodic and calming.

YIELD: 4 SERVINGS

7 or 8 celery stalks with leaves (about ½ bunch), washed
1½ tablespoons olive oil
1 pound fennel bulb, quartered; leaves chopped and reserved
4 ounces walnut halves (about ½ cup), lightly toasted
1 whole star anise, broken into pieces
Kosher salt
Freshly ground pepper

Place a rack in the center of the oven; heat the oven to 375 degrees.

Run the celery through a juicer to make about 1 cup of celery juice. Reserve.

Heat the oil in a heavy, oven-proof skillet over medium-high heat. Sauté the fennel until golden brown, about 4 minutes on each side. Stir in the walnuts, and cook another 4 minutes.

Pour in the reserved celery juice, being careful to avoid splatters. Stir in the star anise and salt and pepper to taste. Bring to a boil.

Cover the skillet and transfer it to the oven. Bake for about 15 minutes, until the fennel can be easily pierced with the tip of a knife but is not mushy. Adjust seasoning, garnish with the reserved fennel leaves, and serve.

CHILI PEPPER
(*Capsicum annuum*)

Hot chili peppers make us warm. They do so internally by stimulating circulation. In large amounts, they make us perspire, which, conversely, cools us down. That's one reason hot, spicy foods are so popular in tropical climates.

But in small amounts, they warm the body. This inner warmth is highly prized in traditional medical systems—as is its clinical counterpart, good circulation, in modern medicine.

"In Greek medicine this warmth is call 'innate warmth' and is said to reside in the heart," Peter Holmes writes in *The Energetics of Western Herbs: Integrating Western and Oriental Herbal Medicine Traditions*. "In Chinese medicine it is known both as the 'authentic Yang' and as 'destiny gate fire' and is seated in the lower warmer in the lower abdomen. In Ayurvedic [traditional Indian] medicine it is the 'fire of life,' *agni*, also housed in the lower abdomen." Warmth, Mr. Holmes writes, is the base upon which the human spirit, including consciousness, the mind, and the self, can develop and thrive.

Chili peppers improve circulation not by making the heart pump faster but by allowing the blood vessels to widen, letting more blood through. Capsaicin, which makes chili peppers hot, stimulates vasodilation, the dilation of blood vessels. Blood flows more easily to your legs, your arms, your fingers, the surface of your skin, so you feel warmer. Animal studies in Japan and Australia reported in 1995 confirm this effect. When small animals were simultaneously given drugs that constrict blood vessels and capsaicin, their blood vessels stayed unconstricted. According to French research, capsaicin inhibits thromboxane A2, a prostaglandin. Prostaglandins are hormonelike substances, produced by the body's tissues. This particular one promotes blood clotting.

Capsaicin may also work in a similar fashion to calcium channel blockers, which inhibit the movement of calcium ions across cell membranes and are used to lower blood pressure and steady irregular hearts, as Bristol-Myers researchers reported in the *European Journal of Pharmacology* in 1995. In animals, it prevents arrhythmias, the irregular heartbeats that can cause sudden cardiac death. Other researchers report that capsaicin acts more like a beta-blocker, another class of drugs used to lower high blood pressure, in this case by blocking the excitatory effects of the "stress hormone" norepinephrine.

Or as Peter Holmes puts it, capsaicin "Supports the Yang, Generates Warmth and Dispels Cold, Stimulates the Heart and Circulation, Balances the Circulation." Holmes, a British herbalist and scholar, writes that chili peppers are indicated for "cold limbs, weakness, palpitations, slow response, melancholic depression." Capsaicin also "Causes Sweating, Releases the Exterior and Scatters Wind Cold; Resolves Fever and Benefits the Throat," he writes, and are used to "Restore and Invigorate the Stomach and Intestines, and to Relieve Pain."

Improving blood flow aids the delivery of nutrients and the removal of waste products in all the tissues of the body. Nowhere is it more beneficial than in the respiratory tract. Chili peppers not only stimulate circulation and perspiration but improve the ability of the lungs and sinuses to "weep," releasing phlegm. Simply dropping a fraction of a teaspoon of hot chili pepper into a cup of hot water, smelling the vapor, and drinking the liquid can relieve sinus congestion. Taken as a tonic over a long period of time, it may improve the functioning of the pulmonary system.

"Capsaicin is far more interesting than most people realize," says Irwin Ziment, M.D., chief of medicine at Olive View, UCLA Medical Center, in Sylmar, California. "It stimulates the mucus-secreting glands in the lungs, and in the bloodstream and then the lungs, it stimulates the airways. In a few people it overstimulates those glands, so they feel more plugged. But in most people it brings relief."

Japanese researchers reported in the *American Review of Respiratory Diseases* in 1991 that in human bronchial tissue, capsaicin regulates substances called tachykinins, which stimulate smooth-muscle contraction. The smooth muscles lining the bronchial passages were more likely to contract when people were given capsaicin, helping them expel phlegm. Another Japanese study, reported in the *American Journal of Respiratory and Critical Care Medicine* in 1994, found that in guinea pigs, capsaicin reduced the airway inflammation caused by exposure to ozone, a major component of smog.

Regular consumption of capsaicin-enriched foods may, over time, have other bronchial benefits, Dr. Ziment says. "In cigarette smokers, for example, it decreases the amount of abnormal sputum, and increases the production of normal sputum. A normal lung produces secretions all the time. People who have chronic bronchial problems suffer from too much of an abnormal, sticky secretion. Consuming capsaicin may lead to an improvement." Not as much of an improvement as quitting smoking, to be sure, or if you live in Los Angeles, moving. But if you can't move, eat hot.

"I think that people who eat a lot of hot foods rich in capsaicin do, over time, show benefits," Dr. Ziment says. "People who are able to tolerate hot foods in their diet may have better lungs."

Chili peppers are irritants. They irritate the tongue, the mouth, the gastrointestinal tract. Several years ago, medical researchers reported a new syndrome that they dubbed "jalaproctitis." Its cause was a college contest in which participants ate as many jalapeños as humanly possible. In some of these students, the hot peppers burned not only going in but coming out.

So amount matters. A little bit of irritation can cause a beneficial physiological response. Too much can overwhelm the system. For years, patients with stomach problems were warned to stay away from spicy foods. This may still be good advice for people who respond badly to spicy foods, but for the rest of us, a normal, culinary amount of chili peppers may actually protect the stomach.

The irritating effect of capsaicin, Japanese researchers reported in the *American Journal of Physiology* in 1995, causes the stomach to release fluid. It slows stomach emptying, which may mean that a spicy meal helps you feel full with fewer calories. But their point was that by increasing the volume of fluid in the stomach, capsaicin protects the stomach lining from potentially damaging substances. (Conversely, milk, once a popular treatment for ulcers, may soothe initially, but then it stimulates the stomach to release more digestive acids.)

Chili peppers can protect the lining of the stomach from the damage caused by aspirin. In a study in Singapore, published in *Digestive Diseases and Sciences* in 1995, 18 healthy volunteers were given a cup of water with 20 grams of chili powder. That's two-thirds of an ounce—a lot of chili pepper. But then, Singapore cuisine can be hot. Then they were given 600 milligrams of aspirin with water. Finally, these lucky volunteers were subjected to endoscopy, in which a tube with a tiny camera is inserted into the stomach, to measure damage to the mucous membranes that protect the stomach. On days when the volunteers took just aspirin with water, they had a "median gastric injury score" of 4. On days when they drank the spicy water first, the score was 1.5, demonstrating, the researchers concluded, "a gastroprotective effect."

In some animal studies, capsaicin protects against cancer, particularly in the lung. In others, it promotes cancer, particularly in the stomach. One Mexican study found that people who eat a lot of chili peppers have more stomach cancers. But other studies don't confirm this. Indeed, a 1995 review by two researchers at Yale University School of Medicine's Department of Epidemiology and Public Health, published in *Life Sciences*, concluded, "Results from recent studies indicate that capsaicin possesses the chemoprotective activity against some chemical carcinogens and mutagens." Researchers at Loma Linda University in southern California reached similar conclusions.

It may have to do with dose. "Very large amounts are toxic to the liver," says Robert Teel, coauthor of the Loma Linda study, "but it appears that moderate use of chili peppers entails benefit." Based on his research, Dr. Teel says, "we would assume capsaicin would inhibit gastric cancer." Capsaicin interferes with a class of P-450 enzymes in the liver that can convert potential carcinogens into actual carcinogens. For example, compounds formed when we fry meat, called heterocyclic amines, can be carcinogenic—but only if P-450 1-A2 converts them. By inhibiting these liver enzymes, capsaicin may protect against some cancers.

So we have a warming spice, which improves blood flow throughout the body, benefits the lungs, and in moderate amounts protects the stomach lining from injuries and may protect against cancer. The most exciting use of capsaicin in modern medicine, however, isn't in food. It is on the skin. Capsaicin, applied topically, is one of the most effective and safest treatments ever discovered for arthritis, as well as shingles and other painful conditions.

When you rub a cream that contains capsaicin on your skin, it burns. That sensation is caused by a chemical called substance P that neurons release at the site of an injury. P stands for pain. So chili pepper burns. (A medical report several years ago documented something called Hunan Hand, an extremely painful condition that occurred when a man who had been sanding wood then handled chili peppers. Cooks are often advised to wear rubber gloves when handling chili peppers.)

Capsaicin doesn't just draw out substance P. It also destroys it. So your nerves send more. It destroys that, too. Soon, the ability of your nerve cells to make substance P is depleted. The pain goes away. Capsaicin-containing creams are available in most drugstores and many health food stores. They have an established ability to reduce dramatically the pain caused by arthritis, diabetic nerve damage (neuropathy), and herpes, among other things. In a New Haven,

Connecticut, hospital researchers make a hot chili pepper candy for patients with mouth pain caused by cancer treatment.

Unlike other topical analgesics, capsaicin only depletes the one substance that causes pain. It doesn't numb. It doesn't affect sensitivity to touch or other sensation. Be aware, however, that when you first apply a capsaicin cream, it will make the pain worse. That's just P coming up. Soon, P will disappear, and you will feel better.

While no panacea for arthritis pain, capsaicin meets Hippocrates's test of doing no harm. This is significant. We do a great deal of damage to ourselves in search of relief from chronic arthritis pain. We take enormous quantities of non-steroidal anti-inflammatories, or NSAIDs, such as Advil and Motrin, and stronger prescription varieties. But by inhibiting the enzyme that regulates inflammation, they also inhibit the stomach enzymes that protect against damage to the stomach lining. U.S. researchers estimate that about four out of ten ulcers are caused by NSAIDs. (The rest are attributed to bacteria; see "Cabbage," page 43.) About one out of every hundred people on high doses of NSAIDs for treatment of arthritis is hospitalized each year for bleeding stomach ulcers caused by medication.

The medical community has responded by developing new drugs that are supposed to protect against the potential of NSAIDs to cause stomach ulcers. But some physicians are crying, "Enough!" NSAIDs, after all, are designed to reduce inflammation, yet osteoarthritis is *not* an inflammatory disease.

Incidental to their anti-inflammatory effect, NSAIDs are also analgesic—they relieve pain. But so does acetaminophen (Tylenol), which has no anti-inflammatory effect. Millions of Americans suffering from osteoarthritis are giving themselves bleeding ulcers by taking expensive NSAIDs for their side effect, pain relief. Now the drug industry wants to sell them additional drugs to curb the negative side effects.

"We've looked at NSAIDs," says Marie R. Griffin, M.D., an associate professor in the Department of Preventive Medicine at Vanderbilt University Medical Center in Nashville, Tennessee. "They are used very commonly, at high doses, with significant side effects, including kidney failure. . . . What we're really treating with these NSAIDs is just pain. So it's a good idea to start with Tylenol, and see if it works for you." (If you are taking acetaminophen, don't have more than one or two alcoholic drinks a day, and don't undertake a fast or other severe diet; otherwise you may be risking liver damage.)

Remember, whatever you try, that the purpose of these analgesics, even the ones your doctor prescribes, is simply to relieve pain. They don't treat the underlying disease. So use them only as you need them; if you feel okay, don't take them.

Often, nothing is totally effective against arthritis pain. That's a sad truth that neither mainstream nor alternative medicine will admit. People who learn to live with arthritis find ways to be physically active, improving their range of motion through exercise. Losing weight can help. So can capsaicin cream.

Let us return, finally, to the inside of the body and to the mind. Some people maintain that capsaicin improves mood by boosting the production of endorphins, natural painkilling compounds. The idea is that your body perceives the "burn" as pain, releasing endorphins. This is a nice hypothesis, but there is no evidence for it. Amal Naj, a *Wall Street Journal* reporter whose book *Peppers: A Story of Hot Pursuits* is a fascinating journey through pepper lore, takes the theory a step further. "The alkaloids in capsicum are chemically related to caffeine, morphine, quinine, strychnine, and nicotine," Naj writes, adding, "but to claim that the pepper itself contains a narcoticlike agent may be stretching it, although the widespread evidence that people get permanently hooked to peppers has led well-known pepper botanists to speculate there may be something to it."

From a scientific standpoint, we are on shaky ground here. Hot chili peppers can improve circulation and are a tonic to the lungs. Improving circulation itself can provide a warm, cozy feeling. If you get more than that from chili peppers, don't tell the federal government.

HOT-PEPPER LEMON TEA

This is a simple, warming, nasal-passage-opening tea. Try it when you feel stuffy or cold. It's a nice pick-me-up.

YIELD: 4 CUPS

1 teaspoon cayenne, or to taste
2 to 3 tablespoons fresh lemon juice
1 tablespoon honey (optional)
1 tablespoon chopped fresh mint leaves (optional)
1 tablespoon ginger juice or grated ginger (see "Note")

Put 4 cups water in a medium saucepan. Add the cayenne and lemon juice. Cover and bring to a boil. Remove the pan from the heat, and stir in any optional ingredients you choose. Drink warm.

NOTE: Japanese-style ginger graters have a compartment that catches the juice. If you don't have one, grated ginger is fine; it will sink to the bottom or can be strained out; alternatively, grate an inch or two of fresh ginger onto a square of cheesecloth, and squeeze out the juice.

BRONCHITIS BROTH

Pulmonary specialist Dr. Irwin Ziment faxed us the recipe he gives his patients, and we started from there. Ours ended up quite different, but it includes the most important thing: plenty of hot chili peppers.

After cooking the chopped vegetables for 30 minutes, you can refrigerate the broth and complete it up to two days later. For a light broth, strain out the vegetables before adding the garlic and other ingredients. (Don't discard the vegetables; they're terrific over brown rice or couscous.)

By the way, this soup is delicious even if your breathing is fine.

YIELD: **8** TO **10** SERVINGS

1 medium onion, peeled
1 pound carrots (6 or 7 medium), peeled and trimmed
1 bunch (1¼ pounds) celery with leafy tops, trimmed
2½ tablespoons olive oil
1 tablespoon curry powder, homemade (page 283) or commercial
2 teaspoons cayenne, or to taste
12 cups Nam Singh's Tonic Chicken Broth (page 270), Basic Vegetable Stock (page 271), low-sodium canned broth, or water
2 heads garlic, cloves lightly smashed, peeled, and thinly sliced
5 dried red chili peppers
2 teaspoons kosher salt
Freshly ground pepper
1 bunch fresh cilantro, leaves chopped medium
1 bunch fresh mint, leaves chopped medium
1 bunch fresh basil, leaves chopped medium (optional)
1 bunch fresh parsley, leaves chopped medium (optional)
Squirt of fresh lemon juice

Chop the onion, carrots, and celery into bite-size pieces.

Heat the oil in a soup pot over medium heat. Stir in the chopped vegetables and curry powder and cayenne. Reduce the heat to medium low, and cook for 15 to 20 minutes, stirring occasionally, until the vegetables are very soft but not too brown. Add the broth, bring to a simmer, and cook, uncovered, for 30 minutes.

Add the garlic, chili peppers, salt, pepper to taste, cilantro, mint, and basil and parsley if using. Cover the pot, bring to a boil, and reduce the heat to a high simmer. Cook for 15 to 20 minutes, until the garlic is soft but not mushy. If you like, fish out the chili peppers with a slotted spoon. Add the lemon juice; taste for seasoning, and add more pepper if you like. Serve hot.

AZTEC CHILI COCOA

The ancient Aztecs discovered cocoa and used it to make a strong, stimulating beverage with hot chili peppers. (Once cocoa got to Europe, it was mixed with sugar and turned into chocolate; you know the rest of that story.) With no sugar to mask its flavor, the cocoa should be the finest you can buy; I use Valrhona. After seeding the vanilla bean, you can dry the pod and store it in a jar of granulated sugar to make vanilla sugar.

This ancient drink warms the body in temperature as well as effect. Though not authentic, the variation with milk and brown sugar is a delicious, soul-warming beverage.

YIELD: 2½ CUPS

1 small dried ancho chili, stem and seeds removed
1 whole vanilla bean, split in half lengthwise
2 tablespoons best-quality cocoa powder

Chop the chili into ¼-inch pieces. Grind it as finely as possible in a spice or coffee grinder or a food mill. Measure out 1 tablespoon of the ground chili, and save the rest for another batch.

Combine the 1 tablespoon ground chili, vanilla bean, cocoa powder, and 2 cups water in a saucepan. Cover and bring to a simmer over medium-high heat. Reduce the heat to low and continue to simmer for 15 minutes.

Remove the pan from the heat, and take out the vanilla bean halves with tongs or a slotted spoon. When the pods are cool enough to handle, use a sharp knife to scrape out the tiny vanilla seeds, and stir them into the hot cocoa. Serve immediately.

Variation

Stir ½ cup hot skim milk and 1 teaspoon dark brown sugar into the hot cocoa.

ANAHEIM STRIPS

This recipe was inspired by the rajas in Diana Kennedy's classic *The Art of Mexican Cooking*. Serve these strips as a condiment or as a topping for rice or baked potatoes. The heat of these peppers can vary enormously, and they will mellow a bit after marinating. (If you have sensitive skin, wear rubber gloves when handling hot peppers; in any case, be careful.) They will keep for up to a week in the refrigerator.

YIELD: ABOUT 1 CUP

3 Anaheim chili peppers
1 small onion, peeled and thinly sliced
1 teaspoon chopped fresh oregano leaves
1 teaspoon kosher salt
Freshly ground pepper
2 tablespoons cider vinegar
¼ cup fresh lime juice

Roast the peppers over a gas flame or under a broiler, using tongs to turn frequently, until the skin has blackened on all sides.

Transfer the peppers to a medium bowl, cover tightly with plastic wrap, and let them steam for 15 minutes.

Peel off the skin with a sharp paring knife. Slit the peppers open, and remove the seeds, veins, and stems. Cut the peppers lengthwise into ¼-inch strips, and return them to the bowl.

Add the onion, oregano, salt, pepper to taste, vinegar, and lime juice. Toss gently, cover tightly, and refrigerate for 3 to 4 hours before serving.

PICKLED WHOLE JALAPEÑOS

All along the border of Texas and Mexico, pickled jalapeños are served with any meal. The best way to have them handy is to make your own.

YIELD: 1 PINT

1½ cups cider vinegar
2 teaspoons kosher salt
1 teaspoon sugar
12 fresh jalapeños

Put a pint canning jar and lid in a large bowl, add boiling water to cover, and let them sit for 5 minutes. Using tongs, set the jar on a clean kitchen towel to dry.

Meanwhile, combine the vinegar, salt, sugar, and 1 cup water in a saucepan, and bring to a boil. Remove the pan from the heat, and let the pickling liquid cool for 10 minutes.

Pack the jalapeños into the sterilized jar, using a chopstick or wooden dowel to poke them down firmly.

Fill the jar almost to the top with pickling liquid, leaving about ½ inch of air. Put on the lid and close it tightly without forcing. Shake it a few times to distribute the liquid.

Label and date the jar, and store it in a cool, dry place for at least a week before using. Chill the pickles before serving, and refrigerate any leftovers.

TOMATILLO CHILI-LIME SALSA

This salsa is great as a dip with corn tortillas; an addition to beans, soups, or stews; or a topping for rice, potatoes, or even toast. You can make it up to a day ahead and refrigerate; add the basil just before serving.

YIELD: 2 CUPS

12 ounces tomatillos (about 10), husked
1 tablespoon extra-virgin olive oil
1 medium red onion, peeled and finely chopped (about 1 cup)
1 medium jalapeño or serrano chili, seeded, deveined, and minced
6 to 8 radishes, trimmed, thinly sliced, and quartered
1 small bunch flat-leaf parsley, leaves chopped
3 tablespoons fresh lime juice
¾ teaspoon kosher salt
Freshly ground pepper
10 fresh basil leaves

Put the tomatillos and olive oil in a food processor, and pulse until the tomatillos are broken up but still chunky. Transfer to a medium bowl.

Add the onion, jalapeño, radishes, parsley, lime juice, salt, and pepper to taste. Toss gently until well combined.

Stack the basil leaves in a neat pile, roll them up in a bundle, and slice them thinly. Toss into the salsa, and serve right away.

CHINESE ANGELICA ROOT
(Angelica sinensis)

Chinese angelica root—known as dang gui, dang quai, dong quai, or tangkuei—is a warming, blood-moving tonic. It improves blood flow at the capillary level and so helps nourish tissue. It is often prescribed for women with painful menstruation, as well as in menopause.

"Angelica root is regarded as the sovereign herb for women because of its power to restore the Blood, regulate menstrual rhythm, and strengthen the womb," write acupuncturists Harriet Beinfield and Efrem Korngold in Between Heaven and Earth: A Guide to Chinese Medicine. "By quickening and enriching Blood, it banishes Cold, Wind, and Dampness."

It's useful not only for women, osteopath Daniel Bensky writes in Chinese Herbal Medicine: Materia Medica, but "when blood deficiency is a problem." Blood deficiency is a broad term that includes such contemporary conditions as anemia and/or poor circulation.

Animal studies reveal that Chinese angelica root stimulates uterine contractions and may make them more regular, which some researchers believe underlies its reputation for treating dysmenorrhea, or painful menstruation. But the main documented action of Chinese angelica root is not particularly related to female physiology. It contains no plant estrogens, for example, although a clerk in a health food store may tell you it does.

Chinese angelica reduces the tendency of blood to clot. In rabbits, for instance, it increases the effectiveness of the anticlotting drug warfarin. In animals, it also acts as a mild sedative and temporarily lowers blood pressure. In human studies, it relieves pain when injected by an acupuncturist into acupuncture points; in China, this therapy has been effective for neuralgia, arthritis, and angina.

The main action of this herb, especially as a tea or in a stew, is to improve circulation. "It doesn't increase the output of blood through the heart or the arteries," explains Dr. Bensky. "It works through the capillaries, improving blood flow in and out of the capillaries." Capillaries are the tiny blood vessels that fan out from small blood vessels to supply oxygen and remove waste from cells.

In Chinese terms, it tonifies Blood. "Blood," though, is not matter but energy—not a substance but circulation. By improving the flow of blood through the tiny capillaries that carry nourishment to tissue and remove waste products, Chinese angelica root can be beneficial for both men and women. But it only helps if you need it.

"In mainstream medicine, if there is a trauma, one puts on ice to cut down on the swelling," says Dr. Bensky. "In Chinese medicine, one gives angelica to increase microcirculation. The patient feels warmer, but the angelica also cuts down on the swelling and protects the integrity of the capillaries."

As a warming, blood-moving herb, Chinese angelica is useful when blood is deficient. A person with such a deficiency "feels limp, restless, irritable, dry, weak-hearted, cold, and fragile," write Beinfield and Korngold.

Conversely, Chinese angelica root is the wrong choice for excessive heat, a condition that generates "inflammation, rapid pulse, and fever," they write. "Heat is distinguished by the appearance of redness and the feeling of increased warmth. . . . Heat conditions are often associated with thirst, dryness, constipation, difficult urination, agitation, a desire for cold."

By enhancing blood flow, Chinese angelica root is useful for women whose menstrual periods are delayed or absent and may be helpful during menopause. But the same action means that it should never be taken by a pregnant woman nor right before or during the menstrual period. "If you are taking dong quai over an extended period of time," herbalist Rosemary Gladstar writes in *Herbal Healing for Women,* "it is suggested that you use it until one week before the menstrual cycle, discontinue its use during the bleeding time, and resume it at the end of the cycle."

Dan Bensky, for one, thinks the beautiful integrity of traditional Chinese herbal medicine is such that an untrained person should not attempt self-treatment. "If a woman is fairly healthy, she shouldn't take anything," he says. "If she needs help, she should find someone to help her. I wouldn't know how to tell the readers of your book how to use this herb."

On the other hand, Chinese angelica root has been part of "kitchen medicine" in China for many, many years, practiced by untrained people who are, to be sure, following folk traditions. If one wants to use the herbs, it seems to me, one should try to understand the traditions.

If you ask for dang gui in a shop that sells Chinese herbs, you will probably be shown large, thin, pressed slices of Chinese angelica root. It is the color of ivory, and good quality is large, long, moist, and oily.

A typical dose is 3 to 15 grams a day, between a tenth and half an ounce. You can eat it—Rosemary Gladstar recommends a piece "about the size of the pink portion of your small fingernail daily"—or grate it into tea. (Toxicity studies show that it is a very safe herb; you would have to eat about 12 pounds to risk your life.)

"Dang gui renourishes, but by itself, it may generate too much heat," says Jacqueline Sa, a Vietnam-born Chinese herbalist. "It needs harmonizing herbs, otherwise it might increase anxiety and irritation. It would harmonize well with red dates," she says. (Chinese red dates, or jujube, are nutritious and calming; see page 186.) She also recommends dried shiitake (see page 240) to enhance immunity.

In a section on menstrual irregularity in *The Book of Jook: Chinese Medical Porridges,* Bob Flaws gives a recipe for Dang Gui Congee, a porridge made with rice, jujube, and the broth from long-simmered Chinese angelica root. "Eat warm each morning and evening on an empty stomach," he writes. "Ten days equals one course of treatment."

Chinese angelica root is an integral part of one of the most famous "kitchen medicine" tonics in traditional Chinese medicine. It is intended for women after childbirth. In traditional Chinese medicine, childbirth is understood as a uniquely depleting event, leaving a woman low in yin and low in blood. In *Chinese Herbal Medicine: Formulas and Strategies,* under "Formulas That Tonify the Blood," Bensky and Barolet give a recipe for "Mutton Stew with Tangkuei and Fresh Ginger." It "warms the interior, nourishes the blood, and alleviates pain," they write. Some versions of the stew include astragalus (page 24).

One can speculate why a folk recipe with lamb, astragalus, angelica root, and ginger would be useful after childbirth. Lamb, like any red meat, is rich in iron and other minerals, nutrients depleted by the heavy blood loss that often accompanies childbirth in countries without modern medicine. Astragalus enhances immune function, which may help protect against infection. Chinese angelica root improves microcirculation, boosting the ability of all body systems to receive oxygen and remove waste. Ginger (see page 146) improves digestion and circulation.

For these reasons, this recipe may also be helpful for women in the days or week *after* their menstrual periods. Try this as a blood-building "tonic"—at the right time of the month. As Bensky and Barolet write regarding their mutton stew, "this formula is an example of 'food as medicine.' Its use has been expanded to include dysmenorrhea [painful menstruation], leukorrhea [thick, whitish vaginal discharge], lower back pain, and abdominal pain associated with cold from deficiency."

If you make the stew *before* your period, just leave out the dang gui. As for us men, it's okay to consume it any time; although we don't need as much iron as women, a little immune boosting and circulatory improvement never hurt anyone.

Even without the Chinese herbs, this is a warming, blood-building dish, so it is most appropriate for someone who is often cold and/or tired, perhaps on the thin side, rather than for an "overheated" person who suffers from obesity, high blood pressure, or frequent headaches. Such a person needs "cooling" foods, including most vegetables, and not red meat.

Nor does every woman who feels tired and cold after her period need to eat lamb. Certainly there are good vegetarian sources of iron and other minerals, including tofu (see page 258), beans (see "Iron," page 180), and dark greens. But food isn't "good" or "bad." Food has characteristics; people have needs. What you need to eat depends on who you are.

If you are low in iron, even red meat can be a tonic.

BLOOD-BUILDING LAMB STEW

YIELD: 6 SERVINGS

2 pounds boneless leg of lamb, cut into ½-inch pieces
1 medium onion, peeled and diced (¼ inch)
¾ cup plain nonfat yogurt
1 2-inch piece of fresh ginger, peeled and coarsely grated
1 tablespoon Curry Powder (page 283)
2 garlic cloves, smashed, peeled, and minced
1 cup chopped tomatoes, canned or fresh
½ cup jujubes (dried Chinese dates)
4 sticks astragalus
4 pieces (about 1 ounce) dang gui (Chinese angelica root)
2 tablespoons olive oil
Zest of 1 orange, grated
½ cup chopped fresh mint
2 tablespoons fresh lemon juice

Put the lamb in a large, nonreactive bowl, and set aside.

Put half the onion in a food processor along with the yogurt, ginger, curry powder, garlic, and tomatoes. Process until smooth.

Pour the yogurt mixture over lamb, toss to coat, and let it marinate at room temperature for 30 minutes.

Meanwhile, bring several cups of water to a boil. Put the jujubes in a small bowl, cover with boiling water, and set aside.

Combine the astragalus, dang gui, and 4 cups water in a saucepan. Cover and bring to a boil. Reduce the heat to a high simmer and cook, uncovered, until liquid has reduced by half, about 30 minutes.

Heat the olive oil in a large pot over medium-high heat. Sauté the remaining onion until translucent but not brown, about 8 minutes.

Stir in the lamb and the yogurt marinade. Cover and bring to a simmer over medium heat.

Meanwhile, strain the astragalus–dang gui broth through a fine sieve or a colander lined with dampened cheesecloth. Discard the herbs, and stir the broth into the stew.

Drain the jujubes. Stir them into the stew, along with the orange zest. Bring to a simmer again, and cook, covered, over medium-low heat for about 45 minutes, until the lamb is tender.

Stir in the mint and lemon juice, and serve over rice or noodles.

CHRYSANTHEMUM
(Chrysanthemum morifolium)

My friend Janet Basu and I had dinner once in San Francisco at the China Moon Café, the kind of cozy place where you can eat alone and not feel lonely. Janet had a little headache. We both ordered chrysanthemum-flower tea, though neither of us knew at the time that it is a classic Chinese remedy for headache. The taste was lovely and gentle, with hints of bitter and sweet. Calming. The Chinese call it "cooling."

Janet's headache improved.

It's not surprising. Studies in animals reveal that chrysanthemum is a vasodilator—that is, it dilates blood vessels. Many headaches, especially those associated with stress, are caused by constriction of blood vessels. According to a 1991 article in the *Polish Journal of Pharmacology and Pharmacy,* chrysanthemum contains compounds that may prove useful in treating migraine headaches as well.

Chrysanthemum, it turns out, is a close botanical relative of feverfew (*Chrysanthemum parthenium*), a medieval European folk remedy for fever (hence the name) and headache. In England, well-designed clinical studies have established that it is indeed useful for treating headaches, especially migraines.

The Chinese concept of "cooling," though, goes beyond headache relief. In one sense, it is quite literal; chrysanthemum is often served in the summer. But cooling herbs are often detoxifying. In animal studies, chrysanthemum extracts protect the liver from the damaging effects of alcohol.

Chrysanthemum may also have cardiovascular benefits. This makes sense if it dilates blood vessels. The Chinese use it clinically for the treatment of hypertension. It inhibits an enzyme, aldose reductase, that can cause the body to retain salt. In one Chinese study, 46 patients with hypertension or coronary heart disease were treated with chrysanthemum and honeysuckle. Within a week, most reported improvements in symptoms such as headache, dizziness, and insomnia, and in 35, blood pressure returned to normal, according to Bensky and Gamble's *Chinese Herbal Medicine: Materia Medica.*

Chrysanthemum tea also contains flavonoids, antioxidants that have been shown to protect the cardiovascular system (see "Tea," page 252).

Chrysanthemum has been reported to have antibiotic effects as well. In the lab, it inhibits staph bacteria as well as shigella, which causes food poisoning. Both chrysanthemum and honeysuckle, it turns out, contain natural antibiotics called sesquiterpenoids. One Chinese study found that a chewing gum containing honeysuckle could inhibit the bacteria that causes strep throat. (In the lab, these natural antibiotics inhibit HIV, but many other substances have done so, too, without clinical benefit.)

Honeysuckle also contains substances that inhibit platelet aggregation—that is, they keep the blood from getting too sticky and forming clots. No wonder the Chinese combine chrysanthemum and honeysuckle to treat people with cardiovascular disease.

If I had a headache, I would certainly make myself chrysanthemum tea. If I suffered from migraines, I might try it and also look into feverfew. If I felt poorly, with a cold or flu coming on, I would make myself a chrysanthemum-honeysuckle tea. If I had high blood pressure or cardiovascular disease, such a tea might help, too.

It's also a relaxing tea for those times when you feel the heat of modern life creeping up your collar. We've added licorice, which soothes the throat and protects the stomach, and Chinese cinnamon (page 78), which helps circulation, though you can omit it for a more "cooling" tea.

CHRYSANTHEMUM-HONEYSUCKLE TEA

Dried honeysuckle has a strong flavor, rather like jasmine, that can throw off the balance of flavors if you use too much.

YIELD: 4 CUPS

2 grams (about ½ cup) dried chrysanthemum flowers
½ gram (about 2 tablespoons) dried honeysuckle flowers
3 sticks Chinese licorice
1 teaspoon freshly ground Chinese cinnamon
1 tablespoon dark brown sugar

Combine the chrysanthemum, honeysuckle, licorice, cinnamon, and brown sugar in a saucepan with 4½ cups water. Stir, cover, and bring to a boil over high heat. Uncover, reduce the heat to medium low, and simmer for 15 minutes. Remove from heat, cover, and let steep 10 minutes. Strain and drink hot. (continued)

Variation

Make the tea as directed, strain, and refrigerate until chilled. Serve over ice with a tablespoon of fresh lemon juice per glass.

CINNAMON

In reading translations of Chinese herbals and books about Chinese food cures, I was puzzled by the universal characterization of cinnamon as a warming spice. Baked into pumpkin pie or sprinkled on winter squash, cinnamon is a little warming, to be sure, but the Chinese texts suggested a much stronger effect. It was hard to reconcile such energies with a spice I think of as simply sweet.

Then I tasted real Chinese cinnamon. It was darker, richer, more pungent, and—yes—warmer; it had a definite bite. It was still clearly cinnamon, but some wilder cousin. So I tried cinnamon tea. It is warming, both in taste and in its physiological effects.

"Cinnamon bark, the part we use, is considered in traditional Chinese medicine to be a deeply warming herb," says Dan Bensky, a Chinese- and American-trained osteopathic physician and the author of several books on Chinese herbal medicine. "It's the kind of tonic for someone who feels cold all the time, and not just in the hands and feet." If that is you, he suggests, cook with more cinnamon, as well as garlic and ginger.

In Chinese herbal formulas, cinnamon is a classic "assisting" herb. It is added to stimulate circulation, to make sure the more specific herbs get to where they are needed, and to protect the body, especially the stomach, from side effects. Cinnamon's reputation for protecting the stomach has some scientific credibility. In a 1989 study reported in *Planta Medica,* researchers gave compounds extracted from Chinese cinnamon to animals and then subjected them to various stresses meant to induce an ulcer: drugs, alcohol, near-drowning. Incredibly small amounts of cinnamon (40 micrograms—that is, $\frac{1}{25,000}$ of a gram—per kilogram of body weight) inhibited the formation of gastric ulcers. The main mechanism by which cinnamon protected against ulcers was by improving blood flow in the stomach. Lab and animal studies have also found that cinnamon has anti-inflammatory properties and may protect against allergic response. It is also antibiotic. These are all good properties to have in an assisting herb, one meant to protect and harmonize.

The most fascinating scientific finding about cinnamon, though, is its effect on insulin. In laboratory studies conducted by the U.S. Department of Agriculture, cinnamon enhanced the effectiveness of insulin, which the body produces to digest sugar. (Brewer's yeast, cloves, and turmeric also had this effect.) The studies are preliminary, but they suggest that, theoretically, as little as $\frac{1}{8}$ teaspoon of cinnamon could, in humans, enhance insulin effectiveness. However, no actual human studies have been carried out.

In a small way, cinnamon may help prevent the common decline in glucose tolerance that often occurs with aging and sometimes leads to adult-onset diabetes. If cinnamon does help a body digest sugar, it would make sense to add it to sweet dishes and drinks such as desserts and cappuccino. Cinnamon sugar, like my dad used to make, would be a good idea, although it didn't save him from adult-onset diabetes.

Cinnamon is a lovely digestive spice, well suited to many dishes. It adds sweetness without sugar. Some American herbalists recommend that their coffee-drinking patients add cinnamon, either as a stick or finely grated, to counter the coffee acids. I'm not sure it works that way, but it probably minimizes the effect of the acids on the stomach.

My blood sugar is normal, and I don't feel deeply cold. But as I write this it is a cool afternoon in early October, and warming the body is what led me to think of cinnamon tea in the first place. As it turns out, Chinese cinnamon makes a delicious warming tea all by itself. As I sip it, it may be enhancing my circulation, warming me deeply, protecting my stomach, making my insulin more effective. At the very least, if it keeps me from drinking too much coffee, it's doing some good.

CINNAMON TEA

There's a touch of sweetness in cinnamon, but if you like a still sweeter taste, add a teaspoon or more of sugar.

YIELD: 1 CUP

About 1 ounce of large Chinese cinnamon bark
1 cup boiling water

Reserve 1 small piece of the cinnamon bark, and steep the rest in the water for about 5 minutes. Remove the cinnamon, and grate the remaining piece of bark into the tea. Let it sit a minute or two, and strain if desired before drinking.

MEXICAN RICE MILK WITH RICE BRAN OIL AND CINNAMON

Rice milk is a cool, refreshing beverage served in Mexico on hot summer afternoons. This version may be beneficial if you have high cholesterol: scientific studies have found that rice bran oil can lower high cholesterol levels. You can buy it in health food stores.

YIELD: 1 SERVING

½ cup brown rice
1 Chinese cinnamon stick
½ to 1 cup skim milk
2 tablespoons rice bran oil
1 teaspoon vanilla extract
⅛ teaspoon ground cinnamon

Combine the rice, cinnamon, and 3 cups water in a saucepan, and bring it to a boil. Reduce the heat and simmer, covered, for about 30 minutes, until just a little milky-looking water remains. Remove the pan from the heat, and leave it covered for 10 minutes.

Strain the water from the rice, pressing down hard to extract as much liquid as possible. Save the rice for another use.

Measure the rice water, and combine it in a blender with an equal amount of skim milk. Add the bran oil, vanilla, ground cinnamon, and a few ice cubes. Blend until chunky, and serve immediately.

CLAM

We Americans eat a paradoxical diet. It is high in calories yet often low in taste. It is rich in fat, especially saturated fat, as well as sugar and salt, yet low in minerals, vitamins, and trace elements. Even as we pig out, we are under-nourished.

Some of us suffer from "white-meat anemia." We eat only white sources of protein—chicken, cheese, yogurt, fin fish—and so fall short on iron. This is especially true for women of childbearing age, who lose iron every month with menstruation. The heavier the flow, the more iron you lose.

If this is you, clams could help. They have just the nutrients semivegetarians need. A three-ounce serving (four large or nine small clams) has only 63 calories. It is a good source of protein (11 grams), with little fat (less than 1 gram), and virtually no saturated fat (0.1 gram). It has some omega-3 fatty acids, which help prevent heart attacks. It contains cholesterol (29 milligrams) but also other kinds of sterols (a broad class of solid alcohol molecules present in fat) that lower blood cholesterol. When human beings eat clams, their blood cholesterol goes down.

Like oysters (see page 218), clams are rich in minerals. One serving has about 40 milligrams calcium, about 5 percent of the U.S. RDA, and 1 milligram zinc, about 8 percent of the RDA. It also has about one-fifth of the lower recommended "safe and adequate" range of both manganese (0.4 milligram) and copper (0.3 milligram).

Calcium can strengthen bones, help regulate blood pressure, protect against colon cancer, and may reduce pain perception and improve mood (see "Calcium," page 45). Zinc is essential for immune function. Copper regulates cholesterol. (Our low-copper, high-fructose diets may contribute to high cholesterol levels; high-fructose corn syrup, a common sweetener in processed foods, interferes with copper metabolism.) Manganese is essential for bone strength.

The best news for those who have forsaken beef, lamb, and pork in their quest for cardiovascular perfection is that a serving of clams provides 12 milligrams of iron, nearly a day's supply. Too much iron (see "Iron," page 180) may not be a good idea, but too little can cause fatigue and perhaps impair concentration.

Fresh clam broth is at once earthy and pure. One evening not long ago I boiled a dozen and a half clams; they were so big I needed two pots. A dozen became sauce for that night's pasta. The rest, simmered in their own broth, went into the refrigerator. The next day, a cup of the pure broth, brought to just below a boil, was heavenly. To a second cup, I added fresh ground pepper, a touch of salt, and a few drops of Tabasco. Perfection.

Which brings us to taste. We swallow the food-industry lie that we need fat, sugar, and salt in large measure to have any pleasure in our food. We swallow the gourmet-lobby lie that we need complicated dishes created by high-priced chefs to enjoy true food. There's no accounting for taste, but clam broth satisfies me.

FRESH CLAMS IN BROTH

Serve this with sourdough bread, a salad of spicy greens, and a glass of sauvignon blanc for a sublime supper. If you want, cook a 6-ounce box of pastina or other small pasta, and add it to the broth just before serving.

YIELD: **4 SERVINGS**

2 dozen small or 1 dozen large, very fresh clams
1 to 2 tablespoons olive oil
1 medium leek, trimmed, washed, and thinly sliced
2 garlic cloves, smashed, peeled, and finely chopped
Kosher salt and freshly ground pepper
Tabasco or other hot sauce

Scrub and rinse the clams to remove all grit.

Heat the oil in a large soup pot over medium heat. Sauté the leek until softened, about 5 minutes. Add the garlic and sauté 1 minute more.

Add 3 cups water to the pot, and bring it to a boil over high heat. Reduce the heat and simmer for about 15 minutes.

Add the clams, cover the pot, and simmer, checking frequently, until all the clams have opened.

Transfer the clams to 4 soup bowls. Season the broth to taste with salt (be conservative) and pepper (be liberal). Ladle the broth into the bowls, and serve immediately, with Tabasco on the side.

CODONOPSIS
(Codonopsis pilosula)

I stopped into a small herb shop in Manhattan's Chinatown to buy codonopsis, known as *dang shen* in Chinese. An old Chinese man, sitting on a three-legged stool, pulled down a jar. I bought a few ounces. He smiled and rubbed his belly. Good for the stomach, he said. Good for digestion.

Codonopsis is the people's ginseng, often used as a substitute in herbal formulas. It's cheaper, less stimulating, and more appropriate for common use. As a "chi tonic," it's used to improve digestion and the assimilation of food and to strengthen the constitution. In Chinese medicine, when a patient is weak (chi or qi deficiency) but needs strong, potentially toxic herbs to "expel the pathogenic influence," as infection is called, codonopsis is added to the mix to "support the normal."

In China, as in many countries where traditional medicine has taken root, your eating habits and digestive ability are the first principles of health. Whether you simply feel sluggish or moody or have a more serious condition, you first attend to improving digestion.

Dang shen, like ginseng, it is said, improves the functioning of the entire body. But unlike ginseng, which is used to treat "collapsed chi with devastated yang," codonopsis is traditionally used to tonify chi, especially of the spleen (read: digestion) and lung. It is often used to treat lack of appetite, fatigue, "tired limbs," and diarrhea.

In *Between Heaven and Earth: A Guide to Chinese Medicine,* acupuncturists Harriet Beinfield and Efrem Korngold write, "If someone is weak, listless, chilly, pale, wants to sleep all the time, and gets frequent colds, this person has a lack of Qi. The module that tonifies Qi matches these symptoms. It is concocted from herbs that affect Qi: astragalus [page 24] strengthens the surface Qi, codonopsis fortifies the interior Qi, dioscorea [page 105] and atractylodes [page 30] build the Nutritive Qi, and licorice [page 199] harmonizes and nourishes Qi."

Medical research, most of it in China, confirms some of the traditional uses of codonopsis. In animals, it protects against ulcers and may increase gastric motility (the stomach contractions that mix food with digestive enzymes), which would indeed improve digestion. It may be helpful in cases of bronchitis, although the only study I could find combines it with another ingredient, so it is hard to tell which is doing what. In animals given liver toxins, it protects the liver. In rabbits, it increases the formation of red blood cells. It may have some beneficial immune-enhancing effects. In one study of 76 cancer patients, codonopsis moderated the immune-suppressing effects of radiation.

The most complete medical research on codonopsis, though, involves the heart. Like garlic, ginger, fish, soy, and many other foods, codonopsis "thins" the blood. It inhibits the action of hormonelike substances called eicosanoids that affect the tendency of blood to clot and tissue to become inflamed. This inflammatory process is increasingly seen as a major risk factor for heart disease, particularly heart attack.

In one Chinese study, 24 patients with angina, the chest pain that often accompanies coronary heart disease, were given 20 grams of codonopsis three times a day for seven days. Ten controls were given aspirin, which is known to reduce the tendency of blood to clot and is a standard treatment for heart disease patients. Like aspirin, codonopsis reduced the clotting factors thromboxane A2 and prostacyclin.

Clots are formed when platelets (small disks in the blood that perform a number of functions) clump together. In another Chinese study, 25 heart patients given an oral codonopsis syrup for a month had a significant decrease in platelet aggregation or clotting. According to contemporary theories, this means their risk of having a heart attack was greatly reduced. (In China, codonopsis is sometimes administered to heart patients along with astragalus, an immune-boosting herb.) In animals, codonopsis dilates blood vessels and lowers blood pressure.

It isn't obvious, to me at least, how to reconcile traditional use and contemporary research. By reducing inflammatory and clot-promoting tendencies, codonopsis may indeed improve the efficiency of the cardiovascular system and so improve the ability of the nutrients we metabolize to get to the right places. But that's stretching it.

Not that I discount traditional use. Even in China, most medical research is just that: medical. It is concerned with the treatment of people with disease. There may be basic nutritional research about the effect of codonopsis on the digestive process and the body's ability to assimilate nutrients, but I haven't found it.

So we are left with an herb with a long history of food use that may possibly modulate immune function in a positive way, may possibly protect the liver, and seems likely to reduce the inflammatory and blood-clotting processes associated with heart attack and stroke. For you and me, protecting the heart and brain may be the most important benefit of all.

You can find codonopsis in herb stores in Chinese neighborhoods, some health food stores, or by mail order (see "Sources," page 321). Look for thick, firm, tight-skinned roots. To make a decoction—the long-simmered tea that is used for many tonic herbs to extract as much active ingredient as possible—boil 1½ or 2 roots with 2 cups water until you have only 1 cup of liquid. Add freshly grated ginger to taste. It doesn't taste all that good to me this way, but it can be an enriching addition to soups and stews that are well seasoned with other herbs.

ENERGY-BOOSTING ASIAN FISH STEW

Serve this colorful stew with cellophane noodles or steamed rice. If you can find one-inch-thick fish fillets, they will hold together better. If you like, add fresh spinach, mustard greens, or chard for the last five minutes of cooking. Siberian ginseng (see page 173), which isn't really ginseng at all but a distantly related botanical cousin *Eleutherococcus,* helps improve performance and stress responses but is less stimulating than true ginseng—and so better for everyday use.

YIELD: **4** SERVINGS

1 5-inch piece codonopsis (about 6 grams)
5 sticks astragalus (about ½ ounce)
2 ounces Siberian ginseng
2 tablespoons brown rock sugar or raw sugar
2 petals from a star anise
1 3-inch cinnamon stick
1 tablespoon canola or mild olive oil
2 to 3 garlic cloves, smashed, peeled, and finely chopped
8 fresh shiitake mushrooms
4 scallions, trimmed, halved lengthwise, and cut into 1-inch pieces
1 2-inch piece fresh ginger, peeled, halved, and thinly sliced
2 cups low-sodium chicken stock (such as Nam Singh's Tonic Chicken
    Soup, page 270) or vegetable stock
¼ cup Lycium berries (see page 86)
4 4-ounce fillets of firm white fish (cod, monkfish, haddock)
2 teaspoons cornstarch or kudzu (page 189, optional)
Kosher salt and freshly ground pepper
½ cup walnut pieces, lightly toasted (page 292, optional)
¼ cup finely chopped fresh mint leaves (optional)

Combine the codonopsis, astragalus, and ginseng in a large pot with 4 cups water. Cover and bring to a boil. Reduce the heat to a high simmer and cook, lid slightly ajar, for 30 minutes.

Add the sugar, star anise, and cinnamon. Cook, uncovered, for another 20 to 30 minutes, until the liquid has reduced to about 1 cup.

Strain the liquid through a fine sieve. (The astragalus sticks may be reserved to chew on for full nutritional value; codonopsis is too bitter for this.) Reserve.

Heat the oil in a large skillet over medium heat. Sauté the garlic until softened, about 2 minutes, stirring constantly. Add the mushrooms, scallions, and ginger, and cook, stirring, for 2 minutes more. Add the stock, scraping the pan with a wooden spoon to dislodge any browned bits.

Add the reserved codonopsis broth and the Lycium berries. Bring the stew to a simmer; then reduce the heat to just below a simmer. Add the fish, and cook uncovered until opaque, about 10 minutes depending on the thickness of the fillets.

For a thicker stew, whisk 1 cup stew broth into the cornstarch, and slowly stir it back into the pan. Simmer for 5 minutes more. Season to taste with salt and pepper. Divide the stew among four bowls, and sprinkle if you like with the walnuts and mint.

LYCIUM BERRIES
(Lycium barbarum or chinense)

You can buy Lycii—small, red, pitted berries with a touch of sweetness—in big bags for a few bucks in Chinese neighborhoods. Unlike some Chinese medicinal herbs, these are clearly food, and maybe more.

Ron Teeguarden, who manufactures tonic formulations in mainland China and sells them in his Tea Garden Herbal Emporium stores in Los Angeles, loves Lycii. "They're tasty, like raisins," he says. "Steam them first, so they get a little plump. Then toss them into muffins, into soups, or put them in the wok along with the vegetables."

Oh, yes, and one more thing. Says Teeguarden, "Lycium berries are one of the best longevity tonics."

In *A Handbook of Chinese Healing Herbs*, Daniel Reid writes that the Lycium berry, also known as Chinese wolfberry, "has been a popular health tonic since ancient times in China, and it appears in many longevity formulas. Among its many benefits, it is especially good medicine for eye problems and improves vision. . . . The herb has nutritional as well as medicinal value, and its sweet flavor lends itself very well to cooking."

Lycii are almost certainly nutritious in the conventional sense. They contain vitamin C; several B vitamins, including thiamin and riboflavin; and various carotenoids, which are precursors of vitamin A. This may have something to do with their reputation for protecting vision; my guess is that among the carotenoids they contain, there is a good representation of lutein, an antioxidant that has recently been shown to prevent macular degeneration, the most common cause of blindness after the age of 65 (see "Spinach," page 247). This is just a guess, of course. Lycium berries contain other antioxidants that may be liver protective: in mice, water extractions of Lycii protect the liver from the toxic effects of carbon tetrachloride.

The Chinese have also identified several antioxidant polysaccharides in Lycium berries that may protect against cancer, perhaps by affecting the immune system. In a study of 75 patients with advanced skin, kidney, colon, and lung cancers, these polysaccharides improved cancer treatment. The patients were being treated with interleukin-2, a natural human immune compound. The interleukin-2 by itself effected measurable remission in 16 percent of the patients. When it was paired with Lycium polysaccharides, the remission rate rose to 41 percent.

One study does not guarantee an effective treatment, to be sure. But it does supply evidence in favor of the traditional use of Lycium berries as a longevity tonic. Closer to food than medicine, they are a good source of vitamins, and perhaps something more.

And they taste good, too.

COFFEE

You drink coffee. It's okay. It won't kill you.

We can state that with some assurance. Coffee has been prodded and probed, tickled, and virtually split open like a frog by medical researchers. And with good reason: it has been accused of sins as diverse as elevating cholesterol levels, causing heart disease, and contributing to benign breast lumps, malignant pancreatic tumors, panic attacks, low-birth-weight babies, and addictive behavior.

Suspicions about this popular drug are nothing new. In 1511, when coffee was new to Islamic society, it was literally put on trial in Mecca. The charge: large amounts could cause insomnia and melancholic anxiety. Defenders of coffee countered that it brought the drinker a sprightliness of spirit and a sense of mental well-being. The anticoffee side prevailed and coffee was banned, but within a year, the prohibition was lifted. (Coffee has often evoked strong passions: in Turkey, well into the twentieth century, the refusal of a husband to supply a reasonable amount of coffee to his wife was considered grounds for divorce, no pun intended.)

In our modern court of opinion, the peer-reviewed medical journal, the consensus on nearly every health concern about coffee has been reassuring. Two recent major studies, for example, found no relationship between coffee consumption and heart disease. For some health risks, such as heart attacks in susceptible people, there remains some concern about heavy consumption, usually defined as five or more cups a day.

On the other hand, coffee could save your life. In the March 1996 *Archives of Internal Medicine,* researchers at Harvard Medical School and Brigham and Women's Hospital in Boston reported a surprising finding in their ongoing study of more than 86,000 nurses: women who consumed two or three cups of coffee a day were 66 percent less likely to commit suicide than those who abstained.

Coffee lifts mood and boosts alertness by the same mechanism: it mimics adenosine, a brain chemical that inhibits certain neurotransmitters. Caffeine is so similar to adenosine that it locks onto adenosine's receptors, blocking them. As a result, neurons fire more frequently, and neurotransmitters that make you sleepy are inhibited. One feels less fatigued. It is easier to concentrate. In short-term studies, the amount of caffeine in about a cup of coffee increases feelings of self-confidence, energy, and motivation to work.

Of course, as anyone who has ever drunk too much coffee under stress knows, such a useful effect can make it easy to ignore the body's signals to rest. In one study of men and women in their early twenties, about half reported drinking more coffee when they were under stress. Feeling stress and ingesting a substance, caffeine, that makes it easier to deprive oneself of sleep is not a healthful combination.

Recent studies also find that coffee exhibits the classic effects of an addictive substance. As a psychoactive chemical, caffeine deserves respect. It can cause insomnia. It can trigger panic attacks in people susceptible to them. Physician-author Andrew Weil likes to joke that he initiates a miracle cure every couple of weeks by suggesting that someone cut back on, or stop drinking, coffee.

So is coffee "good" for mood or "bad"? It depends on you and on how much you drink. If you have trouble sleeping or are subject to anxiety, cutting back on caffeinated coffee might be a good idea. If you are drinking more and more coffee as you get more and more fatigued trying to work too hard, call a halt and make some changes.

On the other hand, if you drink two or three cups of coffee a day, there is no evidence that you are doing yourself any harm, and you are probably improving your mood. If you have asthma, coffee can open your bronchial passages. If you get headaches, drinking a cup of coffee can make an analgesic more effective; that's why Excedrin contains caffeine. If you are an endurance athlete, drinking coffee before an event can free fatty acids in your blood, making them more available for energy and possibly boosting your performance.

For years, medical studies of coffee have tilted between findings that emphasize safety and those that show harm. In the last few years, the pendulum has definitely swung toward safety. For example, an analysis of the relationship between coffee consumption and heart disease over ten years in the nurses' study already cited found no statistical relationship at all. A Danish analysis of major studies found no association either.

Some studies do show that people who drink large amounts of coffee, as much as seven to ten cups a day, have higher rates of angina and heart attacks. But on closer examination, it appears that people who drink that much coffee are more likely to smoke, consume a lot of alcohol, be overweight, and have other unhealthy habits. In such cases, it looks like coffee consumption is a symptom of a stressful life. In fact, overconsuming coffee may allow you to continue a lifestyle that isn't consistent with health. A Canadian study of the link between coffee consumption and lower back pain reached a similar conclusion. While coffee drinking itself was not related to back problems, coffee drinkers were more likely to have lower back pain. "Our findings indicate that dietary caffeine consumption is not related to the global experience of pain and disability in patients with chronic low back pain," the researchers concluded, "although high caffeine use may be embedded in a context of other unhealthy lifestyle behaviors."

Moderation is the watchword. Consider pregnancy. Some studies have suggested that drinking a lot of coffee may inhibit fertility and, if a woman does become pregnant, may result in a low-birth-weight baby. But there is no evidence that consumption of a little coffee contributes to either problem. As a recent review of studies concluded, "prudence might dictate that pregnant women and chronically ill individuals exercise restraint in their use of caffeine, although research suggests relatively low or nonexistent levels of risk associated with moderate caffeine consumption."

Similarly, while coffee can increase the excretion of calcium and would therefore increase the risk of osteoporosis, epidemiological studies fail to document this connection. If you are small, thin, sedentary, and white or have other risk factors for osteoporosis, it may be wise to moderate your consumption of coffee—and get some weight-bearing exercise. Adding a small amount of milk or calcium-fortified soy milk to coffee cancels out any calcium-losing effect; adding a tablespoon or more of nonfat dry milk actually improves calcium balance.

Moderation may also play a role in cancer risk. Over the years, there has been a concern that coffee may contribute to the risk of certain cancers, including pancreatic cancer. A recent Japanese case-control study found a "U-shaped" curve. Those who drank up to four cups of coffee a day actually had a decreased risk of pancreatic cancer, while those who drank more had an increased risk. On the other hand, a major 20-year study in Finland concluded that "the data failed to demonstrate any association between coffee consumption and risk for pancreas cancer."

When I was a child, I would watch my mother make coffee. She would boil water in a kettle while she folded a large circle of filter paper into quarters and placed it in the mouth of a Chemex. Then she would separate the folds so that the filter was one ply thick on one side and three plies thick on the other. She would add the coffee grounds, pour a little boiling water over them so they would "bloom," and then add more boiling water.

Chemex, she told me, was invented by a German scientist who used a beaker and filter paper when he wanted to make coffee in his lab. He believed his method was more healthful than traditional European methods. The filter paper removed the "unhealthful oils," he said, making for a healthier brew. He was right. Filtered coffee doesn't raise blood cholesterol.

Coffee has been accused of raising blood cholesterol. In the early 1990s, however, Dutch researchers discovered that it wasn't caffeine that did it but specific components (diterpenes) of coffee oil. One is called kahweol; the other, cafestol. One study found that as little as two grams of coffee oil raised blood cholesterol in healthy volunteers by 13 percent.

So method matters. Camp coffee, boiled coffee, Turkish coffee, plunge coffee, and any method that doesn't filter out coffee oils may raise cholesterol. One study of Serbian men in Turkey found that just two small cups of Turkish coffee raised their blood cholesterol more than 8 percent.

Filtered coffee contains hardly any cholesterol-raising diterpenes. My Chemex prejudice aside, this is true of all filter-brewed coffee—Mr. Coffee, Melitta, and all the other brands. (Recent studies have found that even filtered American-style coffee may raise cholesterol slightly, but research at Johns Hopkins University suggests this is due entirely to an increase in beneficial HDL cholesterol.)

Even percolated coffee, that dying breed, is okay: the basket of coffee grounds through which the coffee percolates serves as its own filter. Instant coffees are also low in diterpenes. Espresso coffee contains large amounts, but it's consumed in such small portions that a cup delivers only one-quarter of the diterpenes you'd get from a regular-size cup of Scandinavian boiled coffee or Greek or Turkish coffee. (If you drink espresso coffee in American quantities— five or ten ounces at a time—on the other hand, you'll get plenty of cholesterol-raising diterpenes.)

Caffeine itself has little or no effect on blood cholesterol, so switching to decaffeinated coffee won't help; removing caffeine doesn't remove diterpenes. A 1991 Stanford University study found that switching from caffeinated to decaffeinated coffee actually *boosted* harmful LDL cholesterol levels. Others find no effect: in 1994, German researchers gave 119 students about 5 cups (1 liter) of filtered, caffeinated coffee a day, then switched half of them to decaf; there was no change in blood cholesterol levels. Both Arabica beans, used in caffeinated coffee, and Robusta beans, used in decaffeinated coffee, contain cholesterol-raising diterpenes.

Nor is decaf easier on your stomach. Both decaf and regular coffee stimulate gastric acids and may unsettle a delicate stomach; caffeine does relax the muscles that affect acid reflux, however, and thus may contribute more to heartburn.

What removing caffeine does is exactly what you would expect: it makes coffee unstimulating. If coffee makes you nervous, decaf may help. If coffee keeps you up at night, try decaf. If you are breast-feeding and don't want a jumpy baby, it's decaf. Ironically, if you choose decaf, even for the wrong reasons, you're likely to be a pretty healthy person: a 1994 study of 2,677

American women found that those who drank decaf were more likely to exercise regularly, use seat belts, eat cabbage-family vegetables (see "Broccoli," page 38), and take vitamins. A beverage with a healthful reputation, earned or not, attracts the healthy.

With human beings, the role of a psychoactive, stimulating, mood-enhancing, performance-boosting, alertness-promoting, fatigue-masking, addictive, insomnia-producing, anxiety-provoking substance such as coffee's caffeine is bound to be complex. Several years ago, two studies—one in France, one in Italy—looked at the effect of coffee consumption on blood pressure. (Subsequent research has concluded it's nothing to worry about.) The French researchers found that people who drank a lot of coffee had higher blood pressure. The Italians found that people who drank a lot of coffee had *lower* blood pressure. In the end, it wasn't about the coffee at all; it was about society. In France, perhaps, heavy coffee drinkers were under more stress. In Italy, on the other hand, coffee drinking may have been a marker for people who sat around in cafés, talking to their friends.

Into which category do you fall?

Every morning as I write this book, I sip a cup of strong black coffee, brewed in a Chemex, as my mother taught me, from freshly ground beans that I keep in a Ball canning jar in the freezer. Most afternoons, I drink green tea. If I am working hard, though, I'll brew another pot of coffee instead. That's when I know I am working *too* hard.

FRESHLY BREWED COFFEE

YIELD: 4 OR 5 6-OUNCE CUPS

5 tablespoons freshly ground coffee

Put cold, fresh water on to boil. Put a filter in a Chemex pot. Add the coffee grounds.

When the water boils, pour in just enough to wet the grinds, so they "bloom." Then add 4 more cups water (or more or less to taste). Drink in moderation.

CRANBERRY

Cranberries, the tart, red, bog-blooming native American fruit, won't give you more energy, lower your cholesterol, or make your blood thinner. But they do contain some vitamin C (13 milligrams in a cup, about a quarter of the RDA). More important, cranberries prevent, and may even treat, urinary tract infections.

This scientific reputation stems from a 1923 study in which volunteers who ate large amounts of cranberries had acidic urine. An acid medium makes it difficult for bacteria to grow. So cranberries became a twentieth-century folk treatment for urinary tract infections (UTIs). Case studies in medical journals have added to that reputation. But cranberry juice, especially the commercial kind made with lots of sugar, doesn't really make urine more acid. A 1967 study discovered this. Still, people, especially women, reported that drinking cranberry juice helped.

In the 1980s, some researchers postulated a totally different mechanism: cranberries prevent bacteria from adhering to the cells that line the urinary tract, known as epithelial cells. In 1989, Israel researchers reported that, in mice, cranberry juice, as well as blueberry juice, prevented adherence by the common gut bacteria E. coli, which causes most urinary tract infections. A few small human studies also found beneficial effects.

Then, in 1994, in the first significant placebo-controlled double-blind study, researchers at Brigham and Women's Hospital in Boston reported that drinking cranberry juice really does prevent infection. They studied 153 older women—their average age was 78½. Half drank commercial cranberry juice, about 10 ounces a day; the other half got a drink designed to mimic the taste of cranberry juice cocktail without any cranberries. Those who drank the real stuff had significantly lower levels of bacteria in their urine and much lower levels of white blood cells, which signal an infection even before symptoms appear. The researchers speculated that the women drinking the cranberry juice were about 75 percent less likely to develop a urinary tract infection in the next month than the women drinking the fake juice.

"No woman with a urinary tract infection should go on cranberries instead of antibiotics," says study coauthor Jerry Avorn, M.D. "Nor have we proven that they will have fewer UTIs. I would like to believe the study [of younger women] we are now completing will show that, but we don't know that. However, the study does show that yes, when you take cranberry, it does reduce the bacteria count in the bladder."

In *Herbs of Choice*, Purdue University plant drugs expert Varro Tyler recommends drinking about three ounces of cranberry juice cocktail a day as a preventive and 12 to 32 ounces daily as a treatment. There is about an ounce and a half of cranberries in every three ounces of cocktail. It takes about a month for the daily habit of drinking cranberry juice to have its best effect, researchers estimate. So if you are susceptible to urinary tract infections, try drinking a small glass a day. Then, if you feel you may be on the verge of an infection, drink a large glass in the morning and another in the evening.

One interesting finding of the Boston researchers is that cranberry juice appears to be more effective at preventing already existing pathogenic bacteria from adhering to the urinary tract than as a true antibiotic. So it may be particularly useful as a treatment—as a complement to antibiotics. If you have recurring urinary tract infections and are prescribed antibiotics, by all means wash down those pills with a large glass of cranberry juice.

You don't have to rely on heavily sweetened commercial juices, though. We cook the cranberries in our recipes, but that's okay; the protective ingredient survives cooking. Indeed, Ocean Spray, whose "cocktail" Dr. Avorn uses in his studies, cooks their berries in the pasteurization process. The difference is that our recipes contain less sugar.

REAL CRANBERRY JUICE

Making a syrup is the best way to incorporate sugar smoothly into any cold food, but you can also sweeten the juice with plain sugar or honey. Try mixing the juice with equal parts seltzer or Homemade Lemony Ginger Ale (page 151), or with fresh orange juice plus the juice of half a lime.

YIELD: ABOUT 6½ CUPS

1 pound cranberries (4½ cups), fresh or defrosted frozen
Simple Syrup (recipe follows)

Rinse the cranberries and discard any soft or damaged ones. Put them in a large pot with 8 cups water, and bring to a boil over high heat. Reduce the heat to medium, and gently boil for 15 to 20 minutes, until the liquid has reduced but is not syrupy. Set aside to cool.

Strain the cooking liquid into a bowl. Put the berries in a food mill fitted with a fine disk. Hold it over the bowl, and pass the cranberries through the mill. Use a rubber spatula to scrape all the puree into the liquid. Mix well. (Discard solids left in food mill.)

Stir in Simple Syrup to taste; you want a juice that's just sweet enough to enjoy but still has a tart taste. It will keep for about a week in the refrigerator.

SIMPLE SYRUP

YIELD: 1½ CUPS

1 cup sugar

Bring the sugar and 1 cup of water to a boil in a medium saucepan. Reduce the heat to medium, and cook about 5 minutes, until the sugar has dissolved.

Let the syrup cool. Store, in a tightly covered container in the refrigerator, for up to three or four weeks.

CRANBERRY CONCENTRATE

If you want to make enough cranberry juice to last for a few weeks, try this. You can double this recipe if you like. The concentrate will keep for 2 to 3 weeks in the refrigerator and 3 to 4 months in the freezer. We use it in the dessert soup that follows. Here are several more suggestions:

- Add 1 tablespoon per cup to seltzer, Homemade Lemony Ginger Ale (page 151), orange juice, lemonade, or hibiscus tea, hot or cold.
- Sweeten 4 tablespoons with 2 or 3 tablespoons of dark brown sugar or maple syrup, and use it as a topping for oatmeal, millet, or any other hot breakfast cereal.

- Add 1 tablespoon to 1 cup Homemade Yogurt (page 315) and sweeten with honey if desired. Since yogurt appears to reduce the risk of vaginal yeast infections (page 313), this combination might be particularly useful.
- Combine equal amounts of concentrate, honey, and, if you like, low-fat cream cheese and spread on bread or toast.

YIELD: ABOUT 4½ CUPS

2 pounds cranberries, fresh or defrosted frozen

Put the cranberries and 12 cups water in a large pot. Cover and bring to a boil. Reduce the heat to medium and cook, uncovered, for 30 to 40 minutes, until the liquid has reduced and is syrupy. Set aside to cool.

Working in batches over a large bowl, pass the cooled berries through a food mill fitted with a fine disk. Scrape the collected puree from the bottom of the disk into the bowl occasionally, and discard the pulp that accumulates in the mill.

Measure recipe-size amounts of puree—¼ cup, ½ cup, and so on—into small containers. Label with the amount and date, cover tightly, and refrigerate or freeze. You could also freeze the puree in ice cube trays or muffin cups—measure them first—and transfer them to plastic freezer bags when frozen.

CRANBERRY DESSERT SOUP

The flavors of cranberry and hibiscus really work well together. Hibiscus, like cranberry, is rich in vitamin C, which is also helpful in preventing infections. But this soup is delicious without hibiscus. If berries are not in season, use any fresh fruit that will complement the soup's color, which is pale rose-lavender, rather like a Sterling rose. In the winter, thinly sliced Granny Smith apples might be nice. In December, you could call it Christmas Soup.

YIELD: 2 1-CUP SERVINGS

1 cup nonfat yogurt
¾ cup Cranberry Concentrate (page 95)
½ cup brewed hibiscus tea (optional)
2 tablespoons dark brown sugar
Pinch of ground cinnamon
12 to 16 fresh raspberries or strawberries

Put the yogurt in a medium bowl, and whisk in the cranberry concentrate and hibiscus tea. Add the sugar and cinnamon, and whisk until smooth. Refrigerate until chilled but not freezing cold, which will dull the flavor.

Just before serving, spoon the soup into bowls, and scatter the berries on top.

CRANBERRY JAM

Use this as a spread with bread, a dessert folded into Homemade Yogurt (page 315), a glaze for roast chicken, a condiment with any poultry dish, or a topping for hot oatmeal.

YIELD: 2 CUPS

3 cups cranberries, fresh or defrosted frozen
1 cup dark brown sugar
½ cup fresh orange juice (from blood oranges if available)
1 2-inch piece fresh ginger, peeled and grated
½ teaspoon ground cinnamon
1 teaspoon red pepper flakes
Pinch of allspice
Pinch of ground cloves
Pinch of freshly ground pepper

Combine the cranberries, brown sugar, orange juice, ginger, cinnamon, red pepper flakes, allspice, cloves, and pepper in a saucepan. Bring to a boil over high heat. Reduce heat to a simmer and cook, stirring often, for 15 to 20 minutes, until syrupy. *(continued)*

Transfer jam to a bowl and cool. Cover tightly and refrigerate. It will keep for 2 to 3 weeks.

CRANBERRY SORBET

Buttermilk is the secret to making this otherwise acidic sorbet creamy smooth. If you like, drop in a tablespoon of cassis.

YIELD: 1 QUART

1½ cups sugar
2 cups cranberries, fresh or defrosted frozen
1½ cups buttermilk
1 tablespoon vanilla extract

Bring the sugar and 1½ cups water to a boil in a saucepan. Reduce the heat to medium and cook, stirring often, until the sugar has dissolved, about 5 minutes. Remove from the heat.

Puree the cranberries in a food processor for about 2 minutes, stopping once to scrape down the sides.

Stir the puree into the hot sugar syrup. Bring to a simmer and cook 10 minutes. Transfer to a bowl and cool. Cover and refrigerate until cold. It will keep for 3 or 4 days.

When ready to make the sorbet, combine the cranberry syrup, buttermilk, and vanilla in an ice cream maker, and proceed according to manufacturer's directions. The sorbet will keep in the freezer for about a week.

DANDELION
(Taraxacum officinale)

> *Dandelions . . . act as a diuretic, and are believed to cleanse the liver by stimulating the flow of bile . . . all this in the turbid springtime, when everything prepares itself for rebirth.*
> —M. F. K. Fisher, *A Cordiall Water*

In the spring, plants come up from the earth. We forget how significant this once was to human nutrition (and still is, in most parts of the world). One got by in the winter eating root vegetables and cured meats, with nary a fresh fruit or vegetable on the table. Vegetables "put up" from the fall harvest might have retained some vitamins, but by the time the light lengthened and birds sang, one's very tissues cried out for fragile nutrients such as vitamin C found mostly in fresh foods.

When small plants pushed up above the ground, it was time to gather the leaves and edible roots of young plants and make a spring tonic.

It was probably extraordinarily nutritious. A cup of fresh, raw dandelion leaves provides nearly a day's requirement of vitamin A in the form of antioxidant carotenoids (7,840 International Units, or IUs), a third of the daily vitamin C requirement (20 milligrams), plus good amounts of calcium (104 milligrams), iron (2 milligrams), and vitamin E (1.5 milligrams).

Whatever else it does, a spring tonic nourishes. Just as bears will "eat mightily of certain leaves and berries to awaken themselves for the time of frolicking and love," Fisher wrote, "country people instinctively eat such things as dandelions in the spring, in soups and salads, boiled or wilted as a vegetable, kegged the year before as a wine, brewed as a tonic."

In traditional Chinese, Indian, and European medicine, dandelion leaves and roots have long been used as a diuretic, to treat liver and gallbladder problems, and to cleanse. In the *CRC Handbook of Ayurvedic Medicinal Plants,* L. D. Kapoor writes that dandelion root "is a valuable hepatic [liver] stimulant and very useful in obstructions of the liver, chronic disorders of the kidney, and visceral diseases." In *Chinese Herbal Medicine: Materia Medica,* Dan Bensky and Andrew Gamble write that dandelion, both root and leaf, "clears heat and relieves fire toxicity; for any heat disorder, especially Liver heat . . . for damp-heat jaundice and painful urinary dysfunction." In seventeenth-century England, Nicholas Culpeper, in his famous herbal, recommended dandelion for "removing obstructions of the liver, gallbladder, and spleen and diseases arising from them, such as jaundice." In *Herbal Healing for Women,* contemporary herbalist Rosemary Gladstar recommends it for premenstrual bloating.

Contemporary science confirms these uses. In animal studies, dandelion leaf is a strong diuretic. In Germany, dandelion leaf is medically recognized as a diuretic.

One could make a dandelion tea from the dried leaves, for example, or boil down a mess of the greens, eat them, and drink the broth. Dandelion leaf may have potential, under a physician's supervision, as an alternative to standard diuretics in the treatment of high blood pressure. Conventional diuretics rob the body of potassium, but a cup of fresh dandelion leaves has 220 milligrams of potassium, about 10 percent of daily needs. So even as it causes potassium to be lost, it replaces it. A neat trick.

Dandelion root also stimulates bile secretion. Bile acids are secreted by the liver and stored in the gallbladder; they help digest fats. So the root is a general tonic for digestion, as well as a treatment for more serious conditions. In animal studies, dandelion root extracts increase bile secretions by more than 40 percent. The roots also exert a mild laxative effect and have shown anti-inflammatory effects in animals. Paul Bergner, M.D., editor of the newsletter *Medical Herbalism,* recommends dandelion root tea for arthritis (the root has anti-inflammatory properties), acne, gallbladder disease, poor digestion, high blood pressure, constipation, PMS, or problems accompanying menopause (see Dandelion Root Tea, page 101).

Fresh dandelion root may benefit digestion in other ways. In some studies, it lowers blood sugar in diabetics. One reason may be that the fresh root is 25 percent inulin, a soluble fiber that is related to the sugar fructose. Soluble fibers, such as those in psyllium (see page 224) as well as oats, barley, and all manner of beans, tend to lower blood cholesterol and blood sugar. Jerusalem artichokes are a particularly good source of inulin, as are burdock roots (see page 104).

Inulin is not digested in the stomach but broken down by bacteria in the colon. It favors the growth of bacteria that improve health. In a 1995 study reported in *Gastroenterology,* researchers at the Dunn Clinical Nutrition Centre in Cambridge, England, gave eight subjects 15 grams (about half an ounce) of extra sugar a day for 15 days, then 15 grams of inulin for 15 days. (That's the amount in about two ounces of fresh dandelion root.) On the inulin supplementation, there was a significant increase in a beneficial kind of colon bacteria called bifidobacterium. The researchers concluded that "small changes in diet can alter the balance of colonic bacteria toward a potentially healthier microflora."

Serve the sharp, spicy leaves as salad greens or sautéed, wilted, steamed in soup, or as a bed for broiled fish. If you find young dandelions with tender roots, don't hesitate to eat the whole plant. If your bifida could talk, they would thank you.

DANDELION ROOT TEA

Dried dandelion roots are available in health food stores (see "Sources," page 321). If you have access to fresh wild dandelion from a pesticide-free field, or can buy the whole plant, use the leaves for salad, wash the roots thoroughly, and use them in this tea. Use two or three ounces of fresh dandelion root. A small amount of licorice root improves taste and digestibility.

> 1 ounce dried dandelion root
> ⅓ ounce licorice root
> Honey or sugar (optional)

Simmer dandelion root and licorice root in 4 cups water for ten minutes. Add honey or sugar if desired. Drink a cup hot; refrigerate the rest. Drink up to two or three cups a day, either hot or iced, for up to six weeks at a time.

SPRING TONIC

This is a strong, earthy, bracing tonic, a true "root beer." You can easily double the recipe and freeze half (without the seltzer) for up to three months. It will keep in the refrigerator for four or five days. Stir well before drinking, or better yet, zap it in the blender to reincorporate the healthful bits of root that sink to the bottom.

YIELD: ABOUT 8 CUPS (WITHOUT THE SELTZER)

2 ounces dried sarsaparilla root (about ½ cup plus 1 tablespoon; see
  page 104)
½ ounce dried burdock root (about ½ cup; see page 104)
½ ounce dried (2 tablespoons) or 1 ounce fresh dandelion root
½ ounce dried orange peel (2 tablespoons)
8 whole cardamom pods, cracked open
½ teaspoon ground cinnamon
1 2-inch piece fresh ginger, peeled and coarsely chopped
1½ cups fresh lemon juice (6 to 8 lemons)
¼ cup honey
½ teaspoon freshly ground pepper
4 cups apple cider
16 ounces seltzer or other carbonated water (optional)

Bring 5 cups water to a boil in a covered saucepan.

Meanwhile, combine the sarsaparilla root, burdock root, dandelion root, orange peel, cardamom pods, and cinnamon in a heat-proof bowl. Pour on the boiling water, stir, and leave it to steep for 15 to 20 minutes.

Meanwhile, combine the ginger, ½ cup of the lemon juice, and the honey in a blender, and process until smooth. Add the remaining lemon juice and the pepper, and blend until well combined, stopping once or twice to scrape down the sides of the blender with a rubber spatula.

When the root mixture is ready, strain it through a fine sieve, pressing with the back of a spoon to extract all the flavorful tea. Discard the solids.

Add 1 cup of this tea to the blender, and whirl just to combine.

Scrape the contents of the blender into a large pitcher or bowl. Stir in the remaining tea and the apple cider, and chill well. Serve over ice, adding the seltzer for a lighter drink.

Variations

SPRING TONIC SMOOTHIE: For every cup of Spring Tonic, add 1 cup of nonfat plain yogurt. Process in a blender until smooth. Delivers a rich, creamy taste—without the rich calories.

MANGO SPRING TONIC SMOOTHIE: For every cup of Spring Tonic Smoothie, add the fruit of half a fresh mango. Process in a blender until smooth.

SPRING TONIC DESSERT: For every cup of Spring Tonic, add 2 to 3 cups of nonfat plain yogurt. Whisk together. Serve in individual bowls, topped with fresh fruit.

SPRING TONIC APPLESAUCE: For every cup of Spring Tonic, add 2 to 3 cups fresh applesauce, and process in a blender until smooth. Will keep in the refrigerator up to 1 week.

SPRING TONIC OATMEAL: Pour ½ cup of Spring Tonic into your morning oatmeal for a big flavor boost.

FRESH DANDELION-LEAF SALAD

Turn this salad into a light main course by doubling the amount of dandelion greens and serving it with goat cheese and crusty bread. You can prepare the beets up to a day ahead and refrigerate them.

YIELD: **4** SIDE-DISH SERVINGS

¾ to 1 pound beets, scrubbed and tops trimmed to ½ inch
½ pound fresh dandelion leaves
½ cup walnut pieces, lightly toasted
2 tablespoons sherry vinegar or red wine vinegar
½ teaspoon kosher salt
¼ teaspoon freshly ground pepper
1 tablespoon snipped chives
5 tablespoons walnut or olive oil

Place a rack in the center of the oven, and heat it to 425 degrees.

Wrap the beets individually in foil, sealing the edges. Bake until they are easily pierced with the tip of a knife, 35 minutes to 1 hour depending on their size.

When cool enough to handle, slip off the skins, and cut the beets into ½-inch cubes.

Wash the dandelion leaves well to remove all sand and grit. Spin them dry, and put them in a large serving bowl. Add the beets and walnuts.   (*continued*)

In a small bowl, combine the vinegar, salt, pepper, and chives. Slowly whisk in the oil until well combined. Drizzle the vinaigrette over the salad, toss well, and serve.

BURDOCK ROOT
(Arctium lappa)

Burdock root, an ingredient in our Spring Tonic, is a long, skinny brown tuber. Called *gobo* in Japan, it may show up on your plate in a sushi or macro-biotic restaurant.

Burdock has a long folk history as a cancer treatment. Some scientific stud-ies have found that it prevents potentially carcinogenic mutations, and one found an antitumor effect in a test tube, but there has been no significant research to back up this claim.

However, burdock root does, like dandelion root, stimulate bile secretions. It is also a rich source of inulin (see page 100) and so may lower blood sugar and stimulate beneficial colon bacteria.

Be sure you get it from a reliable source, though, as there have been a few cases of substitution with belladonna, a toxic plant (see "Sources," page 321).

SARSAPARILLA ROOT
(Smilax officinalis)

Sarsaparilla root, another Spring Tonic ingredient, is also known as smilax. In the Old West, sarsaparilla beer was often used to treat syphilis. (This fact lends a different interpretation to those old movies in which the hero bellies up to the bar and orders a sarsaparilla.) It was found to be an effective treatment in one Chinese study, though, needless to say, anyone with syphilis should see a doctor and not mess around with sarsaparilla.

Sarsaparilla does have documented diuretic and antibiotic properties. Chinese researchers have identified many plant steroids (saponins)—compounds that are chemically similar to human hormones—in various smilax species, but it's not yet clear exactly what they do. One 1988 Italian study suggested that the sarsaparilla lowers uric acid and may be useful in the treatment of gout.

Sarsaparilla is included in liver-cleansing tonics in many parts of the world. In *The Yoga of Herbs,* a book about traditional Indian herbs, for example, David Frawley and Vasant Lad write that sarsaparilla "purifies the urito-genital tract, dispelling all infection and inflammation." In these tonics, it is often combined with burdock and dandelion roots.

DIOSCOREA
(Dioscorea opposita)

Dioscorea, or Chinese wild yam, is a white root vegetable. It is classified as a "chi tonic" by some practitioners of traditional Chinese medicine and as a replenisher of "chi and essence" by others. In *Between Heaven and Earth: A Guide to Chinese Medicine,* Harriet Beinfield and Efrem Korngold write that dioscorea "relieves weakness, fatigue, generates tissue; promotes growth; enhances fertility."

It is often added to Chinese tonic soups. Beinfield and Korngold, for example, include one ounce of dioscorea root in a soup that also contains astragalus, lotus seeds, codonopsis, jujubes (Chinese red dates), ginger, turnips, yams, and chopped parsley in a vegetable stock. The soup "energizes, builds vital capacity, and increases immunity," they write.

Astragalus (page 24) does enhance immunity, jujubes (page 186) are a mild sedative, codonopsis (page 83) thins the blood and is reputed to improve digestion, and ginger (page 146) has many benefits, especially for digestion. But what does dioscorea contribute?

For one thing, it is a rich source of plant steroids, which are very similar structurally to human hormones. Dioscorea is a particularly good source of diosgenin, also found in soybeans (see "Tofu," page 258). Diosgenin is similar to the female hormone progesterone and, extracted from Mexican wild yam, was once a raw material for birth control pills. (When the price of Mexican yam got too high, drug makers switched to soybeans and other sources.)

In the lab, diosgenin can be converted to DHEA, the "mother steroid" and a precursor to estrogen, progesterone, and testosterone.

We humans produce DHEA in our adrenals, but production peaks at about the age of 30. A 1986 study reported in the *New England Journal of Medicine* found that men with the highest blood levels of DHEA had half the incidence of heart disease of men with lower levels. (This effect wasn't found in women, however.) In animals given carcinogens, injecting DHEA prevents breast tumors. Some small studies have suggested that DHEA may play a role in Alzheimer's disease, lupus, AIDS, obesity, and aging itself. In human studies, people who are given capsules containing DHEA gain muscle mass and say they need less sleep and feel more energetic. It is also said to boost immunity and improve mental acuity.

DHEA was once available in health food stores, but the FDA banned it. It's really a drug, and its long-term side effects are unknown.

Since then, health food supplement manufacturers have been promoting dioscorea as an alternative. One promoter declared over the Internet that dioscorea "contains the basic DHEA compound in precursor form which our bodies can use to manufacture DHEA."

It doesn't work that way, however. The conversion of dioscorea to DHEA "can be done in a chemical laboratory with sulfur, but the body can't do it," says William Regelson, M.D., an oncologist at the Medical College of Virginia and an expert on DHEA.

Dioscorea's diosgenin, on the other hand, is itself very close in structure to the female hormone progesterone. An extract of wild yam that is rich in diosgenin is marketed as a skin cream for women going through menopause. A number of physicians believe that this natural progesterone is better tolerated, with fewer side effects, than the synthetic kind usually prescribed in hormone replacement therapy. The diosgenin (or natural progesterone, if you will) is absorbed through the skin. Like synthetic hormone replacement, diosgenin may help prevent osteoporosis, the risk of which rises rapidly in menopause.

We are still pretty far from the kitchen. It is possible that like soybeans, dioscorea in the diet may affect human hormones. It may smooth the passage to menopause, although a diosgenin-rich cream may be better for this purpose. We really know very little about the effect of plant steroids on humans. Some researchers believe that consuming high levels of these hormonelike substances in foods may actually increase the risk of hormone-related cancers, such as breast cancer. Others believe it may lower the risk dramatically. Only good studies will answer this question and others.

Wild yam cream, for example, is a plant-derived drug. Like any drug, one needs medical guidance to take it safely. If you are a woman going through menopause and want an alternative to synthetic hormone replacement therapy, find a doctor you can talk to about dioscorea cream.

In small amounts in the diet, on the other hand, dioscorea may play an entirely different role. Chinese herbalists recommend it to "tonify" and "augment" the spleen and stomach, which govern digestion. It is used for such spleen-deficiency symptoms as diarrhea, fatigue, and lack of appetite. I hesitate to speculate what physiology may lie behind such traditional use. I suspect that as we understand dioscorea and diosgenin better, we will eventually discover that there is a rational explanation.

On the other hand, I am reasonably certain that consuming dishes that contain dioscorea will lower blood cholesterol. Plant sterols such as diosgenin are similar to cholesterol, which the body uses in synthesizing sex hormones. Because it is so similar, diosgenin interferes with cholesterol absorption. Diosgenin also stimulates the liver to produce more bile acid salts, which require cholesterol. To get more cholesterol to the liver to make more bile acid salts, the body draws it from the blood. As a result, blood cholesterol levels go down. Diosgenin has been shown to lower blood cholesterol in rats, chickens, rabbits, guinea pigs, mice, and dogs. As far as I can determine, it hasn't yet been studied for this effect in humans.

Like other plant steroids—and, indeed, like synthetic steroid drugs—diosgenin and the dioscorea that contains it are markedly anti-inflammatory. In herbal medicine, dioscorea is often used to treat rheumatoid arthritis, an autoimmune inflammatory disease.

So you might consider the recipe that follows as a relaxing (see "Jujube," page 186), cholesterol-lowering, anti-inflammatory, nourishing food. Whether it is a good food to consume during menopause is something you'll have to discuss with your health care practitioner.

CHINESE YAM AND JUJUBE CONGEE

You can simmer this all day in a Crock-Pot, or cook it in a pressure cooker in about 45 minutes.

10 jujubes (dried Chinese dates)
1½ ounces dioscorea (Chinese yam), cut into ¼-inch pieces
1 cup long-grain white or brown rice
Brown sugar, honey, or molasses

Crush each of the jujubes with a pair of pliers or kitchen shears so that the hard nut in the center cracks open.

Put the jujube, dioscorea, and rice in a large pot. Add 8 cups water if using white rice, 6 cups if using brown rice.

Cover the pot and bring it to a boil. Reduce the heat and simmer for about 3½ hours, until the rice has broken down and the liquid is thick with starch.

Remove the hard jujube nuts and stir in brown sugar to taste. Serve hot.

FASTING

He that feeds barely fasts sufficiently.
— Randle Cotgrave (d. circa 1634), *French-English
Dictionary,* quoted in *A Commonplace Book of Cookery*

Fasting or a very light diet is indicated in treating infections.
— Michael Tierra, *Planetary Herbology*

Sometimes, the best thing to eat is next to nothing.

Buddha fasted. Moses fasted. Jesus fasted. They did it for spiritual reasons.

Few in science study the physiology of spirituality, but it is worth noting that in animals, after a day without food, brain levels of natural opiates rise. There may be some physiology behind the idea of fasting in order to attain higher states of consciousness.

But our subject is health. Fasting, the voluntary abstention from food, has a very good reputation in alternative health circles and a rather nasty one in mainstream medicine.

A trip into any health food store will reveal several books endorsing the health-giving powers of fasting—with water only or with juices and broths and often with enemas and high colonics—as the answer to just about any health concern from acne to yeast infection.

Medical studies have burst some bubbles. Fasting is not a good long-term approach to weight loss, for example. In the first few days, you'll lose water; after that, your body will begin to break down muscle, and after that, your body will break down fat, releasing toxic by-products (ketones) that make your breath smell terrible and may make you sick. More significantly, after several days, your body's metabolism will begin to slow down to adapt to starvation, and when you start eating again, you will need fewer calories and so gain weight more easily. (In certain medical situations of life-threatening obesity, however, a short-term, medically supervised semifast that includes protein and electrolytes can be useful.)

Long-term fasts can be acutely dangerous. If all you do is drink water for a week, you may create an electrolyte imbalance, imperiling your heart. A long, water-only fast can deplete the body of iron and zinc and impair immunity. In some studies, a long fast reduces the ability of the body to create antibodies to potential pathogens. Pregnant women, people with diabetes or kidney or liver disease or anyone taking medication should avoid fasting. Even in Ramadan, the Islamic fasting ritual, the sick are exempt from the obligation.

But short-term fasting may enhance immunity. In a 1983 study published in the *American Journal of Medicine,* 15 obese subjects who went on a 14-day fast had a 24 percent increase in their immune system's natural killer cells. Other immune elements increased, too. Many animal studies have found the same effect: short-term starvation temporarily boosted the immune system. This may be a response that evolved to increase the chances of survival under conditions of famine.

Simply eating less may also boost immunity. Feeding animals 20 to 40 percent less than normal has been found to protect T cells, prevent autoimmune diseases, increase the ability of the immune system's macrophages to engulf and devour potential infectious agents, and, in general, retard aging. (The ability to retard autoimmune diseases may be clinically useful: several human studies find that medically supervised fasting can significantly improve the symptoms of rheumatoid arthritis, an autoimmune disease.)

Given the immunity benefits of short-term fasting or caloric restriction, I think it is interesting that when we feel sick, we often don't feel like eating. When we have a fever, there is often a drop in blood levels of many vitamins and minerals. They don't disappear; they get stored in the liver. The body is very smart: it takes nutrients out of the blood, where bacteria and other pathogens can feed on them. That's why if you have a cold or flu, you may want to stop taking a multivitamin-mineral supplement, especially if it contains iron. (Vitamin C is okay.)

Mice underfed by 40 percent live nearly twice as long as mice allowed to eat as much as mice will. Immunity is only one reason. Another is that when food is rare, the body becomes more efficient at utilizing it. In animals, for example, those who are restricted in calories become so efficient at metabolizing carbohydrates that they produce less insulin and have less of a rise in blood sugar than other animals given the same amount of food. Studies published in the *Proceedings of the National Academy of Sciences* in April 1996 reveal that these benefits also occur in monkeys. When fed a nutritious diet with 30 percent fewer calories than a free-eating control group, they had less cancer, heart disease, diabetes, and premature death.

Primates such as monkeys are our closest relatives, so these findings may have real meaning for humans. Although human studies haven't been done, it is reasonable to speculate that eating less than we might want to may help prevent chronic illness. Just a little hunger is not only the best sauce, it is good preventive medicine. As the fighters say, *stay hungry.*

Some ecologists have gone so far as to put forth an evolutionary theory to explain the protective mechanisms that emerge in the famine stage of the feast-or-famine cycle that has characterized most of human history. When food is low, our immune system revs up, keeping the population of pathogens and parasites in check. When food is plentiful, *their* populations rise, keeping *our* numbers in check.

Just how it works is another question. There are many mechanisms. Consider quercetin. It's one of the most powerful cancer-protective substances ever discovered in food (see "Apple," page 15; "Onion," page 211; "Tea," page 252; and "Wine," page 301). It is only effective, however, when it is liberated from the sugars that bind it. Fermentation into wine does that. So do beneficial bacteria in the intestines. Eating more fruits and vegetables promotes—and too much meat inhibits—the growth of beneficial bacteria that are capable of breaking down the sugars.

A sparse diet helps. Like many living things, the beneficial bacteria in the gut go after the easy pickings first. They'll break down easily digested sugars and starches before attacking tightly bound quercetin-containing sugars. "They'll eat the chocolate mousse first," says biochemist Terrance Leighton of the University of California at Berkeley. "It's the starving ones that go after the glycosides [sugar molecules]." Eat less, and those bugs won't have any choice but to liberate quercetin.

True hunger is a terrible thing, but a little hunger is healthful. In Crete in 1960, men had almost no coronary heart disease and the longest life expectancy on earth. They led very active lives on a mountainous island, with few cars, a lot of farmwork, and cold nights without central heating. They ate a mostly vegetarian diet rich in olive oil, vegetables, legumes, fruits, nuts, fish, seafood, cheese, yogurt, fermented foods, and plenty of bread. They ate fruit when it was in season.

But much of the time, they were just a little hungry. This is worth remembering, especially when we read that we can eat as much olive oil as we want and stay healthy. Olive oil (page 208) is a good food, to be sure. But the people on whose diet its reputation is based ate not out of desire but necessity. When they ate, they were hungry. As a recent French study put it, "the Mediterranean diet is characterized by a certain frugality."

Religion plays a role in that frugality. If one follows a strict Greek Orthodox tradition, for example, about half the days of the year have some dietary restriction. On all the fast days, one eats no meat. On some days, one omits dairy and eggs. Then fish. Then wine and oil. On the most restricted days, one can eat only grains, legumes, vegetables, nuts, and fruits, cooked in water. (Of course, there was no limitation on the culinary creativity that might attend such simplicity.)

So let us call a truce between the New Age and the age of science. A look at tradition might help, too. Extreme fasts are used in extreme medical situations. A more moderate desire to improve health is sustained by a more moderate fast: a one-day fast with water only or with fruit juices or vegetable broths. A little temporary underfeeding, a day without food once a week or once a month, might rev up the immune system. That, in turn, as herbalist Michael Tierra suggests, might help the body fight infection.

One can also simply eat *less,* rather than eating until full and then some. We're not talking about dieting here but rather a habit of not overeating. In China, notes Cornell University nutrition researcher Banoo Parpia, "there is an emphasis on balance and restraint. It's yin and yang. We say, 'It is praiseworthy to eat until you are only 70 percent full.'"

In India's Ayurvedic tradition, the most balanced fast—the fast of monks— is to eat nothing but *kitcheri,* a porridge made from brown rice, mung beans, and spices. It is well balanced: beans and rice provide a complete protein and many vitamins and minerals. There are those who say that eating kitcheri alone for two or three weeks will cure all ills.

That may be too much for you—or rather, too little. But try it one weekend. Drink plenty of fluids. If you wish, drink fresh vegetable juices as well. Kitcheri is an anomaly: a nutritionally balanced fast.

KITCHERI

In hot months or if you have a hot constitution, you can omit the ginger. In cold months or if you often feel cold, you can add more.

For a lighter dish, use up to twice as much rice as mung beans. It will still contain plenty of complete protein. Some recipes call for split yellow mung beans; they're good, too. Or you can substitute barley, millet, or other grains for the rice.

Kitcheri can be refrigerated up to a week or frozen up to a month. It reheats very well; just add a bit of water if needed to thin it.

YIELD: 10 CUPS

2 cups dried mung beans, rinsed and picked over
3 teaspoons whole coriander seeds
1½ teaspoons whole cumin seeds
2 cups long-grain brown rice
2 tablespoons olive oil
2 teaspoons ground turmeric
1 tablespoon ground ginger
Kosher salt and freshly ground pepper

Soak the beans in water to cover, leaving them overnight in the refrigerator. (Refrigeration is advisable because mung beans ferment easily.) Or bring them to a rolling boil with 6 cups water, remove the pan from the heat and let them sit, covered, for an hour. Drain the beans.

Dry roast the coriander and cumin seeds in a small skillet over high heat, shaking constantly, until they are aromatic, about 3 minutes. Grind them into a fine powder in a spice grinder. Reserve.

Bring 8 cups water to a boil in a large, covered saucepan over high heat. Add the beans, rice, olive oil, turmeric, ground ginger, and reserved coriander and cumin.

Return the porridge to a simmer and cook, stirring occasionally, for about 1 hour and 20 minutes, until the beans are very tender and all the liquid has been absorbed. Season to taste with salt and pepper, and serve.

FENNEL

After a lovely alfresco lunch in Italy one May, we were served "dessert": small, fresh fennel bulbs, sliced and arranged on a plate like fruit.

It is a common Italian custom and an old one. Ancient Romans were fond of fennel, both as a food and a medicine. Pliny, it is said, listed 22 remedies using fennel. Throughout the ages, though, the most common purpose was the same one for which we were served the sweet, anise-flavored bulbs: as a digestive aid. Fennel bulbs, and even more so fennel seeds, are "carminative"—that is, they dispel gas. Milton, in *Paradise Lost,* called fennel "grateful to appetite."

An old-fashioned remedy for colic is to steep a teaspoon or two of crushed fennel seeds in a half-cup of boiling water for a few minutes, cool and dilute it, and feed it to the squalling baby. It's supposed to calm her right down.

In *Nature's Paradise,* published in England in 1650, herbalist William Coles wrote that "the seeds, leaves and root of our Garden Fennel are much used in drinks and broths for those that are grown fat, to abate their unwieldiness and cause them to grow more gaunt and lank."

In *A Handbook of Chinese Healing Herbs,* Daniel Reed writes, "Like many tonic and restorative herbs, fennel increases the body's supply of available energy by enhancing the digestive system's power to digest, extract, and assimilate essential nutrients and energy from food."

The source of the digestion-enhancing properties of fennel seeds (they are really dried fruits) lies in their essential oils. (The whole bulb also contains some essential oil.) The main active ingredient is anethole, an antispasmodic. It relaxes the smooth muscles of the stomach. In Bulgaria, an herbal formula containing fennel seeds, dandelion root (see page 99), lemon balm (*Melissa officinalis*), and other herbs has been used effectively to treat "chronic nonspecific colitis."

Because anethole relieves muscle spasms, it probably relaxes the muscles of the throat as well. This may help explain why it is sometimes used for sore throats.

Fennel seeds are also weakly estrogenic—that is, they contain plant compounds that are chemically similar to human estrogen but much milder. So it should come as no surprise that fennel-seed tea is used in some folk medicine traditions to stimulate lactation and menstrual periods. It has been shown to have these effects in animal studies. Fennel seeds are also reputed to facilitate birth and increase libido. Again, the active ingredient is anethole, or perhaps specific compounds in anethole. Fennel seeds also contain the antioxidant flavonoid quercetin (see "Onion," page 211), a cancer-protective compound.

So you may want to put out a bowl of toasted fennel seeds as an after-dinner digestive aid. Or slice up small, fresh fennel and serve it for dessert. A cup of sliced raw fennel provides about 10 percent of daily vitamin C needs, plus calcium, folic acid, and plenty of potassium, for a mere 27 calories.

I'm not sure our fennel "broth" will single-handedly turn a person from "unwieldy" to "lank." But it can't hurt. Soup is good for dieting; it slows you down and gives your brain time to know that your mouth has eaten food.

FENNEL SOUP

This half-hour soup is comforting and easy. Use stock for a richer flavor. If you like the taste of caraway seeds, add a teaspoon to the olive oil.

YIELD: 5½ CUPS, ABOUT 4 SERVINGS

1 pound leeks
2 pounds fennel bulb (2 medium)
2 tablespoons olive oil
3 garlic cloves, smashed, peeled, and minced
1 medium baking potato, peeled and cubed
4 cups water, low-sodium chicken stock, or Basic Vegetable Stock
    (page 271)
2 tablespoons tarragon vinegar
Kosher salt and freshly ground pepper
Snipped chives for garnish

Trim the dark green tops and root ends from the leeks; wash well and slice thinly. Trim the fennel bulbs, remove and discard the hard core, and chop the bulbs coarsely; chop the fronds, and reserve them for garnish.

Heat the oil in a soup pot over medium-high heat. Add the leeks and garlic, reduce the heat to medium, and sauté, stirring occasionally, until transparent, about 5 minutes.

Add the fennel and potato, and sauté, stirring occasionally, 5 more minutes.

Add the water or stock, cover the pot, and bring it to a boil. Reduce the heat to a high simmer, and cook for 20 minutes or until potato is soft. Add the vinegar.

Working in batches and taking care not to spill any and burn yourself, puree the soup in a food processor. Season to taste with salt and pepper, sprinkle with reserved fennel fronds and chives, and serve hot.

FENNEL BISCOTTI

Fennel biscotti soothe the tummy. Toasting the fennel seeds brings out their flavor.

YIELD: ABOUT 24 COOKIES

1½ tablespoons whole fennel seeds
1½ cups all-purpose flour
2½ tablespoons sugar
2 teaspoons baking powder
⅛ teaspoon kosher salt
2 large eggs
1½ tablespoons olive oil
1 teaspoon almond or ginger extract
1 cup whole, raw almonds (skins on), toasted
¼ cup chopped, crystallized ginger (optional)
Zest of 1 lemon (about 1 tablespoon)

Place a dry skillet over high heat for 30 seconds. Add fennel seeds and reduce heat to medium. Shake and toast the seeds, moving the pan on and off the heat if necessary to prevent scorching, until seeds are aromatic, about 5 minutes. Transfer the seeds to a spice grinder, and pulse 2 or 3 times, just until partially broken up. Set aside.

Adjust an oven rack so that it's in the center; heat the oven to 375 degrees. Line a baking sheet with parchment paper.

In a medium bowl, sift together the flour, sugar, baking powder, and salt. In a small bowl, whisk together the eggs, oil, and extract. Stir the egg mixture into the flour, working the dough until the ingredients are thoroughly combined; it will be slightly dry. Stir in the almonds, ginger, fennel seeds, and lemon zest.

Turn the dough out onto a well-floured surface. Divide it in two, and shape each half into a log about 1½ inches wide and 8 inches long. Place each log on the prepared baking sheet.

Bake for 25 minutes. Reduce the oven temperature to 225 degrees, and use spatulas to transfer the logs to a large cutting board. Using a sharp knife, cut the logs on the diagonal into ½-inch-thick slices. Return the slices to the baking sheet, cut side down.

Bake for 15 minutes. Turn the biscotti, and bake 15 more minutes, until dry but not too brown. Transfer biscotti to a cooling rack. When completely cool, they may be stored in an airtight container for 3 to 4 weeks.

FENNEL-SEEDED FLATBREAD

This flatbread doesn't need to rise, so the dough is quick to make, though the baking takes a little time.

YIELD: **12** PIECES

¾ teaspoon active dry yeast
½ cup plus 1 tablespoon warm water (110 degrees)
1 tablespoon olive oil, plus more for brushing dough
1 cup plus 2 tablespoons whole-wheat flour
¾ cup all-purpose flour
½ teaspoon cracked pepper
1 teaspoon whole fennel seeds
½ teaspoon ground fennel seeds
½ teaspoon ground ginger
½ teaspoon kosher salt plus more for sprinkling
Cornmeal

Adjust the oven racks so that one is in the center and the other on the next level down. Heat the oven to 375 degrees. Sprinkle 2 baking sheets with cornmeal.

Combine the yeast and 1 tablespoon of the warm water in the work bowl of an electric mixer. Let the yeast activate for 5 minutes.

Add the remaining ½ cup warm water, the oil, both flours, the pepper, whole and ground fennel seeds, ginger, and ½ teaspoon salt. Using a dough hook, mix on low speed for about 5 minutes, until the dough is soft and pliable. (Or knead the dough by hand on a floured surface for 15 to 20 minutes.)

Turn the dough out onto a lightly floured surface, and knead it 6 or 8 times (it will still be a little sticky). Form the dough into a ball, and cut it into 6 wedges. Lightly flatten each piece.

Work with one wedge of dough at a time, and cover the rest with plastic wrap to prevent drying. Pat the wedge into a rectangular shape, and roll it out as thinly as possible into a strip about 3 inches wide and 20 inches long. Cut it in half to form two 10-inch-long pieces. Place them side by side on a prepared baking sheet. Brush lightly with oil, and sprinkle with salt if desired. Repeat with a second wedge.

Bake the flatbread for about 14 minutes, switching the pans, top to bottom, about halfway through. The flatbread is done when the edges have just begun to brown.

Transfer the bread to a cooling rack, and repeat with the remaining dough. The bread will keep for about a week in an airtight container.

WARMING INDIAN TEA

In India, you might be served some version of this aromatic tea if you have a cold. It settles the stomach, calms, soothes, acts as an analgesic, and helps clear congestion. A look at the ingredients helps explain why: both fennel seeds and cloves are carminative (they dispel gas) and stomachic (they settle the stomach). Clove oil is antispasmodic and also kills pain; it contains eugenol, a dental anesthetic. Black pepper, like hot chili pepper, stimulates circulation and acts as a decongestant.

YIELD: 4 CUPS

2 teaspoons whole fennel seeds
6 whole black peppercorns
8 whole cloves

Heat a dry skillet over medium-low heat. Add the fennel seeds, peppercorns, and cloves. Toast lightly, tossing, until aromatic, about 3 minutes.

Transfer the seeds to a spice grinder, and grind into a fine powder.

Bring 4 cups water to a boil. Put the powder in a teapot, and add the boiling water. Let the tea steep for 5 minutes, strain, and serve.

FENUGREEK

Tell me, Lydia, of your secrets
And the wonders you perform,
How you take the sick and ailing
And restore them to the norm.
                    —Nineteenth-century fraternity song

I call Margie Cohen to talk about Lydia Pinkham. I've known Margie for 15 years; we used to be in a book club together. She knows about Lydia Pinkham because she wrote a musical revue about her. It's called *Consuming Passions of Lydia Pinkham and Reverend Sylvester Graham.* It's been on public television in New York. Margie plays Lydia.

The show is an imaginary musical meeting between two great health reformers in the 1800s. Graham believed in whole foods; he gave us Graham flour and, some say, granola. He influenced generations of health reformers, including the Kelloggs. Graham believed in pure, simple food, strict abstention from alcohol, no spices.

Lydia was different.

Lydia Pinkham's Vegetable Compound, first sold in 1875, is the most famous tonic medicine in American history.

It was nearly 40 proof.

The other main ingredient was fenugreek.

Margie shows me a bottle, circa 1900. Lydia's benign, somewhat sad face hovers on the label. "Woman can Sympathize with Woman," it says on one side. On the other: "Health of Woman is the Hope of the Race." The directions say to take one tablespoon every four hours throughout the day. Above the ingredients list is a statement: "Contains 15 Per Cent Alcohol." (Earlier formulations had contained nearly 20 percent.) "This is added solely as a solvent and preservative."

The story of Lydia Pinkham (1819–1883) is part of the hidden history of women in the United States. She was raised in the heady liberal atmosphere of Lynn, Massachusetts, where her parents were Quakers, freethinkers, and abolitionists. She was well educated. But she married Isaac Pinkham, whose primary skill was losing money in real estate. He kept them broke, and then, in the financial crisis of 1873, they were ruined.

Lydia survived. She was frugal. And she had learned a thing or two about medicinal herbs from local Indian women. To keep her family healthy, she made vegetable elixirs. She gave them away to neighborhood women. Then, in 1875, four women from Salem pulled up to the house. They had heard about Lydia's compound. They wanted to buy six bottles. They gave her five dollars.

Her son Dan noted the transaction, and the family business began. It limped. Then they put her face on the bottle—the first time in American history that a real person's image had been used to sell a product. Rebecca A. Foster, curator at the Lynn Historical Society, writes, "It was an enormous success. Not only did her grandmotherly appearance inspire trust in the product, it gave the compound the credibility it needed—many people did not believe there really *was* a Lydia Pinkham." Eventually, the face and the compound became so familiar that jokes and limericks circled the country:

Lizzie Smith had tired feelings,
Terrible pains reduced her weight,
She began to take the Compound,
Now she weighs three hundred and eight.

Business soared. Isaac basked in "a well-deserved leisure," as one contemporary newspaper account put it. Lydia got thousands of letters. Her responses were informed by common sense, a belief in pure food and diet, an understanding of women's physiological and emotional lives, and an intuitive sense of health. She answered letters frankly and clearly, in keeping with her intellectual roots and education. In time, men as well as girls and women were writing her for help in understanding the female body.

Lydia died in 1883, but the business thrived; by 1887, annual sales amounted to $200,000.

The original compound was about 19 percent alcohol, or nearly 40 proof. Perhaps some women, feeling poorly in body or mind and instructed to take a tablespoon every four hours, might have taken a little longer pull on the bottle. If a little feels good, won't more feel better? Lydia Pinkham believed in temperance, but she never considered the alcohol in her medicine to be of concern. The compound remained immensely popular throughout Prohibition.

Lydia Pinkham's Vegetable Compound was more than just an excuse to drink, however. It contained several herbs that we now know to be biologically active. One original recipe is reported to have called for 12 ounces of fenugreek seeds, 8 ounces of unicorn root, and 6 ounces each of liferoot, black cohosh root, and pleurisy root.

Black cohosh root, used by Algonquian and other Indians for gynecological problems and childbirth, contains compounds that are chemically similar to estrogen. In *Herbs of Choice,* plant medicines expert Varro Tyler cites studies that have shown "an alcoholic extract of black cohosh suppressed hot flashes in menopausal women by reducing the secretion of luteinizing hormone (LH)." Contemporary herbals recommend black cohosh for relief of spasms and as a sedative but primarily to promote menstruation. (Like estrogen, it is contraindicated if there is concern over certain hormone-related cancers such as some types of breast cancer, or if one is taking birth control pills or is pregnant, nursing, or at risk from increased blood clotting.)

Liferoot (*Senecio aureus*) is another "female regulator" that was popular in the nineteenth century. However, recent studies have found that it contains small quantities of an alkaloid that is acutely toxic to the liver and may contribute to liver cancer.

Pleurisy root (*Asclepias tuberosa*) is an expectorant.

Unicorn root is another "woman's friend." In *The Handbook of Medicinal Herbs,* botanist James A. Duke describes it as "a folk remedy for rheumatic aches, lack of periods (amenorrhea), backache, colic, dysmenorrhea [painful menstruation], indigestion, fever, stomach ache, and a 'tilted' uterus. It is reputed to prevent miscarriages. Cherokee Indians used the root to treat colic and constipation; to strengthen the womb; to prevent abortion." Unicorn root contains a strongly estrogenic compound, diosgenin, also found in soybeans and dioscorea (page 105), both of which may have cancer-protective properties.

And this brings us to fenugreek. It has a long history of folk medicine use. Dioscorides, a Greek physician who traveled widely with the Roman armies of Nero, wrote of it. The Bible mentions it in Numbers 11 in a passage that begins, "We remember the fish . . . [and] the leeks," which, biblical scholars tell us, were not the member of the onion family we know but fenugreek. Henry VIII (1491–1547), who had a keen amateur interest in the "physic" of his time and concocted many of his own ointments, used fenugreek. (Some of those ointments were to relieve leg sores; others to "comforte the membre.")

Contemporary herbals recommend fenugreek for increasing the milk flow of breast-feeding women. I find nothing in recent medical literature to confirm this effect, but then, some of the most useful properties of plants go unstudied. Since fenugreek has estrogenic properties, it makes sense that it could stimulate lactation.

Contemporary research, including some clinical studies, have, however, found properties in fenugreek that even Lydia Pinkham may not have suspected:

- It reliably lowers elevated blood cholesterol.
- It stabilizes blood sugar.
- It contains anticancer compounds.

Fenugreek is rich in plant sterols, steroidlike compounds that may mimic human hormones, including estrogen. Similar compounds are found in soybeans. In France, researchers at the Laboratory of Vegetable Physiology at the University of Montpelier II report that feeding fenugreek seeds to rats causes an increase in blood insulin, while lowering VLDL (very low density lipoprotein) and LDL cholesterol, which would lower the risk of heart disease. At Hebrew University in Rehovot, researchers report that in dogs, fenugreek lowers blood cholesterol 18 to 26 percent. A 1995 study by the French team provides evidence that it is the plant sterol, a steroidlike compound that is estrogenic, that is responsible for these actions.

Animal studies also point to insulin-sparing benefits. Fenugreek lowers blood sugar in dogs and can prevent the development of diabetes in rats. A 1995 study from the Department of Pharmacology at Pt. B. D. Sharma Medical College in Rohtak, India, found that in both normal and diabetic rats, fenugreek seeds "produced a significant fall in blood glucose"—that is, blood sugar.

What about its effect on people? A study conducted by the National Institute of Nutrition at the Indian Council of Medical Research in Hyderabad, India, and reported in the April 1990 *European Journal of Clinical Nutrition* looked at the effect of fenugreek seeds on insulin-dependent (so-called juvenile) diabetics. They gave the subjects about three and a half ounces of fenugreek for ten days. (That's a lot—more than you or I would want to eat.) There was a 54 percent reduction in the amount of sugar lost in the urine in a 24-hour period. Blood fats, including VLDL, LDL, and triglycerides, also fell. Beneficial HDL wasn't affected. "These results indicate the usefulness of fenugreek seeds in the management of diabetes," the researchers concluded.

A 1988 Israeli study found that fenugreek was beneficial for non-insulin-dependent diabetes, too. Here, the amount was closer to what we might use in food. They fed subjects 15 grams of powdered fenugreek seeds soaked in water.

That's about half an ounce. Within three hours, they report, the fenugreek "significantly reduced the subsequent postprandial glucose levels." In other words, blood sugar levels after a meal fell. Another Indian study found that fenugreek chapatis, an Indian bread often made with chickpea flour, was effective in lowering blood cholesterol levels in men with high cholesterol.

Finally, German researchers, at the Institut für Lebensmittelchemie at the Technical University in Munich, report that fenugreek seeds contain potentially cancer-protective substances. They are in the same family as the Bowman-Birk protease inhibitors found in soybeans. Protease inhibitors are a major factor in soybeans that may explain their cancer-protective effects. Another class of protease inhibitors, developed as pharmaceuticals, has recently proved effective in the treatment of AIDS.

Lydia Pinkham didn't know about cholesterol, insulin, or HIV. Yet she knew fenugreek was good for women. It may still be. If I were a woman feeding a child by breast and I was not producing enough milk, I certainly would try a simple fenugreek tea. I might also try it for menstrual cramps.

Fenugreek has been used as a food for many centuries, and I haven't read about any safety concerns.

If I had diabetes, I might ask my practitioner about trying fairly large amounts of fenugreek, under supervision.

As it is, I'll season my beans with fenugreek from time to time, knowing that the beans and the spice are helping to keep my cholesterol and blood sugar in check and perhaps protecting me from cancer. And I'll sip my Fenugreek Liqueur, knowing that alcohol in small amounts can thin my blood and reduce the risk of heart attack. And I will think of Lydia, who suffered much, and helped many.

FENUGREEK TEA

We don't know if Lydia Pinkham put ginger or cardamom in her tonic, but both are carminative, or stomach settling, and sweeten the somewhat bitter flavor of fenugreek. Licorice was included in some versions of the Vegetable Compound, although the technique of honey roasting is a Chinese one. Fenugreek seeds need to be lightly toasted before being ground.

YIELD: 3 4-CUP BATCHES OF TEA

¼ cup whole fenugreek seeds
4 whole green cardamom pods
1 3-inch piece fresh ginger, peeled and coarsely chopped
6 pieces Honey-Roasted Licorice Sticks (page 203)
1 lime, cut into wedges

Place a small, dry skillet over high heat for 30 seconds. Add the fenugreek and cardamom, and reduce the heat to medium. Shake and toast the seeds, moving the pan on and off the burner if necessary to prevent scorching, until they are aromatic, 3 to 5 minutes.

When cool enough to handle, break open the cardamom pods and transfer the seeds to a spice grinder. Add the fenugreek, and grind into a fine powder. Set aside.

To make one batch of tea, combine 2 tablespoons of the spice mix, the ginger, licorice, and 5 cups water in a saucepan. Cover and bring to a boil. Uncover, reduce the heat to a high simmer, and cook for 20 to 30 minutes, until it has reduced to about 4 cups. Strain, and serve hot with a squeeze of fresh lime juice.

FENUGREEK LIQUEUR

Our version of Lydia's Compound lacks black cohosh and unicorn root, but it may be a relaxing way to lower blood cholesterol.

YIELD: **16** 1-OUNCE SERVINGS

2 cups brewed Fenugreek Tea
Grated zest of one lemon
1 tablespoon dark brown sugar
1 cup vodka

Bring the tea to a boil in a small saucepan, and cook until reduced to 1 cup, about 20 minutes. Let it cool to room temperature.

Place a pint canning jar and lid in a large bowl, cover with boiling water, and let them sit for 5 minutes. Using tongs, set them on a clean dish towel to dry. *(continued)*

Pour the reduced tea into the jar. Add the lemon zest, sugar, and vodka. Close the lid tightly without forcing, and shake the jar a few times to combine the ingredients. Label and date the jar, and store it in the refrigerator for 2 weeks for flavors to develop. Sip slowly, ½ to 1 ounce at a time.

FENUGREEK SOCCAS

Soccas, chickpea crepes, are baked and sold on the streets of Nice in the south of France. Serve them with a fresh salad, goat cheese, or a soup.

YIELD: 7 TO 9 CREPES

1½ cups chickpea flour
½ teaspoon cayenne
2 teaspoons dried marjoram
2 tablespoons whole fenugreek seeds, lightly toasted and ground (see Fenugreek Tea, page 122)
1 teaspoon kosher salt
½ teaspoon freshly ground pepper
⅓ cup olive oil, plus more for sprinkling

Combine the flour, cayenne, marjoram, ground fenugreek, salt, pepper to taste, and oil in a mixing bowl. Add 2 cups water and stir until combined. Cover with plastic wrap and leave at room temperature for 1 to 4 hours.

Turn on the broiler, and place one of the oven racks 3 to 5 inches from the heat source (top position).

Stir the batter, and ladle enough into an 8-inch, oven-proof skillet to cover the bottom, about ¼ cup. (I use a nonstick skillet; if you don't have one, oil the skillet lightly before adding the batter.)

Place the skillet under the broiler for 4 minutes. Remove and sprinkle the socca with a few drops of olive oil. Broil for 3 to 4 minutes more, until golden brown.

Slide the socca onto a large plate, and repeat until all the batter is cooked. The cooking time may decrease as the pan heats up, so watch each batch carefully. Serve warm.

FENUGREEK HUMMUS

Here's another combination of fenugreek and chickpeas, which, like all legumes, can lower blood cholesterol levels.

YIELD: **2** CUPS

1 teaspoon whole fenugreek seeds
1 teaspoon whole cumin seeds
½ teaspoon cayenne
1 20-ounce can chickpeas, rinsed and drained (2½ cups)
2 tablespoons tahini
¾ cup fresh lemon juice
3 garlic cloves, smashed, peeled, and finely chopped
3 tablespoons chopped, fresh flat-leaf parsley
1 teaspoon kosher salt
½ teaspoon freshly ground pepper

Place a small, dry skillet over high heat for 30 seconds. Add the fenugreek, cumin, and cayenne, and reduce the heat to medium.

Shake and toast the spices, moving the pan on and off the burner if necessary to prevent scorching, until they are aromatic, 3 to 5 minutes.

Transfer to a spice grinder, and grind into a fine powder. Set aside.

Combine the chickpeas, tahini, lemon juice, garlic, parsley, salt, and pepper to taste in a food processor. Pulse until smooth. Add the reserved spice mixture, and pulse until well combined, stopping once or twice to scrape down the sides of the work bowl. Taste for seasoning, and add more salt and pepper if desired. Serve with pita triangles and raw vegetables.

FLAX

(Linum usitatissimum)

> *Flax seeds are a good tonic for . . . the colon.*
> —Dr. David Frawley, *The Yoga of Herbs*

> *Unani [an African people] use the oil from the seed . . . for "bad blood."*
>
> *Flax seeds are considered aphrodisiac.*
> —James A. Duke, *Medicinal Plants of the Bible*

Okay, that last one was just to get your attention. There is no scientific evidence that flax seeds are an aphrodisiac. But they may help prevent heart disease, cancer, and a few other unsexy conditions.

Flax seeds are particularly rich in alpha-linolenic acid, an omega-3 fatty acid that prevents blood clotting and does other good things for the cardiovascular system. These special kinds of fats are also anti-inflammatory and immune regulating and may help prevent breast and colon cancer. (For more on omega-3 fatty acids, see "Walnut," page 292, and "Tuna," page 275.)

Flax seeds are also rich in soluble fiber, much like psyllium (page 224), and so improve elimination. In one 1995 study of young healthy men who took 50 milligrams of flax seeds a day for a month, bowel movements increased by 30 percent. (Hence, their reputation in India as a colon "tonic.") Like psyllium, flax seeds also lower blood cholesterol and blood sugar. In the same study, LDL cholesterol, the kind closely linked with heart disease, went down 8 percent, a significant amount. In people with high cholesterol, flax may be even more effective.

Flax seeds—but not flax seed oil—contain yet another potentially beneficial kind of compound: lignans. Lignans are also found in whole grains, nuts, and berries, but flax seeds have the most. These are mildly estrogenic compounds, similar to those found in soybeans (see "Tofu," page 258) but more so. In one 1993 study of 18 healthy women, eating flax seeds greatly increased the likelihood that a woman would ovulate in a particular menstrual cycle. This has implications for fertility, although a lot more research is needed before any recommendations can be made.

Like tofu's isoflavones, flax seeds' lignans may protect against breast cancer and possibly other hormone-related malignancies, such as prostate cancer. If they do help prevent breast cancer, they may do so by binding to estrogen receptors; they are so similar in structure that they take the place of the real estrogens. That's good, because too much estrogen, especially of certain kinds, is linked with increased breast-cancer risk. After menopause, on the other hand, when a woman's estrogen level falls, "plant estrogens" such as flax seeds' lignans may provide beneficial estrogenlike effects.

Lignans have other anticancer actions that may have broader benefits. Dietary lignans are linked with reduced cancer risk in lab studies, animal studies, and population studies. In a 1995 Canadian study of animals given carcinogens, both flax seed oil and flax seeds added to feed reduced the number of tumors. The antitumor effect of the oil is partly due to the omega-3 alpha-linolenic acid; feeding the animals lignan-rich flax seeds, however, had a more powerful antitumor effect. Flax seeds also reduce colon cancer in animals. A 1995 Finnish review of isoflavones and lignans concluded that because they work in many different ways to prevent cancer, they are "strong candidates for a role as natural cancer-protective compounds."

Let me add a note of caution, however: historically, food uses for flax seeds are few. Bartholomaeus Anglicus wrote in 1260 that flax was used to make such things as textiles, fish nets, rope, and thread. *Plants of the Bible,* by Harold and Alma Moldenke, quotes from the Old Testament book of Hosea: "Therefore I will return . . . and will recover my wool and my flax given to cover her nakedness." In the New Testament, Jesus' body, after it was taken down from the cross, was wrapped in linen made from flax.

Maud Grieve wrote in 1931 in *A Modern Herbal* that flax seeds (which she calls linseed) "have occasionally been employed as human food—we hear of the seeds being mixed with corn by the ancient Greeks and Romans for making bread—but it affords little actual nourishment and is apparently unwholesome, being difficult of digestion and provoking flatulence."

We now know that flax seeds may in fact lower blood cholesterol, thin the blood, prevent constipation, help prevent colon cancer, help regulate menstrual cycles, help prevent breast cancer, and do other beneficial things. But it's wise to exercise caution.

Putting a little flax seed in bread or bean cakes, as we do in the recipes that follow, is a reasonable way to incorporate them into our diet. But we know too little about the long-term effect of these plant steroids to start blithely swallowing flax seeds and flax seed oil. Indeed, one shouldn't eat *raw* flax seeds at all: like beans, they contain a toxin that is inactivated by cooking. Like any fiber, taking too much too quickly can cause temporary gastrointestinal distress. So start slowly. Be moderate.

WHOLE-GRAIN BREAD WITH MILLET, RYE, AND FLAX SEEDS

For a crunchier crust, whisk one tablespoon milk into one egg and lightly brush it on the tops of the loaves just before baking.

This bread freezes well; be sure to wrap it tightly and date the package.

Rye flakes are available in natural food stores.

YIELD: 2 LOAVES

½ cup flax seeds
¼ cup millet
2 tablespoons (2½ ¼-ounce packages) active dry yeast
2 cups warm water (110 degrees)
¾ cup unsulfured or black strap molasses
¼ cup vegetable oil
1 tablespoon kosher salt
¾ cup oat bran
¼ cup wheat germ
½ cup rye flakes
2 cups whole wheat flour
4½ or 5 cups all-purpose flour, plus more if needed

Soak the flax seeds and millet in ⅝ cup water for 15 minutes.

Meanwhile, put the yeast in a large mixing bowl with the warm water, and let it activate for 5 minutes.

In a small bowl, combine the molasses, oil, and salt.

Stir the molasses mixture into the yeast. Add the oat bran, wheat germ, rye flakes, soaked flax seeds and millet, and whole-wheat flour, stirring to combine well. Gradually add about 3½ cups of the all-purpose flour. The dough should begin to come together but will still be sticky.

Turn the dough out onto a well-floured surface. Work in as much of the remaining flour as it will take, kneading between additions until the dough is no longer sticky. Knead for about 5 minutes more, until the dough is smooth, elastic, and satiny.

Wash out the large mixing bowl, and coat it lightly with oil. Form the dough into a ball, and roll it around in the bowl so that all sides are lightly coated with oil. Cover with a clean kitchen towel and let it rise in a warm place 45 minutes to 1 hour, until double in size.

Punch down the dough, and knead it 5 or 6 times to remove any air bubbles. Return it to the bowl, cover it with the towel, and let it rise again until doubled, about 1 hour.

Lightly grease 2 loaf pans. Punch down the dough, cut it in half, and shape it into 2 loaves. Put it in the pans, cover with the towel, and let the loaves rest for 20 to 30 minutes.

Adjust an oven rack so that it's in the center, and heat the oven to 350 degrees.

Bake the bread for 50 to 60 minutes. The loaves will be browned after about 45 minutes, but they need a bit longer to bake through. Tent them with foil to prevent them from getting too brown.

BLACK BEAN CAKES WITH FLAX SEEDS

If you don't have time to cook the beans, substitute five 10½-ounce cans, rinsed and drained. Adjust the amount of jalapeño to suit your taste; you can also substitute canned *chipotle* chilies. After forming the patties, you can refrigerate them overnight and cook them the next day. These taste delicious with Homemade Yogurt (page 315) and Fresh Garlic Salsa (page 142).

YIELD: **6 SERVINGS**

7 cups Well-Seasoned Black Beans (page 184), drained and cooking
    liquid reserved
2 heaping tablespoons chopped fresh mint
2 heaping tablespoons chopped fresh cilantro or parsley
⅓ cup finely chopped red onion
¼ cup flax seeds
½ teaspoon ground cumin
½ fresh jalapeño, finely chopped
3 ounces soft goat cheese, crumbled
Kosher salt and freshly ground pepper

Put three-quarters of the beans in a large bowl, and mash them into a thick, lumpy paste. *(continued)*

Add the whole beans and the mint, cilantro, onion, flax seeds, cumin, jalapeño, cheese, and salt and pepper to taste. Mix well. If the mixture seems too dry, add a tablespoon or so of the reserved cooking liquid or water.

Form the bean mixture into 6 patties, about 3 inches across.

Lightly coat a nonstick skillet with vegetable-oil spray, and place it over medium-high heat.

Cook 3 patties at a time for about 3 minutes per side. Once they have a nice crust, reduce the heat to medium low, cover the pan, and cook for about 5 more minutes to heat them through. Keep them warm in a low oven while you cook the remaining patties. Serve hot.

FOLIC ACID

If you follow nutrition, you've heard of the B vitamin folic acid. Its name comes from the Latin word for "leaf" (as in "foliage"), so it's not surprising that the main sources of folic acid are green leafy vegetables. But it's also well supplied by many fruits, vegetables, beans, and other plant foods.

Folic acid is so important to human health that the federal government now requires it to be added to fortified foods such as flour and pasta. The main reason is to protect newborns: folic acid helps prevent neural tube birth defects such as spina bifida. A 1996 study even found that it helps prevent premature births.

Folic acid also protects against colon cancer, in part by protecting DNA. And it protects the heart: adequate folic acid prevents the rise of homocysteine, an amino acid that is proving to be a significant predictor of heart disease risk. In the United States, about a quarter of the people who have heart attacks and nearly half of those who have strokes have elevated blood levels of homocysteine. Having high levels of this toxic substance doubles your risk of developing heart disease.

But that's not why I want you to eat more foods rich in folic acid.

I want you to be happy.

The link between folic acid deficiency and depression has been building for decades. In the 1970s, researchers began to report that women taking oral contraceptives were prone to depression: between 10 and 40 percent of women on the Pill experienced mild to moderate depression. Not coincidentally, early forms of the Pill rapidly depleted folic acid. Today, oral contraceptives are more hormonally balanced and so less folate-depleting. But even so, women who take them are advised to take a vitamin supplement containing folic acid.

Studies of clinically depressed patients—both those brought low by tragic events and those whose depression arises for no discernible reason—often find that these patients are deficient in folic acid. This is not the sole cause of depression, by any means, but folic acid deficiency causes a few cases and exacerbates more. It's one cause of depression in alcoholics, whose heavy alcohol consumption depletes B vitamins, including folic acid.

In a number of clinical studies, depressed patients with mild folic acid deficiencies have improved when given supplements. Often, they remain on antidepressants, but the results are better. In one double-blind study, depressed patients on long-term lithium therapy were treated with folic acid or a placebo. After a year, the patients with the highest folate levels had significantly fewer depressive symptoms.

Most Americans get less folic acid than is optimal. No one has studied whether such suboptimal intakes are associated with mood, but there are reasons to believe it might be. Folic acid, abundant in fresh fruits and vegetables, is needed to convert amino acids in the body into the brain chemical serotonin. When serotonin levels are low, it affects mood. That's why nearly all prescription antidepressants, including Prozac, work by affecting serotonin metabolism.

To make serotonin, our bodies convert the amino acid methionine into a substance with the friendly name of SAM. It stands for S-adenosylmethionine. To turn methionine into SAM, we need—you guessed it—folic acid. In Italy, SAM itself is sometimes prescribed as an antidepressant. It is a precursor of serotonin, so sometimes when you give people more SAM they make more serotonin and feel better.

Folic acid not only helps to convert methionine into SAM; it also converts the SAM not needed to make serotonin back into methionine. When it isn't reconverted, SAM makes homocysteine. That's how adequate folic acid not only helps the body produce enough serotonin but also reduces homocysteine levels. Too little folic acid, and you may feel blue (low serotonin) *and* be at high risk for heart disease (high homocysteine). Before the heart attack, perhaps, comes the sadness.

In nutrition circles, the "standard American diet" is called SAD. The acronym may be more fitting than we know. SAD has too much meat, too few vegetables. The main source of methionine in the American diet is meat and dairy. Eat too much meat, and you'll take in large amounts of methionine. The main source of folic acid is fresh fruits and vegetables. Eat too few of them, and your body won't have enough folic acid to prevent that methionine from turning into homocysteine, nor will it be able to turn methionine into serotonin.

Living plants all contain folic acid. Beans are a good source: a cup of chickpeas, for example, contains 141 micrograms. To put that in perspective, the U.S. RDA is 200 micrograms, while the amount needed to prevent spina bifida and keep homocysteine levels in check is 400.

A tablespoon of brewer's yeast has 313 micrograms of folic acid; a cup of cooked spinach, 262; a cup of cooked asparagus, 176; a cup of cooked turnip greens, 170; two cups of raw romaine lettuce, 154; a cup of parsley, 110; a cup of orange juice, 106; a quarter cup of sunflower seeds, 85.

Folic acid is easily destroyed by heat and air, so it's found mostly in fresh foods, raw or lightly cooked. Like salads.

RISING-SPIRITS SALAD

YIELD: 4 TO 6 SERVINGS

2 ounces fresh flat-leaf parsley, leaves only (1½ cups)
1 bunch arugula, trimmed, washed, and dried
1 bunch watercress, washed and dried
¼ cup fresh lemon juice
½ teaspoon kosher salt
¼ teaspoon freshly ground pepper
¼ cup plus 2 tablespoons olive oil
12 asparagus stalks, woody ends trimmed
A medium head of romaine lettuce (about six ounces), washed and
    dried
¼ cup sunflower seeds, lightly toasted

Process the parsley, 3 strands of arugula, 3 strands of watercress, the lemon juice, salt, and pepper in a blender to combine. Gradually pour in the olive oil, stopping once or twice to scrape down the sides with a rubber spatula. Process until the dressing is thick and fairly smooth. Set aside. Steam the asparagus until just tender when pierced with the tip of a knife, 2 to 5 minutes depending on the thickness of the stalks. Rinse with cold water to stop the cooking. When cool, cut into 1½-inch lengths.

Tear the romaine into bite-size pieces. Toss it in a big salad bowl with the remaining arugula and watercress. Add the asparagus, and sprinkle with the sunflower seeds. Drizzle on the dressing, and toss well.

FRIEND

Friends are not food, not water, not air; one can live without them. One can live without a community. One can live without a lover. One can live without someone to talk to in those quiet moments when one talks from the heart.

But it would not be a good life nor, if we are to believe the tea leaves of epidemiology, would it be a long life. Having a good friend may save your life. It can reduce your risk of getting cancer and keep you alive longer if you do get it. It can lower your blood cholesterol, boost your immune response, protect you from heart disease. If you do develop heart disease, it can cut your risk of dying.

"Having friends, feeling part of a larger network, affects the body," explains Blair Justice, a psychology professor at the University of Texas School of Public Health. It can lower the stress we experience from the problems we inevitably face. And from a health standpoint, feeling less stress means having less stress.

Our modern, individualistic American way of life is an obstacle to having close, confiding friends. Japanese immigrants who retain the group-centered way of life called *amae* have lower rates of heart disease than those who adopt a more American lifestyle. Similarly, Italian immigrants in Pennsylvania who retain close family traditions have been found to be somewhat protected from heart disease. "The younger generation who start splitting off from that way of life don't have any extra protection," Justice says.

Being married isn't enough. "The research shows that those people who are married and place a value on it do have less illness episodes," he explains. "And for people who get divorced, if they have a kind of longing for the marriage that broke up, they are at greater risk. But for some people, divorce is the best thing. People make mistakes." It's also possible to have the wrong kind of friends. "If your friends encourage a lifestyle that's unhealthy, if they are into drugs and promiscuous sex, that could do you in," Justice says.

What really matters, he says, isn't whether you have many friends or few, but the quality of the relationship. Whether it's with a friend, a lover, a spouse, a child, or a parent, a good relationship has elements of commitment and challenge. "You've got to be willing to be open enough to share yourself," Justice says. "You can't be armored. You've got to trust, be open, even be hurt sometimes. Sometimes the hurt is deep, but the dividends are great, and the benefits are what life is all about."

INTIMACY SOUP

YIELD: INTANGIBLE

A friend
A place to walk
Comfortable shoes

Take a walk together.

Tell your friend something that is on your mind, something that bothers you, something you are hoping for. Listen to what your friend says.

Ask your friend how he or she is feeling. Listen. Say something honest.

Don't forget to enjoy breathing.

Let your eyes wander up to the tops of the trees or to the sky. Notice the leaves on the trees or, if it is February, the bare, icy branches and the changes in the light.

Let yourself experience any gratitude you may feel for having a friend, a place to walk, and time together.

Tell your friend about this feeling.

GARLIC

Garlic: A Secret Miracle of God?
> —Title of an article in a German medical journal

I had a garlic-deprived childhood.
> —Restaurateur and cookbook author Alice Waters

Imagine a drug that lowers blood cholesterol, reduces the tendency of blood to form dangerous clots, protects blood cholesterol from the oxidation that initiates the atherosclerotic process (the artery-clogging that causes most heart attacks), modestly lowers blood pressure, protects against infections, helps the body break down toxins, stimulates immunity, protects against cancer, and has no serious side effects even in amounts many times the therapeutic dose.

Now imagine this: it tastes wonderful.

It is garlic, of course, the stinking rose.

A few years ago, I was quoted in the *New York Times* as saying that garlic would be the first food to make the jump from food to medicine.

Now I think we should let it be food.

Perhaps we should take our cue from the Italians. In one study, garlic was added to the feed of sheep, providing demonstrated protection against infection and also, perhaps coincidentally, providing lamb with a mild garlic flavor. Leave it to the serious men and women of Italy to solve an agricultural problem while providing a culinary benefit.

If you have a medical condition such as high blood cholesterol and are not a garlic lover, it might make sense to take a garlic supplement on a daily basis. But pills aren't better than food. It's not clear that they are as good. Says chemistry professor Eric Block of the State University of New York, Albany, "You might want to take garlic supplements for specific medical purposes, such as lowering cholesterol, but the natural approach is to include more garlic, both raw and cooked, as part of meals. To exclude garlic from your diet and rely on pills alone may be unwise. It's also no fun."

Raw garlic has one property that cooking destroys: an antibiotic effect. In the 1800s, Louis Pasteur demonstrated in a test tube that garlic inhibits bacterial growth. Subsequent studies have demonstrated that garlic in very small amounts is effective against a wide variety of potentially disease-causing microorganisms: bacteria, viruses, and fungi. Small amounts do it, such as 1 part of garlic to 100 parts of water.

Today, with antibacterial antibiotics evolving more slowly than their prey and effective antiviral and antifungal medications remaining elusive, liberating garlic's wide-spectrum antibiotic power may prove a safe alternative to more toxic drugs.

When the peace of a garlic bulb is disturbed—when it is cut, crushed, smashed, chopped, bruised, squeezed, or otherwise treated unkindly—it responds by releasing compounds that attack bacteria, viruses, fungi, and, one speculates, small animals. From a garlic point of view, that's why these compounds exist. They protect. Alliin, the primary source of sulfur compounds in untouched garlic, remains intact until the bulb is disturbed, whereupon an enzyme, alliinase, is released. Alliinase turns alliin into allicin, which has antibiotic properties.

Modern medicine doesn't have very effective medications for viruses and few for fungi. Garlic to the rescue? In China, garlic extracts are used intravenously to treat systemic fungal infections, including cryptococcal meningitis, a life-threatening fungal infection that can invade the nervous system. Researchers at the University of New Mexico School of Medicine in Albuquerque have found that garlic extract kills the meningitis fungus in the test tube.

There are potential benefits of a more everyday variety. Consider a Chinese preventive prescription for the common cold: squeeze the juice from a dozen peeled garlic cloves, and put a drop of it in each nostril three times a day. It is said to prevent colds. Makes sense.

Another folk use: if you do catch a cold and get a sore throat, squeeze garlic juice plus ginger juice into a tablespoon of honey. Swallow. The honey soothes, while the garlic and ginger kill pathogens.

Raw garlic may help solve an endemic American medical problem: ear infections. Those medical sleuths in New Mexico have validated the traditional use of garlic to treat ear infections. Both water solutions of garlic and garlic in oil are found, in the test tube, to kill the aspergillus fungus that causes many ear infections. It's good news, because existing antibacterial and antifungal agents for the treatment of ear infections, especially in children, are caustic (that is, they cause a burning sensation) and often toxic. To make the ear oil, thoroughly crush a few cloves of fresh peeled garlic, and add it to a couple of tablespoons of olive oil. After an hour or more at room temperature, strain out the garlic with a cheesecloth—you don't want garlic pieces in your ear. Now, wash the outside of your ear, dry it well, and put in a drop or two of a one-to-one mixture of vinegar and water or a one-to-two-part mixture of vinegar and isopropyl alcohol. Either of these mixtures will clean and dry the ear. Then, drop in a few drops of garlic oil, plug the canal with cotton, and lie down on your other side for a half hour. Repeat with the other ear if necessary. It works with children, too. If symptoms persist, call your doctor, of course.

If you have a cold, or want to prevent one, or if you are traveling and want to protect your stomach from marauding pathogens, try popping a raw clove of unchewed garlic and swallowing it like a pill. Your mouth won't suffer from chewing the raw garlic, but its antibiotics will be released in your stomach. Or do like the Delany sisters, who, at the ages of 102 and 104, wrote in *Having Our Say: The Delany Sisters' First 100 Years,* "Every morning, after we do our yoga, we each take a clove of garlic, chop it up, and swallow it whole."

Raw garlic also belongs in the kitchen, in vinaigrettes and other salad dressings, salsas, Bloody or Virgin Marys. But most kitchen uses call for cooking garlic. "Extracting garlic's oily juice through a press produces the most pungent flavor," writes Marcella Hazan, the doyenne of Italian cooking, in *Marcella's Italian Cooking,* adding dismissively, "it is not suitable to careful cooking." Fortunately, cooked garlic yields most of the benefits we look for: prevention of cardiovascular disease and cancer.

Italy and China, where garlic is consumed regularly, have much less stomach cancer than places where it is less commonly eaten. In the high-garlic provinces of Italy, such as Sardinia, consumption is about a clove a day per person. In China, those who daily consumed an ounce of onion-family vegetables, including garlic, had 40 percent less stomach cancer than people in areas where onions and garlic were less frequently consumed.

Closer to home, a large epidemiological study of women in Iowa reports that those who consumed much less garlic were protected as well. In the Iowa Women's Health Study, which followed more than 35,000 women between the ages of 55 and 69 for five years, those who ate garlic more than once a week had a 32 percent lower risk of getting colon cancer than women who ate less than a clove a month. Rates of breast cancer were also lower. "We can't say for sure that it's garlic that is preventive, but it fits an overall picture," says study author Lawrence H. Kushi, an epidemiology professor at the University of Minnesota. "A few case-control studies show the same thing for colon cancer, and generally speaking, places that have lots of garlic in their cuisine tend to have lower rates of colon cancer."

The cancer prevention story is strengthened by the convergence of biochemistry, animal studies, and epidemiology. In the lab, it is clear that fresh raw garlic inhibits tumors. In a number of studies, animals fed garlic as well as carcinogens developed far fewer tumors.

Both water-soluble (S-allyl-cysteine) and oil-soluble (diallyl sulfide, diallyl disulfide) sulfur-containing garlic compounds appear to protect against cancer.

These have been shown to prevent potential carcinogens such as nitrosamines from forming in the stomach; they also act as antioxidants, bonding to potentially damaging forms of oxygen and thus rendering them harmless. Researchers at Loma Linda University in southern California also find that garlic compounds can boost certain aspects of the immune system, such as macrophages and T cells, that are important in preventing cancer. Perhaps most important, these sulfur compounds play a role in a powerful enzymatic system, glutathione S-transferase, which detoxifies potential carcinogens. Many of these cancer-protective sulfur compounds survive cooking.

Some of the most exciting work is going on with cancers of the breast and prostate; it suggests that garlic may not only play a role in preventing cancer but may also, as an auxiliary to cancer treatment, enhance the effectiveness of conventional treatments such as radiation or chemotherapy. In cell culture, garlic compounds slow breast and prostate tumor cells from proliferating while leaving normal cells alone. Like tofu (see page 258) and broccoli (see page 38), garlic "may modify hormone receptor sites," says John Pinto, M.D., of Memorial Sloan-Kettering Cancer Center in New York City. Although it is hard to translate studies of individual anticancer compounds in garlic into prescriptions for the use of whole garlic, Dr. Pinto believes the same amount of garlic that has been shown to lower blood cholesterol—as little as one clove a day—may also provide anticancer effects. He is currently experimenting with garlic in the treatment of prostate cancer.

Garlic may help the body rid itself of toxic heavy metals such as lead. One of garlic's least well known effects is its ability to bind (chelate) to heavy metals. In the early 1970s, Robert I. Lin, president of Nutrition International in Irvine, California, successfully used this garlic effect to treat inner-city children poisoned with lead.

Garlic's greatest benefit may be to the heart. It has antioxidant effects and so may protect LDL cholesterol from oxidation (only oxidized LDL cholesterol clogs arteries). Garlic's reputation as a heart tonic dates from ancient India and Greece. Dioscorides, the Greek-born Roman author who codified Greek herbal medicine in the first century A.D., wrote in his *Materia Medica* that garlic "clears the arteries." The ancient Indian Ayurvedic text *Charaka* holds that garlic "maintains the fluidity of the blood, strengthens the heart, and prolongs life."

Modern medical research reveals that garlic, in modest amounts compatible with friendship, cooked into gentleness as well as raw and fierce, can simultaneously lower elevated cholesterol levels, lower elevated blood pressure, reduce the tendency of blood to clot, and improve circulation. In some studies, garlic also stabilizes cardiac arrhythmias.

The most well established effect is the ability of garlic to lower elevated cholesterol levels. In 1993, an American analysis of 28 studies, eventually narrowed down to five well-controlled studies, found that about one-half to one clove a day decreases blood cholesterol an average of 9 percent in people who have blood cholesterol levels above 200. A 1994 English analysis of 12 studies reported that half a clove a day lowers blood cholesterol 12 percent. Garlic lowers potentially harmful LDL cholesterol rather than beneficial HDL cholesterol. It also lowers triglycerides, or blood fats, that in combination with high LDL levels increase one's risk of coronary heart disease. (Many of these studies have been done with supplements. But that's primarily because the supplement makers were the ones who financed the studies.)

At Pennsylvania State University in University Park, professor Yu-Yan Yeh has been exploring exactly what it is in garlic that lowers cholesterol. Many different sulfur compounds work, perhaps synergistically. "All these different extracts have similar effects in reducing the synthesis of cholesterol in the liver," says Yeh. "Whatever it is in garlic that lowers cholesterol is soluble in both water and oil. To me, that indicates that there is more than one ingredient in garlic that is lowering cholesterol. It doesn't really matter how you prepare your garlic, whether it is raw, or cooked, or how it is cooked."

Garlic can also lower blood pressure—a little. In 1994, Australian researchers analyzed published and unpublished (but placebo-controlled) trials of garlic preparations on blood pressure. They found a statistically significant reduction in systolic blood pressure, with a smaller reduction in diastolic. A modest effect. Their conclusion: garlic may be clinically useful in mild hypertension.

Garlic dilates blood vessels. That's how it lowers blood pressure. The same effect makes garlic a tonic for other cardiovascular conditions. It treats peripheral cardiovascular disease—the kind that impairs circulation in the legs—increasing the flow of blood through capillaries by 50 percent. In 1993, investigators in Germany tested a daily dose of 800 milligrams of garlic powder (the equivalent of one-half to one clove) on patients with "peripheral arterial occlusive disease stage II"—people who had such poor circulation in their legs that they were in substantial pain after walking a few dozen yards. (This condition is called intermittent claudication.) After five weeks, those on a placebo could walk on average only 31 meters without pain, while those on garlic could walk an average of 46 meters—an improvement of about 50 percent. "It is quite interesting," wrote the authors, "that the garlic-specific increase in walking distance did not appear to occur until the fifth week of treatment."

A tonic can take time. Another study, on lowering cholesterol, found that garlic lowered blood cholesterol in middle-aged men an average of 7 percent in five months—but there was no effect for the first four months.

By dilating blood vessels, garlic may also benefit the lungs. "Allicin, a constituent of garlic, has *systemic* vasodilating effects," says Alan Kaye, M.D., a professor at Tulane University Medical Center in New Orleans. "It has these effects in different vascular beds, including the lung. . . . There are many diseases in which hypoxia—lack of oxygen—plays a significant role: congenital heart disease, chronic obstructive pulmonary disease, and other diseases of the lungs. This compound blunts the effect of hypoxia. It occurs naturally in whole garlic."

By dilating blood vessels, garlic allows more oxygen to get into and out of our lungs. It also contains compounds that help thin mucus, according to pulmonary specialist Irwin Ziment, M.D., of the University of California, Los Angeles. "Cooked garlic contains compounds that are very similar in chemical structure to drugs used in Europe for mucus, such as Mucomist and Mucosolvan," he says. "This agent—or series of agents—probably gets absorbed and preferentially excreted into the lungs, stimulating the bronchial tubes, diluting mucus."

Garlic's greatest benefit to the cardiovascular system, though, may be its ability to inhibit blood clotting. Garlic works similarly to aspirin in inhibiting specific prostaglandins such as thromboxane, which stimulate blood clotting. Unlike aspirin but like ginger (see page 146) and other foods (see "Wine," page 301), garlic "thins" the blood without causing stomach bleeding and increasing the risk of ulcers. German authors, writing in the British *Journal of Clinical Practice* in 1990, were particularly impressed by garlic's ability to increase blood flow through capillaries and its tendency to inhibit blood clotting. "In summary, it can be said that the improvement of blood fluidity and the simultaneous increase in fibrinolytic activity [clot-dissolving activity] are an ideal complement." By reducing the "stickiness" of the blood, they write, garlic improves blood flow, allowing more blood to enter into the tiny capillaries, bringing in oxygen and removing waste products. Thus, they write, garlic has "a cleaning effect, with a 'purification' of the microcirculation."

If a modern pharmaceutical company invented a drug that lowered cholesterol by lowering LDL cholesterol, lowered triglycerides, lowered blood pressure, protected LDL cholesterol from oxidation, reduced irregular heartbeats, reduced the tendency of blood to form artery-clogging clots and also increased the ability to dissolve clots, and improved blood flow throughout the cardiovascular system—all without causing any side effects more serious than occasional heartburn—it would be a billion-dollar-plus product. If it also protected against cancer and tasted good roasted inside a chicken, it might indeed be a secret miracle of God.

EARTHY GARLIC SOUP

Try adding a teaspoon of ground sage or cumin for a flavor variation.

YIELD: 4 TO 6 SERVINGS

2 heads garlic
8 to 10 ounces (half a 1-pound loaf) day-old country or peasant-style white bread
1 tablespoon olive oil
Kosher salt and freshly ground pepper
1 tablespoon chopped, fresh flat-leaf parsley or chervil

Separate the garlic cloves, and smash, peel, and coarsely chop them.

Remove and discard the bread crusts, and cut the bread into 1-inch pieces. Put it in a saucepan with the garlic and 5 cups water.

Cover and bring to a boil. Reduce the heat to a simmer, and cook for 20 to 30 minutes, until the bread starts to disintegrate.

Transfer the mixture to a food processor. Add the olive oil and process until smooth, about 2 minutes. Season to taste with salt and pepper, garnish with parsley, and serve hot.

ELEGANT GARLIC SOUP

Many traditional garlic soups are made with lard, which gives them richness. Lard (pig fat) is hardly a health food, so we have enriched the taste of this soup with a little olive oil, sautéed onions, and port. For an even richer taste, use 2 tablespoons of butter, 1 of olive oil.

YIELD: 4 SERVINGS

3 tablespoons olive oil

3 yellow onions, peeled, and thinly sliced (about 5 cups)

1 head garlic, cloves separated, smashed, peeled, and finely chopped (about ½ cup)

1 tablespoon plus 1 teaspoon rubbed sage

2 teaspoons sugar

¼ cup port or red wine

5 cups Basic Vegetable Stock (page 271), low-salt canned chicken stock, or homemade beef stock

Kosher salt and freshly ground pepper

Heat the oil in a Dutch oven or deep skillet over medium heat. Sauté the onions, stirring occasionally, until golden brown, 15 to 20 minutes.

Reduce the heat to medium low, and stir in the garlic, sage, and sugar. Sauté, stirring frequently, until garlic is soft, 5 to 8 minutes.

Add the port, and increase the heat to high. Stir well to deglaze the pan, scraping up all those flavorful bits. Cook 3 minutes.

Add the stock, cover the pan, and bring the soup to a boil. Reduce the heat to a high simmer, and cook for another 10 minutes. Add salt and pepper to taste. Serve hot with toasted, crusty bread.

FRESH GARLIC SALSA

A good salsa is freshly made for the meal at which it's first served. Which isn't to say it doesn't keep—with all those antioxidants and antibiotic compounds, of course it keeps! The salt draws the juices out of the tomatoes and adds flavor. For a thicker salsa, halve each tomato and squeeze out the seeds and excess juice before dicing.

Taste the jalapeño before you add it—some are hotter than others.

Because you are eating the garlic raw, it's a good idea to remove any green germ you find in the center; it can be bitter.

YIELD: 5 CUPS

5 to 7 large garlic cloves, smashed, peeled, and minced (about ¼ cup)
¼ cup fresh lime juice
2 pounds ripe plum or beefsteak tomatoes, cored and diced (about 5 cups)
1 fresh jalapeño, seeded and deveined, if desired, and minced
¼ cup diced red onion
1 teaspoon kosher salt, or more to taste
½ cup chopped fresh cilantro
Freshly ground pepper

Combine the garlic, lime juice, tomatoes, jalapeño, onion, salt, cilantro, and pepper to taste in a nonreactive bowl. Let it sit for about 20 minutes so the flavors combine. Serve as you would any salsa.

Variations

- Puree half the salsa and leave half chunky.
- Add 1 pound tomatillos, husked and finely chopped or pureed.
- Add finely chopped fresh parsley, mint, or oregano.
- Add 1 chipotle chili, finely chopped or pureed.

GARLIC POUNDED AND BOILED IN MILK

I had a head cold while I was reading Barbara Griggs's wonderful history *Green Pharmacy,* and I came upon a reference to "garlic, pounded and boiled in milk, or eaten freely for a troublesome cough—a remedy found the world over." When I first made it, I didn't let the milk boil, and I came up with a reasonable remedy, the garlic strong as I chewed it, the warm milk balancing its pungency. When I let the milk simmer for a minute or two, it became a truly restorative drink—hot milk with a hint of garlic, and the garlic itself ever so slightly tamed. Boiled only briefly, it retains, I am sure, some allicin, with its antibacterial, antiviral, even antifungal properties. Unlike raw garlic chomped, it didn't send my stomach into revolt. It helped my breathing; my cold left me a few days later—but then colds always do, don't they?

YIELD: 1 SERVING

1 garlic clove
1 cup skim milk

Crush the garlic slightly with the side of a large knife. Peel it, trim off the end, and mince.

Put it in a saucepan with the milk, and bring it to a high simmer. Adjust the heat to keep it from boiling too hard, and let it cook for a minute or two. Drink hot.

CRUNCHY PICKLED GARLIC

Blanching the garlic results in a smoother-tasting pickle. Look for fresh, firm garlic that hasn't started to sprout. If you spot any sticky, moldlike growth as you separate the cloves, don't use that garlic for pickling—it's possible that the mold could surviving pickling, and in any case, it won't taste good. Light pickling such as this retains many of garlic's beneficial properties, especially for heart disease and cancer protection.

YIELD: 1 QUART

2 pounds garlic (about 12 heads)
2 cups rice wine vinegar
2 cups cider vinegar
1 cup sugar
¼ cup kosher salt
1 stalk fresh lemongrass (optional)
4 large sprigs fresh dill
3 to 4 inches fresh ginger, peeled, and thinly sliced

Separate the garlic cloves; discard the excess papery skin, but don't peel the cloves.

Bring a large pot of water to boil. Add the garlic, and let it poach for 4 minutes. Drain in a colander, and rinse with cold water to stop the cooking. When cool enough to handle, peel the cloves, and set them aside in the colander.

Meanwhile, fill a canning kettle or other large pan with water (enough to cover jars by several inches), cover and bring to a boil.

In a saucepan, bring the rice and cider vinegars, sugar, and salt to a boil. Reduce the heat and simmer, stirring, until the sugar and salt have dissolved. Turn off the heat.

Using tongs, put a 1-quart canning jar, its lid, and sealing ring into the boiling water in the canning kettle. Boil for 10 minutes, making sure the jar stays submerged. With the tongs, transfer the jar to a clean kitchen towel to cool. Keep the water boiling.

Meanwhile, trim the lemongrass, if using, and smash the root end with the bottom of a heavy pot or a hammer to release more flavor.

When the jar is cool enough to handle, pack it with a layer of garlic, using a chopstick or long wooden dowel to poke the cloves in tightly. Continue packing and poking, alternating layers of lemongrass, dill, and ginger with layers of garlic, to within about an inch from the top.

Bring the vinegar mixture back to a boil, and pour it into the jar, leaving about a half inch of space at the top.

Using the tongs, remove the sealing lid from the boiling water and place it directly on top of the jar. Remove the metal canning ring and place it on the lid. Use a kitchen towel to screw the hot ring onto the jar, closing it tightly without forcing.

Use the tongs to transfer the filled jar to the canning kettle. Let the water return to a boil, and process (cook) for 10 minutes. Use the tongs to transfer the hot jar to the kitchen towel to cool completely.

You might hear the lid pop, which means the seal has taken and the jar doesn't need to be refrigerated. It doesn't always make a loud pop, though, so check the seal by pressing down on the center of the lid with your finger. The lid should be firm and not move up and down when pressed. If it does give, reprocess the jar in the boiling water bath, or keep it in the refrigerator.

Label and date the jar, and store it in a cool, dark place for 30 days for flavors to develop. If properly sealed, the pickles will keep on the shelf for 6 months. Refrigerate after opening.

Variations

- Substitute white distilled vinegar, white wine vinegar, red wine vinegar, or balsamic vinegar.
- Add a combination of turmeric, mustard seeds, caraway seeds, celery seeds, dill seeds, coriander seeds, hot red pepper flakes, horseradish, whole cloves, peppercorns, citrus zest, or cinnamon sticks to the pickling liquid.

HORSERADISH-HONEY-GARLIC TEA

This should clear out your breathing passages or soothe a sore throat. If you want a cool drink, make a more concentrated tea with only 2 cups water, and add some, according to your taste, to Homemade Ginger Ale (page 151).

YIELD: 4 CUPS

1 1-inch piece fresh horseradish, peeled and grated (¼ cup)
¼ cup honey
2 garlic cloves, smashed, peeled, and coarsely chopped
Juice of 1 lemon

Put 4 cups water on to boil.

In a blender, combine the horseradish, honey, garlic, and 2 tablespoons of water.

Process until smooth, stopping once or twice to scrape down the sides of the blender.

Scrape the puree into a bowl, and pour in the boiling water. Let it steep for 5 minutes. Strain into a teapot, and stir in the lemon juice. Drink hot, inhaling the steam deeply.

GINGER

When a child is born in China, a knob of ginger is tacked onto the entrance of the home to "absorb the harmful character traits of any visitors," according to Bruce Cost in his lovely little cookbook *Ginger: East to West*. That's not surprising, given ginger's salutary reputation in China; it's a common ingredient there in medicines as well as foods.

Ginger is rarely the primary ingredient in herbal formulas. Rather, it is a harmonizing agent, added to improve digestion, protect against ulcers, improve circulation, and warm the body. By enhancing digestion and circulation, traditional Chinese theory goes, ginger helps the body assimilate the active ingredients in stronger herbs, deliver them where they are needed, and minimize any side effects.

Science backs up many of these claims—and adds a few more. One recent animal study from China, for example, reports that adding ginger to another herb, *rhizome pinelliae,* made the latter less toxic.

Ginger's gastrointestinal benefits are among the best established. "It stimulates the release of digestive juices," says Daniel Mowrey, president of the American Phytotherapy Laboratory in Salt Lake City, Utah. "It stimulates the soft muscles of the GI lining, so that there is more vigorous activity, and nutrients are transported into the bloodstream more efficiently. There is also some indication that the flow of bile is increased." Bile acids, secreted by the liver and stored in the gallbladder, help digest fats. Chinese animal studies also find that ginger extracts inhibit gastric ulcers. So adding fresh ginger to foods—it is traditionally paired with pork, chicken, and fish—makes sense.

A larger amount of ginger has a specific therapeutic benefit: it prevents nausea. In Asia, fishermen often chew a piece of ginger in stormy weather. Researcher Mowrey was the first to document this scientifically. He gave volunteers at Brigham Young University either Dramamine (the standard antinausea drug) or 940 milligrams of powdered ginger, then sat them in a chair that moved to simulate a rough, rocky sea. Stop when you feel sick, he said. As he reported in the British medical journal *The Lancet* in 1982, those who took ginger were able to last 50 percent longer than those on Dramamine. Since then, Mowrey has found ginger effective in car sickness, amusement park motion sickness, and, to a lesser extent, morning sickness. A 1988 study of Danish naval cadets found that 1,000 milligrams of dried ginger, compared to an inactive placebo, resulted in "remarkably fewer symptoms of nausea and vertigo."

More recently, ginger has been studied in clinical settings. In 1990, anesthesiologists at Saint Bartholomew's Hospital in London compared ginger, a placebo, and the standard antivomiting drug metoclopramide in 60 women coming out of major gynecological surgery. The purpose: to prevent the nausea and vomiting that often accompany anesthesia. Ginger worked as well as the drug and better than the placebo. In a 1993 study, only 21 percent of those given ginger experienced nausea or vomiting after major surgery, versus 27 percent of those given metoclopramide and 41 percent of those given a placebo.

In 1995, it reached America. At Morristown Memorial Hospital in New Jersey, researchers were studying a new chemotherapy for lymphoma, a cancer of the lymph system. Patients take a drug, 8-MOP (derived from seaweed), which makes their white blood cells sensitive to ultraviolet light; their blood is then removed, exposed to ultraviolet light, and returned. It's called photophoresis. So far it has proven to be an effective new treatment. But 8-MOP can cause severe nausea.

"Thirty to forty percent of patients have some degree of nausea, and in some cases it's so extensive that they can barely tolerate the therapy," says Bonnie Keyes, R.N., of the photophoresis unit at Morristown Memorial Hospital. One of her patients asked about ginger. It seemed to help. So Keyes and her colleagues tested it, and reported their findings in *Dermatology Nursing* in 1995. It worked. In 11 patients who rated their reactions on the "nausea scale," those who took 8-MOP without ginger scored 22.5, those who took ginger, 8.0. The patients took 1.5 grams of dried ginger, but Bonnie Keyes would now recommend 1 gram (1,000 milligrams), because a few patients found that the larger dose caused a burning sensation.

"We now offer it to all our patients," she says. "We keep a big jar in the kitchen, offer them a couple, and after that, they just buy it on their own if they want."

Unlike antinausea drugs, which affect the central nervous system and can cause side effects such as drowsiness, dizziness, dry mouth, blurred vision, or nervousness, ginger has no known side effects. Explains Mowrey, "Ginger works primarily on the digestive system, interfering with the biofeedback between the stomach and the inner ear." The inner ear helps regulate the sense of balance; that's why an ear infection can give you vertigo.

If you want a supplement to prevent motion sickness, start with 1,000 milligrams of dried ginger (that is, one 900-milligram capsule or two to three 400-milligram capsules) before you travel, the same amount while you are traveling, and another 1,000 milligrams if you begin to feel nauseous, Mowrey suggests. "I haven't found an upper limit." A good rule of thumb, he says, is to "consume enough so you can taste it on your breath."

Ginger, used liberally in food, may provide a far more significant benefit: it inhibits blood clotting. Like aspirin, ginger "thins" the blood by affecting prostaglandins, hormonelike substances that affect coagulation and inflammation at specific sites (such as wounds) within the body.

If you get a cut, prostaglandins signal your blood to clot at that site. If you injure your shoulder, prostaglandins tell your muscles to swell painfully. Other prostaglandins inhibit these processes. The proper balance is essential. But our modern meat-centered diet, rich in saturated fat, tilts the balance toward thromboxane, a prostaglandin that promotes both clotting and inflammation. (So do highly polyunsaturated vegetable oils such as safflower and corn oil, although in our diets, they play a smaller role.)

Other foods redress the balance. The most famous is probably fish, which contains omega-3 fatty acids that inhibit thromboxane, reduce the tendency of blood to clot, and, in a number of studies, help prevent heart attacks. Olive oil contains antioxidants that also interfere with clotting. So does garlic, which is a wonderful cardiovascular protector. Alcohol does, too. Ginger, although it isn't as well studied, may be an even more potent agent for preventing blood clots and reducing inflammatory processes.

In India, where the diet often promotes thromboxane, there is great interest in ginger as a protecting factor. In one 1993 study, researchers gave 20 healthy men enough butter (three and a half ounces) to promote blood clotting. They gave ten of them five grams of dried ginger in two doses with their meals for a week. Ginger didn't affect cholesterol, but, the authors report, "there was a significant reduction in platelet aggregation." (The platelets are the part of blood that affect clotting.) An English study found that a smaller amount, two grams of dried ginger, did not have the same effect, causing the researchers to conclude that "the effect of ginger on thromboxane synthetase activity is dose-dependent."

A Danish study finds that fresh ginger is as effective as dried ginger. They gave women five grams of fresh raw ginger—about a heaping teaspoon—a day for a week. Blood levels of thromboxane B2, a potent clot-promoting prostaglandin, fell by 50 percent in the ginger-eating week compared to control weeks.

"Putting ginger in your food may moderate the effects of thromboxane," says Artemis Simopoulos, director of the Center for Genetics, Nutrition, and Health in Washington, D.C. She cautions, however, that few human studies have been conducted. "It may be for the Indian diet what garlic is to the Mediterranean diet. The Mediterranean diet has lots of olive oil, garlic, and fish, so maybe they don't need ginger!"

If ginger capsules do turn out to be a potent thromboxane-inhibiting agent, they could become important holistic treatments in medicine. Migraine headaches, for example, are often treated with anti-inflammatory drugs, with their attendant side effects. According to researchers at the University of Odense in Denmark, "ginger is reported in Ayurvedic [traditional Indian] and Tibb [the Ayurvedic-influenced traditional medicine of Tibet] systems of medicine to be useful in neurological disorders. It is proposed that administration of ginger may [be] abortive and prophylactic in migraine headache [that is, may stop new migraines and prevent future ones] without any side effects." One very small study (seven patients) with rheumatoid arthritis—a highly inflammatory, autoimmune disease—found that ginger reduced symptoms and pain. Other researchers have suggested that it may have clinical relevance for prostaglandin-related conditions as diverse as anxiety, depression, recovery from alcoholism, and ulcerative colitis.

Pungent possibilities, indeed. If ginger does develop into a significant medicine, it will certainly be one of the most delicious ones. But let us not leave this sweet rhizome without mentioning yet another health benefit: ginger is traditionally used in Chinese and Indian medicine for coughs and colds. In 1994, researchers at Wellcome Research Laboratories in England reported that they had identified several compounds, called sesquiterpenes, in ginger that are active against rhino viruses—the kind that cause the common cold.

A classic Indian remedy for a cold with a cough is to squeeze ginger juice with a little garlic juice into a tablespoon of honey. Another popular cold remedy in many cultures is ginger tea (see the recipe that follows).

Finally, what about warming? One might speculate that by thinning the blood, ginger would improve circulation and that all that blood flowing more freely would increase a feeling of warmth. Ginger also stimulates metabolism—that is, the burning of calories. In one study, volunteers who consumed warm spices such as ginger burned an average of 25 calories more a day than on days when they ate blander foods. Whether this means that eating more ginger will help in the battle of the bulge isn't clear, but, as Brett said at the end of Hemingway's *The Sun Also Rises,* "Wouldn't it be pretty to think so?"

The recipes that follow take advantage, variously, of ginger's warming, stomach-settling, antinausea, cardioprotective, and other beneficial properties. Let us not forget pleasure, however. Ginger's unique sweet spiciness and clean pungency cut through fatty fish, enliven stock, and can turn, with a little tweak, into a sweet.

To be sure, use it for specific purposes when you have a cold, feel cold, travel, or want to protect your heart. But if you enjoy the flavor of ginger, use it liberally in your cooking any time. It is food; the pleasure it brings to the tongue is a signal of its healthfulness.

GINGER TEA WITH WARMING SPICES

This refreshing hot tea will warm you from the inside out. It is a wonderful drink when you feel cold and very good if you have a cold. The cinnamon (page 78) adds its own heat, while the cardamom, cloves, and mint help settle the stomach. It's also a lovely afternoon spirit lifter.

YIELD: 4 CUPS

1 1-inch piece fresh ginger, peeled and grated
1 ½-inch piece Chinese cinnamon stick
4 cardamom pods, smashed open to release seeds
5 whole cloves
¼ cup chopped fresh mint leaves
Honey or sugar

Bring 4 cups water to a boil.

Put the ginger, cinnamon, cardamom pods and seeds, cloves, and mint in a teapot. Add the boiling water, and let it steep for 5 minutes.

Strain the tea into cups, and sweeten to taste.

HOMEMADE LEMONY GINGER ALE

Here's a nice one for warm weather. By improving circulation, ginger can also help you cool down. You can substitute two teaspoons ground ginger for the fresh.

YIELD: ½ CUP BASE, ENOUGH FOR 4 CUPS GINGER ALE

1 2-inch piece fresh ginger, peeled and diced (¼ cup)
2 tablespoons fresh lemon juice
¼ cup Simple Syrup (page 95)

Combine the ginger, lemon juice, and syrup in a blender. Blend until smooth, stopping once or twice to scrape around blade with a spatula to make sure all the ginger is getting processed.

Strain the mixture through a fine sieve. It will keep in the refrigerator for 2 to 3 weeks.

For each serving, combine 2 tablespoons base with 1 cup water or seltzer.

FENNEL AND GINGER CONGEE

A congee is a kind of rice soup. By cooking rice for a long period of time, it becomes very easy to digest. In China, congees are given to the very old, the very young, and anyone recovering from illness. They are also a common breakfast food. This congee, with fennel (see page 113), brings out ginger's stomach-settling potential. It is a very comforting dish. The variation is a classic Chinese cold remedy.

YIELD: **8 1**-CUP SERVINGS

1 heaping tablespoon whole fennel seeds
1 ½-inch piece fresh ginger, peeled and thinly sliced
1 cup long-grain white rice
2 tablespoons brown sugar, or to taste
Sesame oil or soy sauce (optional)

Toast the fennel seeds in a small, dry skillet over high heat, shaking them to prevent scorching, until aromatic, about 3 minutes. Transfer them to a spice grinder, and pulse just until the seeds are partially broken up.

Combine the fennel, ginger, rice, and 8 cups water in a soup pot. Cover and bring to a boil. Reduce heat to a simmer and cook until the rice has broken down and the water is thick with starch, about 3½ to 4 hours.

Serve hot—seasoned with the sugar and, if you like, with a drop of sesame oil or soy sauce.

Variation

FOR SCALLION, GINGER, AND CINNAMON CONGEE: Combine 2 teaspoons freshly grated ginger, ½ teaspoon ground cinnamon, 2 thinly sliced scallions, 1 cup long-grain white rice, and 8 cups water in a soup pot, and cook as directed in the preceding recipe.

GINGER JELLIES

These nonfat candies are a delicious treat and a good preventive for motion sickness.

YIELD: **64** CANDIES

2 ounces unflavored gelatin
4⅓ cups sugar
8 ounces fresh ginger, peeled and coarsely chopped
Powdered sugar

Coat an 8-inch square pan with vegetable-oil spray, and set aside.

Put 2 cups water in a heavy-bottomed saucepan, and sprinkle on the gelatin. Let it soften for about 4 minutes.

Add the sugar and warm slowly over low heat, stirring constantly, until the sugar dissolves, about 10 minutes. Wipe down the sides of the pan with a damp pastry brush to remove any sugar crystals.

Increase the heat to high, and bring to a boil. Add the ginger, reduce the heat, and boil gently, without stirring, for 15 minutes.

Let the mixture stand for 10 minutes while the bubbles dissipate. Strain it into the prepared pan, and discard the ginger. Don't scrape out the saucepan.

Let the jelly sit, uncovered and unrefrigerated, for 24 hours.

It can be kept, covered and uncut, in the refrigerator for 4 to 6 weeks. When ready to serve, cut it into 1-inch squares and roll lightly in powdered sugar. Candies will keep in an airtight container for 2 months.

QUICK CANDIED GINGER

Candied ginger is convenient to take along when traveling. This quick version is a little less crystallized than traditional ones but still quite delicious. In spring or early summer, use stem ginger if you can find it.

YIELD: **10** TO **20** PIECES, DEPENDING ON HOW THINLY THE GINGER IS SLICED

1 3½-inch piece fresh ginger, peeled
1½ cups sugar, plus extra for rolling

Shave the ginger lengthwise into paper-thin slices with a vegetable peeler or, better yet, a Japanese mandoline (see "Sources," page 321).

Put the sugar and 2 cups water in a small saucepan. Cook over low heat, stirring, until the sugar has dissolved, about 5 minutes. Cover and bring to a boil. Add the ginger and let it return to a boil. Reduce the heat and simmer until the ginger is translucent, 35 to 55 minutes depending on the thickness of the ginger slices.

Strain and reserve the syrup for Ginger Snow Sorbet (see the recipe that follows).

Use tongs to arrange the ginger slices on a cooling rack. When no longer sticky, roll each piece in sugar to prevent sticking. The candy will keep in an airtight container for several weeks.

Variation

GINGER SNOW SORBET: To make an incredibly light sorbet, mix the ginger syrup with enough water to make 4 cups. Cover, chill, and process in an ice cream maker according to manufacturer's instructions.

PICKLED GINGER (GARI)

Natural pickled ginger is a pale golden color. Commercial ginger often includes food coloring. For a naturally pinker pickled ginger, you may want to add fresh or pickled *shiso* leaves, available in Asian markets.

YIELD: ABOUT 1 CUP

10 ounces fresh ginger, peeled
⅔ cup rice wine vinegar
½ cup sugar
½ teaspoon kosher salt

Put about 4 cups water on to boil.

Shave the ginger lengthwise into paper-thin slices with a vegetable peeler or Japanese mandolin (see "Sources," page 321). Blanch it in the boiling water for 1 minute. Drain and set it aside to cool. (Save the water for making tea or broth if you like.)

Meanwhile, put the vinegar, sugar, and salt in a clean, dry, airtight container. Add the ginger, and poke it down with chopsticks or a wooden dowel to submerge it.

Close the container tightly, and refrigerate for 24 hours for flavors to combine. The pickles will keep in the refrigerator, tightly covered, for a month.

GINGER BRANDY

This one really warms the insides. Between the alcohol and the ginger, you might say this is a cardiovascular tonic. An ounce at a time is plenty; sip slowly.

YIELD: 1 CUP

1 4-inch piece fresh ginger, peeled and thinly sliced (about 1 cup)
½ cup brandy

Put a ½-pint glass canning jar or other lidded glass container and its lid in a large bowl in the sink. Cover with boiling water, and let it sit for 5 minutes. Using tongs, transfer them to a clean kitchen towel to dry and cool.

Pack the ginger into the jar, and add the brandy. Close the jar tightly without forcing, and shake it a few times to distribute the ingredients.

Label and date the jar, and store it in a cool, dark place for 2 weeks for the flavors to develop. If you want, you may then strain out the ginger; if you leave the ginger pieces in, though, you can "top off" the mixture in the jar with fresh brandy from time to time.

GINKGO
(Ginkgo biloba)

In China, the nut of the ginkgo tree is a delicacy, boiled and served over rice. In Europe, the leaf is holistic medicine. In America, it's pure hype.

One night, perusing television, I was addressed by an attractive woman in her late 30s or early 40s who expressed her concern that she was becoming a little forgetful and her excitement about a new supplement she was using that helped her think more clearly. The woman doesn't exist—she was simply an actor in a commercial—but the product is available in most health food stores.

Ginkgo biloba is one of the best-studied of plant medicines. Clinical studies show that active ingredients in the leaf, when isolated and concentrated in supplements, can improve memory and cognitive function in older people who suffer from a lack of oxygen in the brain caused by cardiovascular disease.

It's a wonderful preventive medicine and is quite safe in normal dosages. But is it appropriate for a healthy young woman who would like to think more clearly? Probably not. If our television character actually existed, her forgetfulness would probably be the result of trying to do too much with too little time and too little sleep. It's much less likely that she has cardiovascular disease severe enough to impair blood flow to the brain.

Ginkgo biloba, the leaves of the familiar stinky ginkgo tree, contain a substance that interferes with PAF, or "platelet activating factor." Too much PAF contributes to blood clotting, which can lead to heart attacks and more subtle problems. What's nice about ginkgo is that it doesn't have any direct cardiovascular effects—it doesn't make the heart beat faster, for example. But by "thinning" the blood, it improves circulation, especially in the small capillaries in the limbs, hands, and feet. More significantly, ginkgo leaf extract crosses the blood-brain barrier and so works directly on the delivery of oxygen to the brain.

The effects can be dramatic. In *Spontaneous Healing,* Andrew Weil, M.D., quotes a testimonial from a 60-year-old woman. After the third week of taking *ginkgo biloba* supplements, she wrote, "I lost my depression and began to feel like the world was a wonderful place to live. I began having more energy. . . . I noticed that I wasn't using my cane, and I had a longer stride, a steady stride. . . . I lost the pain in my legs and feet. . . . It is so wonderful to be able to feel life as it should be felt!"

Dr. Weil writes that while he believes the experience of the woman, he nevertheless is not sure he agrees with her statement that it is ginkgo and ginkgo alone that is the cause. The main thesis of his book is that the human body has an innate ability to heal itself, an ability that can be triggered in many ways. Belief in the efficacy of a medical agent, be it ginkgo or surgery, may liberate these innate healing capabilities, according to Dr. Weil. Recent studies have demonstrated that the "placebo effect" is much stronger than previously thought and may explain much of the effectiveness of conventional as well as alternative medicine. Yet Dr. Weil remains open to, if skeptical of, the possibility that ginkgo can indeed provide an extraordinary range of benefits for certain people.

In Europe, an extract of *Ginkgo biloba,* dubbed EGb 761 (it stands for "Extract of *Ginkgo biloba*"), is used clinically for the treatment of cerebral insufficiency, a common occurrence in aging in which there is not enough blood flow to the brain for optimal mental functioning. In Germany, EGb is approved for the treatment of dementia. In one year alone, five million prescriptions were written for the extract in Germany, and more of it was sold over the counter. (Under the German system, the national health insurance will pay for a medication only if your doctor tells you to buy it.)

One review in the French medical journal *Presse Med* reports that the drug "seems to be effective in patients with vascular disorders, in all types of dementia, and even in patients suffering from cognitive disorders secondary to depression, because of its beneficial effects on mood. Of special concern are people who are just beginning to experience deterioration in their cognitive function. *Ginkgo biloba* extract might delay deterioration and enable these subjects to maintain a normal life and escape institutionalization. In addition, *Ginkgo biloba* appears to be a safe drug, being well tolerated, even in doses many times higher than those usually recommended."

Don't expect it to work right away, however; in one double-blind, placebo-controlled study of 166 older patients with "cerebral disorders," ginkgo's benefits were not clinically significant for three months. Its effectiveness continued to increase in the following months. A tonic takes time.

Ginkgo appears to work in several related ways. The extract contains well-known antioxidant phytochemicals such as quercetin (also found in red grapes and yellow onions; see "Onion," page 211) and kaempferol. It also contains specific compounds dubbed "ginkgolides." As plant medicine expert Varro Tyler writes in *Herbs of Choice,* "the therapeutic effects of EGb are attributed to a mixture of these constituents, not to a single chemical entity."

Daniel Mowrey, author of *Herbal Tonic Therapies,* puts it another way: "The extract retains tonic properties. It has a balancing, homeostatic effect on blood flow and neurotransmitter production. If you consume a lot of it you don't screw up specific neurotransmitters, such as acetylcholine, as you would with, say, skullcap or wood betony."

Ginkgo has many beneficial effects. It makes capillaries, the tiny blood vessels that fan out from small blood vessels to remove waste and supply oxygen to cells, less fragile. It is antioxidant, protecting cell membranes from damage by free oxygen radicals (highly reactive and damaging forms of oxygen). Ginkgolides inhibit platelet-activating factor (PAF), which not only can cause blood clots but bronchial constriction and the release of inflammatory compounds. (One might speculate that ginkgo may have a "side effect" of reducing the symptoms of asthma.)

Ginkgolides also improve blood fluidity, making it easier for blood to flow throughout the circulatory system. At Louisiana State University Medical Center in New Orleans, ophthalmologist Nicholas Bazan, M.D., has studied *Ginkgo biloba* extracts as PAF antagonists. "We've studied a specific compound isolated from ginkgo extract, BN52021, that inhibits PAF. PAF is an endogenous chemical—it's in all cells—that regulates cell function. But when it is overproduced, it creates damage to cells. This compound in *Ginkgo biloba* blocks the site of action of PAF—but only when PAF is produced in toxic amounts. Those conditions include many inflammatory diseases, such as in stroke, epileptic brain damage, brain injury. It seems to be neuroprotective"—that is, it protects neurons, or nerve cells. It also seems to help regulate brain neurotransmitters under stress, blocking the neurotransmitter glutamate, which lets calcium migrate inside neurons, killing them. Says Dr. Bazan, "It diminishes the stress response."

The net effect is a safe plant drug that increases the flow of oxygen to the brain even as it protects neurons from excess oxygen free radicals. Says Tyler, "It is used primarily to increase peripheral circulation, not only in the legs for intermittent claudication [pain usually brought on by walking, due to cardiovascular disease] but particularly in the brain. It can improve short-term memory, as well as vertigo, and probably tinnitus. All these beneficial effects are due to improved vascular circulation."

Says Joseph Martarano, M.D., a physician in private practice in New York City, "I've been using ginkgo in my practice for about six years. I'm a psychopharmacologist, and I use it to treat people with memory disorders—impaired memory. I often add it to other medications for drug-resistant depression. It's good for people who are not feeling alert. It's usually used for older people, but it could be used to treat depression at any age. It increases cerebral permeability, so blood vessels in the brain have more access to oxygen and suffer less deterioration. Reduced blood flow to the brain is a common aspect of aging. I personally take two Ginkgo Gold tablets a day. I don't know if it is doing me any good. I'm alert. Maybe it's just helping me maintain baseline."

At the University of Connecticut Health Center in Farmington, assistant professor Arpad Tosaki has been studying ginkgo for nearly a decade, in France and the United States. "Ginkgo is a free radical scavenger," Tosaki says. "In Europe, they use it for aging. It also has some use against arrhythmias. It is also used in Japan. It's helpful in angina pectoris, as well as recovery from stroke or heart attack.

"Mostly, though, this drug is used as prevention—to prevent free radical formation. I've done toxicity examinations, and it is a very, very safe drug. That's a big advantage. We gave animals as much as five grams per kilogram of body weight and found no effects. It is absolutely very safe. People usually take the pills for a long time, for many years, with no side effects."

Everything has some side effects in some people, of course, and Professor Tyler notes that they may include "gastrointestinal disturbances, headache, and allergic skin reactions." To put Tosaki's toxicological studies in perspective, though, let's remember that the *Ginkgo biloba* extracts usually sold in the U.S. contain 40 milligrams per capsule, and recommended dosage is one capsule three times a day. That's 120 milligrams, or about one-eighth of a gram. Five grams is 40 times that amount. So, to give an animal 5 grams per kilogram of body weight means giving it 40 times the human dose—for every 2.2 pounds of weight. A 150-pound man is 68 times this unit weight of 2.2 pounds, which would mean he would receive the equivalent of nearly 3,000 times the recommended dose. Don't take this! The point in animal studies is to find how high a dose one must give an animal to cause harm. But these kinds of studies do indicate that the recommended amount of *Ginkgo biloba* extracts is safe.

From the studies I've read and the experts I've interviewed, it doesn't seem that ginkgo would do a person any harm, whenever they started to take it. But it would seem to have the most benefit for an older person who is beginning to feel a few symptoms of cardiovascular aging, having a little difficulty remembering things, and experiencing ringing in the ears or pains in the leg. For such a person, one would want to start taking ginkgo supplements, standardized to contain specific amounts of EGb 761, on a daily basis—forever. It's not particularly cheap, although it's a lot cheaper and more beneficial than most of the drugs physicians prescribe for those conditions. Remember, you may not feel many benefits for the first few months. But you will be addressing your symptoms in a way that is improving the functioning of your cardiovascular system and particularly the functioning of your brain.

Says Tyler, "If you are under medical care, do talk it over with your physician, but don't expect too much. We know little about drug interactions with phytomedicines, for example. But do sit down with your physician, assuming him to be an intelligent creature, and say, 'Here's this information, I would like to try ginkgo. Would you monitor me carefully, so I can do it without harm to my health?' Of course, if you have any problems, stop. Conversely, if after many weeks you find no benefit, stop taking it. But it is very safe. Do make sure you are dealing with a standardized product, and follow directions on the label."

If you are 35 or 40 or 45, any problems you have with mental clarity are much more likely the result of stress, lack of sleep, lack of exercise, and general burnout than a lack of oxygen-rich blood reaching your brain. For you (me, too), the best brain tonic is probably a diet rich in fruits and vegetables, a break from drinking too much coffee or alcohol, a vacation, yoga, therapy, deep breathing, sitting quietly, a daily walk. Aerobic exercise is about as good a way to reduce blood clotting and get more oxygen to the brain as has been discovered. Take *Ginkgo biloba* if you want; it certainly seems to be safe. As for me, I'll wait until I really need it.

MEMORY LIQUEUR

Unlike most of the tonics in this book, *Ginkgo biloba* is not best taken in some sort of food preparation. You can't even make a very effective tea from it because the active ingredient isn't very water soluble. The best way to take it is as a supplement or tincture standardized to provide a guaranteed potency of ginkgolides. Tinctures are alcohol-based, which makes sense, because ginkgolides, the active ingredients, are alcohol soluble. So the only reasonable homemade approach is an alcohol-based tonic. If you want a specific amount of ginkgolides to treat a medical condition, take a supplement; quantities of active ingredient in this tonic vary with each batch. On the other hand, one might say it makes a memorable nightcap.

YIELD: 2½ CUPS

1 ounce dried, crushed ginkgo leaves
2 cups vodka

Put a pint canning jar or other lidded glass container and its lid in a sink or large bowl. Pour on boiling water to cover, and let it sit for 5 minutes.

Use tongs to transfer the jar to a clean kitchen towel.

When cool enough to handle, pack the jar with the ginkgo leaves, and pour in the vodka.

Remove the lid from the hot water. Use a clean towel to close it tightly without forcing. Shake the jar a few times to distribute the ingredients.

Label and date the jar, and store it in a cool, dark place for 2 weeks for flavors to develop. After that, keep it in the refrigerator.

To serve, strain the liqueur through a fine strainer or cheesecloth. Sip slowly no more than ½ to 1 ounce (a shot) at a time.

GINSENG
(Panax ginseng)

Ginseng has been in continuous use in China for over 4,000 years. The first written reference to it appears in the oldest Chinese pharmacopoeia, *Shen-Nung Pen T'sao Ching,* from the first century A.D. What is extant is a revision by Tao Hung-Ching (452–536), who wrote that ginseng was used for "repairing the five viscera, quieting the spirit, curbing the emotion, stopping agitation, removing the noxious influence, brightening the eyes, enlightening the mind, and increasing the wisdom. Continuous use," he added, "leads one to longevity with light weight."

Ginseng is used to restore vital energy ("chi" or "qi"), especially in the elderly, people weakened by disease, and in cases of exhaustion. According to one textbook of traditional Chinese medicine, ginseng is used for "extreme collapse of the qi" and "devastated yang." It is often combined with other herbs as a kind of constitution-strengthening tonic that bolsters the chi while the other herbs do their more specific tasks. It is not a cure. Rather, it is a "superior" medicine that improves general functioning and restores balance and strength, helping the body heal itself.

Ginseng may be ancient and esteemed, but it is also greatly misunderstood, at least in the West. It is expensive, which provides a profit motive for companies and countries to support its reputation as a cure-all, a "panacea," which is what its Latin name, *Panax,* implies. A German scientist, Carl Anton Meyer, so named it in 1842, and to this day, its full scientific name is sometimes given as *Panax ginseng C. A. Meyer.*

The Chinese do not call it a panacea. They call it *ren-shen*—literally, "man root." The root often does look like a human body, with legs, a trunk, arms, and a head. According to the ancient "doctrine of signatures," this makes it good for the entire human body. The doctrine of signatures holds that a thing is what it looks like. Thus walnuts, which look like the human brain, are good for the brain. (They are—see page 292—but that's another story.)

In the 1960s, a Japanese scientist, Shoji Shibata, at the Meiji College of Pharmacy in Tokyo, identified a unique set of chemicals that are largely responsible for ginseng's actions. They are saponins, biologically active compounds that foam in water. Ginseng's unique saponins were dubbed "ginsenosides."

Modern research reveals that ginseng can have beneficial effects on metabolic function, immunity, mood, and physiological function at the most basic cellular level. It doesn't benefit everyone; recent studies of elite athletes reveal that it has no demonstrable effects on athletic performance. Yet in older people, studies show that it reduces fatigue, improves performance, and boosts mood. This makes sense in classic terms. Why would Olympic-class athletes, with their superior yang energy, want to take a root for people with "devastated" yang?

Ginseng is best used according to traditional criteria. If you are young, or even middle-aged, or suffering from an "overheated" condition such as high blood pressure, headaches, insomnia, heart palpitations, asthma, acute disease, a cold, or the flu, this is one herb to avoid. Paul Bergner, M.D., editor of *Medical Herbalism: A Clinical Newsletter for the Herbal Practitioner,* recently wrote about learning this the hard way: "I took ginseng while attending a stressful professional conference. The day after the convention, I experienced heart palpitations, and went to the doctor for a complete cardiac workup. The tests revealed nothing wrong, and the problem went away so the cause remained a mystery— until I took ginseng a year later at the same annual conference. The palpitations returned. In each instance I was also drinking coffee, and as I discovered, ginseng should not be taken with stimulants of any sort."

On the other hand, if you are recovering from a drawn-out illness, feeling fatigued, or feeling the effects of age—if, in other words, you are experiencing a "collapse" of your "chi," ginseng may be just right for you. As an old Chinese adage puts it, "If you use ginseng when you are young, what will you use when you are old?"

Let's look a little deeper into how modern science is unlocking some of the workings of this ancient rhizome. Then we can repair to the kitchen for some classic southern Chinese chi-strengthening soup.

"Repairing the Five Viscera"

The five viscera—liver, heart, spleen-pancreas, lungs, and kidney-bladder—are functional categories rather than specific organs; they relate, respectively, to the elements wood, fire, earth, metal, and water. They are central concepts in traditional Chinese medicine. According to Steven Fulder, author of *The Book of Ginseng: And Other Chinese Herbs for Vitality,* "the traditional Chinese physicians view the body as a set of purely functional processes such as storage, heating, digestion, elimination and energy production."

Scientific studies suggest than *Panax ginseng* may be particularly useful in the treatment of one particular metabolic disorder: diabetes. In dogs that were given diabetes, which was then controlled by injected insulin, ginseng led to a lowering of blood sugar levels. It had a synergistic effect with insulin but was not a substitute for it.

"In animal studies, ginseng has a glycogen-sparing effect," says sports physiologist Mel Williams of Old Dominion University in Virginia. That is, it helps the body make more efficient use of glycogen, the stored form of sugar in the liver.

A recent study finds that ginseng helps people with non-insulin-dependent diabetes, the common form that often appears with age. In a placebo-controlled study of 36 such patients, published in the journal *Diabetes Care* in 1995, Williams reported that ginseng "reduced fasting blood glucose levels, had a beneficial effect on body weight, elevated mood, and was associated with an improved outlook."

The effect on people with cardiovascular disease is more uncertain. In animals, small amounts of ginseng raise blood pressure, while larger amounts lower it. In patients with heart disease, ginseng may improve cardiac function. However, the research is so scant, the disease so serious, and the alternative herbs so attractive (see "Garlic," page 135, and "Hawthorn," page 178) that there is little reason to experiment with ginseng. And some authorities warn against using ginseng for "hot" conditions such as hypertension.

"Quieting the Spirit, Curbing the Emotion, Stopping Agitation"

"We have found an active ingredient in ginseng that acts like an opiate," says Edwin W. McClesky, a professor at the Vollum Institute for Advanced Biomedical Research at Oregon Health Sciences University in Portland. "It's a strong compound, but it is present in very low quantities, which makes ginseng a very mild medicine. We found it in *Panax ginseng,* but not in American ginseng.

It affects the rate at which nerve cells fire. "It's a hormonal type of inhibition, acting through receptors. That's what hormones do—they are not on-off switches but modulate [regulate] biological events. There is a real advantage to drugs that behave like that. You're not just hitting the system with a hammer.

"Our research suggests that ginseng may be an analgesic—that is, it can suppress pain. The compound we have discovered is a beautiful mimic of an opiate. If ginseng makes people feel a little better, that could explain a lot."

"Removing the Noxious Influence"

"Pharmacological investigations show that crude ginsenosides can increase non-specific resistance of an organism to various untoward influences," wrote two physicians from King's College Hospital in London in a 1988 article in the *Journal of Postgraduate Medicine* entitled "Ginseng: Is There a Use in Clinical Medicine?"

Nonspecific resistance is a big thing these days. It refers to the ability of an organism to respond to various stressors—to adapt—rather than a specific immune response to infection. One name for such a substance, coined by a Russian researcher, is "adaptogen." It helps us adapt to stress. An adaptogen may do so by supporting the adrenal system, which regulates hormones, and at the cellular level, by allowing cells to use oxygen and eliminate waste products more efficiently.

In *Chinese Herbal Medicine: Materia Medica,* Dan Bensky and Andrew Gamble give an example of how this might work in the case of ginseng. "Based on animal experiments using EEG and conditioned reflexes, it enhances both stimulatory and inhibitory processes in the central nervous system, thereby improving the adaptability of nervous responses"—that is, it improves the ability of our nervous system to speed up *and* to slow down. It helps the system respond more efficiently to the environment.

Another word for an edible substance that helps the body's regulation is—you guessed it—*tonic.*

"A tonic is an herb that balances body functions," says Daniel Mowrey, president of the American Phytotherapy Laboratory in Salt Lake City, Utah, and author of *Herbal Tonic Therapies.* "It can be minute physiological functions, or whole-body systems. Under the influence of a tonic, the body processes are driven toward homeostasis"—that is, equilibrium. Ginseng, he notes, improves immune processes "at the cellular level, making cells more resistant to damage from infection—as well as less susceptible to allergic reactions."

The adrenal glands produce hormones such as corticosteroids, known as "stress hormones." We produce them when we are under stress. If we are under chronic stress or chronically overstimulated, our adrenals can become less efficient and less responsive. They tend to overproduce stress hormones, overrespond to stressful events, and are less efficient at breaking down the stress hormones once they have begun to circulate in the body.

There is some evidence that ginseng, taken in small amounts over a long period of time, improves regulation of the adrenals so that stress hormones are produced rapidly when needed and broken down rapidly when not needed. Says Mowrey, "Small amounts of whole *Panax ginseng* can gradually rebuild the adrenal gland. The adrenal gland, once it becomes drained, is very difficult to build back up. Ginseng, along with licorice root and vitamin C, can help in the rebuilding process."

Whole root is best. Extracts, even those that contain specific guaranteed-potency ginsenosides, don't have some of the other compounds in ginseng that may be beneficial. "An extract loses its tonic action," says Mowrey. "It's okay to use a good-quality extract, such as Ginsana, for two or three weeks, but don't take it for a year. On the other hand, good whole ginseng root, in small amounts, can be taken every day for a year or more."

Research at the University of Alberta supports the benefit of whole ginseng. Dr. Benishim's colleagues there have discovered another compound in ginseng that stimulates antibody production. But it is not a ginsenoside, the putative "active ingredient" in ginseng. So it may not be in an extract.

Other researchers have helped define ginseng's immunological effects. At the Kyoritsu College of Pharmacy in Tokyo, researchers are studying "ginsenan PA," a polysaccharide isolated from whole ginseng root. Polysaccharides—literally, the word means "many sugars"—are large molecules found in foods that often have immunological effects. Ginsenan PA stimulates phagocytosis, the process through which the immune system "engulfs and devours" foreign bodies. Researchers at the Norman Bethune University of Medical Sciences in Changchun, China, also report that ginseng extracts promote phagocytosis and, in the lab, inhibit the growth of tumor cells.

At the Institute of Immunological Science at Hokkaido University in Sapporo, Japan, researchers have been studying another ginsenoside, Rb2. In mice given lung tumors, "oral administration of ginsenoside Rb2 caused a marked inhibition of both neovascularization and tumor growth," they write. Neovascularization, also called angiogenesis, is the tendency of tumors to create tiny blood vessels that feed their malignant growth.

Preventive medicine is very interested in compounds that can arrest this process; if a tumor doesn't get access to blood and thus oxygen, it cannot grow. Soybeans contain a potent antivascularization compound; so does shark cartilage. The authors conclude, "These results suggest that the inhibition of tumor-associated angiogenesis by ginsenoside Rb2 may partly contribute to the inhibition of lung tumor metastasis."

Yet another ginsenoside, Rh2, has recently been found to inhibit the growth of lab-cultured melanoma cells and human ovarian cancer cells, according to research at the National Defense Medical College in Saitama, Japan. In mice given tumors, those also given Rh2 had smaller tumors and lived longer. Those given both Rh2 and an anticancer drug, cisplatin, lived longest.

Finally, a case-control study in Korea compared about 2,000 patients admitted to the Korea Cancer Center Hospital in Seoul to another 2,000 noncancer patients. Those with cancer were about half as likely to use ginseng as those without cancer. Cancer risk was lower with those who took ginseng for a year but much lower for those who took ginseng for up to 20 years. Fresh ginseng, white ginseng extract, white ginseng powder, and red ginseng were all associated with reduced cancer risk.

Let's take these ginseng studies with a grain of salt, however. It takes more than a few lab and animal studies and a single case-control study to make a case. In case-control studies, people are already sick, and when somebody goes to their bedside to ask questions, they are likely to search for reasons why they may have gotten sick. In addition, for what it's worth, much of the ginseng research in Korea is supported by the ginseng industry.

On the other hand, by helping to restore adrenal function, improving cellular metabolic function, stimulating cellular immunity, and perhaps preventing incipient tumors from getting access to the blood supply, ginseng seems like an excellent adjunct for patients undergoing chemotherapy and a good preventive for the rest of us. You might even say it helps "remove the noxious influence."

"Enlightening the Mind, Increasing the Wisdom"

At the University of Alberta School of Medicine's Department of Physiology, associate professor Christina Benishim has focused on the effect of a particular ginsenoside, Rb1, to improve memory. In animal research, she has found that Rb1 increased the rate at which choline, an amino acid, is taken up in the brain, where it is turned into acetylcholine, a neurotransmitter that plays an essential role in memory.

"We compared Rb1 with Cognase, a drug used in the treatment of Alzheimer's disease which has an antiamnesiac effect," says Benishim. "But Cognase has a lot of side effects—it's really quite unpleasant. We found that in animals, the ginsenosides Rb1 and Rg1 were able to reverse amnesia effects of another drug, scopolamine, just as well as Cognase."

That was the first step. "Then we found, in in-vitro [lab] studies, that these ginsenosides stimulate the release of the neurotransmitter acetylcholine in specific regions of the brain associated with memory, the hippocampus. Rb1 and Rg1 have pronounced effects on the nerves in that region, improving the ability of the brain cells to absorb choline." She and her colleagues have a few patents on the ginsenosides for treatment of Alzheimer's disease, and she is working toward clinical studies. She readily admits that her research is preliminary.

"The study of the brain is very complicated. I don't advocate that people take medicinal herbs for any old reason. Any substance you put in your body has the potential to do you harm. But ginseng has been used for thousands of years with very few side effects. When people ask me whether they should take ginseng, I tell them I don't think it's a bad idea. I drink ginseng tea almost every day myself. . . . If you have an underlying illness, however, please consult your physician first."

Clinical studies in England, China, and elsewhere also suggest that ginseng can improve mental function. In one English study, wireless operators and telegraphists who took ginseng made fewer mistakes than those who didn't. In another double-blind study, 33 students were asked to trace a complex spiral maze on paper and to select certain letters from randomized groups of letters according to special rules. Those who took ginseng performed better. In another British study, nurses, both male and female, on night duty at a London hospital were given either Korean white ginseng or a similar white-powder placebo for three days. The nurses who took ginseng were both more alert and more tranquil during their work and performed better during a test of speed and coordination.

A double-blind study of 120 subjects, both male and female, ages 30 to 60 revealed the age-specific benefits of ginseng. In subjects over 40, ginseng increased the capacity to perform visual and acoustic reaction tests; it also improved pulmonary function, which is interesting, because the traditional Chinese interpretation of ginseng is that it "enters the lung meridian." However, in subjects ages 30 to 40, it had no such effects.

"Ginseng is considered to be tonic for the elderly," says Benishim. "In Western terms we have a hard time understanding that, but older persons might take ginseng and feel better, stronger, more resistant to infections and disease, with mental capacities improved."

"Longevity with Light Weight"

Ginseng is portrayed as a magic bullet in some circles, but it is more likely just what it is esteemed to be in traditional Chinese medicine: a unique root that helps support vital energy at a deep level, especially when one's chi has collapsed, one's yang is devastated. I haven't found any evidence in science that it improves longevity, helps one lose weight, or indeed "brighten[s] the eyes." However, taken in small amounts over a long period of time, it may help the body respond to stress. Don't take it if you don't need it, if you have energy but suffer from other health problems such as headaches or high blood pressure, or if you have an acute condition, such as a cold. If you want to take supplements, try ginseng for a month on, a month off. Whole root, in food or tea, can be taken for a longer period of time, a year or more.

Today, a walk through an American health food store will reveal such delightful inventions as ginseng soda, ginseng chewing gum, even ginseng candy. No need to worry about getting too much ginseng from these products; they aren't likely to contain much ginsenoside. Again, a better bet is the whole root.

Good whole ginseng root is thick, long, and intact. Commercially grown ginseng root is often very soft and, when you break it, spongy. This is inferior. Good ginseng, especially wild or woods-grown ginseng, is compact; the roots are much harder, with plenty of wrinkles around the top. The best ginseng root is at least five or six years old. To determine the age, count the scars; each one represents a year.

Whole root is more balanced and beneficial as a tonic than concentrated extracts or supplements. In China, Korea, and other Asian countries, there is a tradition of cooking with ginseng, of integrating it into the diet. It is often cooked with chicken to make a strengthening soup or stew. One might make the soup every month or two or at the beginning of each season, supplemented by other appropriate culinary-medical herbs, to prepare the body and mind for the changing season.

Traditionally, different forms of ginseng have different "energies." The strongest, most "yang" is red Korean, followed by red Chinese; this is ginseng that has undergone a process that may concentrate ginsenosides. American ginseng is purported to have a cooler, milder, more balanced yin-yang energy. (Siberian ginseng, another purported adaptogen, is only distantly related to *Panax ginseng*; see page 173.) Modern pharmacological studies, such as those of Shibata, confirm that red Korean ginseng tends to contain more ginsenosides that stimulate the central nervous system than white ginseng does and that American ginseng (*Panax quinquefolius*) tends toward less stimulatory, more sedating ginsenosides.

GINSENG TEA

In Chinese medical traditions, a daily "dose" of ginseng is three to nine grams, decocted (simmered until reduced by half) into a tea. The one ounce of ginseng called for in this recipe is 28 grams, so if you divide this tea into seven daily cups, you'll be taking in four grams a day. If you drink it in four days, it will give you seven grams a day.

Ginseng is a safe herb with low toxicity, but too much can cause headaches, insomnia, heart palpitations, or a rise in blood pressure in some people. As with any medicinal herb, if it makes you feel bad, stop taking it. And don't take it if you have high blood pressure.

It is not a quick-acting remedy but a long-term tonic. You may want to take a "course" of ginseng for a month or two and then refrain for at least two or three months.

YIELD: ABOUT A WEEK'S WORTH

1 ounce whole dried ginseng root
⅓ ounce whole licorice root
⅓ ounce fresh ginger root (about a ⅓-inch thick slice), plus more for
    serving

Put the ginseng and 8 cups of pure water in a medium saucepan (use a porcelain or Pyrex pot if available). Bring it to a boil, reduce the heat, and cook at a low simmer for an hour or more, until the liquid is reduced by half. (Because ginseng is so expensive, you may want to pour off that tea, add fresh water, and continue to cook it as directed to extract as much ginsenoside as possible.)

Add the licorice root and ginger, simmer for 30 minutes more, and strain. Drink a small amount, about a half cup a day, preferably in the morning.

Store the leftovers in a tightly covered container in the refrigerator. For subsequent servings, heat a half cup of tea, add more water to taste and another slice of ginger to freshen the flavor. The tea will keep, refrigerated, for up to 7 days.

INNER-STRENGTH POACHED CHICKEN

This is a traditional strengthening Chinese herbal soup. We learned the appropriate measurement of the medicinal herbs from the *Oriental Herbal Cook Book for Good Health,* a privately published book from the Shun An Tong Group, a Queens, New York, Chinese herb importer. This beautifully illustrated book represents the folk cooking of Guangdong (formerly Canton), in southern China. Our point of departure was the recipe for Dark Bone Chicken Soup with Wild Ginseng, which the book asserts is good for "curing all weaknesses and enforcing vitality."

We make no such claims, to be sure. But this soup is good. Combining American and Chinese (or Korean) ginseng balances its stimulating effect. And astragalus (page 24) and reishi (page 228) are both good for the immune system. If you are seriously run down, chronically fatigued, or immune compromised, you may want to add this soup to your regimen, but you should, of course, consult your physician first.

YIELD: ABOUT 3 QUARTS SOUP, PLUS THE CHICKEN; SERVES 6 TO 8, WITH
      BROTH LEFT OVER

¼ cup dried American ginseng pieces (about 6 grams)
10 disks dried red Chinese or Korean ginseng (about 6 grams)
5 sticks astragalus
1 4-inch dried reishi mushroom (about 3 grams), rinsed
1 3½-pound chicken, preferably organic, rinsed and patted dry
Nam Singh's Tonic Chicken Soup (page 270) or Basic Vegetable Stock
    (page 271) (optional)
2 stalks celery, trimmed and sliced (about 1 cup)
1 medium leek, trimmed, quartered, washed, and thinly sliced (about 1 cup)
1 bay leaf
1 1½-inch piece fresh ginger, peeled and thinly sliced
Fresh lemon or lime juice (optional)
Chopped fresh parsley or chervil (optional)

Combine both ginsengs, the astragalus, and reishi in a saucepan with 6 cups water. Cover and bring to a boil. Reduce heat to a high simmer and cook, uncovered, until the liquid has reduced to 2 cups, 45 to 60 minutes.

Strain the liquid through a very fine sieve. Reserve it, along with the ginseng and astragalus. Discard the reishi.

While the ginseng is cooking, put the chicken in a large pot with water to cover. (For fuller flavor, substitute chicken or vegetable stock for all or part of the water.) Add the celery, leek, bay leaf, and ginger. Cover and bring to a boil. Reduce the heat to a high simmer, and cook for about 30 minutes, skimming off any scum that rises to the surface. To keep the chicken submerged, place a heatproof plate on top of it.

Add the reserved ginseng broth, ginseng, and astragalus. Cook for another 30 minutes, or until the chicken is cooked through.

Serve the chicken and broth with a squirt of fresh lemon juice and a garnish of parsley if desired. Chew on the astragalus and ginseng to get all their valuable compounds.

Leftover broth will keep in the refrigerator for 2 or 3 days.

CHICKEN BREAST WITH FRESH GINSENG

Foraging in New York City's Chinatown, I came across fresh ginseng, vacuum-packed in plastic and refrigerated. Fresh ginseng has the same properties as dried ginseng—the active ginsenosides are quite stable—and it doesn't require long cooking to extract its essence. It's closer to food. If you can find fresh ginseng, this is a nice way to serve it, for general strength and energy.

YIELD: 4 SERVINGS

1 medium cucumber, peeled
7 scallions, trimmed
1 pound boneless, skinless chicken breasts
½ cup white wine or water
6 grams kudzu (see page 189) or 2 teaspoons cornstarch
1 teaspoon kosher salt
½ teaspoon freshly ground pepper
2 tablespoons canola or olive oil
1 cup (1 25-gram can) bamboo shoots, drained and rinsed
1 2-inch piece fresh ginger, peeled, quartered, and thinly sliced
15 grams fresh ginseng root, trimmed and thinly sliced
1 tablespoon chopped fresh cilantro
¼ cup chicken or Basic Vegetable Stock (page 271)
1 teaspoon sesame oil (optional)

Cut the cucumber and scallions into matchstick slices, about ⅛-inch wide and 2 inches long. Set aside.

Trim the fat from the chicken; flatten the chicken slightly with the palm of your hand, and cut it into ½-inch strips.

Pour the wine into a nonreactive bowl large enough to hold the chicken. Gradually whisk in the kudzu until dissolved, and add the salt and pepper. Add the chicken strips, toss gently to coat, and set aside.

Heat 1 tablespoon of the oil in a large skillet or wok over medium-high heat until very hot but not smoking. Add the chicken and cook, stirring constantly, until almost done, about 5 minutes. Transfer it to a plate.

Wipe out the skillet with a paper towel. Heat the remaining tablespoon of oil over medium-high heat until very hot. Add cucumber, bamboo shoots, ginger, scallion, and ginseng and cook, stirring constantly, until just slightly softened, about 5 minutes.

Return the chicken to the skillet and cook, stirring, another 3 minutes. Add cilantro and chicken or vegetable stock, and cook 5 minutes more. Season to taste with salt and pepper.

Just before serving, drizzle with sesame oil if desired. Serve with rice to sop up all the juices.

AMERICAN GINSENG LIQUEUR

The active ginsenosides in ginseng are alcohol soluble. This gives scientific credence to the age-old practice of making an alcohol-based ginseng tonic. This pleasant tonic liqueur is likely to contain the active ingredients of American ginseng. If you drink, this is a nice way to take ginseng.

YIELD: 2 CUPS

25 to 30 grams (about 1 ounce) American ginseng
1 2-inch stick Chinese cinnamon
1 1-inch piece fresh ginger, sliced
3 tablespoons honey
2 cups vodka or gin

Put a pint canning jar or other lidded glass container and its lid in a sink or large bowl. Pour on boiling water to cover, and let it sit for 5 minutes.

Use tongs to transfer the jar to a clean kitchen towel.

When cool enough to handle, pack the jar with the ginseng. Add the cinnamon, ginger, and honey. Pour in the vodka or gin.

Remove the lid from the hot water. Use a clean towel to close it tightly without forcing. Shake the jar a few times to distribute the ingredients.

Label and date the jar, and store it in a cool, dark place for 2 to 4 months for flavors to develop.

To serve, strain the liqueur through a fine strainer or cheesecloth. Drink about a half ounce at a time, as a shot or in hot water.

SIBERIAN GINSENG

Eleutherococcus senticosus is sometimes called Siberian ginseng. It is not ginseng at all but a member of the larger botanical family Araliaceae. Like ginseng, it contains saponins, dubbed "eleutherosides."

It owes its origins as a tonic to a Russian physician, I. I. Brekman, who was searching for plants that improve human performance in the 1950s. He studied ginseng, but it was too expensive for the Soviets to consider giving to millions of workers. So Brekman turned to eleuthero, a plant that grew in abundance in Russia. He concluded that it acted as an "adaptogen"—that is, it helped stabilize and normalize many physiological functions. He believed it lowered blood sugar when it was too high, raised it when it was too low, and balanced other physiological functions.

Brekman didn't do controlled clinical studies. But he did try eleuthero on thousands of workers, from telegraph operators and proofreaders to factory workers and truck drivers. In many studies, he found that it countered fatigue, improved performance, and strengthened immunity to disease.

His findings were impressive, but clinical studies without control groups have very limited relevance. And because eleuthero is a new plant drug, one cannot look back on traditional use to interpret scientific research.

Eleuthero appears to be quite safe, without the potential stimulating effects of ginseng, especially red ginseng. Contemporary herbalists recommend 5 to 15 grams a day for two to nine months as an antistress tonic—a pick-me-up. You can take it in tea; in tincture, the dose is two droppersful at a time, morning and evening. (For a recipe that includes Siberian ginseng, see Energy-Boosting Asian Fish Stew, page 85.)

Scientists, meanwhile, argue about whether such a thing as an "adaptogen" exists at all. Some are impressed by the sheer quantity of Brekman's research, arguing that the consistency of his findings must point to something. The extent of our ignorance is neatly evoked by botanist James Duke in *Ginseng: A Concise Handbook:* "Perhaps many adaptogenic responses result from a mere stimulation of the immune system. Or, contrarily, immunological responses may result from adaptogenic stimuli. At the threshold of the immunological era, we have many surprises awaiting us."

GRAPEFRUIT

Fresh grapefruit juice is tart, bracing, refreshing. So is fresh, whole grapefruit. This morning, I sliced a yellow grapefruit in eighths and ate it like an orange. Ahhh.

Good thing I'm not taking a calcium channel blocker such as felodipine or nifedipine to lower high blood pressure.

Or that I'm not a woman taking 17-beta-estradiol to minimize the symptoms and risks of menopause.

Nor an organ transplant recipient taking cyclosporine to prevent rejection.

Nor a hay fever sufferer taking the nonsedating prescription antihistamine Seldane.

Nor an anxious person taking prescription Halcion, a Valium-like drug.

I am, however, drinking coffee, so I had better watch it.

The curious ability of grapefruit and grapefruit juice to potentiate drugs—that is, to increase blood levels of the drug without an increase in the dose—was discovered by accident a few years ago at Victoria Hospital in London, Ontario.

In 1991, David Bailey, M.D., and his colleagues were studying the potential interaction of alcohol and felodipine, a drug used to treat hypertension. To keep the study "blind," so the subjects didn't know what they were getting, Bailey used grapefruit juice to mask the taste of the alcohol. Some subjects got grapefruit juice with alcohol, some just grapefruit juice. But blood levels of the drug soared in all the volunteers.

Bailey tested it again on six men, ages 48 to 62. Some took their pills with water, others with orange juice, others with grapefruit juice. The first two beverages had no effect. But those who washed their pills down with grapefruit juice had blood levels of the drug 300 percent higher than normal. They felt dizzy. Their faces were flushed. Their hearts raced. One man got a headache. When your blood pressure falls too low, your heart pumps faster to make up the difference.

Scientists around the world rushed to figure out what was happening. In the last year or so, the answer has emerged. An antioxidant flavonoid in grapefruit inhibits a liver enzyme that breaks down many drugs. The flavonoid is called naringin, which includes an active ingredient, naringenin. The liver enzyme is P–450, class 3A4. There are about 40 types of P–450 enzymes, but 3A4 "metabolizes about 60 percent of drugs," Dr. Bailey says. "It's promiscuous." (He is speaking in a strictly scientific sense, of course.)

Grapefruit has the same effect on caffeine, although it is not as dramatic. If animal studies translate to human experience, which sometimes happens, the cup of coffee I had this morning will result in blood levels of caffeine that are about 23 percent higher than they would be if I hadn't eaten that delicious grapefruit. That's the equivalent of drinking another quarter cup of coffee. Recent research finds that grapefruit juice does *not* affect metabolism of theophylline, the caffeinelike substance in tea, so if I had been drinking tea, there would have been no effect.

The grapefruit-drug interaction has made it into clinical literature, so there is a chance your physician will mention it to you. It's worth watching out for.

The Grapefruit Effect, however, may have some benefits, as well: it may allow patients to take lower doses of drugs. Sometimes, organ transplant patients are given drugs to make cyclosporine more effective, and those drugs are toxic; grapefruit juice, of course, is not. It may also be possible for patients on several other drugs to take lower doses, which, at the very least, would save money.

If I were ever prescribed a blood-pressure-lowering drug, I might ask my physician if I could take half a dose, with a grapefruit chaser. (First, though, I would try to lose weight, get more exercise, eat more fresh fruits and vegetables and fewer sodium-enriched processed foods, get enough calcium, and munch a couple of stalks of celery a day; see "Celery," page 57.)

Medical researchers may also try to use a drug made from grapefruit to ensure that a specific dose of a target drug has a standardized effect. "We could use the active ingredient in grapefruit juice to have better confidence that we will get the same blood level of a drug with the same dose," says Dr. Bailey. That dose would also be lower than it would be without the grapefruit boost. "We may also be able to convert some medications that are now given intravenously into an oral form."

But that is medicine. What about health?

When epidemiologists study diet and cancer, citrus fruits consistently pop up as protective foods. To take one study almost at random, 1994 research conducted by the Environmental Epidemiology Branch at the National Cancer Institute and reported in *Cancer Causes and Control* looked at the relationship between diet and the incidence of non-Hodgkin's lymphoma, a kind of cancer. Researchers compared 385 Nebraska men and women who had the disease with 1,432 healthy people. The main statistically significant difference between the two groups: men who didn't have lymphoma tended to consume more dark green vegetables and more citrus fruit. As a result, they consumed more vitamin C and carotenoids. (In women, the results were similar but less statistically significant, perhaps because there were fewer women in the study.)

This is one of about 200 studies showing a link between fruit and vegetable consumption and reduced rates of cancer. That's one reason public health authorities tell us to eat at least two servings of fruit and three servings of vegetables a day. (A better goal would be four servings of fruits and five of vegetables.)

Vitamin C has a lot to do with it. It is a significant dietary antioxidant, along with vitamin E and various carotenoids. Antioxidants protect the body from potentially damaging forms of unstable oxygen and may help protect against heart disease and cancer. (And, yes, vitamin C does help reduce the severity of the common cold; some scientists believe that popping a gram or two of vitamin C a day helps them ward off colds.) According to nutrition tables, the grapefruit I ate this morning gave me 78 milligrams of vitamin C—more than the U.S. RDA of 60 milligrams. It also provides about 80 calories and one and a half grams of dietary fiber. (Juice has no fiber.) If I had eaten the white pith, I would have taken in some pectin, which can lower blood cholesterol levels. (Apples are a more appetizing source of pectin; see page 15.)

If I had eaten the whole grapefruit skin, I would have consumed some limonene, a potent cancer-protective compound found in the oil of lemon, orange, and other citrus fruit. It is now being studied as a potential source of cancer-protective drugs. Given the use of pesticides, I'm not sure I trust citrus peels unless they're organic. Besides, one scientist estimates that to get the same amount of limonene needed to prevent cancer in laboratory animals, one would have to eat 400 oranges a day.

There is, however, another class of antioxidant compounds in citrus fruits that may protect against cancer. They are the flavonoids, chemically related to the anticancer compounds found in apples, onions, green and black tea, red wine, and, in varying amounts, in all fruits and vegetables. Naringin, the flavonoid in grapefruit that enhances drug effects, also seems to have cancer-protective properties. Recent studies have identified two other anticancer flavonoids found in citrus: tangeritin and nobiletin; these may be more widely protective.

In lab and animal studies, tangeritin and nobiletin inhibit cancer. In one study, reported in *Cancer Letters* in 1991, researchers at the State University of New York, Buffalo, treated human skin-cancer cells in test tubes with these two flavonoids. By the fifth day, these cells were growing 60 to 80 percent less rapidly than untreated cancer cells. Japanese researchers have reported similar effects. Among other benefits, these flavonoids may prevent the formation of carcinogenic nitrosamines in the stomach.

My morning's grapefruit, it seems, may interfere with medications if I were taking any and may make my coffee deliver a stronger jolt. But it may also be protecting me in ways that are, in the end, more important. And I didn't even have to eat 400 peels.

MINTED PINK GRAPEFRUIT SORBET

If you can find ruby-fleshed grapefruit for this light, refreshing dessert, snap them up. The sorbet is not diluted with water, so the finished product is an appealing, tea-rose color. When juicing the fruit, scoop up lots of the pulp and add it to the juice. If yellow-fleshed grapefruit are all that you can find, you might want to add two more tablespoons of sugar as these grapefruit can be bitter. Taste one first to find out.

YIELD: 4 CUPS

½ bunch fresh mint
4½ pounds ruby- or pink-fleshed grapefruit (4 to 6 depending on size)
½ cup sugar, or more to taste
16 whole cloves
1 tablespoon fresh lemon juice
1 teaspoon vanilla extract

Wash and stem the mint. Reserve several whole leaves for garnish, and coarsely chop the rest.

Juice enough grapefruit to yield 4 to 4½ cups juice; if there's a little extra, it's fine. Collect the pulp from the juicer and add it to the juice.

Combine 1 cup of the juice with the sugar, chopped mint, and cloves in a saucepan. Bring it to a boil over medium-high heat, stirring occasionally. Reduce the heat to medium and cook until the sugar has dissolved, about 5 minutes. Reduce the heat to low and simmer, stirring occasionally, until the mint has wilted, 10 to 15 minutes. Set it aside to cool.

Strain the cooled liquid through a fine sieve into the reserved juice, pressing down with the back of a spoon to extract all the liquid. Stir in the lemon juice and vanilla.

Pour the mixture into an ice cream maker, and process according to manufacturer's instructions.

If you don't have an ice cream maker, pour the mixture into 2 metal pie tins or 4 ice cube trays, and freeze until hard. Let it sit at room temperature a few minutes to loosen up. If using pie tins, break it into chunks. Process it in a food processor until it's smooth and light in color, about 3 minutes. Serve topped with the reserved mint leaves.

The sorbet can be packed into tightly covered plastic containers and frozen. Since it doesn't contain a lot of sugar, which acts as a preservative, it should be used within 3 or 4 days.

HAWTHORN
(Crataegus oxyacantha)

The Chinese use hawthorn for "food stagnation," and it was used in fourteenth-century Europe to treat gout. In 1695, it was already being used in Europe to treat high blood pressure. Therein lies its truth.

It wasn't until the end of the nineteenth century, though, that the usefulness of the berries of the English hawthorn bush as a heart tonic was fully realized. In 1894, upon the death of a Dr. Green of Ennis in County Clare, Ireland, his daughter revealed the secret of his famous cure for heart disease: a tincture, or alcoholic extract, of ripe English hawthorn berries. Two years later, a scientific article on hawthorn berries as a cardiovascular tonic appeared in the *New York Medical Journal*. More medical articles followed. By 1898, it was part of many medical practices. In 1931, Maud Grieve wrote in *A Modern Herbal* that hawthorn was "mainly used as a cardiac tonic in organic and functional heart troubles."

Its use was eclipsed by the rise of modern medicine in the United States, but in recent years, it has returned to mainstream medicine in Europe. Animal studies reveal its actions, and clinical studies, its usefulness.

The hawthorn berry contains water-soluble compounds that dilate blood vessels, lowering blood pressure and increasing blood flow to the coronary arteries and brain. They also steady the heartbeat, reducing arrhythmias. Hawthorn has been found to be effective in the treatment of angina. It is also a mild sedative.

As Purdue University professor Varro Tyler, an expert on plant-derived medicines, writes in *The New Honest Herbal,* hawthorn "has a direct, favorable effect on the heart itself which is especially noticeable in cases of heart damage. Hawthorn's action is not immediate but develops very slowly. Its toxicity is low as well, becoming evident only in large doses. It therefore seems to be a relatively harmless, mild heart tonic."

The main ingredients in hawthorn berries (as well as other parts of the plant, such as the leaves) that so benefit the heart are antioxidant flavonoids, similar to the ones found in green tea. There are many different flavonoids that together yield a synergistic effect.

In Europe, hawthorn extracts, in tablet form, are prescribed for various cardiovascular conditions. In the United States it is available in many forms, unregulated, in health food stores. An odd effect of the separation of herbal medicine from "mainstream" medicine in this country is that some very useful plant-based drugs, best taken under medical supervision, are not available from doctors but can be bought with no guidance as "dietary supplements."

If you have a cardiovascular condition, from mild hypertension to serious heart disease, the hawthorn berry or its extract may be a very useful treatment. But as the saying goes, he who treats himself has a fool for a patient. Hawthorn-based drugs can have similar effects as digitalis, the anti-angina medication, for example, so if you take the two together, you can cause serious problems. If you have a heart condition, you need to be working with a health care professional, preferably a cardiologist. If you find one who will let you experiment with hawthorn berry, you are lucky indeed.

Whole hawthorn berries, made into tea, are something else. They are food. Taken over time—and most tonics do need to be taken over a long period to have their best effect—they may be good for the heart.

As Rob McCaleb, president of the nonprofit Herb Research Foundation in Boulder, Colorado, writes, "Hawthorn is one of the herbs that perfectly straddles the line between foods and drugs. . . . Indeed, the current worldwide uses of hawthorn cover this entire range [between food and drug], and show how a medicinal agent effective enough to be used as a prescription drug for heart disease can also be safe enough to consume in jellies, jams and herbal teas."

Hawthorn tea, blended with mint, honey, and lemon, is a gentle, relaxing beverage. For people who are free of heart disease and are looking for a soothing way to wind down, a cup or two in the evening is fine. For people with heart disease, working with their physicians, it may be even better.

HAWTHORN MINT TEA

YIELD: **4 1-CUP SERVINGS**

¼ cup dried hawthorn leaves (¼ ounce)
⅓ cup packed fresh mint leaves, or ¼ cup peppermint tea leaves
2 teaspoons honey
1 tablespoon fresh lemon juice

Put the hawthorn and peppermint leaves in a teapot. Bring 4 cups water to a boil. Pour boiling water over leaves, stir, and let steep for 5 minutes. Strain into cups, stir in honey and lemon juice, and enjoy.

IRON

Iron signifies strength. No one competes in a Zinc Man Triathlon or rules with a Potassium Will. Yet we worry about iron. We watch our children, nibbling on who knows what, and wonder if they are getting enough. Careful studies with children find that even modest iron deficiencies can result in subtle cognitive deficiencies that affect their ability to learn.

A woman, feeling fatigued, worries about iron deficiency anemia. It's a common enough occurrence, even in our country. If she is anemic, dietary or supplemental iron would indeed restore strength.

When I was an editor at a now defunct magazine, *The Runner,* we ran articles about a mysterious condition called runner's anemia. Athletes were losing iron, one theory went, because red blood cells circulating through the soles of their feet were being systematically squashed, leaking iron.

For children, women, and elite athletes, iron seemed to be the kind of thing that gave strength. Then, like any media darling, iron fell. We carry iron in our red blood cells and store it in our tissues.

Cancer researchers found evidence that people with high body stores of iron were more likely to get colon cancer. Finnish researchers reported that men with high body stores of a biochemical marker for iron were more likely to have heart attacks. The media jumped on the story as if it were the last train leaving Paris in 1944. "Well, blow me down," lamented *U.S. News & World Report* in a 1992 cover story, "Iron and Your Heart." Popeye's habit of downing iron-rich spinach, the reporters wrote, "might make him a candidate for Toonland General's cardiac care unit." *Time* magazine followed.

Nutrients aren't heroes or villains, though; they are naturally occurring chemicals that our bodies need in a certain proportion to function well.

Runner's anemia, it turns out, doesn't exist. A few vegetarian runners who habitually popped anti-inflammatories, which can cause mild bleeding ulcers, thus depleting iron, became anemic. But it was their habit of relying on over-the-counter remedies for overuse injuries that made them so. "The scientific evidence for runner's anemia is just not there," says Alvin R. Loosli, M.D., of the Center for Sports Nutrition at Saint Francis Memorial Hospital in San Francisco.

There may be a subtle effect on iron, but it may even be beneficial: a 1995 Canadian study found that men who exercised aerobically for 45 minutes a day had modestly lower levels of blood iron than sedentary men. If your blood iron levels are too high, it may be beneficial to lower them. But those researchers didn't find a statistically significant increase in iron loss in men who exercised more intensively.

The heart disease story hasn't held up very well either. Several studies have failed to find the original Finnish link. The hypothesis, so attractive to journalists (including me), was that iron, an oxidant, would increase coronary heart disease by increasing the likelihood of injury to LDL cholesterol. It's LDL cholesterol that clogs arteries. According to the Antioxidant Theory of Heart

Disease, it's only when LDL gets damaged by free radicals—oxidants—that it festers. If only oxidized LDL causes heart disease, then iron, a potent oxidizer, isn't good.

The Antioxidant Theory helps explain why some people who eat a lot of fat—say, the French—have less coronary artery disease than other people who eat the same amount of fat—say, Americans. The French consume less meat, more bread, more vegetables, fewer trans fats (hydrogenated fats found in many processed foods that raise blood cholesterol), and more wine than Americans. The vegetables and the wine (see page 301), especially the red wine, provide antioxidants. An interconnected web of evidence, from cellular tests to population-wide studies, support the antioxidant theory.

Yet we seem to have stretched the point to make iron fit. A 1995 study from Finland reported that in more than 12,000 men and women followed for 14 years, "no association was found with dietary iron intake and coronary mortality." The cardiovascular system, it turns out, is more resilient than the iron theory of heart disease would have it. Ferritin, which binds iron in the circulation and is endogenous, or made by the body, is a natural antioxidant. Ferritin protects LDL from becoming oxidized by iron. It's not simply a question of more iron, more oxidation. The body is more subtle.

Cancer remains a concern. Kaiser Permanente epidemiologists reported in October 1995 that in a study of nearly 40,000 men and women, followed for an average of 18 years, elevated body stores of iron were associated with an increased risk of stomach cancer in women and colon and rectal cancer and non-Hodgkin's lymphoma in men. It's free radicals again. Take in too much iron-rich red meat, and you'll be giving your lower intestines a bath of iron, an oxidative cascade. Rust never sleeps.

And we haven't even mentioned the million-plus Americans who carry an extra iron-storing gene, a condition called hemochromatosis, who can develop potentially fatal symptoms if they supplement with iron. Then there are the millions of women who get too little iron in their diets to restore the iron lost in monthly periods. And the children.

Everyone, it seems, is getting the wrong amount of iron. Men, who need less, eat more red meat. Women, who need more iron than men, eat less; if they become vegetarians without developing a taste for iron-rich dark, leafy greens and legumes, the problem is compounded. So whether iron does you good or harm depends on whether you need it, it seems.

There is another possibility, however. Perhaps the problem isn't the iron itself but its dietary source. From childhood, we have been taught that beef and other red meats contain a special kind of iron that our bodies can absorb most efficiently. It's called heme iron, meaning it comes from hemoglobin, the iron in animal blood. Vegetable sources of iron—non-heme iron—tend to get second billing. They are acceptable, we have been told, but they don't contain as much iron as steak, and under certain circumstances, we might absorb very little iron from them. A hamburger, though, is always reliable!

It's true that a wide variety of environmental factors affect absorption of vegetable sources of iron. If you eat your beans with tomatoes, the vitamin C in the tomatoes helps your body absorb more iron from the beans. Too much tea can reduce absorption. Cooking foods in an iron skillet, especially in an acidic medium such as tomato sauce, lets food pick up iron from the pan. A little flesh food, such as a few ounces of fish, chicken, or lamb, improves the absorption of non-heme iron.

The body's iron stores also affect how well we absorb non-heme iron: the more we have, the less we take in. So perhaps plant sources of iron, long dismissed as inferior, actually help us regulate our internal stores of iron.

Perhaps if our iron came more from beans and greens and less from ribs and bratwurst, we would run less risk of becoming overloaded with iron. The absorption of heme iron is "not as well regulated by the body as the absorption of non-heme dietary iron," write Harvard School of Public Health epidemiologists Alberto Ascherio and Walter C. Willett, M.D. "People with normal reserves of iron will not absorb much non-heme iron, decreasing the likelihood of storing too much iron in the body."

So is iron a tonic? If you need it, certainly. It shows up in Lydia Pinkham's Vegetable Compound (see "Fenugreek," page 118), not to mention Geritol. If you are deficient in iron, something easily determined by a blood test, an iron supplement will help. If you have a genetic disposition to iron overload, an iron supplement could kill you over time.

The real "tonic" effect, however, comes from the whole diet. If your diet is primarily plant based, with plenty of legumes and greens, you'll be supplying your body primarily with non-heme iron. This is the kind of diet—plenty of greens, small amounts of lean meat—on which humans evolved. When we give ourselves the kinds of foods to which evolution has adapted us, we can take what we need.

A tonic is sometimes defined as a substance that helps the body regulate itself. In that sense, one might consider the recipes that follow, and the largely plant-based diet they represent, a tonic. Black beans are rich in iron, so these dishes will help someone who is iron deficient move toward homeostasis—the ability of organisms to self-regulate toward a desirable biological norm; in this case, this would mean to self-regulate iron absorption.

If you need iron, you absorb more iron. If you have enough iron or more than enough, the iron in black beans won't be well absorbed. Nice how it all works out. If you are a vegetarian, eat more greens and beans, plus whole grains, plus sea vegetables. If you are an omnivore, modest amounts of animal foods within a more plant-based pattern may prove an ideal way to supply iron, balancing heme with non-heme sources.

The trick about nutrition is to learn each new thing without forgetting everything else, and then to apply it to your own life. Look for animal foods that are not only rich in iron but low in saturated fat. Clams (see page 81) are one example. Another is dark-meat poultry, which has more fat (mostly monounsaturated) but also about a third more iron than white meat. If you are anemic, medical attention, including supplements, may be needed to replenish lost iron stores.

Nutrition is individual. What you need may be different from what the next person needs. There are, so to speak, no ironclad rules.

WELL-SEASONED BLACK BEANS

Here is a simple recipe for flavorful, tender black beans. (To keep them from toughening, be sure not to add salt until they're done.) Black beans don't need to be soaked before cooking. Once cooked, they freeze well. Serve them with rice, or use them in Black Bean Cakes with Flax Seeds (page 129) or the soup recipe that follows.

YIELD: 3½ QUARTS

4 cups dried black beans (1½ pounds)
4 garlic cloves, smashed and peeled
1 medium onion, peeled and coarsely chopped
1 1½-inch piece fresh ginger, peeled and diced (¼ cup)
2 jalapeños or other hot peppers, whole
1 tablespoon fenugreek
1 bay leaf
2 teaspoons ground cumin
¼ cup sherry
Kosher salt and freshly ground pepper

Rinse the beans in a colander, and discard any impurities or discolored beans.

Put them in a large pot, and add enough water to cover them by at least 5 inches. Add the garlic, onion, ginger, peppers, fenugreek, bay leaf, cumin, and sherry. Cover and bring to a boil.

Reduce the heat to a high simmer, and cook until tender but not overly soft, 45 minutes to 1 hour and 15 minutes, depending on their freshness. Season with salt and pepper to taste. Remove the bay leaf and, if desired, the hot peppers.

BLACK BEAN SOUP

Adding fresh herbs and vegetables to the cooked beans brightens the flavors. Always taste chili peppers before adding them to a dish to check their heating punch; it can vary from batch to batch and pepper to pepper. Yogurt is not only a nice complement to the black beans but an excellent soother of burned palates. This soup uses half the recipe for Well-Seasoned Black Beans; if you want more, use all the black beans, and double the other ingredients.

YIELD: 6 TO 8 SERVINGS

7 cups Well-Seasoned Black Beans (page 184)
¼ cup chopped fresh cilantro, plus extra for serving
¼ cup finely chopped red onion
2 to 3 tablespoons fresh lime juice
3 tablespoons minced fresh hot peppers, or to taste
1 medium tomato, chopped (optional)
Homemade Yogurt (page 315) or plain nonfat yogurt (optional)

Stir together the beans, cilantro, onion, lime juice, peppers, and tomato in a saucepan. Heat over medium heat, stirring occasionally, until warmed throughout, about 12 minutes. Serve in individual bowls, topped with yogurt and chopped cilantro if you like.

JUJUBE
(Ziziphus jujuba)

You can buy a big bag of jujubes, or Chinese red dates, for a dollar or two in Chinatown here in New York. They're usually sold dried, and they have a unique taste, sweet yet slightly tart. Jujubes are "one of the tonic herbs that help make a person at peace," says Ron Teeguarden, who manufactures tonics in China and sells them in Ron's Tea Garden Herbal Emporium in Santa Monica, California. He adds jujubes to his "shen," or "heart," formulas.

Jujube fruit is almost certainly nutritious. From its tart taste, I would bet it has significant vitamin C; from its deep, reddish-brown color, vitamin A in the form of carotenoids. Jujube doesn't show up in standard U.S. references to nutritional values, but according to Dan Bensky and Andrew Gamble in *Chinese Herbal Medicine: Materia Medica,* its "major known ingredients" include "vitamin A, vitamin B2, vitamin C, calcium, phosphorus, iron."

It's the jujube seeds that get the most attention in Chinese medicine. That's why Daniel Reid, who practices and writes about traditional Chinese medicine, recommends that you crack open the seeds before cooking the fruit. "Crush the kernels inside in order to release their active constituents," he writes in *A Handbook of Chinese Healing Herbs.* "Ordinary pliers do the job very well."

Reid adds, "Jujubes are frequently included in formulas for warming tonic herbal liquors . . . [that] are said to 'clear the nine openings,' the apertures that connect the human system to the external environment, such as eyes, ears, nose, throat, anus, and so on. The herb facilitates the flow of energies . . . throughout the entire human system."

In traditional Chinese medicine, jujubes are considered "herbs that tonify the chi"—thus, a chi, or energy, tonic. According to Bensky and Gamble, jujube "nourishes the blood and calms the spirit" and is indicated for "wan appearance, irritability, and severe emotional lability"—that is, quick mood changes, from elation to despair. Jujube is recommended, they write, for people who are weak, tired, fatigued, with little appetite. By the same token, it is not recommended for people who are overweight or "damp" (retaining water).

It's easy to imagine that this dark, sweet-tart, nutritious fruit would "nourish the blood." In one study of mice given a toxin, carbon tetrachloride, those that also drank a long-simmered jujube tea recovered faster than mice that didn't. One might expect that of any nourishing food, though, so it doesn't prove a specific liver-protective effect. Another animal study found that jujube lowered fever. In China, patients recovering from hepatitis or cirrhosis are sometimes given jujube tea, along with peanuts and brown sugar, at bedtime.

It probably helps them sleep. Jujube contains flavonoids, antioxidants related to tannins; these exert a mild sedative and hypnotic effect in animals. They calm the central nervous system.

One 1987 Japanese study conducted by a pharmaceutical firm, Kyushin, looked at the effects of a water extract of jujube seed on mice. The mice had already been given sedative drugs. When they were also given jujube tea, the drug effects were made stronger—that is, the mice slept longer. A 1993 Chinese study, from the Hehei Provincial Academy of Medical Sciences in Shijiazhuang, confirms that the seeds inhibit central nervous system function, while the fruits make sedative drugs more effective.

So we have a nutritious, calming food. Much nicer than a dangerous, addictive, sedative drug.

In *Chinese Herbal Medicine: Formulas and Strategies,* in a section entitled "Formulas That Nourish the Heart and Calm the Spirit," Dan Bensky and Randall Barolet give a simple recipe for "Licorice, Wheat, and Jujube Decoction." A decoction is a kind of long-simmered tea. To make a tonic decoction, you typically simmer an herb in several cups of water for 20, 30, even 40 minutes to extract its active ingredients fully. Under "actions" for their jujube version, Bensky and Barolet list, "Nourishes the Heart, calms the spirit, and harmonizes the middle burner," which governs digestion.

What is it recommended for? "Disorientation, frequent attacks of melancholy and crying spells, inability to control oneself, restless sleep . . . frequent bouts of yawning." Yawning? Well, this description comes from an very ancient text. Modern practitioners of traditional Chinese medicine believe the term is better translated as "moaning" or "deep sighing." In modern practice, it is prescribed for "hysteria" and "neurosis," as well as menopausal symptoms and, sometimes, fever. It helps "lost souls."

Basic Questions, one of the ancient texts Bensky and Barolet quote, suggests a dietary approach to this kind of emotional distress: "When the Liver is in a bitter and urgent state, quickly eat sweet things to moderate it." The authors add, "This formula is an example of 'kitchen medicine' and is quite popular. Note that it should be taken long term for best effect."

Sweet things for bitter emotions. This, too, makes sense. Who hasn't found solace in sweets? Contemporary nutrition finds that when we eat carbohydrates, it tends to calm us down. Often, we get a little drowsy. The current hypothesis is that carbohydrates indirectly stimulate the levels of tryptophan in the blood and brain. The body uses tryptophan, an amino acid, to make serotonin, a neurotransmitter whose lack is involved in depression. Some researchers believe that people who suffer from seasonal and other forms of depression may "self-medicate" with carbohydrates in order to boost brain serotonin levels. I'm not sure we know enough about this to dot all the scientific *i*'s, but the clinical research does show that carbohydrates calm.

So we have taken the formula into the kitchen. The original recipe provided by Bensky and Barolet calls for a long-simmered tea made from ten pieces of jujube fruit with seed, 9 grams of licorice, and 9 to 15 grams of wheat. Instead of a tea, we offer a sweet wheat-berry porridge and a jujube-licorice tea (with chamomile, another calming herb). To get the appropriate dosage, drink one cup of tea and eat one cup of porridge. When your heart is breaking.

HEARTBREAK HOTEL PORRIDGE WITH JUJUBE-LICORICE TEA

The porridge and tea can be made ahead and refrigerated, tightly covered, for up to two days.

YIELD: 4 SERVINGS

FOR THE TEA:
30 dried jujubes
1 cup dried chamomile flowers
15 pieces Honey-Roasted Licorice Sticks (page 203)

FOR THE PORRIDGE:
1 cup wheat berries, dark or light, rinsed
1½ cups Homemade Yogurt (page 315) or plain nonfat yogurt
¼ cup plus 2 tablespoons honey
30 poached jujubes from Licorice-Jujube Tea

First, make the tea. Crush each jujube with a pair of pliers so that the hard nut in the center cracks open. Combine them in a large pot with the chamomile, licorice, and 6 cups water. Cover and bring to a boil. Reduce the heat to a simmer and cook for 20 minutes.

Meanwhile, put the wheat berries in a saucepan with 3 cups water. Cover and bring to a boil. Reduce the heat to a simmer and cook, uncovered, until the wheat berries are tender but not mushy, 30 to 50 minutes. (Timing will depend on how fresh they are.)

When the tea is done, remove it from the heat and let it sit, uncovered, until the fruit is cool enough to handle, about 10 minutes.

Remove the jujubes from the pan with a slotted spoon, and rinse off any chamomile residue. Remove and discard the hard pits; dice and reserve the fruit.

Strain the tea through a fine sieve into a teapot, and cover. Discard the chamomile leaves; save the licorice sticks for chewing.

When the wheat berries are tender, remove them from the heat, and let them sit for 10 minutes. Drain well.

Stir together the wheat berries, yogurt, and honey in a medium bowl. Stir in the diced jujube fruit.

Serve the porridge in individual bowls with the tea on the side, sweetened (if you want) with honey or sugar. Heck, add honey to the porridge, too, if you like. Life is hard.

KUDZU
(Pueraria lobata)

In the American south they tell the story of a farmer who planted kudzu vines far out in his fields. By the time he walked home, the vines were creeping up his porch. It's a fast-growing vine.

That kind of thing can drive you to drink. Or still your hand.

For nearly 2,000 years, the Chinese have used kudzu roots, along with its leaves and flowers, to treat drunkenness and hangovers. The first known reference to it appears in *The Divine Husbandman's Classic of the Materia Medica* from the Later Han period (25–220 A.D.). A standard dose is 6 to 12 grams a day. It is often combined with chrysanthemum flower (see page 76). Both are classified as cooling, and both treat headaches.

Now Harvard biochemists are on the brink of discovering how kudzu works. They started with hamsters in 1993. These hamsters liked to drink. Given a choice between water and an alcoholic beverage, they bellied up to the bar. In human terms, they drank the equivalent of a case of wine a day. Biochemist Wing Ming Keung and his team injected the hamsters with kudzu and gave them their choice of water or alcohol. Their alcohol consumption dropped by more than 50 percent. Then the researchers tried injecting daidzin and daidzein, two compounds found in kudzu that they suspected were the alcohol-inhibiting agents. They were. Daidzin was more effective than daidzein.

Then they tried it on a strain of rats prone to alcohol addiction. Once again, both kudzu and daidzin, injected, inhibited alcohol appetite. "It's one step closer to the human situation," says Keung. "We want a substance that limits alcohol intake only in people who cannot limit it themselves. We don't want to treat social drinkers, don't want to destroy that joy."

The Harvard researchers went back to the hamsters. This time, they gave them kudzu and daidzin in their chow rather than in a shot. Once again, it worked.

Japanese researchers have found that it works in mice, too. In their studies, mice given kudzu compounds not only drank less alcohol but had significantly lower levels of alcohol in the blood, even taking into account their lower consumption. In 1994, researchers at Indiana University School of Medicine confirmed that in rats, daidzin reduces blood alcohol levels by nearly 50 percent. One might say it prevents laboratory animals from getting drunk, in addition to inhibiting their appetite for booze.

In one Chinese study of nearly 300 human alcoholics, treatment with kudzu (and other herbs) greatly suppressed alcohol cravings. After a month, 80 percent reported they no longer craved alcohol. No adverse side effects were reported.

So it works. But how?

In 1993, Keung and his colleagues thought they knew. In a test tube, they found that both daidzin and daidzein inhibited a human enzyme, aldehyde dehydrogenase. That's the liver enzyme that detoxifies alcohol. When the liver comes in contact with alcohol, it begins to break it down. The first by-product is very toxic, but aldehyde dehydrogenase renders it harmless.

Drugs used to treat alcoholism, such as Antabuse, work by blocking aldehyde dehydrogenase. Then, when an alcoholic drinks, toxic by-products build up, and he or she gets very sick. The idea is that if you associate drinking with getting sick, you won't want to drink again.

But in 1995, Keung and his colleagues found that at the levels needed to persuade animals to stop drinking, daidzin didn't significantly inhibit aldehyde dehydrogenase. "We've ruled out that mechanism." They haven't ruled out a role for this enzyme, though. Daidzin may act in a more subtle way.

"This enzyme, aldehyde dehydrogenase, isn't just sitting in the liver waiting for alcohol to come in," Keung says. "What other function does it have? Daidzin may modulate its action on a physiological level, and it may trigger a signal, telling the animal to drink less. That possibility is still alive."

Nor has daidzin revealed its last secret. For it may not only help reduce blood alcohol levels and the desire for alcohol. It may help prevent cancer.

Daidzin is abundant in another, more common food: soybeans. And Keung believes that soy foods, such as soy milk, may be similarly useful in moderating alcoholic consumption. Daidzin is in a class of compounds called isoflavones. A 1994 study in the *Journal of Nutrition* found that the daidzin in soy milk is more bioavailable than another, more famous soybean isoflavone, genistein.

Daidzin, daidzein, and genistein are famous in scientific circles. They may help prevent cancer, especially breast cancer. They affect a genetic signal, kinase, which tells cells when to replicate and when to stop. By helping to regulate cell growth, they may prevent potential cancer cells from growing. It happens in the test tube and in laboratory animals. It may be one reason Japanese women, who eat many more soy foods than American women, have much lower rates of breast cancer. Populations with high soybean consumption also have lower rates of prostate and colon cancer (see "Tofu," page 258).

So if you have a problem with alcohol, it might be wise for you to work kudzu and soybean products into your diet. Make a tea with ground kudzu and use it in stir-fried vegetables or blender fruit drinks, as we do in the recipes that follow. Try kudzu with a cup of chrysanthemum tea (page 76). If you have never had a problem with drinking but want to eat good-tasting foods and perhaps reduce your risk of cancer, do the same thing.

Kudzu has other traditional medicinal uses. Herbalist Michael Tierra writes in *Planetary Herbology:* "Kudzu root is good . . . for treating colds, flu, headache and diarrhea. . . . As a simple folk remedy for most acute colds, flu, fevers and digestive problems, it is prepared with ginger root, bancha [green] tea, and umeboshiplum (Japanese salt plum), any or all of these."

Kudzu, a bland, slightly chalky-tasting white root, is usually sold in chunks in health food stores and Asian specialty markets. If you grind it finely in a spice grinder or crush it with the back of a spoon, you can measure it out; a heaping teaspoon is about six grams. (You can also purchase a pharmaceutical-grade scale at a drugstore or fine foods store to measure it exactly.) It is a very good thickener, more subtle than cornstarch or arrowroot. Mix a little with cold water and you get a fine, translucent paste.

VEGETABLE STIR-FRY WITH KUDZU AND GREEN TEA

In this recipe, we combine ginger, kudzu, and green tea in a delicious vegetable stir-fry. You can substitute any fresh, seasonal vegetables for the cabbage.

YIELD: 4 SERVINGS

2 tablespoons canola oil
3 or 4 garlic cloves, smashed, peeled, and minced
1 2-inch piece fresh ginger, peeled, and cut into ¼-inch sticks
1 or 2 tablespoons low-sodium tamari soy sauce
3 celery stalks, leafy tops and stalks chopped separately
1 red bell pepper, cored, seeded, and chopped
¼ head green cabbage, cored and thinly sliced
1½ tablespoons (23 grams) ground or crushed kudzu
1 cup brewed green tea
Kosher salt and freshly ground pepper

Heat the oil in a large, heavy skillet or a wok over medium-high heat. Sauté the garlic, stirring, until it begins to soften, about 2 minutes.

Add the ginger, soy sauce, chopped celery stalk, and bell pepper. Reduce the heat to medium, and cook, stirring, for another 2 minutes. Add the cabbage and cook, stirring occasionally, for 4 minutes more.

Meanwhile, dissolve the kudzu in 3 tablespoons of water, and whisk it into the green tea. After the cabbage has cooked, add the tea and the reserved celery tops. Cook 3 minutes, stirring often. Season to taste with salt, pepper, and soy sauce. Serve with brown rice.

STRAWBERRY KUDZU FRUITY

A traditional dose of kudzu in Chinese medicine is 6 to 12 grams. Each cup of this provides about 3 grams. You can substitute any fresh fruit for the strawberries.

YIELD: 2 CUPS

1 heaping teaspoon (6 grams) ground or crushed kudzu
½ cup soy or skim milk
8 ounces strawberries (about 10), hulled
¼ cup plain nonfat yogurt or Homemade Yogurt (page 315)
2 teaspoons good-quality balsamic vinegar
1 tablespoon sugar
1 tablespoon vanilla (optional)

Whisk the kudzu into the milk until dissolved, and set aside.

Combine the strawberries, yogurt, vinegar, and sugar in a food processor or blender, and process until smooth.

Add the kudzu mixture, and process until smooth. Taste for seasoning, adding more sugar if needed. Add the vanilla if you like, and serve.

STRAWBERRY-MANGO KUDZU SMOOTHIE

YIELD: 2 CUPS

1 heaping teaspoon (6 grams) ground or crushed kudzu
½ cup seltzer or fizzy spring water
1 ripe mango, peeled and cut into chunks
8 ounces strawberries (about 10), hulled
1 1-inch piece fresh ginger, peeled and grated
⅛ teaspoon ground cloves
⅛ teaspoon ground nutmeg
½ teaspoon vanilla
2 tablespoons fresh lime juice

Whisk the kudzu into the seltzer until dissolved. Set aside.

Combine the mango, strawberries, ginger, cloves, nutmeg, vanilla, and lime juice in a food processor or blender. Process until smooth.

Add the kudzu mixture, and process until well combined. Serve over crushed ice.

PEACHY-ORANGE KUDZU FRUITY

YIELD: 2 CUPS

1 heaping teaspoon (6 grams) ground or crushed kudzu
⅓ cup seltzer or fizzy spring water
2 ripe peaches, rinsed, pitted, peeled if desired and cut into chunks
¼ cup fresh lemon juice
¼ cup soy or skim milk
½ cup fresh orange juice

Whisk the kudzu into the seltzer until dissolved. Set aside.

Combine the peaches, lemon juice, milk, and orange juice in a food processor or blender. Process until smooth.

Add the kudzu mixture, and process until well combined. Serve over crushed ice.

LAVENDER
(*Lavandula officinalis*)

> *Lavender is of especiall good use for all griefes and pains of the head and brain.*
>
> —John Parkinson, *Theatrum Botanicum,* 1640

Taking a hot bath infused with essential oil of lavender is like immersing yourself "in a giant cup of calming tea," herbalist Rosemary Gladstar writes in *Herbal Healing for Women.* Just smelling the intoxicating essence of the lavender flower, it seems, is enough to get some insomniacs off very toxic drugs.

At the Greenwood Institute of Child Health at the University of Leicester, David Stretch, M.D., tried lavender aromas on four nursing-home patients with severe insomnia. He knew that lavender oil had sedative effects in animals and that it has been used in folk remedies for insomnia for at least a thousand years. The Romans perfumed their baths, even their underwear, with lavender.

One of Dr. Stretch's patients had been taking temazepam for a year; a second, promazine hydrochloride for three years; a third, chlormethiazole for seven months. The fourth was not on medication. Each drug has potentially serious side effects. Temazepam, sold under the brand name Restoril, for example, can cause amnesia, poor concentration, and daytime sedation, increasing the risk of hip fractures through falls. It is better than some drugs, to be sure. But it is not better than lavender.

According to a report published in *The Lancet* in 1995, Dr. Stretch and his colleagues took the patients off sedatives for two weeks and then, for another two weeks, infused their nursing-home ward with lavender oil. They used an infuser, a little machine that atomizes essential oils and diffuses them thoroughly into the air. (You can buy these in shops that specialize in aromatherapy and, sometimes, in health food stores. The best ones don't use heat, which can destroy some of the active ingredients in oils.)

The three patients who had been taking sedatives suffered worse insomnia when they went off medication and then returned to the same level of sleeping with the lavender oil. The fourth patient, who hadn't been taking medication, slept better with the lavender. The researchers are now repeating the experiment with children.

Jean Valnet, M.D., the father of essential oil aromatherapy, writes in *The Practice of Aromatherapy* that the essential oil of lavender, used externally, is antiseptic, disinfectant, and a "regulator of [the] nervous system."

A clinical study with women who had just given birth found that the combination of relaxation and antiseptic properties can be very useful. Researchers at Hinchingbrooke Hospital, Huntingdon, Cambridgeshire, England, reported in the *Journal of Advanced Nursing* in 1994 on the use of lavender oil to reveal "perineal discomfort" following childbirth. In the double-blind randomized trial of 635 women, each woman was instructed to take a bath every day. One group put lavender oil in the bath, another put in synthetic lavender fragrance, and a third, an inactive placebo. Between the third and fifth days, the women using true lavender oil reported less discomfort. This is usually the point at which British hospitals discharge new mothers, as well as the point at which discomfort is high, the authors report, so a lavender bath may be quite useful. (In the U.S., women who give birth are typically told to take showers rather than baths for a few weeks to minimize infection, so this approach may not be as useful here.)

Another study, this one published in the May 1993 *Nursing Times,* found that when lavender oil was applied to patients after open-heart surgery, it reduced their stress levels. In that study, some kinds of lavender were more effective than others, which suggests that it was indeed the lavender and not just the caring touch of a nurse's hands that did the job.

But enough of clinical medicine. Let's take a hot bath.

In these days of pills and potions, of chronic sleep insufficiency, of caffeine days and melatonin nights, we might pause for a moment to appreciate the soporific power of a hot bath. Adding a few drops of lavender oil makes a bath more relaxing, aromatic, and antiseptic. But a bath itself is hot stuff. Taken at the right time, at the right temperature, a bath is an elegant bioregulating agent. It can influence body temperature, making it easier to fall asleep.

When you take a hot bath, it cools your body. It's a rebound effect: your body strives to maintain a temperature of roughly 99 degrees (few of us are actually 98.6), but moment to moment, it varies. Get cold and your body will burn energy to warm up. Get hot and your body will respond, within the next hour or two, by cooling off.

There's a natural daily rhythm to temperature swings. Most of us are warm in the morning, hotter by midmorning. By midafternoon, we start to cool off. By six or seven in the evening, most people warm up a little. Later in the evening, we cool down and, if we're lucky, fall asleep for the night. Our body temperature usually falls to its lowest level about two-thirds of the way through the night. Then, core body temperature begins to rise. By the time we wake up, we're warm again. (If you disrupt this natural rhythm with, say, an alarm clock, you may wake up colder than you would like.)

The majority of us feel most alert when our body temperature is highest. (This is core *body* temperature, not room temperature.) When we're cool, we feel sleepy. Some chronobiologists theorize that we get cool in the early afternoon as an evolutionary adaptation to the danger of the midday sun. It's a good time to take a nap. Napping in the early afternoon is an almost universal trait in mammals. Nearly every human culture in a warm environment has a siesta custom.

We fall asleep for the night when we start to cool, too. When people are isolated from all time cues (natural light, clocks), they go to sleep when their bodies start to cool, according to Deborah E. Sewitch, a sleep disorders specialist and the director of the Thermal Regulation Laboratory at the Institute of Pennsylvania Hospital. What drives our desire for sleep isn't cooling to the low point—that will take most of the night—but the onset of cooling. And the speed. Says Sewitch, "The steeper the fall in body temperature, the shorter the sleep onset."

Which brings us to the hot bath. English researcher James Horne has studied it extensively, reporting his findings in such journals as *Electroencephalography and Clinical Neurophysiology*. In a typical study, Horne found that young women who took a hot, 90-minute bath two or three hours before bedtime slept more deeply, passing through the animated dream state to delta sleep—deep sleep. On days without baths, their sleep was lighter.

A hot bath raises body temperature, causing a "compensatory reverse response to maintain balance," Sewitch explains. That is to say, two or three hours after a hot bath, we tend to be pretty cool and should be better able to fall asleep. But don't bathe right before bedtime. "It takes a period of time for temperature to rebalance," Sewitch says. "An elevated temperature is not conducive to sleep, not at all."

A run, or other exercise, a few hours before bed may accomplish the same thing. It raises body temperature, which cools down over the next few hours. When you sleep, keep the room slightly cool. Not cold but cool. A hot room can interfere with a good night's rest.

So take a hot bath early in the evening. Add a little lavender oil to make it even more relaxing.

Never drink lavender oil; it's so concentrated it can be toxic. But lavender flowers, in small amounts, can be an aromatic and relaxing addition to herbal teas and other foods. Lavender is so sweet, so feminine, so floral that a little imparts a pleasant smell and taste.

It may also impart cancer-protective properties. Lavender flowers (and their essential oils) contain a substance called perillyl alcohol. In the laboratory, perillyl alcohol causes regression of breast cancer in animals, according to researchers at the University of Wisconsin Medical School. In animals, it also has antitumor effects against liver and pancreatic cancers and leukemia. Howard Bailey, M.D., a professor at the medical school, is so impressed with the effects of the lavender extract that he has begun a two-year study of it with about two dozen breast cancer patients.

The amount of perillyl alcohol in lavender oil, let alone lavender flower, is very small, and the amount necessary to have an effect on tumor growth is large enough to cause side effects. So our Sweet Dreams Tea, which follows, is no cancer therapy. On the other hand, small amounts of cancer-protective substances from many different foods may, taken together, play a role in helping our bodies stay healthy.

LAVENDER BATH

YIELD: 1 BATH

Hot water
6 drops pure oil of lavender essence (preferably French)

Run a hot bath. Pour in the lavender essence. Climb in and relax.

LAVENDER PILLOW

Austrian researchers, reporting in 1991 on their success at calming caffeine-jangled mice with the scent of lavender, referred to "the aromatherapeutical use of herbal pillows employed in folk medicine since ancient times in order to facilitate falling asleep or to minimize stressful situations of man." It certainly works in our house.

You don't need to sew your own pillow slips. Small muslin bags are available at most herbal and potpourri supply stores. The bags are also handy for holding herbs that are steeped in broths or teas; they're much easier to remove. Baby pillowcases, available at department stores, are a nice way to keep the muslin bags close at hand.

When purchasing lavender, let your nose be your guide. Good lavender has a strong scent; old, faded lavender has lost its punch (see "Sources," page 321).

YIELD: 1 PILLOW AND MANY RESTFUL NIGHTS

1 cup (1 ounce) aromatic dried lavender
1 5½-by-3½-inch muslin bag

Lightly pack the lavender into the bag. Close with the drawstring, if it has one. If not, thread a needle and chain-stitch the opening closed, or attach strips of Velcro. (The latter would make it easy to renew the lavender every six months or so.) Lightly flatten the bag with your hand. Insert it into your favorite sleeping pillow, slipping it to the bottom of the pillowcase so it won't fall out.

SWEET DREAMS TEA

Chamomile, like lavender, is mildly antispasmodic and sedative. Lemon balm (*Melissa officinalis*), like many members of the mint family, helps settle the stomach and is cooling.

YIELD: 4 CUPS

¼ cup (4 grams) dried chamomile
¼ cup (2 grams) lemon balm
Scant ¼ cup (4 grams) dried lavender
Fresh lemon juice (optional)

Combine the chamomile, lemon balm, and lavender in a saucepan with 4 cups water. Stir well, cover, and bring to a boil over high heat.

Reduce heat to a simmer and cook for 10 minutes.

Remove from the heat and steep for 10 minutes.

Strain the tea into cups, and add a drop of lemon juice if you like.

LICORICE
(*Glycyrrhiza glabra*)

In Holland, shortly after World War II, a pharmacist-herbalist named Revers was in the habit of boiling down licorice root into a paste and then drying it. He sold the dried licorice extract to patients who had sore throats.

Licorice—real licorice root, not the red or black anise-flavored candy ropes you may have eaten as a child—is "demulcent"—that is, it soothes the throat. It's been used that way for thousands of years. Licorice root was found in King Tut's tomb. King Hammurabi of Babylon reportedly had his scribes carve information about licorice on stone tablets in the eighteenth century B.C.—in other words, nearly 4,000 years ago.

In modern-day animal studies, licorice simultaneously inhibits coughing (antitussive) while promoting phlegm release (expectorant). That's why it is often added to cough drops, lozenges, and syrups. In 1979, Italian researchers reported in *Nature* that licorice extract inhibits the growth of several unrelated viruses, including the herpes virus, which causes cold sores. Says botanist James Duke, "Licorice root is a great thing to chew if you have a hacking cough."

It may very well be a great thing for other, much more serious problems, too. But let's get back to our Dutch pharmacist-herbalist for the moment. Revers also recommended his licorice extract for patients with Addison's disease, a condition in which the body's adrenal glands are unable to produce enough (or any) cortical hormones, which regulate blood pressure. It's a terrible disease: the skin turns bronze; the patient is weak, anemic, nauseous; blood pressure falls to dangerously low levels. Revers's licorice extract seemed to help.

Then a funny thing happened. Patients with stomach ulcers reported that their ulcers had gone away. It's not clear whether Revers knew about this effect or whether people he had treated for sore throats and Addison's disease told him about it. But this sweet-tasting ulcer cure caught on in Europe. English researchers, working with Revers, isolated glycyrrhizic acid, the active ingredient in licorice responsible for its ulcer-healing properties. By the 1950s it was synthesized and made into a drug: carbenoxolone.

It quickly became a wonder cure. Then its reputation crashed. To this day, people are warned about the dangers of licorice, as if this demonstrated the problem with herbal medicine. Yet licorice has been used for millennia, and problems didn't arise until modern medicine made it into a drug.

It's a fascinating and revealing story. After Revers's licorice extract was turned into a synthetic drug, medical researchers quickly established its efficacy in human trials. Research continued. In March 1978, a review of 29 randomized trials in the *American Journal of Gastroenterology* concluded that carbenoxolone, the synthesized licorice component, "has been shown to be clearly effective."

There was only one problem—a problem Revers himself had noted. Licorice extract, and most of the drugs made to mimic its effects, made some people very sick. About one in five patients developed edema, or bloating, in the face. They had headaches, shortness of breath, stiffness, pain in the upper abdomen. It seemed like an allergic reaction, but antihistamines didn't help. For some patients, reducing the dosage was enough to get rid of these symptoms, but for others, discontinuing treatment was the only answer. In some patients, blood levels of potassium fell to dangerously low levels, and blood pressure soared. This didn't just happen with ulcer patients, either. Once identified, the syndrome was reported in children and adults who snacked on licorice, usually in large amounts.

The roots of the problem, it turns out, are more than two billion years old. It was then that several animal enzymes branched out in different directions. One set inhibits certain prostaglandins, hormonelike substances that appear at the site of injury and orchestrate the healing of a wound. Another set breaks down cortisone, a steroid produced by the adrenal gland, into an inactive form, cortisol. The two sets of enzymes have nothing to do with each other now, but they share a common evolutionary root.

Licorice, even older than those enzymes, is similar in structure to both. So it binds to receptors for both. Without a receptor to bind to, an enzyme is powerless. So licorice inhibits both enzymes.

By inhibiting the enzymes that in turn inhibit certain prostaglandins, licorice promotes wound healing. In the stomach, it promotes mucus secretion and cell proliferation, thus healing ulcers.

But by inhibiting the enzyme that breaks down cortisone, licorice can indirectly raise blood pressure. Cortisone affects the balance of sodium and potassium in the bloodstream. Too much cortisone, and potassium starts to become depleted. When potassium is depleted, the body retains water, causing edema, and eventually, blood pressure rises.

"You have to take a lot of licorice extract to raise blood pressure," says Michael Baker, M.D., a steroid expert in the department of medicine at the University of California, San Diego. "But drug companies won't deal with it. They wouldn't risk a lawsuit."

So licorice's stock plummeted. Today, it's rare to see an article in a mainstream periodical that mentions licorice without warning readers that it is potentially dangerous.

How can we reconcile this conclusion with the fact that licorice has been used in traditional medicine for centuries? The Chinese add licorice to hundreds of formulas. It "moderates and harmonizes the characteristics of other herbs, by virtue of its sweet, neutral, and moderating properties," according to Bensky and Gamble's *Chinese Herbal Medicine: Materia Medica*. While some herbs only cool, or only heat, the text continues, "this herb moderates hot and cold herbs, and mitigates the violent properties of other herbs." In *Herbal Tonic Therapies,* herbal researcher Daniel Mowrey is positively evangelical: "Licorice can be recommended for just about everybody, for male and female alike, young and old, well or sick. It is the grand tonic of the world, in this author's opinion."

Part of the answer is certainly dosage. A 1995 study reported in the *Journal of Human Hypertension* by researchers from Reykjavik City Hospital in Iceland found that even in men and women with normal blood pressure, consuming nearly a quarter pound (100 grams) of real licorice candy every day can raise systolic blood pressure a modest yet potentially significant amount: 6.5 mm/Hg. (Thus, if your blood pressure is 120 over 80, it might become 126.5 over 80 on days you are eating licorice.) The effect is reversible, to be sure, but it's probably not a good idea to eat a quarter pound of licorice every day.

Once we get beyond candy, though, the effect is less pronounced. In a 1994 study reported in *Life Sciences,* researchers from the University of Bologna in Italy looked at the effect of pure licorice extract on 24 healthy men and women for a month. Only at the highest dosages were they able to find evidence of a drop in blood potassium, an increase in blood pressure, or water retention.

In traditional Chinese medicine, a typical dosage is 2 to 12 grams of ground licorice root—not concentrated glycyrrhizin but whole licorice root. Even here, the Chinese recommend against licorice use by people who are prone to "dampness" or water retention. Though at that dosage, the University of California's Dr. Baker says, "there would be no harm at all. Licorice tea is a popular hot drink in Egypt, and Syria, and other parts of the Mediterranean. . . . Oh, it's possible you might get a slight transient increase in blood pressure. That's what gives you a buzz. It happens when you exercise, too—or drink a cup of coffee."

One of the mistakes of the modern pharmaceutical approach may have been to isolate the active ingredient in licorice and turn it into a drug. Potent drugs have potent side effects. At a more modest level, licorice will, very subtly, stimulate wound healing in the stomach and, ever so slightly, deplete you of potassium. (All fruits and vegetables contain potassium; see our recipe for Baked Licorice Apples on page 18.)

In recent years, scientists have discovered other beneficial effects of licorice. It is a legume, like soy, and like soy, it has mild estrogenlike properties. So it is sometimes added to formulas for women during menopause. It is rich in flavonoids, natural antioxidants. A recent Japanese study identified 11 flavonoids in licorice, including five new ones.

In animals, licorice extract inhibits colon, breast, and prostate cancer. It stops cells from proliferating rapidly and prevents the conversion of testosterone to dihydrotestosterone, a substance that promotes prostate cancer. It boosts levels of interleukin-2, an immune factor. It augments the activity of the immune system's natural killer cells. It protects DNA from damage that can lead eventually to cancer.

In Japan, glycyrrhizin is used clinically to treat chronic hepatitis, in the form of an intravenous solution named Stronger Neo-Minophagen C. Glycyrrhizin is antiviral and, in lab tests, inhibits the HIV virus. It also has antiallergenic effects. Licorice, it turns out, not only inhibits enzymes that affect wound healing and blood pressure, it also inhibits enzymes in the liver that turn potential carcinogens into actual carcinogens.

"We have found that licorice extract affords protection against cancer of the skin," says Hasan Mukhtar of the Department of Dermatology at the University Hospitals of Cleveland. "It inhibits certain enzymes that are key players in the process of cancer induction."

The amount necessary for this subtle effect is modest. "The concentrations are certainly achievable in the amounts used in Chinese cookery," Mukhtar says. "A few milligrams of the active agent present in licorice is capable of this effect."

So let's welcome licorice back into our diet. From time to time, a little true European licorice candy is fine. Just don't eat more than a quarter pound every night, especially if you are prone to high blood pressure. As for licorice itself, the whole food, the root, is a real find. The little sticks are fun to chew on. Candy twigs, some call them—not surprising, since glycyrrhizin is 50 times sweeter than sugar.

We add licorice to a number of recipes in this book for the classic reasons: to improve taste, protect the stomach, harmonize the formula. In extract form, licorice has real medical uses, with some caveats. In food, it's quite wonderful and, perhaps, offers something more.

HONEY-ROASTED LICORICE STICKS

Honey-roasting makes licorice sweeter, more flavorful, and, the Chinese would say, gives it a warmer energy. The same could be said for honey-roasted ginger. When roasted with licorice, the ginger releases liquid that keeps the pan moist.

YIELD: **10** STICKS

10 Chinese licorice sticks
1 tablespoon honey
1 3-inch piece fresh ginger, peeled and thinly sliced lengthwise
    (optional)

Position one of the racks in the center of the oven; heat the oven to 450 degrees. Line a small roasting pan with foil.

Put the licorice in the pan, drizzle it with honey, and add the ginger, if using. Turn the pieces to coat. (*continued*)

Roast for 5 minutes. Turn, and roast for 2 to 3 minutes more, watching carefully to make sure the pieces don't burn.

Transfer immediately to a cooling rack or the pieces may stick. If not using all right away, the licorice and ginger may be refrigerated, tightly wrapped, for up to 2 days.

HONEY-ROASTED LICORICE TEA

YIELD: 4 CUPS

5 pieces Honey-Roasted Licorice Sticks (see preceding recipe)
1 ½-inch piece of roasted ginger (optional; see preceding recipe)

Combine the licorice, ginger if using, and 5 cups water in a saucepan. Cover and bring to a boil over high heat. Reduce heat to a high simmer and cook for 20 minutes.

Strain, and drink hot or warm.

LONG PEPPER
(Piper longum)

Trikatu works for me.

It's the most famous stimulant digestive tonic in India's Ayurvedic medicine tradition. It's very simple: equal parts black pepper, ground ginger, and long pepper. You drop a small amount in a half glass of hot water, add honey, and drink it down. It wakes you up, like coffee. But it makes you feel better—less stimulated but more awake.

Unlike coffee (page 87), which merely improves mood, trikatu also improves health, stimulating the liver's ability to break down toxins, improving digestion, reducing inflammation, opening up the lungs, enhancing immunity.

All three major ingredients contribute. Ginger (page 146) improves digestion by stimulating the release of digestive "juices" as well as stimulating the liver to release bile, which helps digest fats. It protects against ulcers; improves circulation, thus warming the body; is antioxidant; and has strong anti-inflammatory and anticlotting properties.

Black pepper (*Piper nigrum*) is also a warming stimulant. And like hot chili pepper (page 61), it "thins" the mucus, thus improving breathing if you are congested.

Long pepper is in the same family as black pepper. It has similar actions, but they are more pronounced and have been better studied. In Ayurvedic medicine, long pepper, known as *pipali*, is used to treat coughs, colds, asthma, bronchitis, arthritis, and indigestion. Recent scientific studies help explain its traditional use as an expectorant: it reduces the movement of cilia, tiny hairlike structures in the esophagus that can suppress the cough reflex.

In trikatu, long pepper's main function is to stimulate digestion, including liver function—an effect confirmed by animal studies. When mice were given two chemicals, including carbon tetrachloride, a powerful liver toxin, along with an active chemical in long pepper (piperine, also found in black pepper), it reduced the breakdown of the fatty tissue by free radicals. It prevented the "leakage" of enzymes that rise with liver damage and prevented the depletion of glutathione, one of the liver's most important detoxifying antioxidants.

Indian long pepper is added to many Ayurvedic formulas to enhance their effectiveness. In *Ayurvedic Healing: A Comprehensive Guide,* David Frawley recommends an "herbal absorption compound" of equal parts nutmeg, cardamom, cyperus (not to be confused with cypress), long pepper, chamomile, and licorice for "lack of appetite; indigestion; gas and abdominal distention; colic; nervous indigestion; candida; chronic diarrhea or loose stool; malabsorption."

The absorption-enhancing capability of Indian long pepper also has scientific support. In one study, when two drugs were administered along with piperine, the blood levels of both drugs increased by more than 100 percent. It increases the availability of biologically active compounds by several mechanisms: boosting the transport of compounds from the stomach to the blood, improving absorption in the intestines, and protecting drugs from being broken down by the liver. Improving intestinal absorption may also enhance the assimilation of nutrients.

Like black pepper, long pepper is very safe. In Ayurveda, trikatu is recommended for indigestion and lack of appetite, as well as cough and congestion. It is said to boost low *agni,* or digestive fire, and to help rid the body of *ama,* or toxins. Modern science agrees. It's also a nice morning pick-me-up.

TRIKATU

You'll need a very accurate scale, the kind you get in a drugstore or a fancy food market, to measure these small quantities accurately. You'll also want to purchase empty gelatin capsules in one-gram quantities, available in health food stores. The coriander, nutmeg, and cloves are added because they are "carminative" (stomach settling) and so help to harmonize the formula. If you want to grind up a much larger quantity, make sure each ingredient is represented in equal amounts.

YIELD: 12 1-GRAM DOSES

2 grams freshly ground black pepper
2 grams ground long pepper
2 grams ground ginger
2 grams freshly ground coriander
2 grams ground nutmeg
2 grams ground cloves

Combine the black pepper, long pepper, ginger, coriander, nutmeg, and cloves in a spice mill. Grind into a fine powder, stopping to toss the ingredients from time to time.

The powder may be measured out in 1-gram doses as needed or measured into gelatin capsules. Store in a bottle or sealed plastic bag in a cool, dry place.

Take from 1 to 4 grams in ½ cup warm water or milk with honey to taste. Take as often as three times a day, preferably before meals. It's particularly good before breakfast to get the juices going.

TRIKATU MUFFINS

Try these for breakfast. Each muffin has one gram, the smallest "dose," of trikatu.

YIELD: 12 MUFFINS

1 cup all-purpose flour
¾ cup whole-wheat flour
1 teaspoon baking soda
1 tablespoon baking powder
¼ teaspoon kosher salt
1 recipe Trikatu (page 206)
1 large egg
2 large egg whites
1½ teaspoons vanilla
⅓ cup unsulfured molasses
1 cup low-fat or nonfat buttermilk
1 ripe banana, mashed
½ cup raisins or other dried fruit

Position one of the racks in the center of the oven; heat the oven to 400 degrees. Spray a 12-muffin tin with vegetable-oil spray.

In a medium bowl, sift together both flours, the baking soda and powder, salt, and trikatu powder. Set aside.

In a large bowl, whisk together the egg and egg whites, vanilla, molasses, and buttermilk.

Add half the flour mixture to the egg mixture, and stir lightly until partially combined. Add the remaining flour mixture, mashed banana, and raisins, and mix just until combined. A few streaks of flour in the batter are fine. Fill each muffin cup to the rim.

Bake for 15 to 18 minutes, until a cake tester or toothpick inserted in the middle of a muffin comes out clean.

Serve warm. You can refrigerate extras in an airtight container for up to 4 days, or freeze them for up to 2 weeks.

OLIVE OIL

Olive oil is the best fat for cooking, and a valuable article of diet for both sick and healthy of all ages.
—Maud Grieve, *A Modern Herbal*, 1931

Ancel Keys walks me around his garden. We are in Pioppi, Italy, several hours south of Naples. The garden is terraced. There are roses and orchids; tiny potatoes and artichokes; rows of onions, lettuces, and chardlike vegetables; and lemon, grapefruit, loquat, fig, and olive trees. Last year was terrible for olives, Keys tells me, but this year looks better. He bends an olive branch and shows me a cluster of new buds.

Without Ancel Keys, an academic physiologist, we wouldn't know much about olive oil. In the 1950s and 1960s, he discovered that saturated fat raises blood cholesterol and causes heart disease and that replacing it with unsaturated fat such as olive oil lowers cholesterol. He also identified the healthfulness of what we now call the Mediterranean diet with his pioneering Seven Countries Study of the United States, Holland, Finland, Yugoslavia, Italy, Greece, and Japan.

"There's no evidence that olive oil has a special virtue," says Keys. "It's simply a matter of changing the distribution of fatty acids. The diet should certainly be low in saturated fatty acids. It probably shouldn't be too high in polyunsaturates, because none of the world's populations consume a diet that is high in polyunsaturates. When saturates are high in these populations, they have coronary heart disease. When saturates are decreased, as they were markedly in Finland, coronary heart disease goes down." (His next-door neighbor in Pioppi is Martti Karvonen, M.D., who ran the Finnish part of the Seven Countries Study with Keys. He remembers Finland in the 1950s. "In those days, in the winter time, we had bread, potatoes, milk, and pork with layers of fat on it. There was nothing green seen on the table—maybe the tablecloth.")

The Mediterranean diet, rich in monounsaturated olive oil, may be an alternative to a very low-fat, high-carbohydrate diet for the prevention of heart disease and diabetes. In some people, substituting carbohydrates for fats lowers their beneficial HDL cholesterol and raises blood sugar levels because they can't produce enough insulin to handle all those carbohydrates. Diabetics, for example, are now often advised to consume a moderate-fat, low-saturated-fat diet, replacing the saturated fats with monounsaturates such as olive oil.

Simply adding olive oil to a high-fat diet, on the other hand, will do no one any good. If you want the benefits of the Mediterranean diet, you should emulate the Mediterraneans' entire way of eating, not to mention their high level of physical activity.

Olive oil, the main fat in the Mediterranean countries, is good because of what it is not: it is not rich in saturated fatty acids, like butter and cream, nor in trans fatty acids, like those found in the hydrogenated fat of stick margarine and many processed foods. Both saturated fats and trans fatty acids raise blood cholesterol.

Nor is olive oil rich in polyunsaturated fatty acids, as are corn oil and safflower oil. Polyunsaturated fats increase the likelihood of blood clotting and, in animal studies, promote the growth of cancer. By *not* being polyunsaturated, olive oil may help the body transform vegetable sources of omega-3 fatty acids (see "Walnut," page 292) into their heart-protective forms, EPA (eicosapentaenoic acid) and DHA (docosahexaenoic acid). Polyunsaturated fats interfere with this beneficial process.

So the Mediterranean diet, with vegetables rich in omega-3 fatty acids and olive oil as the main fat, is a good mix. (In many areas of the Mediterranean, the diet also includes plenty of fish, which is rich in elongated, heart-healthy omega-3 fatty acids.)

Olive oil is also good because of what it is. Olive oil is a traditional agricultural product, a whole food. It is more than the sum of its fatty acids. Extra-virgin olive oil, which undergoes the least processing, is particularly rich in antioxidants, some of which are lost in later pressings. Extra-virgin olive oil contains significant amounts of vitamin E, for example, which reduces blood clotting. It contains something else that prevents blood clotting, too, although no one is quite sure what. In a 1994 study of the effects on blood clotting of fish oil rich in omega-3 fatty acids, the researchers used olive oil as an inactive "placebo." But something in olive oil also made the blood of the healthy young men and women less likely to clot. A 1995 study found similar results.

Like many other plant foods that predominate in the Mediterranean (greens, onions, garlic, red wine), olive oil is rich in antioxidant phenolic compounds. These may contribute to its anticlotting capability. The antioxidants may protect unhealthful LDL cholesterol from becoming oxidized, the first step toward the development of coronary heart disease. A 1995 Italian laboratory study found that extra-virgin olive oil, even in small amounts, prevents the oxidation of blood cholesterol.

Perhaps it's those phenolics that account for a surprising new finding about olive oil: it may protect against breast cancer. Many phenolic antioxidants inhibit cancer in many stages along the way, from the initiation of a potential tumor to its progression into actual cancer. It's too early to tell what, if anything, in olive oil protects. But population studies in Spain, Greece, and Italy show a lower rate of breast cancer in women who use olive oil as their principal fat. The relationship isn't proved, to be sure, but it's a potential benefit. When one consumes whole foods, the benefits are not linear.

It is dusk in Pioppi. Ancel's wife, Margaret, invites me to pick peas; white flowers bloom on the vines. We come back inside. Cocktails are served. Dinner is simple. She sets out a carousel of wine and water and a pretty pottery bowl of steaming bow-tie pasta. In the center of the table is a bowl of aromatic, maroon-colored octopus sauce. Margaret says it's made by sautéing fresh octopus and adding tomatoes, garlic, parsley, salt, pepper, and olive oil. After pasta, she brings out fresh green beans and mushrooms, sautéed in olive oil. Crusty whole-wheat bread appears. For dessert, perfectly ripe pears and apples on a plate with a sharp knife. Margaret is in her late eighties; Ancel, his early nineties. They have been eating this way for about half a century, and it appears to agree with them.

HOT CHILI OLIVE OIL

Flavored oils are a shortcut to aromatic cooking. Use them as you would any oils: in stir-fries, pasta sauces, marinades, and vinaigrettes.

Of late, fresh herb oils have fallen out of favor because fresh herbs in oil can harbor the botulin bacterium. (If you want to use fresh herbs, sauté them first, which drives out the water and makes the oil safer.) Dried chili peppers are not a concern, but it's still a good idea to make only a cup or two, so the flavors stay fresh, and to store the oil in the refrigerator. Let it come to room temperature before using. The strength of the infusion will vary with the quantity of peppers; a little practice will give you the results you like best.

YIELD: 2 CUPS

8 to 10 dry small hot chili peppers
2 cups extra-virgin olive oil

Wash and dry the peppers to remove any grit or dust. Using a small knife, make tiny slits in the peppers but leave them whole.

Put the peppers in a clean, dry 1-pint glass container. Add the olive oil, and close with a tight-fitting lid.

Refrigerate the oil for 2 weeks before using in order for flavors to infuse. Strain it through a fine sieve or dampened cheesecloth before using. Keep refrigerated.

ONION
(Allium cepa)

Slowly, layer by layer, the onion is revealing its secrets. It has few calories, a little fiber, a small amount of vitamin C and folic acid. But forget nutrition; family resemblance is a better place to start. Like all allium vegetables, especially garlic (see page 135), onions contain sulfur compounds that protect against heart disease and cancer.

Like garlic, onions reduce the tendency of blood platelets to clump together and form clots. The effect is so well established that it shows up in scientific review of foods that might interact with prescription blood-thinning drugs. When British volunteers were given two ounces of fried onions along with a proper English breakfast, it significantly inhibited the clot-promoting tendency of the high-fat meal. (In rabbits, adding onion to a diet loaded with dietary cholesterol prevents heart disease, but since rabbits are vegetarians and cholesterol exists only in animal-based foods, the relevance of such studies eludes me.)

Like raw garlic, raw onions are powerfully antibiotic against a wide range of bacteria, as well as fungi. Like garlic, onions inhibit cancer in lab animals, and in population studies, people who eat lots of garlic, onion, chives, and other allium vegetables have lower rates of various cancers. In the Vidalia onion-growing region of Georgia, for example, stomach cancer rates are particularly low.

Let's peel back a few more layers.

The onion has a reputation that is somewhat different from that of garlic. In India's Ayurvedic medicine tradition, for example, onions are considered a sedative, and Russian researchers report that they contain small amounts of lithium, the antidepressant. To be sure, this is not a well-documented link, but it's suggestive.

A better-documented effect: onions may lower blood sugar. This has been suggested with garlic, but there is more evidence with onions. In 1975, researchers gave allyl propyl disulfide, a sulfur compound found in onions, to six nondiabetic volunteers and reported that blood levels of insulin rose while blood sugar fell. In 1983, researchers studied onions in 20 diabetic patients in Indonesia. In that country, both green beans and onions are believed to have medicinal benefit, so each day, half the patients ate green beans and the other half ate almost two ounces of fresh onions. After a week, blood sugar levels were significantly lower in the onion eaters. Then the two groups switched: onion eaters ate green beans, green bean eaters ate onions. Again, the onion eaters had lower blood sugar. In diabetic rats, adding onion- and garlic-derived sulfur compounds to the chow reduced glucose intolerance and reversed weight loss, according to a small 1995 study reported in *Planta Medica*.

In 1984, another compound, diphenylamine, was isolated as one of the blood-sugar-lowering agents in onions. It also exists in green and black tea (page 252). That's a clue. Here's another: in 1996, Finnish researchers reported in the *British Medical Journal* that Finns who ate the most onions were the least likely to die from heart attacks. Same thing for apples (page 15).

This is because of our old friends, the flavonoids. These antioxidant compounds, found in onions, apples, black and green tea, and red wine (page 301), thin the blood and protect against cancer at many stages. In Japan, tea supplies most of the flavonoids; in Italy, red wine is a major contributor. In the United States, apples and onions together contribute 40 percent of our flavonoid intake.

Which brings us to asthma.

Onions have a reputation for improving breathing. In *Kitchen Pharmacy*, British alternative health practitioner Carlo de Paoli and food writer Rose Elliot state that onions, especially raw, "are valuable for . . . colds and flu when there is shivering and blocked sinuses; also for bronchitis and asthma with mucus." In the United States, alternative health practitioners often recommend onions and garlic as a dietary adjunct to treating asthma.

At the University of Munich in Germany, researcher Walter Dorsch, M.D., has isolated several compounds in onions that prevent asthmatic and allergic attacks. They are sulfur compounds but different ones from the sulfur compounds in garlic. They are called thiosulfinates. One particular thiosulfinate, diphenylthiosulfinate, is more active at preventing inflammation than prednisolone, a synthetic steroid similar to hydrocortisone that's prescribed as an anti-inflammatory and antiallergenic drug. Prednisolone is also used to treat cancer.

In guinea pigs, tablets of diphenylthiosulfinate prevent bronchial asthma-like reactions induced by inhaling histamine, which causes allergic inflammation. In humans, onion-alcohol extracts injected just under the skin prevented allergic reactions to IgE, the compound that causes these reactions.

This helps explain the folk use of onions for asthma. But whole foods are more complicated than the magic bullets medical researchers search for.

Consider quercetin, one of those life-protecting flavonoids that has public health researchers so excited. It's in red wine, broccoli, yellow summer squash, green beans, some types of kale, and, particularly, yellow onions. It is quercetin that gives these vegetables their color. You won't find any in white onions of any sort, but yellow onions, red onions, and shallots are loaded with quercetin. It is in highest concentration in the outer parts of the onion, which have more color. It's also in the papery skin, but no one eats that. (You might want to leave the skin on, though, the next time you add onions to your stockpot.)

Quercetin is a potent antioxidant. It prevents LDL cholesterol from being oxidized, which is the crucial first step in the formation of artery-clogging plaque. It also prevents platelet aggregation; in other words, it thins the blood. Quercetin is one of the most powerful cancer-protective substances ever studied. In lab and animal studies, it inhibits breast cancer, ovarian cancer, leukemia, and melanoma, the dangerous form of skin cancer. It inhibits the initiation of cancer—that is, the mutation of a normal cell into a cancer-causing cell. Much more important, it strongly inhibits the progression of an initiated cell into an actual cancer.

"There is more quercetin in the human diet than vitamin E and beta-carotene combined, but it is not well studied at all," says Terrance Leighton, a biochemist at the University of California, Berkeley, who has been studying quercetin for over a decade. "It's a better antioxidant in preventing lipid peroxidation"—the oxidation of LDL cholesterol—"than vitamin C."

Quercetin "has well-documented anticarcinogenic, antioxidant, and antithrombotic [anti-blood-clotting] activity in animal and biochemical models," Leighton adds. "It works to target and regulate cancer gene expression. It also inhibits some viral enzymes needed for replication in the life cycle of viruses."

Quercetin even kills *Helicobacter pylori,* the bacteria that causes most human ulcers, German researchers reported in 1995 in the medical journal *Arzneimittelforschung.* They concluded that "flavonoids are a group of compounds which could have a therapeutic potential for treatment of gastrointestinal diseases associated with *Helicobacter pylori* infection."

Oh, yes, and one more thing. "Quercetin down-regulates immune response," says Leighton.

In a 1995 study reported in the *Journal of Immunology,* researchers at the National Heart, Lung, and Blood Institute looked at the effect of quercetin on mast cells in the laboratory. These are the cells that release histamine and create the biochemical cascade of inflammation in allergic reactions; when this happens in the lungs of people susceptible to asthma, an asthmatic attack occurs. The researchers were looking in particular at arachidonic acid, which causes an inflammatory response. Quercetin inhibited the inflammatory cascade, including the release of arachidonic acid, by 50 percent.

So raw onions are not only antibiotic and full of sulfur compounds that inhibit inflammation but yellow onions and shallots are rich in quercetin, which dramatically inhibits the inflammatory response. This is more clinical support for onion's folk reputation for opening the lungs.

In the end, these actions are interrelated. Arachidonic acid causes not only inflammation but promotes blood clotting and the carcinogenic process. You can purchase quercetin in a health food store, and that may be useful for certain purposes. But traditional foodways are better.

It makes a difference how you consume foods rich in quercetin. Right now, one of the most active areas of research involves bioavailability—whether these potentially protective quercetin molecules actually get to the cells in the human body where they may do the most good. Most quercetin is bound with sugars. These are digested in the intestines by bacteria, but they are hard to break apart; beneficial bacteria like to go after the "easy" sugars first.

One way to "liberate" quercetin may be to eat less. If you are constantly eating, your good-guy bacteria always have plenty of easy sugars to live on. But if you are just a little hungry, these bacteria will start to break down the harder sugars, including the ones that bind quercetin. This may be one way in which fasting (see page 108), always an enigma to mainstream medical researchers, can enhance health.

Traditional foods also liberate quercetin. In making wine, for example, the quercetin-rich wine skins are in contact with yeasts, which break down their sugars. This may be one reason red wine is so beneficial.

Then there's vinegar. "Any type of quercetin-rich food produced with vinegar will have more liberated quercetin," says Leighton. This may be one reason fermented foods such as sauerkraut and kimchi have such a healthful reputation: they contain antioxidants bound with sugars that are liberated by the fermentation process. Sauerkraut, the German saying goes, is good for a cold. "In folk lore, boiling red wine with onions is supposed to be good for certain ailments," Leighton says. "It may be related to these reactions."

We take advantage of these traditional foodways in our recipe for Chilean Pickled Onions. When pickling in vinegar, Leighton notes, it may take two or three months for the sugars to be fully broken down and the quercetin fully released.

In the meantime, if you have allergies or asthma or just feel stuffy, try our Pink Onion Juice. Keep your inhaler on hand, to be sure; this is dietary support, not medicine. This juice is also a tonic for the stomach; it may kill bacteria, including those that cause ulcers. It's also a refreshing, bracing cocktail. The Onion Relish recipe is also a lung-opening bracer, as well as a delicious condiment.

If you have diabetes, consider adding substantial amounts of onions to your diet, raw or cooked, and see if it improves your condition; inform your physician first, though. If you are concerned about heart disease or cancer—and who isn't?—eat onions, cooked or raw, as often as you may.

That's the best advice for general health, as well. Eat onions, especially red and yellow ones but also shallots, chives, and green onions, as often as you like. Quercetin is remarkably stable, so it is just as available in cooked onions as raw. Raw onions, on the other hand, have one advantage: they are antibiotic. So if you have a cold, you'll want to take your onions raw. Just be careful that the cure isn't worse than the illness. Consider M. F. K. Fisher's experience, recounted in *A Cordiall Water,* after taking her husband's advice and devouring a particularly strong onion to remedy her cold:

> Love as well as despair blinded me before the tears did, of course, and I still hope they all acted as a kind of anesthetic for the wild blasting of my senses that followed that first resolute bite. I was on fire. I was in Hell. From the shoulders up to the last hair on my head I buzzed like an agonized bee in every atom of my skin and flesh and bone. When I gasped, my husband whacked me and said, "Good, good. That's the way it should be. Clearing you out. Killing the germs. Excellent reaction. You'll be fine before you know it."

As M. F. K. Fisher tells it, she spent the next three days in bed with severe blisters in her mouth and throat. On the other hand, her cold was gone. "It had been routed. It is almost literally the last one I have ever had, just as that onion is the last one I have eaten raw for a cold cure since 1929, when the stock market and I crashed."

PINK ONION JUICE

The sweetness of the red grapefruit softens the bite of the raw onion juice. If only yellow grapefruit are available, add a teaspoon or two of sugar.

YIELD: 2½ CUPS

1 large onion (10 ounces), peeled and cut into 2-inch chunks
2 cups fresh Ruby Red grapefruit juice (from 1 or 2 grapefruits)
1 1½-inch piece fresh ginger, peeled and cut into chunks
Juice of ½ lemon

Process the onion in a juicer; it should yield about ½ cup juice. Combine it with the grapefruit juice in a large glass measuring cup or other nonreactive container.

Process the ginger in the juicer, and add 3 tablespoons of the juice to the onion-grapefruit juice. Stir well, cover, and chill.

Just before serving, stir in the lemon juice. The juice will keep in the refrigerator for a day but will separate, so stir well before serving.

ONION RELISH

Between the raw onions and the hot chili peppers, this will really open up those sinus passages. Serve this Indian-inspired relish with roasted fowl, as a filling for warm corn tortillas, or as a topping for soup or rice. If it's the middle of winter and all you can find are harsh-tasting storage onions, soak them in cold, salted water for 30 minutes after chopping. Then rinse and drain.

YIELD: 1½ CUPS

1 large onion, peeled and diced into ¼-inch pieces (about 1 cup)
Juice of 2 limes
1 fresh jalapeño pepper, seeded if desired and minced
½ bunch fresh cilantro or parsley, leaves chopped
½ teaspoon cayenne, or more if you can take it
Kosher salt and freshly ground pepper

Stir together the onion, lime juice, jalapeño, cilantro, cayenne, and salt and pepper to taste. Let the relish sit at room temperature for at least 30 minutes for the flavors to combine. It will keep, tightly covered, in the refrigerator for 2 or 3 days.

CHILEAN PICKLED ONIONS

One of the best ways to release the protective antioxidant quercetin in onions from the sugars that bind it is with vinegar. Our recipe developer, Stephana Bottom, adapted this recipe from one given to her by a Chilean friend. Because of the high acid content, "you don't need to boil it, or even put it through a hot water bath," Stephana says. "So there are no excuses not to make it—it takes about 10 minutes." The pickles are sweet-sour, and the liquid is eminently useful in marinades, soups, stews, and vinaigrettes. If you don't consume alcohol, you can substitute 2 additional cups of red wine vinegar for the red wine.

YIELD: 1½ QUARTS

2 cups red wine vinegar
2 cups red wine
¼ cup sugar
3 pounds small yellow onions, peeled and cut in quarters or eighths
2 tablespoons mustard seed
1 4-inch piece fresh ginger, peeled and cut into ½-inch pieces
8 garlic cloves, peeled
4 ounces fresh horseradish, peeled and cut into ½-inch pieces (a heaping ½ cup; optional)

Wash a 1½-quart glass container with a tight-fitting lid in hot, soapy water. Rinse the jar and lid with boiling water, and set them aside on a clean kitchen towel to dry.

Combine the vinegar, wine, and sugar in a large, nonreactive container, preferably one with a pouring spout. Stir to dissolve the sugar.

Pack the onions into the jar, sprinkling the mustard seed, ginger, garlic, and horseradish (if using) between layers. A chopstick or wooden dowel is helpful to poke the ingredients down tightly. Pack to within an inch of the top.

Pour the vinegar brine up to the top of the jar. (You may not need it all.) Close the lid tightly without forcing. Label and date the jar, and store it in a cool, dark place for 30 days for flavors to develop. (The refrigerator is fine.) Refrigerate the pickles after opening.

OYSTER

I have a certain obsessive passion for raw oysters. It is related to summers, swimming, sea love, and the sensory experience of evanescent perfection. It would be a cruel world that did not have oysters in it. Not for the deep ecology of the oyster, mind you, but for me and my friends to eat.

Eating a raw oyster is a dangerous gustatory joy. Oysters, like all mollusks, are intimate with their environment. They swallow and filter seawater in enormous quantity. That is why they taste like the local bays. Oh, that our bays tasted better! Oysters are sensitive environmental signals to ecological decline, aqueous canaries in coal mines. Pollution can kill them en masse; more commonly, they survive, harboring bacteria and viruses. This makes eating a raw oyster a risky proposition, especially for people with diabetes, cancer, or an immunological deficiency such as HIV infection.

As a journalist who writes about public health, I would never advocate eating raw oysters—or sushi, for that matter. There is no public health gain to be had from consuming raw seafood. Yet something in me feels that intelligent risk, especially in the pursuit of pure, clean flavor, has something to do with health, and I eat them both myself.

For sushi, I trust the Japanese-influenced supply system from fish in the boat to sushi chef in the restaurant. For oysters, I trust locale, proximity, and to a degree, season. If the water is pure and the season cold, the taste of a raw oyster subtly and sharply reflects its watery home. In *A Moveable Feast,* Ernest Hemingway described walking around Paris, hungry and a bit desolate, and then entering an eating establishment and ordering: "As I ate the oysters with their strong taste of the sea and their faint metallic taste that the cold white wine washed away, leaving only the sea taste and the succulent texture, and as I drank their cold liquid from each shell and washed it down with the crisp taste of the wine, I lost the empty feeling and began to be happy and to make plans."

In oysters, as in other real foods, taste itself is a signal. The saltiness is mostly mineral. A half dozen raw, medium Eastern oysters have only 94 milligrams of sodium, along with 192 milligrams of potassium. So it is balanced; our problems with sodium come not just from too much sodium (mostly in processed foods) but too little potassium and other minerals.

The same six oysters have 58 calories, a low two grams of fat (a half a gram is saturated), and 46 milligrams of cholesterol—a rather misleading figure. An oyster's cholesterol is balanced with noncholesterol sterols. These interfere with cholesterol absorption, so they actually lower levels of cholesterol in the blood. Oysters are also good sources of omega-3 fatty acids. These lower triglyceride levels, inhibit blood clotting, reduce inflammatory processes, and have beneficial immune effects (see "Walnut," page 292, and "Tuna," page 275). Oysters protect the heart.

What makes an oyster a nutritional "tonic" is signaled by their "strong taste of the sea" and their "faint metallic taste": minerals. Our modest half-dozen serving provides nearly half the recommended dietary allowance of iron, nearly twice the recommended amount of copper, and more than five times the recommended dietary allowance for zinc. They also have a modest amount of manganese, a trace element that plays a role in keeping bones strong.

What really makes oysters a nutritional tonic, though, isn't the oyster. It's us. Foods aren't absolute. They have qualities. Whether they are "good" or "bad" for us depends on what our needs are. If you eat a lot of red meat, the minerals in oysters are superfluous (although their omega-3s would help). But if you aren't eating a lot of red meat these days—if you're primarily a vegetarian who also eats seafood—they may make a difference.

Zinc supports immunity. Copper is an antioxidant, protecting our cells from the damage highly reactive forms of oxygen can inflict. Iron is tricky; too much isn't good, but too little can cause fatigue and impair learning (see "Iron," page 180). Much is made of oyster's zinc content in the vain search to support its aphrodisiac reputation. There's no question that zinc is needed for sexual development and performance; it is well supplied in semen, for example. But there is little evidence that subclinical deficiencies impair sexual performance. Too little zinc, however, may raise blood cholesterol. It may also subtly impair immunity. We need our minerals. And if you, like me, eschew beef most or all of the time, oysters are a particularly delicious way to get minerals.

In keeping with the theme of danger and health, let me tell you the other way I like oysters: deep-fried. The Chinese say that oysters are both yin and yang: they nourish the blood and treat indecision. Frying them would certainly make them more yang. But not necessarily unhealthful. Frying oysters, just like eating raw oysters, depends on picking the perfect moment.

John Martin Taylor taught me that. He writes cookbooks, runs Hoppin' Johns, a wonderful cookery bookstore in Charleston, South Carolina, and is passionate about frying. "If the oil is the right temperature and clean, frying is a dry-cooking technique," he told me—that is, no oil is absorbed. "That hissing sound you hear is the moisture leaving the food. It is vaporizing. As long as it is leaving the food, no oil is being absorbed.

"After the food stops releasing water, then it immediately starts to absorb oil. That will also happen if you fry at too low a temperature, so the water isn't instantaneously vaporized. The oil temperature should be 365, 370 degrees. Never let the temperature go below 340.

"So get yourself a frying or candy thermometer. Another way to tell that the oil is hot enough, if you don't have a thermometer, is to drop in a cube of bread first; it should become golden exactly at one minute. But a thermometer is better. . . . For oysters, I like peanut oil. Heat the oil on medium or medium high; don't use the highest heat—you want to have the ability to increase the heat if the temperature goes down. When the oil temperature is 365 degrees, or a little hotter, drop the oysters in."

Here is his—and now my—favorite recipe for fried oysters.

PERFECT GREASELESS DEEP-FRIED OYSTERS

If you try to fry all the oysters at once, the oil temperature will plunge and they won't cook properly. If you want to make more than 12, strain the oil to clean it, or start fresh with new oil. A thermometer is essential to achieve the correct oil temperature and to be able to fry quickly.

YIELD: 4 APPETIZER SERVINGS OR 2 MAIN-COURSE SERVINGS

¼ cup dry mustard
1 cup stone-ground yellow cornmeal
Peanut oil
12 freshest shucked oysters, strained but still damp
Kosher salt and freshly ground pepper

Put the mustard in a small bowl. Put the cornmeal in a larger bowl. Set up a cooling rack over newspaper or paper towels.

Pour oil into a heavy skillet, preferably cast iron, to a depth of ¾ inch. Heat it over medium-high heat to 365 degrees, measured with a candy or frying thermometer.

While the oil is heating, pat each oyster in the dry mustard, then dredge it in cornmeal. Transfer them to a clean plate, or leave them in the cornmeal.

When the oil is hot, shake off the excess cornmeal and carefully place 4 oysters in the skillet. There will be a lot of sputtering and hissing. After about 15 seconds, when the hissing stops, the oysters are done. Use tongs or a large slotted spoon to transfer them to the cooling rack.

Check the oil temperature; when it returns to 365 degrees, fry 4 more oysters the same way. Repeat with the last batch.

Eat warm, sprinkled with salt and pepper, or make a delicious sandwich with thick crusty bread.

PARSLEY

Parsley thrown into fish ponds will heal the sick fishes therein.
—William Turner, *Turner's Herbal,* 1551

Fresh parsley is incredibly nutritious. A cup has only 22 calories, yet it provides 30 percent of the U.S. RDA for vitamin A (3,120 International Units, or IUs), more than 100 percent for vitamin C (80 milligrams), about a quarter for iron (4 milligrams), more than half for copper (0.9 milligram), about half for folic acid (92 milligrams), and about 10 percent for calcium (82 milligrams) and magnesium (30 milligrams).

Even assuming that the U.S. RDA underestimates optimal levels for many nutrients, which it does, these figures are significant. For example, recent studies find that the optimal dietary intake of vitamin C is probably 200 milligrams, in which case, our cup of parsley supplies nearly half. Its vitamin A equivalents are in the form of mixed carotenoids, which may protect against disease in many different ways. Iron from plant sources may be preferable to iron from animal sources (see "Iron," page 180), copper helps regulate blood cholesterol, and magnesium, an underappreciated nutrient, is important for blood pressure regulation.

Parsley may also help prevent cancer. It has a folk reputation for treating tumors of the bladder, breast, eyes, liver, throat, and mouth, and modern research is bearing this out. Not bad for a garnish.

Parsley, a member of the carrot family, contains small amounts of substances called coumarins. The main one is psoralen. (In large amounts, it can induce light sensitivity; if you ate a lot of parsley and went to the beach, you could conceivably have a skin reaction.) Synthetic coumarins are used in medicine to prevent blood clotting in heart disease patients. They may also prevent and treat cancer; several clinical trials are under way testing that possibility, and there is already evidence that they do. In a 1989 study in Ireland, for example, 13 people who had melanoma, an often deadly form of skin cancer, were given 50 milligrams of coumarin a day for three years. None had a recurrence of melanoma. In 10 of 14 who didn't get coumarin, melanoma returned. The results were so dramatic that the researchers, at Beaumont Hospital in Dublin, stopped the study and gave coumarin supplements to all their melanoma patients.

Coumarin has also been used to treat cancers of the kidney. In a 1992 Austrian study, patients with metastasized kidney cancer—that is, cancer that had spread beyond the kidney—who were given 100 milligrams a day of coumarin lived an average of 38 months. Similar patients given no coumarin lived an average of 11 months. Coumarin may also be useful in treating prostate cancer, and in animals, it inhibits breast and lung tumor growth.

Parsley itself hasn't been well studied, but then, foods aren't as exciting or as lucrative as drugs. You can't patent a plant that's been grown by humans since before recorded history. There is a little bit of research, however, that's tantalizing, like that sprig of parsley on your plate. In 1987, Japanese researchers gave three healthy nonsmoking men a meal of fried salmon. Burnt, fried foods can contain carcinogens. When the men also ate about 2½ ounces (70 grams) of parsley, the amount of potentially cancer-causing mutagens in their urine dropped by 50 percent.

In 1992, researchers in Minneapolis looked at myristicin, a compound found in the oil of parsley leaves. In mice, it induced the powerful cancer-protective detoxifying enzyme glutathione S-transferase. When the mice were given a cancer-causing chemical as well as myristicin, they developed significantly less lung cancer.

Myristicin is a rather famous chemical. Along with apiole, another component of the oil found in parsley leaves, root, and seeds, myristicin is a uterine stimulant. Parsley oil has been used to bring on menstrual periods and misused to induce abortions. (Thus, parsley oil should never be given to pregnant women.) Parsley oil is also what makes parsley root and seed an effective diuretic in folk medicine.

In the tiny amounts found in the fresh leaves of parsley, on the other hand, parsley's oils may help prevent cancer. In that regard, its vitamin C, carotenoid, folic acid, and calcium, all cancer protective, are a nice part of the package. Unlike synthetic coumarin, parsley also freshens the breath. Whether it heals sick fish is, at present, unknown.

GREEN GLORY JUICE

This light, fresh-tasting juice is a mild diuretic and stimulates the liver's detoxification function. If you can find parsley with the roots attached, wash them well and use the whole plant.

YIELD: 2 CUPS

½ bunch flat-leaf parsley (leaves and stems), well washed
½ cup fresh mint leaves, well washed
1 medium carrot, trimmed and peeled
4 celery stalks with leafy green tops
1 apple
4 ounces romaine (about half a medium head), red oak leaf, or Bibb lettuce
¼ to ½ cup fresh lemon juice

Cut the parsley if necessary to fit the juicer, and juice it with the mint. Cut the carrot and celery if necessary and juice. Core and juice the apple. Juice the lettuce.

Stir the juices together, add lemon juice to taste, and drink immediately.

PSYLLIUM
(Plantago psyllium)

Let me tell you about an exotic little seed. It comes from India.

When pounded into powder, it dissolves in water. It is soothing. It goes by the name plantago or, more commonly, psyllium seed.

In the late Middle Ages, according to historian Barbara Griggs, Arab physicians used it to tame a vicious laxative plant known as scammony (*Convolvulus scammonia*). Scammony was enormously popular in Europe at the time. It was an era of purges, laxatives, emetics, bloodletting, and other enlightened practices. Even then, scammony was considered extreme, Griggs writes in *The Green Pharmacy,* with "some physicians maintaining that its action was so violently irritant that it should never be used, others that they could not possibly do without such a marvelous purge."

The first thing the Arab physicians did was boil scammony in quince, a fruit we know from preserves. Then they threw away the scammony, which was the smartest thing. Finally, they mixed the scammony-infused quince pulp with psyllium seeds and gave it to patients who were constipated. They called it diagridium. In a marvelous bit of subterfuge, they also sold it at great expense to Europeans, purportedly as their favorite purging laxative, when the true curatives were quince and psyllium.

Both quince and psyllium are rich in soluble fibers, which tend to lubricate the intestines and have other beneficial effects. Psyllium by itself treats constipation by absorbing large quantities of water, acting as a "bulking" agent through the digestive tract. You may know that. You may purchase Metamucil or over-the-counter "colon cleansers" that are nothing but psyllium. Just look at the label. A recent scientific review found that psyllium is as effective as any laxative on the market.

Psyllium does more than move bowels, however. It is as effective as some drugs at lowering high blood cholesterol. What's more, when combined with a good diet, it enhances the effect of certain cholesterol-lowering drugs. It is safe enough to give to children with elevated cholesterol levels. It also lowers blood sugar levels and can be helpful in the treatment of diabetes.

In principle, the soluble fiber found in psyllium seeds isn't any different from the soluble fiber in apples, pears, quinces, beans of all kinds, barley bran, or oat bran. (Yes, oat bran does lower cholesterol—just not when it's sprinkled on chocolate doughnuts.) Soluble fiber causes the liver to synthesize more bile acids, which are then harmlessly excreted. The liver makes bile acids from cholesterol, so the more it makes and excretes, the more cholesterol it removes from the system.

A 1994 review in the *Journal of the American Dietetic Association* looked at 77 human clinical studies of soluble fiber, including some that used psyllium. In 68 studies, soluble fiber significantly reduced total blood cholesterol. Of the 49 studies that looked specifically at LDL (low-density lipoprotein) cholesterol, the "bad" cholesterol that clogs arteries, 41 reported significant reductions. Psyllium does so without lowering beneficial HDL cholesterol, which helps return excess LDL cholesterol to the liver.

A tablespoon of psyllium seeds provides about 8 grams of dietary fiber, just about all of it soluble. Most nutritionists recommend that we get from 25 to 35 grams of total dietary fiber a day. (Insoluble fiber, such as that found in wheat bran, also plays a role in preventing constipation by moving undigested food through the intestines. As Hippocrates wrote, "whole-meal bread cleans out the gut.")

The small act of adding psyllium to your diet can produce significant reductions in cholesterol. Consider a study published in 1993 in *Annals of Internal Medicine* involving 118 healthy men and women, ages 21 to 70, with high blood cholesterol. Researchers at the University of Cincinnati gave some of them about five grams of psyllium twice a day (a total of ten grams daily) and others a placebo. Some ate a low-fat diet, some a high-fat diet. Psyllium dropped cholesterol in both groups. Those on a high-fat diet, whose blood cholesterol was more elevated, had a drop of 5.8 percent total cholesterol and 7.2 percent LDL cholesterol on psyllium. For those on a low-fat diet, whose cholesterol had already fallen, psyllium dropped total cholesterol an additional 4.2 percent and LDL 6.4 percent. Concluded the researchers, "Psyllium, when added to a prescribed low-fat diet, may obviate the need for typical lipid-lowering medications."

So, if you have high blood cholesterol, tackle your diet first. The most effective thing to do is to cut down on saturated and trans fats (see "Olive Oil," page 208) by eating less fatty meat, high-fat dairy products, and processed foods made with hydrogenated vegetable oils. Choose monounsaturated olive or canola oil for cooking, and eat more grains, beans, fruits, and vegetables. Then add two tablespoons of psyllium husks (seven grams) to your juice or hot cereal, or enjoy it in our Banana Smoothie (page 227). The psyllium alone may drop your total cholesterol 5 percent, which would reduce your heart attack risk by 10 percent. It should do even more for your LDL.

Cholesterol-lowering drugs can drop high blood cholesterol levels by as much as 30 percent, but there is concern that some of them may also increase cancer risks. That's happened in animal studies, though not in human studies to date. It's not a clear-cut danger, to be sure. But it's there.

One intriguing possibility is to use psyllium along with medication. For example, cholestyramine is a very safe drug that lowers cholesterol, but it isn't very popular because it can cause constipation. So researchers at Victoria Hospital in London decided to combine it with anticonstipating psyllium. Working with 121 patients with moderately high blood cholesterol, they gave some a placebo, some 5 grams of cholestyramine, others 5 grams of psyllium, and still others 2.5 grams of the drug plus 2.5 grams of psyllium. They reported in 1995 in the *Annals of Internal Medicine* that in patients who took the drug-psyllium combination, the ratio of total to HDL cholesterol fell an average of 18.2 percent. That was better than the results from the drug alone (10.6 percent) or psyllium alone (6.1 percent). Other studies have confirmed the effect—and the benefits in terms of counteracting cholestyramine's constipating effects. So that's another option: half a dose plus psyllium. Ask your doctor.

But we've strayed from food, and the best way to lower cholesterol with psyllium, it turns out, is to add it to food. A 1994 study at Saint Michael's Hospital in Toronto, reported in the *American Journal of Clinical Nutrition,* looked at 18 people with mildly elevated blood cholesterol. For two weeks, they took psyllium (7.6 grams) in cereal, and their blood cholesterol fell an average of 8 percent. For another two weeks, they took the same amount of psyllium between meals, and it didn't have significant cholesterol-lowering effects.

Psyllium, like other soluble fibers, may also benefit people who have or are at risk of developing adult-onset (type II) diabetes. It seems to do so by moderating the blood sugar spike after a meal, thereby lowering the amount of insulin needed to handle the blood sugar load. For example, in a 1991 study published in the *American Journal of Clinical Nutrition,* researchers at the University of Virginia added psyllium to the diets of 18 diabetic patients. On days when they ate it, their blood sugar levels were an average of 14 percent lower after breakfast and 20 percent lower after dinner than on days when they didn't. Other studies have reported similar effects. Because diabetes increases the risk of heart disease, anything that can moderate blood sugar levels and at the same time lower total and LDL cholesterol is a welcome addition. What drug can match that combination?

Psyllium may slow blood sugar rise by a simple mechanism: slowing the rate at which food empties from the stomach. It may seem odd that a fiber that promotes elimination actually slows down stomach emptying, but it makes sense. Soluble fibers absorb water. They expand. So they slow down digestion at first. But they also make it easier for waste to travel through the intestines. By increasing bulk, they stimulate the small intestines to contract, helping them to work better.

This filling action also makes us feel fuller after eating. In 1992, researchers reported in the gastroenterologic journal *Gut* that healthy volunteers given 10.8 grams of psyllium with their meals had a greater "sensation of satiety" and felt less hungry even six hours after eating. A 1995 English study found that healthy women given 20 grams of psyllium three hours before a meal not only said they felt fuller after eating but they tended to eat less fat. Psyllium, the researchers concluded, "may be a useful supplement in weight control diets as it affects fat intake, and may have some effect on the subjective feeling of fullness."

Psyllium, especially combined with wheat bran, may also reduce the risk of colon cancer. As researchers at the Institute for Disease Prevention at George Washington University, in Washington, D.C., put it in *Cancer Letters* in 1993, "wheat bran and psyllium seed fiber alone, and to a greater degree in combination, can offer protection against colon cancer."

That's why we include both in our Banana Smoothie. (To make it, buy the cheapest bulk psyllium you can find; the only differences between it and the prepackaged stuff sold in drugstores are artificial flavors and inflated prices.) A daily serving of our smoothie will also significantly increase your dietary fiber intake, improve regularity, and may lower your cholesterol (especially if it is elevated), lower your blood sugar, and help you stave off hunger. Made with skim milk, the smoothie contains no saturated fat. Made with soy milk (see "Tofu," page 258), it probably has an extra cholesterol-lowering effect. Just as important, though, it's a tasty, healthful drink that the whole family can enjoy.

BANANA SMOOTHIE

Each cup of this drink contains about an ounce of psyllium, which equals about eight grams of dietary fiber—about a third of your optimal daily intake. Try it for breakfast or as a cool refresher on a summer afternoon. Says our food maven, Stephana Bottom, "This is one of my favorite drinks." Because the psyllium "sets," you can also use this recipe to make creamy banana custard; see the Variation at the end.

YIELD: **4** 1-CUP SERVINGS

3 ripe bananas (about 1½ pounds total)
1½ cups cold skim or soy milk
2 teaspoons honey
1 teaspoon vanilla
¼ cup ground psyllium husks
¼ cup wheat bran

Peel the bananas, and cut each into chunks.

Combine them in a food processor or blender with the milk, honey, and vanilla. Process until smooth. Add the psyllium and wheat bran, and process until smooth. Serve cool.

Variation

BANANA CUSTARD: Make the smoothie as directed, and pour it into 4 1-cup custard dishes. Cover tightly with plastic wrap, and chill until set, about 2 to 3 hours. Serve cold.

REISHI
(*Ganoderma lucidum*)

Our immune-enhancing Vegetarian Wei Qi Soup (page 27) contains not only astragalus and ligustrum but another remarkable tonic food: *reishi* mushroom. That's the Japanese word for it. The Chinese name is *ling zhi* or *ling chi*. It is sold in Chinese herb stores, dried, often whole. It looks lacquered.

Reishi belongs to a class of mushrooms called polypores. Many of them have been used for medicinal purposes. In China, *ling zhi* was first mentioned in medical texts more than 2,000 years ago. It was believed that one could bring the dead back to life by laying a tincture of reishi mushroom on the body's chest.

The medicinal use of other polypores is even more ancient. In 1991, Italian hikers in the Alps discovered the body of a man who had been frozen intact more than 5,300 years earlier. In his knapsack, there was a flint ax and a string of dried birch polypores (*Polyporus betulinus*, or *Piptoporus betulinus*). As mushroom scholar Paul Stamets writes in *Growing Gourmet and Medicinal Mushrooms,* "these polypores, like many others, can be used as tinder, for starting fires, and medicinally, in the treatment of wounds. Further, by boiling the mushrooms, a rich tea with anti-fatiguing, immunoenhancing, and soothing properties can be prepared."

At the time of Christ, notes Stamets, the Agaria of Sarmatia, a pre-Scythian culture, used a polypore to combat illness. Its use was passed on to the ancient Greeks. Dioscorides, a Greek-born surgeon in the Roman army who gathered nearly all the available knowledge of herbal medicine around 200 A.D., called it *agaricum.* (Its botanical name is *Fomitopsis officinale.*) Dioscorides, herbalist Christopher Hobbs notes in *Medicinal Mushrooms,* prescribed it for bruises, liver and kidney disease, hysteria, dysentery, asthma, colic, "wasting diseases" (probably tuberculosis), and hip pain.

Stamets writes, "Cultures from tropical Amazonia to the extreme northern sub-polar zones of Eurasia have discovered the power of polypores in preserving and improving human health."

Which brings us to reishi. Let's use the name *Ganoderma* for the moment. That way we won't just be referring to the Japanese mushroom, for *Ganoderma* is used in many cultures. Himalayan guides use a species of *Ganoderma* to combat altitude sickness. It is used in China for the same purpose. It works by increasing the level of oxygen in the blood. In one uncontrolled (read: not very reliable) study, Chinese mountain climbers who took *Ganoderma lucidum* before climbing peaks as high as 17,000 feet felt minimal effects.

The main effects, though, are immunological. *Ganoderma* is rich in polysaccharides, large sugar-bound molecules that stimulate immune function and may help fight cancer. These polysaccharides appear to stimulate the immune system's T cells. In mice fed carcinogens, one particular polysaccharide, D-beta-glucans, inhibits the formation of tumors. *Ganoderma* doesn't appear to kill cancer cells outright; rather, it appears to enhance immune response. *Ganoderma* also contains unique proteins that may stimulate immunity. Researchers suggest that rather than a one-directional immune-stimulating effect, *Ganoderma* exerts "immunomodulating" effects—that is, it helps the immune system function better. To be sure, there are no well-controlled human clinical studies yet.

Ganoderma also has cardiovascular effects. The Chinese consider it a heart tonic, though this reputation refers more to its mild sedative effect; it is calming. But *Ganoderma* also contains compounds, dubbed ganoderic acids, that thin the blood and lower cholesterol levels. A 1990 Chinese study with 15 healthy patients and 33 heart disease patients found that *Ganoderma lucidum* tea reduced blood platelet aggregation—it "thinned" the blood.

It may also lower blood pressure. According to pharmacological researchers at Oral Roberts University School of Medicine in Tulsa, Oklahoma, the blood-pressure-lowering effect of *Ganoderma* is related to its sedative effect: it mildly depresses the actions of the central nervous system. No wonder Dioscorides and ancient Chinese texts prescribe it to treat hysteria and anxiety.

Ganoderma is also anti-inflammatory and may inhibit allergic response. As one 1988 Japanese study published in *Agents and Actions* noted, "for centuries, *Ganoderma lucidum* has been used in Oriental medicine for the treatment of chronic bronchitis." In their study, the Japanese researchers reported, a sulfur compound found in the mushroom inhibited the release of histamine from mast cells in animals. It is histamine release that causes allergic reactions.

So we have a mushroom that may stimulate the response of the immune system in some cases and may simultaneously inhibit the allergic overresponse of the immune system that can cause allergic reactions. These effects have certainly not been conclusively established in humans, but if they are, what we have is a substance that tones the immune system. And that is one definition of a tonic.

Reishi may also reduce the tendency of blood to form artery-clogging clots, reduce inflammation, lower blood pressure, and calm. In animal studies, it is very safe. In one study of mice, for example, very large amounts taken for a month produced no adverse effects. However, large amounts of reishi can cause diarrhea in some people and allergic reactions in others.

Given that, I would suggest, if you want to try reishi, to use small amounts for no more than a month at a time. As Paul Stamets writes, "if a daily regimen of Ling Chi is followed, as little as 3–5 grams per person has been traditionally prescribed." In *Reishi Mushroom: Herb of Spiritual Potency and Medical Wonder,* Terry Willard writes that while 9 to 15 grams is used to treat heart disease, "3 to 6 grams a day is generally regarded [as] efficacious in everything from bronchial asthma to insomnia, hepatitis, nervousness and neurasthenia."

REISHI TEA

If you buy whole dried reishi mushrooms, break them into small pieces with your hands, then crush them to a fine powder in a spice grinder. They will turn into a fine, airy fluff. Twelve grams, the amount used in this tea, will fill about one and a half cups.

YIELD: **4** 1-CUP DAILY SERVINGS

12 grams (1½ cups) reishi powder

Bring 8 cups water to boil in a large pot.

Put the reishi powder in a small muslin bag (see page 198) and close the bag tightly. Drop it into the boiling water, and reduce the heat. (If you don't have muslin bags, just put the reishi into boiling water, let simmer as directed, then strain before drinking or refrigerating.)

Let the tea simmer until it is reduced by half, about 1½ hours. Drink 1 cup in the evening, and store the rest, tightly covered, in the refrigerator. It will keep refrigerated for a week.

Drink no more than 1 cup daily, reheated if you like, for no more than a month.

ROSEMARY

That's rosemary, that's for remembrance.
— Ophelia, in *Hamlet*

"Pray you, love, remember," says Ophelia, mad with despair. Hamlet has returned her letters, her ring. He says, "I did love you once." So she tosses rosemary leaves, which from ancient times have been reputed to strengthen memory.

More telling, rosemary is linked with sexual fidelity, which is, after all, a kind of memory. Traditionally, a bride wears a wreath of rosemary, often dipped in scented water. Rosemary is also traditional at funerals, where memory matters, too. Perhaps Ophelia was thinking of both kinds of ceremonies when she tossed the rosemary leaves.

In *Bancke's Herbal*, published in England in 1525, Richard Bancke prescribed rosemary flowers, leaves, and even the smoke and ashes of rosemary wood for readers wanting to "become light and merry," "have a fair face," ward off evil dreams and rotten teeth, prevent wine from souring, and remedy feebleness, gout-swollen legs, and breathing difficulties. Finally, he wrote, "Make thee a box of the wood of rosemary and smell to it and it shall preserve thy youth."

In particular, rosemary seems to have been recommended for the head. "Rosemary helpeth the brain, strengthening the memorie, and is very medicinable for the head," English religious eminence Roger Hacket wrote in *A Marriage Present,* a sermon published in 1607.

Modern herbals continue to praise it. In *Herbal Delights,* published in 1950, C. F. Leyel wrote that "a tisane of Rosemary will cure a nervous headache and has a beneficial effect on the brain. Its constant use will greatly improve a bad memory." Forty years later, in *The Practice of Aromatherapy,* French physician Jean Valnet, M.D., recommended rosemary tea for "physical and mental strain," as well as "migraine."

I wouldn't say that modern scientific studies confirm these uses, but they certainly make them more understandable. Rosemary oil, present in the plant's spiky, aromatic leaves, contains some of the most powerful natural antioxidants ever discovered. Some are many times more potent than the commercial synthetic antioxidants BHA (butylated hydroxyanisole) and BHT (butylated hydroxytoluene). Rosemary's antioxidants are also antibiotic. Applied topically to the gums, they kill many of the germs that cause gum disease.

In the body, rosemary's antioxidants may also keep the oils in our bloodstream from becoming rancid. This is called lipid peroxidation, and it refers to the tendency of blood cholesterol, especially LDL cholesterol, to be attacked by oxygen free radicals. Our bodies create these highly reactive forms of oxygen all the time. Dietary antioxidants such as those in rosemary render them harmless. When these defenses fail, however, and LDL cholesterol is oxidized, it begins to form plaque, clogging arteries.

This "oxidative stress" is also implicated in cancer. In one 1995 Japanese study published in *Planta Medica,* the researchers concluded, "Agents from the leaves of *Rosmarinus* were shown to be effective to protect biological systems against oxidative stresses."

Rosemary's antioxidants, which are in the same class (flavonoids) as protective compounds in tea (page 252), onions (page 211), red wine (page 301), and apples (page 15), also stimulate the liver to rev up its protective mechanism. They stimulate enzymes that detoxify poisons, including carcinogens. One study in animals found that a diet that contains 1 part of rosemary in 400 parts of food can "significantly enhance liver activities [of] . . . important enzymes for detoxification of carcinogens and xenobiotics." A xenobiotic is a foreign substance that the body must break down.

In animal models, rosemary turns out to be a strong inhibitor of cancer. "We don't know yet what the overall protective effect might be," says cancer researcher Allan H. Conney of Rutgers University in New Brunswick, New Jersey. "But we have found that compounds in rosemary oil inhibit chemically induced skin cancer." Other researchers have found that when added to the diet, rosemary compounds "inhibit chemically induced lung and breast cancer" in animals.

Another compound in rosemary oil is a strong anti-inflammatory agent. In recent years, scientists have realized that inflammatory processes play a large role in the development of atherosclerosis, the most common form of heart disease, which results in coronary artery disease and, in turn, in heart attacks. Rosemary oil's anti-inflammatory compounds also reduce the tendency of blood to form clots, a process that is related to inflammation.

To be sure, these findings come from lab and animal studies. To establish that rosemary is a preventive agent or a source of potential disease-preventive drugs, human studies are needed. As for now, the best one can say is that rosemary, an integral part of many Mediterranean diets, may be yet another protective component that makes that eating pattern so remarkably healthful.

But what about headaches? Reducing swelling in the legs? Becoming light and merry? Remembrance? Let's speculate for a moment. Headaches, that's easy. If rosemary thins the blood and prevents inflammation, it may be a useful antidote to the vascular kind of headache triggered by tension. As an anti-inflammatory, it could reduce swelling in legs afflicted by gout. As an antioxidant, it could protect wine from becoming "sour." We already know that rosemary oil can protect the teeth from bacteria that cause gum disease, although how burning rosemary into coals and rubbing them onto your teeth might work, as Richard Bancke prescribed, I'm at a loss to say. By reducing inflammation, rosemary may even help some people who have difficulty breathing, though not everyone. By stimulating the liver to break down toxins and harmlessly excrete them, rosemary may, finally, help keep us young and even help restore those who are feeble.

The final mystery is remembrance. Botanist James Duke has speculated that because many forms of dementia are caused by oxidative stress in the brain, rosemary's powerful antioxidants may help preserve brains from these memory-robbing diseases. Hence, rosemary for remembrance.

Personally, I think it has something to do with the scent. One doesn't mistake rosemary for basil, bay leaf, or even thyme. It is a heady aroma that stays in the nose, a boon to baked bread and broiled fish. In recent years, scientists have discovered that the nose contains nerve cells that communicate directly and immediately with the brain. This is one reason aromas are so emotionally powerful.

Strong, distinctive scents evoke strong associations, such as those that make strong memories. Someday we may even discover something in the aroma of fresh rosemary leaves that affects the brain in such a way that it wards off evil dreams.

In the meantime, we must satisfy ourselves with the realization that there may be more things in rosemary than are dreamt of in our philosophy.

ROSEMARY WALNUT BREAD

If you like a hard crust, whisk one tablespoon milk into an egg, and brush it lightly on the tops of the loaves before baking.

YIELD: 2 LOAVES

2 tablespoons (2½ ¼-ounce packages) active dry yeast
2 cups warm water (110 degrees)
¼ cup unsulfured molasses
¼ cup honey
¼ cup vegetable oil
1 tablespoon kosher salt
¼ cup chopped fresh rosemary, or 1½ tablespoons dried
1 cup chopped walnuts, lightly toasted
2 cups rye flakes
2½ cups whole-wheat flour
About 4½ cups all-purpose flour

In a large mixing bowl, dissolve the yeast in the warm water. Let it sit for 5 minutes; the yeast should begin to bubble.

In a small bowl, combine the molasses, honey, oil, and salt. Stir this combination into the yeast mixture.

Add the rosemary and walnuts, and then the rye flakes and whole-wheat flour, mixing well between each addition.

Gradually stir in about 3½ cups of the all-purpose flour. The dough should begin to come together but still be sticky.

Turn the dough out onto a well-floured surface. Work in as much of the remaining flour as the dough will take (use more if needed), kneading between additions until the dough is no longer sticky. Knead for about 5 minutes more, until the dough is smooth and satiny.

Wash out the large bowl, and coat it lightly with vegetable oil. Put the dough in the bowl and turn it so that it's coated on all sides with oil. Cover with a clean kitchen towel and it let sit in a warm place until the dough has doubled in size, 45 minutes to 1 hour.

Punch down the dough, and knead it 5 or 6 times to remove any air bubbles. Return it to the bowl, cover it with the towel, and let it rise until double again, about 1 hour.

Lightly oil 2 loaf pans. Punch down the dough, cut it in half, and shape it into 2 loaves. Put it in the pans, cover it with the towel, and let it rise for 20 to 30 minutes, until dough has risen near the rim of pan.

Meanwhile, put the rack in the center of the oven; heat the oven to 350 degrees.

Bake the bread for 50 to 60 minutes. The loaves will look browned at 45 minutes, but let them cook a bit longer so they will be cooked through to the center; tent them with foil to prevent overbrowning if necessary.

Turn the bread out onto a cooling rack. Serve warm or at room temperature. Extra loaves can be frozen, tightly wrapped, for up to a month.

ROSEMARY RUB

A batch of this flavorful rub is enough for two roasting chickens, eight quail or Cornish game hens, eight lamb chops, or a pan full of potatoes. For a hot variation, omit the sage, reduce the rosemary to about one-third cup, and add one-half cup of grated horseradish root (about a two-inch piece).

YIELD: ½ CUP

½ cup fresh rosemary needles (from 6 or 8 sprigs), coarsely chopped, or
    ¼ cup dried
½ cup fresh sage leaves (from 5 or 6 sprigs), coarsely chopped, or 2
    tablespoons dried
½ cup olive oil
4 garlic cloves, smashed, peeled, and coarsely chopped
¼ cup fresh thyme leaves (from 3 or 4 sprigs), or 2 tablespoons dried
1 teaspoon kosher salt
1 teaspoon freshly ground pepper
Zest of 1 lemon

Combine the rosemary, sage, and olive oil in a blender. Blend until smooth, stopping once or twice to scrape down the sides with a rubber spatula. Add the garlic and blend well. Add the thyme, salt, pepper, and lemon zest, and blend well.

Use immediately, or refrigerate, tightly covered, for up to a day.

HIBISCUS, ROSEMARY, AND CARDAMOM TEA

If you have a headache, try tea made with fresh rosemary sprigs, rich in anti-inflammatory oils. With antioxidants from the rosemary and hibiscus, it's quite healthful. Cardamom settles the stomach. Dried hibiscus flowers, also called sorrel, are available in many Middle Eastern and Latin American groceries.

YIELD: 4 CUPS

3 or 4 whole cardamom pods
⅓ cup (½ ounce) dried hibiscus flowers
1 large sprig fresh rosemary, coarsely chopped, or ½ teaspoon dried

Toast the cardamom pods in a dry skillet over medium-low heat for 2 to 3 minutes, until lightly toasted. Smash the pods open with the bottom of the skillet.

Combine the cardamom, hibiscus, and rosemary in a saucepan with 4 cups water. Cover and bring to a boil. Let it boil 1 minute.

Remove it from the heat, and let it steep for 5 to 10 minutes. Strain it into a teapot, and serve.

Variation

HIBISCUS, ROSEMARY, AND CARDAMOM SORBET: Stir ¼ to ½ cup sugar or honey and ⅓ cup fresh lemon or lime juice into a batch of hot tea. Let it cool to room temperature, and then chill. Process it in an ice cream maker according to manufacturer's instructions.

SCHISANDRA
(*Schisandra chinensis*)

> *I guess I'll go through life just catching colds and missing planes.*
> —Billie Holiday singing "Everything Happens to Me"
> by Matt Dennis and Tom Adair

"Taste this," Stephen Brown demands. He is half sitting on a stool, one foot braced under the counter of his herb store in Brewster, Cape Cod. He offers me a little dried reddish-black berry; it looks like a peppercorn. "It has all five Chinese tastes," he tells me. "That's why they call it five-flavor berry." It tastes peppery but without heat.

In Chinese medicine, taste is revered; it is understood as a signal to a food's effect on the body. Sweet nourishes. Bitter cools and detoxifies. Salt condenses, holding moisture in. Sour stimulates digestion. Spiciness warms. It is not a question of a food being healthy or not healthy but whether it is appropriate— for you right now. A well-balanced meal, which helps create a well-balanced eater, has all five flavors.

Imagine, then, how enthusiastically the Chinese embrace Schisandra, which contains all five flavors.

"This herb is widely used for its balanced energies and broad spectrum of therapeutic effects," writes Daniel Reid in *A Handbook of Healing Chinese Herbs*. "Schisandra has long been popular in Chinese households as an all-round sexual tonic and balanced energy rejuvenator for both men and women. It lends itself well to use in tonic longevity formulas."

Chinese medicine practitioners Harriet Beinfield and Efrem Korngold are effusive in their lovely book *Between Heaven and Earth: A Guide to Chinese Medicine.* Schisandra "fosters the generation and storage of *Essence,* awakening sexual potency and sensitivity," they write. "It calms the *Spirit.*" They recommend it for "chronic cough and asthma, insomnia, diarrhea, thirst, fatigue, sexual debility, and memory loss; it regulates blood sugar and assists recovery following prolonged fever and illness."

I can't attest to all these wondrous qualities, but I can tell you that Schisandra shows some quite promising scientific effects on the ability of the body to protect itself from toxins. The studies are in small animals, so from a conservative scientific standpoint, they aren't much to write home about. But when science reveals a physiological effect, even in mice, that conforms with the traditional use of a botanical, it's worthy of attention.

The studies have taken place at the University of California, Berkeley; the University of North Carolina, Chapel Hill; and at research facilities in Taiwan, China, Russia, and Japan. What scientists have found is that Schisandra contains substances called lignans that stimulate the liver to produce enzymes that break down toxins, including carcinogens. In a typical study, mice are fed Schisandra in pretty high amounts, such as 5 percent of their diet. Then these protective enzymes are measured. They go up. In one study, they went up 300 percent. The mice's ability to detoxify two carcinogens, one synthetic (benzoapyrene) and one natural (aflatoxin, a potent carcinogen found in moldy peanuts), goes up, too.

In a Chinese study, animal immune function that had been depressed by steroids came back to normal when Schisandra was added to the diet. In another study, it protected against potentially toxic effects of carbon tetrachloride, a carcinogenic chemical used in dry cleaning. The Japanese also report that it stimulates the liver to synthesize proteins, which may facilitate the repair of damaged liver tissue. No wonder the Chinese use Schisandra to treat hepatitis.

Whether this adds up to a sexual tonic is beyond me. But I wouldn't underestimate the powers of a well-functioning liver. When your body functions better, you feel better. When you feel better, you have energy. When you have energy, you may feel like sharing it with someone else.

At the very least, Schisandra, the five-flavor berry, is a safe herb that can help protect us from many of the poisons in this mortal world.

FIVE-FLAVOR TEA

Schisandra is a mild stimulant, certainly less so than coffee. In some people it can cause indigestion, so we have added licorice (page 199) and ginger (page 146) to our tea. This recipe makes enough for about two days. Refrigerate it in a tightly covered container, and drink it cold or rewarmed. A standard "dose" would be a half cup in the morning and another half cup in the afternoon or evening.

YIELD: 2½ CUPS

8 grams (about 1 tablespoon) dried whole Schisandra berries
4 sticks Chinese licorice, each cut into 4 pieces
1 ½-inch piece fresh ginger, coarsely chopped
Honey or brown sugar

Grind the Schisandra berries in a spice mill to a medium-fine powder.

Combine the powder in a saucepan with the licorice, ginger, and 5 cups water. Cover and bring to a boil over high heat.

Uncover the pan, reduce the heat to medium, and let the tea simmer until reduced by half, 15 or 20 minutes. Don't let it reduce more, or the bitter tones of Schisandra will become too strong.

Strain through a fine sieve into a teapot, add honey or sugar to taste, stir well, and serve.

Variations

FIVE-FLAVOR FENNEL TEA: Add 1 tablespoon lightly toasted and finely ground fennel seeds before cooking.

FIVE-FLAVOR CHAMOMILE TEA: Make a separate pot of chamomile tea with ¼ cup dried chamomile flowers and 3 cups boiling water; combine the two teas and drink warm or iced.

ICED FIVE-FLAVOR TEA: Combine 1 batch cooled Five-Flavor Tea, 2½ cups sparking mineral water, and freshly squeezed lemon juice and honey or brown sugar to taste.

FIVE-FLAVOR PINEAPPLE JUICE: Combine 1 batch cooled Five-Flavor Tea with 2½ cups pineapple juice, and serve over ice.

SHIITAKE
(Lentinula edodes)

"The shiitake is the sexiest mushroom," exotic mushroom importer John Gottfried once told writer Jane Merrill. Cut off the stem, paint it with a little olive oil, broil it until the gills are crisp, he said, and it's like "nibbling on an earlobe."

In Japan, lentinan, a large sugar-bound molecule (polysaccharide) isolated from shiitake mushrooms, is used to treat cancer.

Somewhere between these two approaches, we may form our opinion.

In medical circles, primarily in Japan, lentinan has been well studied. It appears to stimulate the immune system, especially in people who are ill. It boosts interferon production, which fights flu viruses.

It boosts levels of natural killer cells, which help suppress tumors. In animals, both injections and oral administration of lentinan suppress the ability of carcinogens to cause cancer.

In Japan, lentinan is often given to cancer patients undergoing chemotherapy to support the immune system. In one randomized, controlled trial, 275 patients with stomach cancer were given chemotherapy with or without lentinan injections. In patients who had never had chemotherapy before and did not have complications, lentinan treatment had positive effects on immune function and modestly prolonged life.

Lentinan also appears to support the function of T cells. The HIV virus attacks T cells, so there has been clinical interest in using lentinan to treat patients at risk of, or already suffering from, AIDS. Some hospitals use lentinan along with the anti-AIDS drug AZT to retard secondary infections. "We found that the drug was fairly well tolerated," says Donald Abrams, M.D., of the University of California, San Francisco. In Dr. Abrams's trials, lentinan appeared to improve immune function, such as CD-4 count (a crucial measure of immune competence), in several AIDS patients, but, he notes, it's too early to tell how effective it might be.

Because drying the fruit body of shiitake (the mycelium) both preserves and concentrates lentinan, a preparation called LEM (*Lentinula edodes* mycelium extract) is sometimes used in Japan as an adjunct to treatment of hepatitis B and tuberculosis. Tablets made from the dried water-extract of shiitake mycelium, standardized as to lentinan content, are available in health food stores. They're not magic, but they may be useful to take for a month or more if you find you are suffering from frequent colds and flu.

Shiitake mushrooms are a wonderful food. Cooking, which breaks down their tough cell walls, makes the protein more digestible. Like beans, shiitakes' amino acid profile neatly complements those of grains. Rice and shiitakes make a complete protein. Cooked shiitakes are also a rich source of B vitamins. If you substitute these chewy, meaty mushrooms for beef in your stir-fry, you are almost certainly improving your health.

Whether you are doing more is unclear. It's not that shiitake doesn't contain medically marvelous compounds. It does. But no one has done the exacting research to determine whether we absorb significant enough quantities to enhance our health when we add a few ounces to our meals. You would have to eat a huge amount of mushrooms to get the amount of lentinan used in cancer research. And you wouldn't want to do that, because too much can actually suppress immune function.

One reasonable assumption is that regularly eating a normal amount of shiitakes may lower blood cholesterol. That's a function of another compound they contain called eritadenine, and here we do have human studies. In young Japanese women, as little as a third of an ounce (9 grams) of dried shiitake mushrooms, eaten every day for a week, lowered blood cholesterol 7 percent. In another study, eating 90 grams of fresh shiitake (about 3 ounces) a day for a week lowered total blood cholesterol 12 percent. Fresh and dried shiitake also have been found to lower blood cholesterol in people over 60.

Normal amounts of shiitakes may have other benefits, too. One study found that a compound in cooked shiitake (thiazolidine-4-carboxylic acid) can prevent the formation of potentially carcinogenic nitrites in the stomach. Says Bill Breene, a University of Minnesota food scientist who has reviewed the literature on these mushrooms, "If you eat shiitake on a regular basis, it could prevent cancers from occurring."

That sounds sexy to me.

FRESH SHIITAKE SUSHI

I make only vegetarian sushi at home; I trust neither my fish store nor my eyes enough to try it with raw fish. Look for bamboo sushi-rolling mats in Japanese, gourmet, or health food stores. You can make delicious sushi without one; it just won't be as neat. This is a fun meal to prepare with a group of friends. Buy "sushi rice," a special kind of sticky short-grain rice, in health food stores or Oriental markets, and prepare it according to the package directions.

YIELD: ABOUT 20 PIECES

2 tablespoons wasabi powder (green horseradish)
6 ounces fresh shiitake mushrooms (about 16), stems reserved for
    another use
2 tablespoons mirin (Japanese sweet cooking wine)
2 tablespoons rice wine vinegar
3 cups cooked sushi rice
5 or 6 sheets of preroasted nori, about 6½ inches square
Pickled Ginger (page 154)
Low-sodium tamari soy sauce

Put the wasabi powder in a small bowl, and stir in just enough water to make a thick paste. Cover and refrigerate.

Place an oven rack 2 to 4 inches from the heat source, and turn on the broiler.

Cut the shiitake caps into ¼-inch slices, and arrange them in a single layer on a rimmed baking sheet. Sprinkle them with mirin and vinegar, and toss to coat. Spread them out again in an even layer.

Broil the shiitakes for 6 to 8 minutes, turning them halfway through. Don't let the slices burn or shrivel. Transfer them to a plate to cool.

Spread out a bamboo rolling mat or set out a large cutting board on a work surface. Place the sushi rice, a shallow pan of cool water, and a roll of paper towels nearby.

Soak a sheet of nori in the water until just dampened, about 15 seconds. Pat it dry with a paper towel, and spread it flat on the rolling mat or cutting board.

Scoop up about ½ cup rice and spread it out on the center 3 inches of the nori. Dampen your fingers and use them to spread the rice as evenly as possible. Spread about ⅓ cup mushrooms along the center of the rice.

With the line of rice and shiitake parallel with you, roll up the nori in the rolling mat or on the cutting board as tightly as you can. Dampen the nori a bit if necessary to make the roll stick. Cover the roll with plastic wrap and refrigerate. Repeat until all the ingredients are used.

To serve, use a very sharp knife to cut each roll into 4 pieces. Arrange on a platter, along with the reserved wasabi and Pickled Ginger. Pour soy sauce into small bowls, and dip away.

SPICY SHIITAKE DUMPLINGS

When you serve these, everyone will want one, then another, then the recipe. The dumplings are also excellent steamed and added to Traditional Miso Soup (page 264). You can add shredded cabbage, water chestnuts, or hot peppers to the filling. If you have a large bamboo steamer, you can cook all the dumplings in one batch.

YIELD: ABOUT 20 DUMPLINGS

2 teaspoons olive oil
1 2-inch piece fresh ginger, peeled and minced (¼ cup)
6 or 7 garlic cloves, smashed, peeled, and minced (¼ cup)
4 to 6 scallions, trimmed and minced (¼ cup)
3 ounces fresh shiitake mushrooms, caps minced (about 1¾ cups) and
    stems reserved for another use
½ medium red bell pepper, cored, seeded, and diced in ¼-inch pieces (⅓
    cup)
Kosher salt and freshly ground pepper
½ cup packed fresh mint leaves
½ cup packed fresh cilantro leaves
½ teaspoon sesame oil
20 to 22 square wonton wrappers
¼ cup low-sodium tamari soy sauce
Juice of 1 lemon

Heat the oil in a skillet over medium-high heat. Sauté the ginger and garlic, stirring, until the garlic is soft, 3 to 5 minutes.

Stir in the scallion, shiitake, and bell pepper. Cook, stirring, until the shiitake softens, about 5 minutes. Add ½ teaspoon more olive oil if mixture begins to stick. Season to taste with salt and pepper.

Transfer to a medium bowl. When cool enough to handle, stir in the mint, cilantro, and sesame oil.

Set out the filling, wonton wrappers, and a small bowl of water on a work surface. Line a baking sheet with parchment paper.

Spread out one wrapper, and place about 1½ teaspoons filling in the center. Wet your index fingers, and run them around the edges of the wrapper. Fold the wrapper in half to form a triangle. Press the edges together to seal the dumpling; remoisten if necessary to form a tight seal. Set the dumpling on the baking sheet, wipe the work surface dry, and repeat until all the filling is used.

The dumplings may be covered with plastic wrap and refrigerated for a day, or packed between layers of wax paper in an airtight container and frozen for up to 2 weeks.

To cook the dumplings, put a steamer insert in a Dutch oven or large, deep skillet. Add enough water to reach just below the bottom of the steamer, cover the pot, and bring the water to a boil.

Meanwhile, combine the soy sauce and lemon juice in a small dish to make a dipping sauce, and set it aside.

When the water boils, reduce the heat to a high simmer. Using tongs, arrange as many dumplings as you can in the steamer without letting them touch. Cover and steam until the dumplings are transparent, about 5 minutes. Transfer them to a large serving platter, cover to keep warm, and steam the rest of the dumplings. Serve with the dipping sauce.

SOBA NOODLES WITH LEMON-SHIITAKE SAUCE

Substitute rice noodles if you prefer, or omit the noodles and serve the sauce over brown rice. Save the shiitake stems in a plastic bag in the freezer, and add them the next time you cook stock.

YIELD: **4** FIRST-COURSE SERVINGS OR **2** GENEROUS MAIN-COURSE PORTIONS

Kosher salt
1 8.8-ounce package of soba noodles
3 tablespoons canola or olive oil
8 garlic cloves, smashed, peeled, and finely chopped
½ pound fresh shiitake mushrooms, caps thinly sliced, stems reserved
    for another use
1 lemon, zested and juiced
1 to 2 tablespoons low-sodium tamari soy sauce
¼ cup white wine, chicken broth, or water
Freshly ground pepper
A sprinkle of hot red pepper flakes (optional)
1 teaspoon sesame oil (optional)
2 or 3 scallions, trimmed and thinly sliced lengthwise

Bring a medium pot of water to a boil, and add ¼ teaspoon salt. Cook the noodles, stirring occasionally, until just al dente, 4 to 6 minutes. Drain, rinse with cool water, and set aside.

Heat the oil in a large skillet over medium-high heat. Reduce the heat to medium, and sauté the garlic, stirring, until tender, 2 or 3 minutes. Don't let it get too brown.

Add the shiitakes and cook, stirring occasionally, until soft and shiny, about 5 minutes. Stir in the lemon zest, soy sauce, and wine. Add the reserved noodles, and stir just until warm through. Stir in the lemon juice, pepper to taste, and pepper flakes if using. Drizzle on the sesame oil if using. Sprinkle with sliced scallions, and serve.

WILD MUSHROOM SOUP

Herbalist Jacqueline Sa recommends combining fresh shiitakes with the more concentrated energy of dried ones for balance. If you can't find or afford chanterelles or other fresh wild mushrooms, replace some or all of them with common white button mushrooms. This savory soup is healthful for anyone anytime. We've built more immune-boosting power into the variations; as always, if you have a medical condition, get the help of a qualified health professional, and ask about using a tonic soup in your regimen.

YIELD: 8 1-CUP SERVINGS

1 1-ounce package dried shiitake mushrooms
8 ounces (about 20) fresh shiitake mushrooms
1 pound assorted fresh wild mushrooms such as chanterelles, hen-of-the-woods, oyster, trumpet, or cremini
2 tablespoons olive oil
3 large garlic cloves, smashed, peeled, and minced
1 heaping tablespoon chopped fresh thyme leaves
1½ teaspoons balsamic vinegar
¼ cup Basic Vegetable Stock (page 271), Nam Singh's Tonic Chicken Soup (page 270), low-salt canned broth, or water
1 heaping tablespoon chopped fresh flat-leaf parsley
8 ounces soft tofu, drained and cubed (optional)
Kosher salt and freshly ground pepper

Bring 6 cups water to a boil. Put the dried shiitakes in a large bowl, pour on the boiling water, and let them soak for 30 minutes.

Meanwhile, wipe the fresh shiitakes clean with a paper towel, reserve the stems for another use, and thinly slice the caps. Wipe the wild mushrooms clean, trim the stems, and thinly slice them.

Heat the oil in a soup pot over medium-low heat. Sauté the garlic, stirring occasionally, until transparent, 3 to 6 minutes. Add all the fresh mushrooms and thyme. Sauté, stirring often, until the mushrooms have released all their liquid, about 8 minutes. Stir in the vinegar, stock, and parsley, and simmer 5 minutes.

Meanwhile, transfer the dried shiitakes to a colander (reserve the soaking liquid), and rinse to remove any grit. Remove and discard the woody stems. Slice the caps into very thin strips, discarding any hard center bits, and add them to the pot.

Strain the soaking liquid into the pot through a very fine sieve or a strainer lined with dampened cheesecloth.

Bring the soup to a simmer, and cook for 20 minutes for flavors to blend. Add the tofu if using, and heat just until warm. Season to taste with salt and pepper.

Variations

IMMUNE-BOOSTING, BLOOD-THINNING WILD MUSHROOM SOUP: At the beginning of your soup preparations, soak 1 ounce dried tree-ear mushrooms (page 273) in 3 cups boiling water for 30 minutes.

Meanwhile, rinse and coarsely chop ¼ ounce dried reishi mushrooms (page 228), and simmer them, uncovered, in 4 cups water for 30 to 45 minutes, until liquid has reduced to 1 to 1½ cups.

While the soup is simmering for the final 20 minutes, transfer the swollen tree-ear mushrooms to a colander and rinse to remove any grit. Strain the soaking liquid into the soup pot through a very fine sieve or a strainer lined with dampened cheesecloth. Puree the mushrooms in a food processor, and add to the pot.

Strain the reishi broth into the soup, and discard the mushrooms. Proceed with the recipe as directed.

STRONGER IMMUNE-BOOSTING WILD MUSHROOM SOUP: At the beginning of your soup preparations, combine 6 to 8 sticks astragalus (page 24), ¼ cup ligustrum (page 29), and 4 cups water in a saucepan. Cover, bring to a boil, reduce heat to a simmer, and cook for 45 minutes to 1 hour, until the liquid has reduced to 1 to 1½ cups.

While the soup is simmering for the final 20 minutes, strain the cooking liquid into the pot through a fine sieve, and discard the astragalus and ligustrum. Proceed with the recipe as directed.

SPINACH
(Spinacia oleracea)

Spinach . . . is . . . more nourishing than other vegetables.
  —Maud Grieve, *A Modern Herbal,* 1931

Spinach, with its delicate, curly leaves in deep shades of green, has fascinated nutritionists for decades. No wonder: a cup of chopped, raw spinach leaves has only 12 calories. That cup cooks down to a few tablespoons, yet it supplies 1.5 grams dietary fiber, a modest step toward a daily goal of 25 to 35; 16 milligrams vitamin C, about a quarter of the U.S. RDA; a modest amount of vitamin E; and 108 micrograms of folic acid, more than half the U.S. RDA and about a quarter of the 400 micrograms the government recommends daily to prevent birth defects.

Not to mention colon cancer: in a recent Harvard study of about 10,000 men and 16,000 women, those who consumed the highest amount of folic acid were, respectively, 29 and 35 percent less likely to test positive for colon or rectal cancer than those who got the least amount. (The nutrient may also help prevent heart disease, stroke, and perhaps even depression; see "Folic Acid," page 130).

Spinach's iron (1.5 milligrams) and calcium (56 milligrams) are not inconsiderable, but you can't have them. These minerals are bound up in a form that makes them relatively unavailable. If you're a vegetarian who doesn't consume dairy products, you'd best rely on broccoli, beans, soy products, and, perhaps, a calcium supplement (see "Calcium," page 45).

The nutrient most strongly represented in spinach is vitamin A, or rather carotenoids, including beta-carotene, which the body converts to vitamin A. (Only animal flesh supplies preformed vitamin A.) That cup of raw spinach alone supplies 36 percent of one's daily needs. Vitamin A is needed for normal cell growth and development, keeping skin smooth, and preventing night blindness. Spinach may protect eyesight, too, but this has hardly anything to do with vitamin A. Or even beta-carotene.

Today, the most common cause of blindness in people over 65 is a condition called macular degeneration. The macula is in the center of the retina in the back of eye. In some people, it gradually breaks down with age, making vision blurrier and blurrier and ultimately destroying it altogether. Medical science can't do much to help, but spinach can.

If you eat spinach and similar greens such as kale, collard, mustard, and turnip greens two to four times a week, your chance of developing macular degeneration is 46 percent less than if you eat them only once a month or less. If you eat greens five times a week or more, your chance of getting it falls by 86 percent. Those were the findings of the Eye Disease Case-Control Study, which compared 356 men and women over the age of 55 diagnosed with age-related macular degeneration with 520 age-matched men and women who didn't get the disease. It was reported in the *Journal of the American Medical Association* in 1994.

At first glance, beta-carotene seemed to be protective, but when the researchers teased apart the carotenoids, it was two others that stood out: zeaxanthin and lutein.

In the delicate anatomy of the eye, the macula plays a crucial role. It is a tiny yellow spot located at the center of the retina, where visual perception is most acute. What turns the macula yellow are two pigments: zeaxanthin and lutein.

The zeaxanthin-lutein yellow pigment helps the eye filter out visible blue light, which can cause damage to the delicate tissues of the retina. The cornea and lens nearer the outside of the eye can filter out ultraviolet light, with the help of various antioxidants, including vitamin C, E, and beta-carotene. Some studies find that people who eat more fruits and vegetables rich in antioxidants have lower rates of cataracts, which is a clouding of the cornea due to ultraviolet light damage. So eating a plant-based diet may help protect against cataracts. (So does wearing sunglasses and a hat with a brim.)

Even when the cornea and lens filter out ultraviolet light, however, blue light still sneaks through to the retina. There, the macula's yellow pigment catches it. Without enough lutein and zeaxanthin, however, the macula can't do its job; it falls victim to the power of blue light, which destroys cells.

"It seems prudent," the researchers concluded, "to concur with the recommendation of increasing the consumption of vegetables in the diet, and, in particular, to include dark green, leafy vegetables that are rich in lutein and zeaxanthin."

Lutein, which is also found in such leafy cruciferous vegetables such as collard greens, mustard greens, turnip greens, and kale, may do more than protect the eyes. In Chile in 1995, researchers looked at 61 men with lung cancer and 61 men without. The men who remained free of lung cancer ate more spinach. They also ate more Swiss chard, beet (perhaps including beet greens—the study doesn't say), chicory, and cabbage.

In Honolulu, also in 1995, researchers at the Cancer Research Center of Hawaii at the University of Hawaii, tried to figure out why lung cancer rates are lower in Fiji than elsewhere in the South Pacific. They found that cigarette smoking explained 61 percent of the difference in lung cancer rates between individuals and that dietary intake of lutein explained another 14 percent of the difference. They concluded, "These ecological data provide evidence for a protective effect of lutein against lung cancer."

If you go to a health food store, you can probably find a pill that contains lutein. But the folly of relying on supplements rather than whole foods was well illustrated by a study conducted at Iowa State University in Ames, Iowa, and published in the *American Journal of Clinical Nutrition* in 1995. The researchers gave lutein, beta-carotene, or both to eight volunteers and then measured blood levels. When the subjects were given lutein, blood levels of beta-carotene declined in five but went up in three. When they were given beta-carotene, blood levels of lutein went down. It is not entirely clear what is going on, although the researchers remarked that "carotenoids clearly interact with each other during intestinal absorption, metabolism, and serum clearance."

Let us, then, respect our ignorance. We don't know enough about these phytochemicals yet to design a pill that will have reliable effects. I'm not sure we ever will. But we do know—and epidemiological studies show—that people who eat more plant foods, such as spinach, are healthier.

Eating whole foods has synergistic advantages. For example, the fiber in spinach helps us fill up. In a 1995 study published in the *International Journal of Food Science and Nutrition,* Swedish researchers gave ten healthy male volunteers mixed meals. Some had spinach, others didn't. The total calories were the same, as were the amounts of carbohydrates, protein, and fat. Those who ate the most spinach felt the most full, and their blood sugar levels were better regulated. Spinach's fiber, the researchers concluded, was responsible.

So let's eat spinach, along with its dark green cousins, a few times a week. Even if scientists could come up with a supplement that had all its health-promoting benefits, it wouldn't taste nearly as good.

SIZZLED SPINACH

The trick to this French style of cooking spinach is to keep the pan very hot. Spinach is full of water, which prevents it from being scorched. The entire dish takes five minutes to prepare. Make it just before you are ready to eat, so it goes straight from pan to mouth.

YIELD: **4** SERVINGS

2 10-ounce bags fresh spinach (or 1¼ pounds loose)
1 tablespoon olive oil
2 garlic cloves, smashed, peeled, and minced
1 teaspoon balsamic vinegar

Trim and discard the stalk ends of the spinach, and roughly tear the leaves. Swish the spinach around in several changes of cold water until all the sand and grit are removed. Set aside in a colander to drain.

Heat the oil in a large, heavy, nonstick skillet over high heat until hot but not smoking. Add half the spinach and sauté, stirring, until wilted, about 2 minutes. Transfer to a plate, and cook the remaining spinach the same way.

Pour off excess liquid, and add the first batch of spinach back into the pan. Stir in the garlic, and sauté 1 minute. Stir in the vinegar, sauté 30 seconds, and serve immediately.

SPINACH-WATERCRESS GOMAE

Watercress, slightly chewy and peppery, combines well with the smoother, sweeter spinach in this classic Japanese dish.

YIELD: **2** OR **3** SERVINGS

1 10-ounce bag (or bunch) of fresh spinach, stems trimmed
1 small bunch watercress, stems trimmed
2 tablespoons white sesame seeds, toasted
1 tablespoon sugar
2 tablespoons low-sodium soy sauce

Bring a large pot of water to a boil.

Meanwhile, rinse the spinach and watercress in several changes of cool water until all the sand and grit are removed.

Blanch the greens in the boiling water for 1 or 2 minutes. Drain, rinse with cold water to stop the cooking, and drain again. Squeeze dry, and chop into ½-inch pieces.

Grind the sesame seeds with a mortar and pestle or in a small blender. Stir in the sugar and soy sauce, toss with the greens, and serve.

LEAFY GREENS CONGEE

Congee, a long-simmered, easily digested rice soup, is standard breakfast fare in China and other Asian nations. Here, spinach cooks right in the congee, preserving its vitamins. Try it with a touch of soy sauce. You can simmer the rice in a Crock-Pot, or cook it in a pressure cooker in 45 minutes or so.

YIELD: **8** ONE-CUP SERVINGS

1 cup long-grain white rice
8 ounces spinach, mustard greens, Swiss chard, or beet tops, stems
    removed
Kosher salt to taste

Combine the rice and 8 cups water in a large pot. Cover, and bring to a boil. Reduce the heat to a simmer and cook until the rice has broken down and the water is thick with starch, about 3½ hours.

Rinse the greens to remove sand or grit. Pat dry, and cut into ½-inch strips. Add to the rice, and simmer for 15 to 20 minutes. Salt to taste. Serve warm.

TEA

Tea is different.

For coffee (page 87), the questions have been whether too much increases heart attack risk and whether some kinds of coffee brews raise cholesterol levels. The answers have been reassuring, but no one is seriously suggesting that coffee benefits health, beyond improving one's mood.

For tea, the question is this: How beneficial is it?

New benefits keep accruing. In March 1996, Dutch researchers who have been following more than 500 men ages 50 to 69 for 15 years reported that those who drank more than 4.7 cups of tea a day had a 69 percent lower risk of stroke than those who drank less than 2.6 cups daily. The tea of choice among these men was black, but green tea may be even more protective.

One theory holds that it is the drinker, not the tea, who makes the difference. Tea drinkers tend to be more health conscious. Coffee drinkers, especially heavy coffee drinkers, are more likely to smoke and to drink more alcohol. A 1994 study from the Institute for Social Medicine at the University of Vienna Medical School illustrates the point. Researchers looked at 2,400 men and women between the ages of 25 and 64. Those who regularly drank coffee were more likely to smoke, eat more meat and sausages, and drink lemonade (who knows?) than those who regularly drank tea. Conversely, those who drank more tea were more likely to eat more fresh fruit, drink juice or mineral water, and walk to work.

As a coffee drinker myself, I hasten to repeat that moderate coffee consumption has been found to have psychological benefits and minimal or no health risks. But I also drink tea, especially green tea. When I drink it, I am usually calmer, which isn't surprising: given standard brewing time, a cup of black tea has only about a third the caffeine of an average cup of coffee, and green tea has even less.

Which raises an interesting philosophical question: Am I a different person when I drink tea? Are you?

We needn't delve into epistemology and social medicine, however, to explain tea's benefits. Epidemiology and material medicine will do just fine.

Tea and coffee drinkers may indeed be different, but in recent years it has become clear that tea itself has powerfully protective compounds. They are called flavonoids. They are in green, oolong, and black tea. Flavonoids are natural antioxidants that may protect against heart attack, stroke, and coronary heart disease, as well as certain cancers.

Flavonoids have existed in nature for more than a billion years. They are pigments; they turn tea green or tan. They contribute red, yellow, and orange colors to fruits, vegetables, and flowers.

In plants, flavonoids protect against solar radiation; they are natural sunscreens. So it is not surprising that when applied topically to animals exposed to ultraviolet radiation, they protect against skin cancer. Some researchers have suggested that tea compounds be added to topical sunscreens for people, too, as well as to cosmetics and shampoos. Perhaps this is already being done. But there is another possibility: drinking tea. Animals given tea compounds in their diets—the equivalent of about four cups of tea for a human—also had less skin cancer.

As a class, flavonoids are generally strong antioxidants and protect low-density lipoprotein (LDL) cholesterol in the bloodstream from being attacked by oxygen free radicals, highly reactive forms of oxygen that can damage many different kinds of cells. LDL is the "bad" cholesterol that can form artery-clogging plaque. But it is only when LDL cholesterol is damaged by free radicals that it becomes toxic to arterial cell walls. Anything that protects LDL from oxidation may, in theory, protect against coronary heart disease. Many flavonoids do this.

Flavonoids, including those in tea, also inhibit blood clotting. They are "platelet aggregation inhibitors." By "thinning" the blood and making it less likely for clots to form, flavonoids and the tea that contains them prevent the most common kind of stroke, as well as heart disease. A number of studies have found that people who eat plenty of fruits and vegetables have a markedly reduced risk of stroke. Until recently, most researchers chalked this up to potassium, but now many believe the real benefactor may be flavonoids. Tea's flavonoids may also lower blood pressure. Many flavonoids are strongly protective against cancer as well.

In the Dutch stroke-prevention study, tea provided about 70 percent of the flavonoids in the diet. Tea, mostly green tea, is the major source in Japan, too. But in the United States, as well as Greece and the former Yugoslavia, the major contributors are fruits and vegetables, mainly apples (page 15) and onions (page 211). In Italy, 40 percent of the flavonoids come from red wine (page 301).

How many flavonoids you have in your diet may play a role in how likely you are to develop cardiovascular disease. Consider a 1995 study published in the *Archives of Internal Medicine* that looked at flavonoid intake in the Seven Countries Study. One of the world's longest epidemiological research projects, the Seven Countries Study has looked at the diets (among other things) and disease rates of people in the United States, Japan, Finland, Holland, Greece, Italy, and the former Yugoslavia over nearly 30 years.

It turns out that flavonoid intake among these countries varied by a factor of almost 30. It was lowest in western Finland, averaging 2.6 milligrams per day, and highest in Ushibuka, Japan, averaging 68.2 milligrams per day. Holland was in the middle at 25 milligrams. Those differences explained about 8 percent of the difference in the coronary heart disease rate among the countries. Smoking explained another 9 percent. Saturated fat intake explained 72 percent. So drinking tea may not do you much good if you use it to wash down your cheeseburger.

If you consume few foods rich in flavonoids, however, increasing your intake may have dramatic effects. In Finland, with the lowest intake of flavonoids, a 1996 study looked at more than 5,000 men and women from 30 communities over 25 years. Among men, those with the highest dietary intake of flavonoids were 69 percent less likely to die from coronary heart disease in that quarter century. Among women, risk was reduced 76 percent. Consumption of apples and onions explained nearly all the difference in risk.

Tea's specific flavonoids have come in for some serious study. Green tea has one set, black tea another. But each kind acts similarly. Green tea is made from raw dried tea leaves. Oolong tea is partly fermented. Black tea is fully fermented. Fermentation causes oxidation, so some of the antioxidant flavonoids in black tea are spent in processing.

This means that green tea has more antioxidant flavonoids; the major flavonoid in green tea makes up 20 to 30 percent of its dry weight. In recent years, it has been established that the specific flavonoids in black tea are also quite effective in preventing heart disease and, perhaps, cancer. To my mind, green tea has a slight edge, but black tea is also a pretty healthful brew.

The cancer story is still evolving. In the lab, the flavonoids found in tea are effective cancer-protective agents. They protect against the kind of DNA damage that can initiate the cancer process. They inhibit a class of liver enzymes (phase I) that can turn potential carcinogens into actual carcinogens, and they enhance another class (phase II) that turn potential carcinogens into inactive forms. They block the transformation of nitrates into carcinogenic nitrosamines. In a few lab studies, tea extracts have actually shrunk existing tumors.

In Japanese studies, the main flavonoid in green tea prevents tumor promoters and the hormone estrogen from interacting with receptors in breast cancer cells. Human studies reveal that tea's flavonoids are absorbed, according to researchers at the Department of Science and Dietetics at the University of Nebraska in Lincoln, so their beneficial effects would be expected not only in the lining of the colon, where they come into direct contact, but everywhere in the body.

In the Seven Countries Study, there was no consistent relationship between tea or flavonoid consumption and the risk of cancer. A few new studies, however, are finding a link. In a 1995 study of more than 35,000 postmenopausal women in Iowa, tea drinkers tended to have less cancer of the stomach, throat, and kidney. Daily tea consumption reduced mortality from these cancers by 50 percent.

A 1993 Japanese study found that green tea consumption reduced the risk of gastric cancer. A 1993 Polish study found that lifetime consumption of tea reduced risk of pancreatic cancer. A 1994 Chinese study found that green tea protects against esophageal cancer in women; the more tea the women drank, the lower their risk. A 1994 Swedish study found that while black tea drinking didn't affect colon cancer risk, it reduced rectal cancer risk by 44 percent. Finally, a 1996 Chinese study, which compared 711 subjects with stomach cancer with 711 people who were cancer free and followed them for 27 months, found that people who drank green tea were at lower risk. Drinking as little as a cup of freshly brewed green tea a week for six months or longer was linked with a 30 percent lower risk of stomach cancer.

Drinking tea after a meal, as the Chinese do, may have special benefits. At the Institute of Nutrition and Food Hygiene of the Chinese Academy of Preventive Medicine in Beijing, researchers gave three volunteers several kinds of tea and studied how effective they were at inhibiting the conversion of nitrates into carcinogenic nitrosamines. Green tea was 89 percent effective; black tea, 87 percent; jasmine tea, 85 percent; oolong, 82 percent; and sun-dried tea, 62 percent. The effect was most pronounced when volunteers drank their tea after a meal rather than before. You might think of the practice as bathing your stomach in protective compounds.

On the other hand, the Western habit of adding lemon to black tea isn't such a bad idea, either. Black tea has more tannins, and tannins can interfere with the absorption of minerals such as iron and calcium. In studies at the University of Wisconsin, adding lemon to black tea made both minerals more bioavailable; the vitamin C in the lemon made the minerals more soluble and absorbable.

Tea has a few other benefits. It inhibits bacteria, including the bacteria that cause cavities. In 1994, Japanese researchers studied the effects of oolong tea, which is partly fermented and thus somewhere between green and black tea, on 35 volunteers, ages 18 to 29. They were told to refrain from all oral hygiene for four days, except a mouth rinse. On some days, the rinse had oolong tea extract; on other days, it did not. Oolong significantly inhibited plaque deposits. A Chinese study found that green tea had the same effect; one would expect that black tea would, too. In addition, tea of all kinds contains fluoride, which, of course, also protects teeth from cavities.

Tea also significantly inhibits bugs that cause diarrhea, including the cholera bacteria (*Vibrio cholerae*) and several salmonella bacteria, which cause food poisoning. Tea has been found to inhibit the influenza virus, too. Tea's tannins, by themselves, also treat diarrhea.

So it is not surprising that a cup of tea is the first thing we think of when we feel poorly. Gastroenterologists sometimes recommend the BRATT diet for people with diarrhea: banana, rice, applesauce, tea, and toast. The banana and applesauce replace lost potassium. Rice and toast supply easily digested carbohydrates. Tea's tannins treat diarrhea and may kill the stomach bugs that made you sick in the first place.

BANCHA LEMONADE

Food historian William Wos Weaver writes that one of the most popular punches in eighteenth-century America was made with five ingredients: lemon or lime juice, rum, water, sugar, and green tea. The concoction, with or without rum, is delicious. It also tastes good with orange pekoe tea or gunpowder tea, which is a fine grade of green tea.

YIELD: **2** 2-CUP SERVINGS

4 tea bags bancha green tea or ½ ounce loose tea
2 tablespoons sugar, or to taste
¼ cup plus 2 tablespoons fresh lemon juice
2 sprigs fresh mint (optional)
Rum (optional)

Combine the tea and sugar in a teapot. Bring 2 cups water to a boil, pour into the teapot, and stir to dissolve the sugar. Cover and let steep for 10 to 15 minutes.

Remove tea bags (strain if using loose tea), and add the lemon juice. Add mint and rum to taste if using. Serve warm, or chill and serve over ice.

THYME

Jim Duke wakes me up early to see the frost flower before it melts. Jim, a botanist who retired after 25 years with the U.S. Department of Agriculture, is an inspiration. For decades, without official support, he has been building a database of science and folklore about food; he's a bridge between the communities of science and alternative health. I've come to his six-acre Maryland farm to interview him about some of the issues that will eventually help to form this book.

On this particular late winter morning, we hike to a county park after breakfast to find *Cunila origanoides*, a.k.a. mountain dittany. It secretes water so that in a frost a delicate ice collar, like the ruffle on a Lalique crystal clown, forms around the stem. Jim picks up a frost-flower stem, crushes it, and hands it to me.

The smell is unmistakable: wild thyme.

"It's got thymol in it, the same ingredient that's in thyme," he explains. Thymol is antiseptic; in the lab, it inhibits staph bacteria. It's also an expectorant and a tracheorelaxant—that is, it relaxes the muscles of the throat. So it's not surprising that thyme tea has been used for hundreds of years as a remedy for a sore throat or nagging cough.

In Germany, thyme preparations are often prescribed for whooping cough and emphysema. Culpeper, a popular seventeenth-century English herbalist, said of thyme, "It purgeth the body of phlegm." In 1931, English herbalist Maud Grieve recommended thyme tea for "wind spasms," colic, and whooping cough.

Thyme is antispasmodic—it relieves spasms—so it makes sense that thyme tea is also used to relieve menstrual cramps. It is also anti-inflammatory; Jim drinks thyme tea when his lower back flares up.

Thyme also contains strong antioxidants, primarily phenolic compounds including quercetin that display an extraordinary cancer-protective capacity in animal studies (see "Onion," page 211). In German studies, thyme extract stimulates an increase in the human immune system's white blood cells.

Still holding the frost flower between his fingers, Jim says, "There's also some carvacrol [a phenolic compound] in that flower; the two compounds tend to run in tandem and have similar effects, though not necessarily by the same mechanism. I have a hunch that one part of carvacrol and one part of thymol may be better than two parts of just one. That's the synergy concept."

Whole plants, rather than isolated "active ingredients" you might buy in a "guaranteed potency" herb supplement, often contain compounds that have similar effects. Chinese herbal formulas often contain more than one botanical with similar actions; the synergistic combination may produce a benefit with fewer side effects.

By the same token, whole foods contain hundreds of antioxidant carotenoids that may work together to create a more balanced and potent antioxidant effect than single isolated compounds such as beta-carotene taken in a pill (see "Carrot," page 51).

THYME TEA

Sometimes simple is best. We tried many combinations of thyme and other herbs and spices, only to find that thyme, by itself, makes the best tea. Try it if you have a cough, a cold, a backache, menstrual cramps, or if you just want to flood your body with natural cancer-protective antioxidants. The tea becomes so rich after long simmering that it also makes an excellent soup base or risotto stock.

YIELD: 4 CUPS

1 bunch fresh thyme (about 1½ ounces)

Combine the thyme and 6 cups water in a saucepan. Cover and bring to a boil. Reduce heat to a high simmer and cook, uncovered, about an hour, until liquid has reduced to 4 cups. Strain, and drink hot.

TOFU

I have a lovely little red-covered book with tofu recipes. It's called *Shojin Cooking: The Buddhist Vegetarian Cook Book,* and it was published in 1977 by the

Buddhist Bookstore in San Francisco. It lets me make all the foods I love to order in Japanese restaurants: cold spinach (oshi-tashi), simple buckwheat noodle dishes, and, especially, tofu.

Mixing tofu with vegetables is the thriftiest form of tofu cookery, the little red book says, because by using broken or crushed pieces, one can make "tempting fried or steamed dishes even from those things that might be thrown away."

How frugal, humble, philosophical. My desires are more gustatory, however: I want to cook the way these recipes sound. Cooking tofu this way may be good for my soul, and eating it is unquestionably good for my body, but I want to learn because I like the way it tastes when it is prepared well.

Tofu, "meat without the bones," is a remarkable food. It contains a balance of amino acids that makes it a nearly perfect protein source. Although soybeans are difficult to digest, tofu—made by fermenting ground soybeans—is quite readily digested. When we eat tofu, our stomach produces less acid than it does when it digests, for example, beef.

Tofu contains some fat, but 80 percent of it is unsaturated. Each three-ounce serving contains about three grams of the omega-3 alpha-linolenic fatty acid, which, like fish oils, reduces the tendency of blood to clot.

Tofu is a good source of iron, and it is much more bioavailable than the iron in other soy products. When made with calcium salts, as most tofu is, it is also rich in bioavailable calcium. Tofu is a good source of dietary fiber, magnesium, copper, zinc, and manganese as well.

Tofu became big news in the summer of 1995 when a study published in the *New England Journal of Medicine* demonstrated the cholesterol-lowering effect of soy protein. In a statistical analysis of previous research, a so-called meta-analysis, the researchers found that consuming an average of 47 grams (about 1½ ounces) of pure soybean protein lowers blood cholesterol an average of a little over 9 percent. That's a lot of soy—the equivalent of 1½ cups of tofu a day—but it got plenty of press.

The main reason for excitement over soy foods, though, is that they are a potent source of isoflavones, natural plant hormones also called phytoestrogens. These may lower cholesterol (see the discussion of diosgenin in "Dioscorea," page 105) and protect against cancer, particularly breast cancer (see the discussion of daidzin in "Kudzu," page 189).

Tofu is especially rich in isoflavones in a form the body can use. A 1994 study of phytoestrogen levels in various soy foods conducted at Tufts University School of Medicine in Boston found that tofu had by far the highest levels. Soy milk had less but still had significant amounts. (Soy-based formulas, the kind sold to adults as nutritional supplements, had no detectable levels. Zip.)

The fermentation process that creates foods such as tofu may increase its usefulness. In one 1995 study, University of Minnesota researchers gave 17 men about four ounces of either soybeans or tempeh, another fermented soy food. Although tempeh has lower levels of isoflavones than plain cooked soybeans, the researchers found that the men who ate it had much higher levels of a marker chemical for isoflavones in their urine. "This finding suggests that fermentation increases availability of isoflavones in soy," they concluded. Other traditional fermented soy foods, including soy sauce, natto, and miso, have demonstrated cancer-protective properties in lab and animal studies.

One isoflavone called genistein can, at high doses, inhibit nascent tumors from developing a blood supply. So it may have potential as a cancer drug or even as a preventive drug for people at high risk of cancer. At much lower levels—one-tenth the level needed to prevent new blood vessel growth—genistein inhibits an enzyme that promotes the development of cancer. This enzyme, tyrosine protein kinase, is between five and ten times more active in cancer cells than in normal cells. Inhibiting it helps potential cancer cells become normal cells. This may be genistein's main dietary contribution to cancer prevention.

These plant hormones are similar to human hormones, although weaker. In premenopausal women, they may latch onto estrogen receptors, effectively lowering levels of estrogen. Excess estrogen, particularly specific kinds of estrogen, is associated with increased risk of a common kind of breast cancer. In animal studies, soybeans can prevent breast cancer. In Japan, where breast cancer rates are much lower than in the United States, the consumption of soy foods of all kinds is much, much higher.

"The exciting thing to me is, based on the epidemiological studies, there are an impressive number that suggest that one serving of a soy product a day is enough to lower cancer risk," says Mark Messina, who left his job as a National Cancer Institute researcher to study and write about soy foods and vegetarian diets. "There aren't many instances where one serving of a food decreases cancer risk."

Soy foods may protect not only against breast cancer but also against other hormonal cancers, such as prostate, Messina notes. "The hypothesis about prostate cancer is very attractive, but there are not a lot of data. If I had prostate cancer, I'd be eating soy every day, but as a professional, I can't say there are enough data to prove it would be beneficial." (Tofu consumption has also been linked with lower rates of nonhormonal colon and rectal cancers, perhaps through the enzyme-inhibiting mechanism already noted.)

Besides having low breast cancer rates, Japanese women seem relatively free from the hot flashes and other symptoms that many American women experience during menopause, when production of estrogen rapidly declines. This is the flip side of these plant hormones: though weaker than human estrogens, they may serve as a kind of dietary estrogen replacement therapy (ERT). As one study put it, "in postmenopausal women, endogenous circulating estrogen concentration declines by about 60 percent, compared with premenopausal levels. Therefore, the likelihood of estrogen receptors being unoccupied is enhanced. Isoflavonoids of dietary origins may occupy these sites, thereby increasing total estrogens available to these women." By locking onto estrogen receptors, these plant estrogens free human estrogens to circulate in the bloodstream. A higher level of circulating estrogens may mean fewer symptoms and, perhaps, less risk of, for example, osteoporosis.

Messina doesn't find the research so far on soy foods and menopause conclusive, but he notes that animal studies show that soy foods may stop bone breakdown, another consequence of postmenopausal estrogen loss. "Over the course of a lifetime," he says, the phytoestrogen in soy "may be significant."

The isoflavones as well as the protein in soy may benefit the heart. They may modestly lower cholesterol while inhibiting the oxidation of LDL cholesterol and stimulating "vasodilation"—that is, opening up the blood vessels, potentially lowering blood pressure. Says Messina, "Phytoestrogens in soy may mimic the beneficial effects of estrogen on cardiovascular disease."

Messina is a big promoter of soy foods, but he is cautious about the emphasis on phytoestrogens and, indeed, the entire field of "phytochemicals"—compounds in foods that may affect health. "When you take phytochemicals out of plant foods, there's the possibility that they may be harmful," he says. "The main reason I feel comfortable promoting soy is that it is not meat. It is part of a plant-based diet. It's a good food from a nutritional standpoint. And one serving a day—one half cup of tofu, a cup of soy milk—may prevent certain diseases."

Soybeans have been a food staple in Japan for about a thousand years and in China for two millennia. The medicine, as one scientist once wrote about wine, already exists in highly palatable form. We needn't pop it in pill form, or add powders to our drinks, or consume faux meat products to benefit from soy. Fermented, it is more nutritious and, perhaps, contains more bioavailable protective compounds.

It wouldn't surprise me to learn that the way tofu is traditionally cooked and how it is served with other foods may play a role in its healthfulness. My little red *Shojin* book doesn't concern itself with achieving a certain number of grams of soy protein in order to lower cholesterol. Nor are there tofu cheesecake recipes, or creamy tofu dips, or tofu ice creams. Rather, the recipes begin with tofu, season it with fermented soy foods such as soy sauce, miso, and natto, and serve it in small amounts with a wide variety of vegetables, greens, and rice.

Whole foods, produced by traditional methods and developed over hundreds or thousands of years as part of culinary traditions that in turn developed slowly, may protect health in ways we can spend the rest of our lives trying to understand.

How to Drain Tofu

My *Shojin* book, which, unfortunately, is out of print, recommends this very effective way of removing excess moisture from tofu. You can use paper towels in place of cloth toweling:

Leave the tofu on a wooden chopping board placed at a slant for 30 to 40 minutes. Much of the water will run off. If in a hurry, place a clean dry towel over the tofu and weight it with a medium-sized dish.

Take the tofu from the chopping board, place it in a finely woven cloth, and squeeze out the remaining moisture. Knead gently so as not to force the tofu itself through the cloth. Stop when the water being pressed out becomes milky white.

TOFU AND FRESH SPINACH SOUP

If you can find spinach with the stems or, better yet, the roots, wash them well and toss them into this classic Chinese soup.

YIELD: 4 TO 6 SERVINGS

1 pound soft tofu
10 ounces fresh spinach
2 tablespoons fermented black beans or salted black beans with ginger
Sesame oil

Rinse the tofu, and drain it as directed in the preceding section. Cut it into ½-inch cubes.

While the tofu is draining, swirl the spinach around in several changes of clean water until all the sand and grit are removed. Put it in a colander, give it a final rinse, and set it aside.

Combine the beans and 6 cups water in a soup pot. Cover and bring to a boil. Reduce to a simmer. Remove the beans with a slotted spoon and discard. (If a few are left floating around, that's fine.)

Stir the spinach and tofu into the broth. Simmer just until the spinach has wilted and tofu is warm, about 5 minutes.

Drizzle with sesame oil, and serve.

TOFU AND BOK CHOY STIR-FRY

YIELD: 2 TO 4 SERVINGS

1 pound firm tofu
2 tablespoons canola oil
5 garlic cloves, peeled and sliced thinly lengthwise
1 3-inch piece fresh ginger, peeled and sliced thinly lengthwise
1 pound bok choy, trimmed and cut into 1½-inch pieces
½ teaspoon kosher salt
16 cherry tomatoes, halved
1 teaspoon low-sodium tamari soy sauce
Sesame oil

Rinse the tofu, and drain it as directed. Cut it into ½-inch cubes.

Pour the oil into a wok or large skillet. If using a wok, swirl the oil around to coat the sides. Heat the oil over medium-high heat for a minute or two, until hot but not smoking.

Sauté the garlic just until soft, about 30 seconds; scoop it out with a slotted spoon, and reserve.

Add the ginger and bok choy, and sprinkle it with salt (use more or less to taste). Cook, stirring, until the bok choy softens, 3 to 4 minutes. Add the tofu, tomato, reserved garlic, and soy, and cook, stirring, for 3 or 4 minutes more, until juices have thickened. Drizzle with sesame oil, and serve with rice.

TRADITIONAL MISO SOUP

There are two main varieties of miso: white and red. White miso is lighter, sweeter, and more often used in summer soups. Thicker, saltier, punchier red miso is traditionally used for winter soups. Don't let the miso come to a boil; it will deaden the flavor. Look for kombu, a sea vegetable, in health food or Japanese markets. (If you can't find it, you can make the soup with Shiitake Broth; see the variation that follows.)

YIELD: 4 TO 6 SERVINGS

8 ounces soft tofu
1 sheet kombu, about 7 by 4 inches, cut into 1-inch strips
3 tablespoons red miso paste
3 scallions, cut into 2-inch lengths and thinly sliced lengthwise

Rinse the tofu, and drain it as directed. Cut it into ½-inch cubes.

While the tofu is draining, combine the kombu and 6 cups water in a saucepan, and let it soak for 10 minutes. Put the miso in a small bowl.

Cover the saucepan, and bring the water just to a boil over high heat. Immediately scoop out and discard the kombu.

Reduce the heat to a simmer, and add the tofu. Cook gently for a minute or two. Pour ½ cup of the soup over the miso, and stir until well combined. Pour the lightened miso paste into the saucepan, and reduce the heat to just below a simmer. Add the scallions, and heat through, 2 or 3 minutes. Serve hot.

Variation

FOR SHIITAKE BROTH: Empty a 1-ounce package of dried shiitakes into a large bowl, cover them with 6 cups boiling water, and let them soak for 30 minutes. Scoop out the mushrooms, rinse them to remove any grit, and drain. Remove and discard the woody stems, and slice the caps into thin strips, discarding any hard center bits. Strain the broth through a very fine sieve or a strainer lined with dampened cheesecloth, and use it in place of the kombu broth in the preceding recipe. Add the sliced shiitakes to the soup with the scallions.

VERMONT SOY MILK

Soy milk isn't tofu, of course, but a cup of it contains about as many isoflavones as a half cup of tofu. Drink this on a cold day, and you can almost see the snow fall when you look out the window. On a hot day, omit the spices and serve it cold.

YIELD: 1 SERVING

1 cup soy milk
2 teaspoons maple syrup
Dusting of ground cinnamon, nutmeg, and cocoa powder (optional)

Combine the soy milk, maple syrup, and spices, if desired, in a saucepan, and heat until steaming. Serve immediately.

TOMATO

Lycopene turns tomatoes red. It also protects against cancer.

It's a carotenoid, in the same family as beta-carotene, which turns carrots orange. Color matters. So does taste. Those tasteless, pale pink winter tomatoes have hardly any lycopene.

Lycopene is showing up in pills in health food stores: another trap.

The best way to get lycopene is the old-fashioned, grandmotherly way: cook tomatoes, with a touch of olive oil, into a richly aromatic sauce.

Studies find that lycopene is the most powerful antioxidant in the carotenoid family; it is turning out to be one of the most effective cancer-protective compounds in our diet. When you go out in the sun, lycopene protects your skin from the oxidative damage of solar rays. In mice given carcinogens, adding lycopene to their chow prevents mammary tumors. Lycopene consumption has also been associated with reduced risk of cancer of the bladder, stomach, colon, and rectum.

But it is in the prostate that lycopene may be most protective. This should not be surprising. Lycopene is the primary carotenoid in the testes.

At the end of 1995 in the *Journal of the National Cancer Institute,* researchers at the Harvard University School of Public Health reported on a study of prostate cancer involving 48,000 men. From a scientific viewpoint, it was the best kind of study: prospective. The researchers started with healthy men, had them fill out dietary questionnaires, and then observed them over six years. Then the researchers compared the dietary data of the 773 men who developed prostate cancer to the data of the men who did not. This kind of study eliminates the bias that can creep in when you ask people with a disease what they used to eat that may have made them sick.

The Harvard researchers looked at 46 fruits and vegetables. One food, the tomato, and one compound, lycopene, stood out as protective. The four most protective foods were tomato sauce, tomatoes, pizza, and strawberries. (Strawberries, like other aromatic berries, are rich in ellagic acid, a powerful cancer-protective compound.) Men who ate at least seven servings a week of tomatoes, tomato sauce, tomato juice, or pizza had 20 percent less risk of getting prostate cancer. Those who ate ten servings or more a week had a 45 percent lower risk.

If you want to prevent prostate cancer, the best dietary tack is to cut back on saturated fat. It's a proven contributor. Saturated fat is found primarily in fatty meats, such as ribs and bologna.

The next most important thing to do is to eat more tomatoes. Ripe ones, to get lycopene. Cooked ones, so your body can use it. "Cooked is best," says Edward Giovannucci, M.D., lead author of the Harvard study. "The strongest association was with cooked tomato foods, such as tomato sauce."

In 1992, German researchers looked at the link between dietary sources of lycopene and blood levels. They tested tomato juice, and tomato juice boiled in 99 parts of water and 1 part corn oil. Two to three days later, blood levels in volunteers who drank cooked tomato juice rose to their peak levels; in those who drank uncooked juice, blood levels didn't increase at all.

The reason: cooking breaks down tomato cell walls, releasing lycopene. Oil absorbs it. "Lycopene is fat soluble," says Dr. Giovannucci. "So cooking ripe tomatoes in oil is ideal for absorbable lycopene." That's one reason we use olive oil in our Fresh Tomato Sauce. Of course, I'd probably have added it anyway.

FRESH TOMATO SAUCE

Make this with the freshest vine-ripened tomatoes you can find. When tomatoes are cheapest and most plentiful, make large batches and freeze the extra in 1- or 2-cup containers; it will keep well for 6 to 8 months. You can modify this simple sauce at serving time by, for example, adding sautéed garlic and pine nuts.

YIELD: **2** QUARTS

5 pounds fresh, ripe tomatoes, rinsed and coarsely chopped
2 tablespoons olive oil
Kosher salt and freshly ground pepper

Heat the tomatoes and olive oil in a large soup pot over medium-high heat. Stir occasionally until the tomatoes begin to release their juices.

Stir in ¼ cup water, and reduce the heat to the lowest possible level. If your soup pot is not heavy, a flame tamer, a metal device that sits on top of a burner, is a good idea to keep the heat low and even.

Cook, stirring occasionally and skimming off the foam that rises to the surface. The cooking time will depend on the juiciness of the tomatoes. Taste the sauce after about 3 hours; if it's still watery, continue cooking until it thickens to your liking. Season to taste with salt and pepper.

Process the sauce in batches in a food mill fitted with a medium disk. Serve over pasta, or use in recipes calling for tomato sauce.

Variations

FOR TOMATO SOUP: Season the sauce with a sprinkling of fresh dill, rosemary, or tarragon. Alternatively, add ½ teaspoon of Curry Powder (page 283) for every 2 cups sauce.

FOR CREAMY TOMATO-RICE SOUP: Add ½ cup cooked rice and ½ cup skim milk for every 2 cups sauce.

FOR COLD TOMATO SOUP: Add ½ cup low-fat yogurt for every 2 cups sauce, and puree in a food processor or blender.

TONIC SOUP

When I was researching this book, people kept telling me to talk to Nam Singh. If you are interested in Chinese tonic herbs and the traditional Chinese use of food as medicine, they said, he's the one.

Christopher Hobbs, an herbalist in Capitola, California, told me. So did Vietnamese-born Chinese herbalist Jacqueline Sa, who runs a small spa in Mill Valley, just north of San Francisco, where Nam Singh sometimes teaches. Harriet Beinfield, an acupuncturist in San Francisco, gave me his number. In *Between Heaven and Earth: A Guide to Chinese Medicine,* she and her husband, Efrem Korngold, write, "Countless herbal meals were shared with Nam Singh, who initiated us into the tradition of cooking Chinese medicinal food."

So I called him.

He was busy, he said, but he could make a little time. Our appointment was at noon. I rang the bell of his modest apartment near Golden Gate Park in San Francisco. The door opened, and I stared. I couldn't help it: before me stood a tall African-American man wearing clothes that resembled Chinese silk pajamas. He had an Oriental wisp of a beard on his chin, but his skin was a deep purple black.

He smiled, beckoned me inside, and offered green tea.

"My background is from East and West Africa," he explained. "My grandfather, who was Ethiopian, emigrated to Taiwan, where he studied Chinese medicine and took over a doctor's practice. He introduced me to Chinese medicine. My most formative years were living with him in Taiwan."

I sat in his living room for nearly four hours. He showed me foods and herbs, delicious and strange things, roots and mushrooms and dried caterpillars. He talked in a sweet, mellifluous, earnest, and at times mischievous way. The essence of his message: listen to your body, be aware of your environment, and simplify, simplify, simplify.

Chinese food theory is much less restrictive than many food-health systems Americans have embraced, such as macrobiotics, Nam Singh said. The Chinese classify foods as relatively yin or yang—hot or cold, damp or dry. In general, Americans eat too much meat and so are overstimulated, or "hot," he said. (Still, when we look to Chinese herbs for help, we often choose stimulating, heating ginseng—the last thing in the world most of us need.) "In our culture, the more the better. We are obese. We are overambitious. Even our vegetables are too big. Smaller carrots taste sweeter."

What you need at a particular time, he said, depends on how you are. If you are weak and cold, you need strengthening and heating foods, such as ginseng. If you are strong and hot, you need cooling, detoxifying foods, such as steamed greens.

Our food needs depend on our external as well as internal climate, he said. In the summer, we need to eat less and to eat lighter, even more cooling foods, including raw foods. But raw foods are hard to digest, so adding a digestive herb such as ginger to a salad is a good idea. In the fall, warm salads and braised, roasted, and stewed foods are called for; in the winter, stewed, boiled, slow-cooked foods are best.

Few of us truly nourish our essence, he explained. We don't eat with the seasons. "In the spring, make yourself a soup of sprouted grains, such as sprouted wheat and barley, with mung beans and fresh bok choy, napa cabbage, young greens such as dandelion greens. Put in a little lettuce for a nice flavor. Put in young vegetables."

We eat foods that don't nourish, so we have cravings. We may be overstimulated, hot, so we crave ice cream. But this doesn't cool the body down as a truly cooling food would. We try to gratify ourselves with foods, but they are empty, so they don't satisfy. Empty foods create empty persons.

"The Chinese call these 'ghost people,'" Nam Singh said. "They have cravings but no body. It's like a child who has never been hugged."

Most of the time, we forget the most basic lesson: eat simply. "Moderation is key. Use meat as a condiment, as a flavoring, along with vegetable proteins."

We eat too much, we exercise too little, and perhaps we drink too much, maybe even smoke and can't quite quit yet, and we don't feel great. So we try to add something. If we are constipated, we take laxatives; if we are retaining water, diuretics; if we have sinus congestion, decongestants; headaches, analgesics. If we are "holistic," we may simply replace these conventional medicines with over-the-counter herbal nostrums: echinacea for colds, senna for laxatives, corn silk for diuretics, Chinese ephedra for sinus congestion. But senna is a strong, irritating laxative; ephedra can raise blood pressure; and echinacea gives the immune system only a temporary boost.

What we need most is less, Nam Singh said—not addition but subtraction. One can find this principle in traditional healing systems throughout the world: to heal, give your body a small amount of simple, light, easily digested food. For example, David Frawley, a Vedic scholar who has translated many ancient Indian texts from Sanskrit into English, writes in *Ayurvedic Healing* that "most remedial measures in Ayurveda are generally of a *sattvic* (harmonious) nature." This includes a pure diet, with raw or freshly cooked vegetarian food, pure air and water, and proper exercise "of a calming nature."

"Everything you put in your mouth has a purpose," Nam Singh said. "Chinese tonic foods are preventive. Ginger, black [shiitake] mushrooms—they are preventive. The Chinese have a highly developed soup knowledge. There are thousands of recipes that deal with soup."

Tonic soups are very simple; often, the only seasoning is a little salt, perhaps some ginger. They don't include heating spices such as garlic or chili powder. To prepare to take a tonic soup, Nam Singh said, "you need to gear your eating program so that you are receptive," especially in the 24 hours before eating the soup. "Eat simply—steamed foods or stir-fried with a little oil, but nothing too invigorating."

You can use Nam Singh's Tonic Chicken Soup or the Basic Vegetarian Stock, which follow, as a model for any tonic soup. Better yet, once you understand the Chinese principles of food and health and the individual personality of foods, you can practice "medicinal" cooking without tonic herbs, Nam Singh said. Astragalus, codonopsis, black fungus (shiitake), *Ganoderma* (reishi), and other tonic herbs are helpful in balancing a body, he said, but they can only augment diet, not replace it. Food is the place to start and, perhaps, the place to finish. "You don't need herbs. Food itself is medicinal. Food is the best way to get control over health, over destiny."

NAM SINGH'S TONIC CHICKEN SOUP

This soup can be refrigerated for up to three days or frozen for up to three months.

YIELD: 8 CUPS

4 whole chicken legs
1 cup kosher salt
1 3-inch piece of fresh ginger, peeled and thinly sliced

Trim and discard the skin and fat from the chicken legs. Cut through the joint that separates the thigh from the drumstick.

Put the chicken in a large, nonreactive bowl, and cover it with the salt. Use your fingers to pack the salt all over the chicken, and let it sit for 10 minutes to draw out blood and impurities.

Meanwhile, heat 14 cups water in a large stockpot over high heat.

Rinse the chicken under cool water to remove all the salt. Add it to the stockpot along with the ginger. Cover and let it come to a boil. Uncover the pot, reduce the heat to medium low, and add any tonic herbs (see the variations that follow). Simmer for 2 to 4 hours, occasionally skimming and discarding any foam.

Strain the stock and discard the solids. Use it right away, or let it cool to room temperature before refrigerating or freezing.

Variations

TO BOOST ENERGY: Add ½ ounce American ginseng, which is less stimulating than Chinese or Korean, and 8 to 10 sticks astragalus. Though both are "chi tonics," Nam Singh says they balance each other.

TO IMPROVE DIGESTION AND THE ASSIMILATION OF NUTRIENTS: Add 8 pieces (about 1 cup) tree-ear mushrooms (page 273), soaked until pliable and then cored; 8 1-inch pieces dioscorea (wild yam, page 105); 1 cup polygonatum (*Polygonatum sibiricum*); 1 tablespoon Lycium berries (page 86); and 1 cup shredded fresh kelp or ½ cup dried kelp, soaked and rinsed.

TO BOOST THE IMMUNE SYSTEM: Add 2 cups fresh shiitake mushrooms, stems and caps separated; 8 to 10 sticks astragalus; 1 large *Ganoderma* mushroom (reishi); ½ cup white fungus; and ½ ounce cordyceps. (Cordyceps, a caterpillar, bears a fungus that the Chinese believe boosts energy—they give it to their Olympic athletes. I couldn't bring myself to cook with it, but if you are more adventurous than I, go right ahead.)

BASIC VEGETABLE STOCK

Use the stock as is in any soup recipe, or use one of the herbal variations described in the preceding recipe.

YIELD: ABOUT 8 CUPS

1 bunch parsley, washed
2 celery stalks, washed and roughly chopped
2 medium carrots, scrubbed and roughly chopped
2 small onions, peeled and roughly chopped

Trim the leaves from the parsley, and save for another use. Put the parsley stems, celery, carrots, and onions in a stockpot with 10 cups water.

Cover and bring to a boil. Reduce heat to medium high. If you are using tonic herbs, add them now. Continue to cook for 30 minutes.

Working in batches, puree the soup in a food processor or blender. Strain, and discard the solids. Use immediately, or cool to room temperature and refrigerate for up to 3 days or freeze for up to 3 months.

CHICKEN SOUP FOR A COLD?

Consider the ideal liquid for a cold sufferer. It should do no harm; it should comfort, relieve symptoms, restore fluids, nourish. If the patient is dehydrated, potassium and sodium would restore electrolytes. Even better if our liquid nourishes the recovering body with calories, with carbohydrates for energy, with easily digested proteins, and with minerals. Antioxidant vitamins—including the hero of holistic cold relief, vitamin C—can't hurt. A warm, salty broth might soothe a sore throat. Steam would open up nasal passages.

This tonic we imagine—this warm, salt-seasoned, potassium-rich, water-based, steamy, soothing, nourishing broth—is, of course, chicken soup. In the twelfth century, the Jewish philosopher Maimonides recommended chicken soup for the common cold. It's a folk cure in Eastern Europe, a "Jewish penicillin" that has followed Jews in diaspora from Tel Aviv to Miami.

Solid scientific evidence for poultry-based nostrums is scarce. It's hard to attract grant money, after all, to fund a double-blind study for symptomatic relief of a condition that goes away without treatment, usually in a week or less. What there is, though, is promising. In the late 1970s, Marvin Sackner, M.D., a pulmonary specialist in Miami Beach, tested cold patients at Miami Beach's Mount Sinai Medical Center. Compared to cold water, chicken soup hastened the "velocity" of mucus expulsion, the study found. But then, so did hot water.

More recently, Irwin Ziment, M.D., who specializes in pulmonary medicine and teaches at the University of California, Los Angeles, has found more evidence for chicken soup's decongestant properties. Cysteine, an amino acid from chickens that's in the soup, is similar chemically to acetylcysteine, which is prescribed for bronchitis; indeed, the drug was originally derived from chicken skin and feathers. It "thins" mucus.

The spices many cultures add to chicken broth add to this effect. Hot chili peppers (page 61), curry, mustard, and horseradish all irritate nose, throat, and bronchial passages slightly, making tissues "weep," according to Dr. Ziment. Garlic (page 135) is another well-known expectorant. In India and Mexico, hot, pungent spices are a standard therapy for respiratory congestion. In Russia, you are likely to be given warm water with horseradish and honey for a cold.

So don't knock chicken soup. It can't stand up to penicillin, but then, nobody has ever really put it to a fair test. With carrots, celery, onions, parsley, perhaps turnips or rutabagas, even greens, some rice or matzo balls, it's got a lot of balanced nourishment—especially for people with colds, who may not be up to eating a full meal.

If you have a cold or a stuffy nose from allergies, add hot spices such as hot chili peppers, as well as plenty of garlic, to Nam Singh's Tonic Chicken Soup. You can also use the soup, which is really a broth, instead of water in Bronchitis Broth (page 67).

TREE-EAR MUSHROOM
(Auricularia polytricha)

Tree ears are the thin, black, crinkled, chewy mushrooms you sometimes find in hot-and-sour soup.

They thin the blood—that is, they are anticoagulants, or, to use more technical language, they inhibit the aggregation of platelets. When you cut yourself, disklike platelets in your blood aggregate, or clump together, to stop the bleeding.

The saturated fats in meat, dairy, and other foods make it easier for platelets in the blood to stick together, promoting heart disease. So for most of us, thinning the blood is a very good idea.

Tree-ear mushrooms are also called black tree fungus, wood-ear mushrooms, and, in Chinese transliteration, *mo-er* mushrooms. In *The Thousand Chinese Recipe Cookbook,* Gloria Bley Miller says each one resembles a "convoluted flower" or a "well-shaped ear." They were once called Judas's ears; legend holds that they appeared on the tree from which Judas hanged himself after betraying Christ.

In 1749, the famous Swedish botanist Linnaeus wrote in his *Materia Medica* that these mushrooms are good for treating angina—the pain that often accompanies heart disease.

When the blood-thinning attribute of tree ears was first reported in the *New England Journal of Medicine* in 1980, it got attention. The mushrooms thin the blood as effectively as aspirin. They contain adenosine, a blood-thinning compound also found in onions and garlic.

A few years later, researchers reported in the journal *Thrombosis and Haemostasis* that even when tree-ear mushrooms are chemically treated so they contain no adenosine, they still inhibit blood clotting in animals. "Mo-er extracts contain an agent (or agents) in addition to adenosine that blocks platelet aggregation," they wrote. We may speculate, once again, that whole foods contain ingredients that act synergistically in ways that isolated compounds don't.

In *Spontaneous Healing,* Andrew Weil, M.D., recommends that if you want or need to thin the blood, a "reliable dose" of dried tree-ear mushrooms would be a tablespoon, measured after soaking. If you are taking anticoagulants, talk to your doctor first.

Recent studies have revealed blood-thinning effects from shiitake mushrooms as well (see page 240). Although shiitakes are only about 15 percent as effective as black tree-ear mushrooms, we tend to eat a lot more of them.

White tree fungus (*Auricularia auricula*), a close cousin of black tree ear, also contains blood-thinning adenosine. White tree fungus has another worthwhile attribute, too: it contains polysaccharides that inhibit cancer in animals.

The soup we have developed contains black tree-ear mushrooms and shiitake. It also contains tofu, which is a good source of alpha-linolenic acid, a plant-based omega-3 fatty acid that also thins the blood. So this is a good soup to have if you are concerned about your cardiovascular health.

The idea of making soup with rock sugar may seem odd at first, but the result is subtle and light. One food-as-medicine cookbook we consulted called this kind of traditional Chinese soup "double lucky." Considering the potential benefits of black tree-ear and shiitake mushrooms, we can guess why.

LUCKY-HEART SOUP

Rock sugar, which is cooked to an amber shade, is not as sweet as regular granulated sugar. It's often used in Chinese dishes.

YIELD: 4 SERVINGS

⅓ ounce (10 grams, about 9 pieces) tree-ear mushrooms
2 ounces (about 5) fresh shiitake mushrooms
3 tablespoons rock sugar
1 scallion, trimmed and thinly sliced
4 ounces silken tofu, cut into ½-inch cubes

Put the tree-ear mushrooms in a large bowl, and cover them with 4 cups boiling water. Let them soak for about 30 minutes.

Meanwhile, wipe the shiitakes clean. Remove the stems and save them for another use; cut the caps into ¼-inch slices, and set aside.

Remove the tree-ear mushrooms from the water, and rinse them to remove any clinging bits of dirt or grit. Cut the mushrooms into ¼-inch pieces, cutting around the hard, woody center stem. Discard the hard centers.

Strain the soaking liquid into a saucepan through a very fine sieve or a colander lined with dampened cheesecloth. Add the tree-ear and shiitake mushrooms and the sugar. Cover and bring to a boil. Reduce the heat to a simmer, and cook, partially covered, for 30 minutes.

Add the scallion and tofu, heat just until warmed through, and serve.

TUNA

Fresh tuna, marinated in soy sauce, lime juice, and ginger and grilled rare, is one of my favorite foods.

It's a clean food. Tuna are deep ocean fish. They aren't predators, so they don't accumulate toxins like bluefish do. They don't frequent polluted inland rivers, lakes, or bays; they swim in the open ocean, where the waters are cleanest.

A 7-ounce serving of bluefin tuna, before cooking, has about 10 grams of fat. About 2½ grams are omega-3 fatty acids. Salmon has about the same amount, although it has half again as much fat. Tuna packed in water in a can has less fat but also much less omega-3, anywhere from 0.2 to 1.5 grams.

So I'll choose fresh tuna. Those fish fats are doing me some good.

One definition of a tonic is an edible substance that helps restore physiological balance. As Daniel B. Mowrey puts it in *Herbal Tonic Therapies*, "the events of any given body system have an optimum operating range that is regulated through dozens of feedback loops to help keep various push-pull tendencies of the events in balance. . . . A substance that tends to maintain the optimum state or that moves a system back toward the optimum state is a tonic."

I nominate tuna.

It has taken science a few years to understand omega-3 fatty acids, a class of highly polyunsaturated fats. These include alpha-linolenic acid, found in plant foods such as soybeans and walnuts and certain greens such as purslane. Some animals elongate these polyunsaturated fats into even more unusual omega-3 fatty acids, EPA and DHA. (For the record, EPA stands for eicosapentaenoic acid and DHA for docosahexaenoic acid.) In Greece, for example, where free-range chickens eat wild green things including purslane, their eggs are rich in DHA and EPA. American eggs aren't. For you and me, just about the only significant source of elongated alpha-linolenic acid is seafood.

A quarter century ago, scientists thought fats were just fats, sources of calories. Now we know they are the building blocks of exquisitely balanced physiological compounds called eicosanoids. Eicosanoids affect many bodily processes, including immunity, wound healing, inflammation, and blood clotting. Some eicosanoids promote clotting, for example, while others inhibit it. Such a "push-pull," as Mowrey puts it, is a good thing. One wants blood to flow without undue clotting. On the other hand, if you cut yourself, a little clotting is a good thing.

The polyunsaturated fats called omega-6 fatty acids are the building blocks for eicosanoids that promote clotting, inflammation, allergic response, and (it turns out) in excess, heart disease and cancer. Omega-6 fatty acids are found in highly polyunsaturated fats such as corn and safflower oil, as well as in animals fed corn and similar grains. Saturated fats also promote similar eicosanoids.

Omega-3 fatty acids, on the other hand, serve as building blocks for eicosanoids that have the opposite effects: less clotting, less inflammation, less allergic responsiveness, less promotion of tumors.

Improving the balance between omega-3 and omega-6 fatty acids is in some ways paradoxical. It suppresses some aspects of the immune system yet boosts others. It reduces the tendency of the immune system to overrespond and thus may be beneficial for people who suffer from such autoimmune diseases as rheumatoid arthritis and, possibly, lupus; but improving that balance also improves the immune response to nascent tumors in the breast or colon.

One might say it tones the immune system.

Omega-3 fatty acids most famously tone the cardiovascular system. In 1985, Dutch researchers found that eating as little as an ounce of fish a day on average—that is, seven ounces of fish a week—cut the rate of heart attack death in middle-aged men by 50 percent. In 1995, they found that the same holds true for older people. (A 1995 Harvard study of male physicians found that there was no difference in cardiovascular effect between eating fish once a week and six times a week, but that may be because once a week is enough.)

The eicosanoids unleashed by eating more fish reduce the tendency of blood to clot, lower blood pressure, raise beneficial HDL cholesterol, and lower triglycerides in the blood. (If you have high cholesterol, high triglycerides are an additional risk factor for heart disease.)

If you stick with a high-fat diet, though, just adding fish fats may actually raise total cholesterol—LDL as well as the beneficial HDL. That's what Australian researchers found in 1994 when they added fish to the diets of men who took in 40 percent of their calories from fat. When the men switched to a more moderate diet with 30 percent of calories from fat and kept eating fish, their total cholesterol and harmful LDL and triglycerides fell, while beneficial HDL-2 rose.

What protects is not the substance but the balance. Too much omega-3 fatty acid may even be harmful. Omega-3 fatty acid supplements may be beneficial for some patients with heart disease or a high risk of heart disease, such as elevated triglycerides. But tuna is good for everyone. One 1991 study found that EPA is better absorbed by human beings when it comes from fish than when it comes from pills.

Then there's the breast cancer connection. In 1993, researchers in Norway reviewed health statistics of more than a half million women who had been between the ages of 35 and 55 in 1970. They tracked them over 15 years, to 1985. In particular, they were interested in the wives of fishermen, assuming that they ate a lot more fish than other women. They found that fishermen's wives developed breast cancer one-third less often than did their fellow Norwegians. Eskimos, who eat a lot of fat in the form of seal blubber without getting heart disease, also have very low rates of breast cancer. One 1995 study, looking at fish consumption in 24 European countries, found that when current intake was high, rates of both breast and colon cancer were low.

That's another effect of balancing eicosanoids and toning the immune system. In animals given carcinogens, omega-3 fatty acids added to their feed suppress breast tumors. In test tubes, omega-3 fatty acids, primarily EPA and DHA, stop breast cancer cells from replicating. In France, omega-3 fatty acids were studied in the breast tissue of 56 women undergoing chemotherapy for breast cancer. In those who responded best to chemotherapy, omega-3 tissue levels were highest.

The beneficial effects of omega-3 fatty acids on the immune system are also being applied in an entirely different arena: surgery. After surgery, infection is a big concern. One clinical supplement, Impact, which contains omega-3 fatty acids along with several other compounds, has been found to cut postsurgical infection rates by 75 percent by enhancing immunological competence and reducing inflammation.

Many drugs that reduce inflammation actually depress immunity. But not omega-3 fatty acids. Omega-3 fatty acid supplements have proved effective in treating autoimmune diseases such as rheumatoid arthritis and psoriasis and may have potential for multiple sclerosis and lupus. One study even suggests that eating more fish may modify a common inflammatory response: sunburn.

Tuna is looking juicier all the time. If I were a pregnant woman, it would look even better. One study finds that pregnant women who get adequate omega-3 fatty acids are less likely to deliver prematurely. The DHA in fish oil is necessary for the development of a baby's brain and eyes. In animals, including primates, that get too little DHA during gestation and breast feeding, visual acuity drops by 50 percent. Some researchers even believe that the DHA that we store in our brains in the womb and during the first two years of life may, at the end of life, help prevent Alzheimer's disease.

DHA may play a role in adult brains, too. It may prevent depression, including the depression that sometimes occurs after childbirth, as part of PMS, in people with heart disease, and among alcoholics. Each is linked with low levels of DHA. A current hypothesis goes like this: DHA is needed to keep cell membranes fluid. Without it, membranes become more rigid, less efficient. This can affect the ability of the brain to take in adequate serotonin and norepinephrine, two neurotransmitters linked with mood. Depression is almost always linked with low serotonin levels. By keeping our membranes fluid, we may be improving our moods.

"I think there should be some DHA in the human diet at all stages of life," says William E. Connors, M.D., of Oregon Health Sciences University in Portland, one of the pioneering researchers on the effect of omega-3 fatty acids on human health. "I suspect what we need is the amount that's in human milk. It's not a great amount. One or two servings of fish a week probably provide a very healthy amount." That's also the amount that cuts heart attack rates in half.

"Great civilizations," notes Connors, "arose on the banks of rivers or oceans." Maybe, he suggests, it was the fish.

SEARED TUNA WITH GINGER-SOY MARINADE

YIELD: **2** SERVINGS

2 8-ounce tuna steaks, about 1 inch thick
1 2-inch piece fresh ginger, peeled and grated
2 tablespoons olive oil, plus more for grilling
3 tablespoons fresh lime juice
3 tablespoons low-sodium tamari soy sauce

Put the tuna in a nonreactive container. Stir together the ginger, oil, lime juice, and soy sauce, and pour it over the fish. Turn to coat. Let the fish marinate at room temperature for 20 to 30 minutes. (If you won't be grilling for several hours, cover and refrigerate the fish, but take it out 30 minutes before cooking.)

Prepare a fire in the grill if using. Place the rack 3 to 5 inches from the heat source, and brush it with olive oil. Wait until it is hot before putting the tuna on.

Alternatively, heat a cast-iron skillet or grill pan over medium-high heat for a full 5 minutes.

Transfer the tuna to the grill or pan. If cooking on the stove top, reduce the heat to medium. For medium rare, cook 3 to 5 minutes per side. Serve immediately.

TURMERIC

"Perfect piquant peppery" is how the English makers of Madras Curry Powder describe their blend. The first ingredient is coriander; the second, sunny turmeric. Then come chilies, salt, cumin, fennel, black pepper, garlic, ginger, fenugreek, cinnamon, cloves, anise, and mustard. It's a sensual combination, an aromatic invitation to a thousand dishes.

Of course, you can make your own. Pan-toasting and grinding the seeds at home makes for a fresher, richer curry. Use our recipe (page 283) as a template, and vary it with the seasons. In colder regions of India and in cold weather, a curry will likely contain more hot chilies, ginger, and pepper; in winter, more cumin; in summer, more coriander.

"The basis of Indian curry is three important spices," herbalist Michael Tierra writes in *Planetary Herbology*. "Cumin seed, which is heating and carminative and has a strong, spicy flavor; coriander seed, which has a cooler energy and milder spicy flavor; and turmeric root, which is pleasantly bitter and only slightly spicy-tasting, imparts a golden color to food, and has liver detoxifying, blood moving and digestive properties. The three spices used together are balanced within themselves and are most important in promoting optimal digestion and assimilation of complex carbohydrates."

Of these, turmeric is the most interesting. In *The Yoga of Herbs*, Ayurvedic scholars David Frawley and Vasant Lad write that it is "an excellent natural antibiotic, while at the same time it strengthens digestion and helps improve intestinal flora. . . . It purifies the blood."

Animal studies confirm that turmeric stimulates the liver to produce bile acids, which help in the digestion of fats. But this is only the tip of the iceberg. The tip of the tip.

In the past five years, medical researchers in ten countries have collectively published hundreds of scientific papers on turmeric. In the United States, turmeric studies have been conducted at dozens of research centers, including the National Cancer Institute and Harvard Medical School.

The scientists are looking for more than a digestive balm. They want to prevent cancer. And heart disease. And AIDS.

Traditional use offers a clue: turmeric is anti-inflammatory. "In the form of paste it is applied externally in [cases of] wounds and inflammatory troubles of the joint," L. D. Kapoor writes in the *CRC Handbook of Ayurvedic Medicinal Plants*. In India today, turmeric is sometimes given for postoperative inflammation.

I wouldn't recommend the paste; it works, to be sure, but anyone who cooks with turmeric knows that it can stain skin, clothing, countertops, even white china. A potent pigment called curcumin makes up about 1 part in 200 of turmeric. And colorful curcumin is where the power lies.

Curcumin inhibits inflammation in much the same way that aspirin does, although at least one study finds that it is more effective. It interferes with hormonelike substances called eicosanoids—in particular, a class of eicosanoids called arachidonic acid. Arachidonic acid does two nasty things. It promotes carcinogenesis (it makes it easier for a damaged cell to turn into a tumor), and it makes it easier for blood to clot. Our bodies have different sets of eicosanoids; some promote clotting, others inhibit it. When you cut yourself, you want your blood to clot, but too much clotting action contributes to the development of heart disease. So you need both kinds of eicosanoids, in balance.

The standard American diet, however, creates an imbalance. It's high in saturated fats from meat and dairy products and in trans fats from hard margarines and commercial baked goods and fast foods, both of which trigger the formation of cancer- and clot-promoting arachidonic acid. (So do some polyunsaturated vegetable oils, especially the most unsaturated ones such as corn and safflower.) By contrast, olive oil, nut oils, and fish oils inhibit arachidonic acid and promote the formation of prostacyclin, an eicosanoid that inhibits clotting and so prevents heart attack.

Aspirin does the same thing, and that's why it's prescribed for people who have had heart attacks or are at great risk of having one. In a 1986 animal study, aspirin and turmeric were compared in animals. Both inhibited adenosine, which promotes blood clotting. Both inhibited platelet aggregation, the medical term for the tendency of disklike platelets in the blood to stick together, forming clots. But turmeric also caused a slight increase in clot-inhibiting prostacyclin. The researchers concluded, "Curcumin may, therefore, be preferable in patients prone to vascular thrombosis [blood clotting]."

And unlike aspirin, which can cause bleeding ulcers, turmeric may actually protect against ulcers. It's a traditional ulcer treatment in India, and in animal studies it's been shown to stimulate the stomach lining to produce more protective mucus.

Turmeric has another advantage over aspirin in terms of prevention of heart disease: it's a powerful antioxidant. In lab and animal studies, it's been shown to protect LDL cholesterol from being "oxidized," a process that precedes the development of heart disease. It is only LDL that has been damaged by oxygen free radicals, highly reactive and damaging forms of oxygen, that can initiate coronary heart disease. In India, in 1992, researchers gave ten healthy volunteers a half a gram of turmeric a day for seven days. That's an amount you might get in your diet if it includes curry. They measured the level of oxidative by-products of blood cholesterol. After a week, it fell 33 percent. Blood cholesterol fell, too, by 12 percent; this often happens with foods that stimulate bile acid secretion because bile acids are made from cholesterol.

The prostacyclin turmeric stimulates does one more thing: it dilates blood vessels. So it may lower blood pressure. In animals, turmeric itself lowers blood pressure.

Sprinkling curry on your cheeseburgers won't save you. But turmeric, like garlic and ginger, may be yet another food that protects the heart.

Aspirin does more than prevent heart attacks and strokes. If you take four to six aspirin tablets a week for ten years or more, it can lower your colon cancer risk. Harvard School of Public Health researchers found that after 20 years, risk dropped 44 percent in the 87,000 women they studied.

Could turmeric have similar benefits?

"Many chemicals that inhibit the carcinogenic process also inhibit arachidonic acid," says Allan H. Conney, chairman of the Department of Chemical Biology and Pharmacognosy at Rutgers University in New Brunswick, New Jersey. "It is thought that substances that inhibit arachidonic acid also inhibit cancer. We think turmeric works by inhibiting two enzymes that are involved in arachidonic acid metabolism."

In the lab and in animals, turmeric's curcumin exhibits a remarkable range of protective actions. It is an antioxidant, as we've mentioned. It inhibits so-called phase I enzymes in the liver, which can convert potential carcinogens into actual carcinogens. At the same time, it stimulates production of phase II enzymes, which detoxify potential carcinogens. It protects cells from mutations that may initiate the carcinogenic process. It inhibits the formation of carcinogenic nitrosamines from nitrates in the diet. It inhibits the expression of "oncogenes," or cancer genes, which can damage DNA and make cancer more likely. In animals, it inhibits cancers of the breast, colon, stomach, and when applied topically, the skin. One study suggested that turmeric may inhibit cancer "at initiation, promotion and progression stages of development."

There have been, however, few human studies. One in 1992 in India, published in *Mutagenesis,* looked at 16 chronic smokers. When given one and a half grams of turmeric a day for 30 days, they excreted significantly lower levels of mutagens in their urine, researchers found. But Conney cautions, "There have been no epidemiological studies with curcumin or turmeric. So we can't say anything about humans yet."

In India, turmeric mixed with hot milk is a traditional cold remedy. One explanation: curcumin is antiviral. It also kills *Staphylococcus aureus,* a bacteria that causes food poisoning, and herpes simplex, the virus that causes cold sores.

Turmeric's sunny pigment may also play a role in inhibiting HIV. At the Dana Farber Cancer Institute at Harvard Medical School, researchers have found that curcumin inhibits a gene expression integral to the transformation of HIV to full-blown AIDS. Most people infected with HIV progress to full-blown AIDS, but some live for a decade or more without developing AIDS. Why? One necessary step for HIV replication is something called the "long terminal repeat" or LTR. Says Harvard researcher Chiang J. Li, "It is a crucial fragment of DNA that controls the activity of this virus. We think it's very important. When LTR activity is zero, then virus replication is zero."

The most effective use of such a genetic brake on virus replication would be to give it to a patient as soon as he or she tests positive for HIV. But curcumin may also slow down replication of HIV after the process has begun.

Several clinical trials with curcumin are under way. One was reported in August 1994 at the International Conference on AIDS. A group called Staying Healthy with HIV in San Francisco gave 18 HIV-positive volunteers an average of two grams of pure curcumin a day and compared them with 18 HIV-positive volunteers who didn't take curcumin. After nearly three months (83 days), "there was a significant increase [in T cell counts] for those taking curcumin over the matched controls," researchers reported. In particular, there was a large increase in counts of CD-4 T cells, low levels of which are associated with increased risk of opportunistic infection. There were no side effects.

To get the dose of curcumin used in the HIV studies, you'd have to swallow nearly a pound of turmeric. That's ridiculous; it would probably make you sick. So that amount of curcumin is clearly a drug.

In Chinese medicine, a dose of turmeric is between three and nine grams—about a teaspoon—still much more than you would put in a single serving of food for pure culinary pleasure.

The Yoga of Herbs recommends 250 milligrams to one gram. A gram is about a fifth of a teaspoon. That's culinary. If you eat our lovely potato salad, you'd get between half a gram and a gram in a serving. Even half a gram of turmeric a day may protect the cholesterol in your blood from becoming oxidized and so protect against coronary heart disease.

And it makes the potato salad such a pretty color.

CURRY POWDER

To grind your own spices, buy a small coffee grinder and use it solely for that purpose, or use a mortar and pestle. Use this recipe anywhere you would use curry powder: in soups and stews, as a rub on chicken, to flavor rice.

YIELD: ⅓ CUP

1 tablespoon whole coriander seeds
2 teaspoons whole cumin seeds
1 teaspoon mustard seeds
2 teaspoons whole fenugreek seeds
6 small dried red chilies, about ¾ inches long
1½ teaspoons peppercorns
1 teaspoon ground ginger
2 teaspoons ground turmeric

Heat a dry skillet over high heat for 30 seconds. Add the coriander, cumin, mustard, and fenugreek, and reduce the heat to medium. Toast, shaking the pan and moving it on and off the heat as necessary to prevent scorching, until the seeds are aromatic, about 5 minutes.

Transfer the seeds to a spice grinder, and pulse 2 or 3 times, until coarsely ground. Add the chilies, peppercorns, ginger, and turmeric, and grind into a fine powder. Store in an airtight container, and use within a month.

GOLDEN NEW-POTATO SALAD

Turmeric gives this comfy salad its golden glow.

YIELD: 6 TO 8 SERVINGS

1¾ pounds new potatoes (about 12), scrubbed
½ teaspoon whole cumin seeds
2 teaspoons ground turmeric
½ teaspoon yellow or brown mustard seeds
⅓ cup plain nonfat yogurt or Homemade Yogurt (page 315)
⅓ cup low-fat mayonnaise
¼ cup fresh lemon juice
1½ tablespoons snipped chives
Kosher salt and freshly ground pepper
2 celery stalks, diced
1 medium bell pepper, seeded and diced
1 small red onion, peeled and diced

Put the potatoes in a large pot, and cover them with cold water. Cover the pot, and bring it to a boil over high heat. Reduce the heat to a high simmer, and cook, uncovered, until the potatoes are easily pierced with the tip of a knife but not mushy, 20 to 30 minutes. Drain and set aside to cool.

Heat a dry skillet over high heat for 30 seconds. Add the cumin, turmeric, and mustard seeds, and reduce the heat to medium. Toast, shaking the pan and moving it on and off the heat as necessary to prevent scorching, until the spices are aromatic, 3 to 5 minutes. Transfer to a spice mill, and grind into a fine powder.

In a medium bowl, combine the yogurt, mayonnaise, lemon juice, and chives. Stir in the ground spices, and salt and pepper to taste.

Put the potatoes in a large bowl, cutting any large ones in halves or quarters. Add the celery, bell pepper, onion, and dressing. Toss gently so that potatoes don't fall apart until all the ingredients are well combined. Cover and chill for at least an hour for the flavors to combine. The salad may be made a day ahead.

VITAMIN E

I like food better than pills. If you eat a wide variety of fruits and vegetables each day, you'll take in amounts of the antioxidants vitamin C and carotenoids (including beta-carotene) that are much greater than the government's recommended daily allowances. You'll be getting levels that are linked with reduction in chronic diseases, including cancer and heart disease.

Vitamin E is a different story. The U.S. RDA for vitamin E is only about 10 milligrams, but that's irrelevant, because we are not interested in deficiency but in optimal health. In human studies, vitamin E intakes above 100 milligrams a day have been shown to reduce the risk of heart disease. It not only prevents the oxidation of harmful LDL cholesterol but also prevents blood clots. In two large population studies, people who took vitamin E supplements for more than two years had about a 40 percent lower risk of developing heart disease.

Even higher doses may have therapeutic potential: one 1996 English study of 2,000 patients who already had heart disease found that taking between 400 and 800 milligrams a day reduced the risk of heart attacks by 75 percent.

There may be other benefits.

A number of studies have suggested that people who take vitamin E supplements tend to have lower rates of certain cancers, although this is far from established. One study of healthy older people found that vitamin E supplementation enhanced immune function (especially T cells), which tends to decline with age. It also improves sperm function, helps treat leg cramps, and protects diabetics from disease complications.

If you exercise avidly or want to start, taking a vitamin E supplement may help prevent muscle soreness and inflammation. In one study of healthy but sedentary men, those who took 800 milligrams of vitamin E for seven weeks before they ran vigorously downhill on a treadmill had less damage and inflammation than unsupplemented men. The effect was there with guys in their 20s, but it was even more pronounced in men in their 50s and 60s. The mechanism: disarming free radicals. When we jump-start an exercise program or push an existing one, we push more oxygen-rich blood through our muscles, throwing off more potentially damaging oxygen free radicals. Unchecked, they damage muscle tissue. Vitamin E renders them harmless. (For more on exercise, see "Walking," page 289).

Our need for vitamin E goes up as we expose ourselves to more sources of oxidation: air pollution, illness, excessive exercise, a diet rich in highly polyunsaturated fats such as corn or safflower oil, and age itself.

Vitamin E is fat soluble. A tablespoon of virgin olive oil will supply about 2 milligrams; an ounce of dried almonds, about 6 milligrams; a quarter cup of wheat germ, 4 milligrams; an ounce of sunflower seeds, 14 milligrams; a medium avocado, 2 milligrams; a medium sweet potato, 6 milligrams; four spears of asparagus, 2 milligrams.

It's hard to make those numbers add up to 100. Besides, many of these foods are high in fat. We would do well to replace saturated and trans fats in our diets with unsaturated fats rich in vitamin E, to be sure. But simply adding oils and oil-rich nuts to a fat-laden diet won't improve health, let alone the waistline.

Vitamin E doesn't work alone. It needs other antioxidants to work best. Vitamin C, for example, is water soluble, while vitamin E is fat soluble, as is beta-carotene. Vitamin C protects against oxygen free radicals in a watery medium such as blood; vitamin E protects against oxidation in a fatty medium such as cholesterol. Vitamin C protects vitamin E itself from damage. Too much vitamin E without enough vitamin C may even cause the vitamin E to act not as an antioxidant but as a pro-oxidant (it promotes oxidation). That's why public health scientists tend to recommend taking vitamins E and C and beta-carotene together.

It may be nearly impossible to take in disease-preventive quantities of vitamin E from food alone, but I don't think that has to be a discouraging fact. A plant-based diet has hundreds of different antioxidants. A well-balanced diet contains small amounts of many different natural antioxidants, which may act synergistically. I believe that many of the benefits we want from taking vitamin E supplements can be achieved from a diet rich in a wide mix of natural antioxidants from whole foods.

Such a diet would include nuts, seeds, nut oils, and other foods rich in vitamin E. It would include only cold-pressed oils such as virgin olive oil, little saturated fat, no trans fats, and hardly any highly polyunsaturated fats such as corn or safflower oil, which are easily oxidized and so eat up vitamin E.

Such a diet may provide only 15, 20, or 25 milligrams of vitamin E a day. But it may be as effective, or more so, in protecting health. After all, people in Asia and Mediterranean Europe who eat a pound or two of plant foods a day and drink antioxidant-rich tea or red wine have very low rates of heart disease and certain cancers. And, for the most part, they don't take supplements.

To be sure, adding a little extra vitamin E to this diet can't hurt and might well help if you make it a regular habit, but nothing can replace a good diet.

Recipes for Supplementation
If you want to take an antioxidant supplement, here are a few choices, in order of preference:

1. **200 to 400 milligrams vitamin E:** Take daily, at any time, and combine with a plant-based diet rich in vitamin C, beta-carotene, and other carotenoids and in folic acid and other antioxidants from such foods as citrus fruits, dark green leafy vegetables, winter squash, melons, berries, cruciferous vegetables including broccoli, red peppers, mangoes, spinach, sweet potatoes, apricots, carrots, pumpkins, and legumes. Take for at least two years to achieve a reduction in heart disease.

2. If you eat enough fruits and vegetables, here's another alternative: **200 to 400 milligrams vitamin E plus 250 to 500 milligrams vitamin C:** Combine with the diet just listed. Take for at least two years to achieve a reduction in heart disease.

3. If you want to add beta-carotene, remember that there are no established benefits to these supplements. If you are a smoker or a heavy drinker,

there may be a risk to high doses. But the amount that a plant-based diet would provide is around 3 to 6 milligrams, and that is safe. (Many supplements provide 15 milligrams or more, so read labels carefully.) Then your supplement would look like this: **200 to 400 milligrams vitamin E, 250 to 500 milligrams vitamin C, and 3 to 6 milligrams beta-carotene or mixed carotenoids:** Combine with the diet described in the first item in this list. Take for at least two years to achieve a reduction in heart disease.

4.   A multiple-vitamin and -mineral supplement with the quantities of vitamins E and C just listed and RDA levels of other nutrients, but no iron: Combine with the diet we've described. Take daily. (If you think you need iron, have your doctor run a diagnostic test; taking extra iron if you don't need it can do more harm than good. See "Iron," page 180.)

NOTE: If you do eat a plant-based diet with plenty of fruits and vegetables, you won't need to take extra vitamin C and carotenoids. Conversely, if you don't eat plenty of fruits and vegetables, you can't expect the same benefits from taking antioxidant supplements.

AVOCADO NUT SHAKE

This delicious drink is high in fat, but it is full of "good" fat, low in saturates and free of trans, rich in monounsaturates, with some omega-3 fatty acids and plenty of vitamin E. Drink it right away; the avocado doesn't keep its green color long.

YIELD: 4 1-CUP SERVINGS

1 cup raw, unpeeled almonds (5–6 ounces)
½ cup raw, unsalted walnuts (3 ounces)
¾ cup raw sunflower seeds (4 ounces)
1 tablespoon vanilla extract
2½ cups soy or skim milk
1 small, ripe avocado (about 8 ounces)
⅓ cup honey
1 tablespoon wheat germ
1 teaspoon ground cinnamon (optional)

Place a rack in the center of the oven, and heat the oven to 350 degrees.

Spread the almonds, walnuts, and sunflower seeds on a rimmed baking sheet, and bake them for 5 to 7 minutes. Turn them and bake about 5 minutes more, until very aromatic and just browned. Watch the nuts carefully; they can brown very quickly and then burn.

Transfer the toasted nuts to a food processor, and grind to a fine powder. Add the vanilla and milk, and process until smooth, stopping once to scrape down the sides with a rubber spatula.

Peel and seed the avocado, and cut it into chunks. Add it to the processor, along with the honey, wheat germ, and cinnamon if using. Process until smooth. Serve immediately, over ice.

WALKING

You've observed, surely, how a person's limbs drag and his feet dawdle along if his spirit is a feeble one? And how the lack of moral fiber shows in his very gait if his spirit is addicted to soft living? And how if his spirit is a lively and dashing one his step is brisk?

—Lucius Annaeus Seneca (c. 4 B.C.–A.D. 65),
Letters from a Stoic

Nothing in excess.

—An ancient Greek proverb

In 1983, when I was an editor at a magazine called *The Runner,* I went out to Randalls Island, just outside Manhattan, to cover a six-day race. The winner, a German named Siegfried Bauer, ran 511 miles and 4,320 feet; he also suffered tendinitis, swollen legs, blisters, and plenty of pain. When another competitor, Stu Mittleman, finished with 488 miles, 3,993 feet, an American record, I described the scene: "Someone helps him across the field, and he stands waiting for his award, his arms around someone's shoulder, his sore feet dangling on top of each other, like a cripple, or a Christ."

Around the same time, a more famous runner, Alberto Salazar, was rushed from winning the New York City Marathon to a hospital, because his core body temperature had risen so high that it threatened to kill him.

Marathoning remains a popular sport, and for many runners, meeting its challenges remains a peak personal experience. But competitive long-distance running has claimed its share of knees, bones, backs, and marriages.

And there may be a limit to the health-promoting advantages of increasing exercise. (I, for one, don't have to worry about reaching that limit any time soon.)

For example, regular aerobic exercise can enhance immunity; every time you run, you raise your body's core temperature just a bit, which may kill off potentially pathogenic bacteria as effectively as the fever you get when you are sick. But exhaustion from overtraining can make you more susceptible to colds and flu. When you push your body, it sometimes pushes back.

If what you want is health, there is an easier way. To prevent premature death from heart disease, one needs to be physically active nearly every day. But a funny thing began to show up in long-term population studies about a decade ago: the fitness advantage began to melt.

In terms of preventing heart disease, there is probably still a small additional advantage to being very aerobically fit. Great fitness may have psychological advantages as well. But the striking difference is between being sedentary and being active. What matters is not how fast you can run a mile, or 511 miles, but how many minutes a day you spend being active: walking, climbing stairs, running, swimming, bicycling, carrying groceries, carrying children, roller-skating, chopping wood, shoveling snow, walking your dog. It turns out that even people who garden several times a week live longer than people who are totally sedentary.

A few years ago, the prestigious American College of Sports Medicine changed its formula for physical activity and health. Gone are the measurements of target heart rate and the like. Instead, it recommends that every American strive to "accumulate" at least 30 minutes of physical activity at least five days a week. Accumulate means it doesn't have to be all at once: you can take a ten-minute walk in the morning, climb the stairs at work, and take another ten-minute walk when you get home.

More vigorous exercise is fine. It's great. It will give you more energy, continue to improve the efficiency of your cardiovascular system, and improve your mood. In particular, there is increasing evidence that maintaining lean body mass—that is, muscle—helps stave off the metabolic changes of aging that may lead to heart disease and diabetes. Some studies find that even people in their nineties can dramatically improve their strength, thus improving their ability to function and elude disability. Weight training can also strengthen the bones, reducing the risk of osteoporosis.

But the main thing is to get moving. A daily walk can lower blood pressure, increase beneficial HDL cholesterol, reduce the risk of osteoporosis, reduce the complications of diabetes, and if you have arthritis, increase your mobility. In a recent study of older men and women taking blood pressure medication, for example, walking two miles in under 30 minutes three times a week for six months dropped blood pressure 17 mm/Hg systolic and 8.5 mm/Hg diastolic.

In human studies, aerobic exercise or strength training three to five times a week effectively treats some forms of depression. Exercise also improves the body's ability to respond to stress and enhances self-esteem.

"A short brisk walk is one of the most reliable mood elevators I've ever encountered," says California State University psychology professor Robert Thayer, who studies such things. As the Roman philosopher Seneca wrote, "the feeling that one is tired of being, of existing, is usually the result of an idle and inactive leisure."

There are similar benefits from swimming, bicycling, cross-country skiing, tap dancing, rock climbing, canoeing, hoeing, hiking, jumping rope, dancing. And, of course, running. While Alberto Salazar was burning himself out, another marathoner, Bill Rodgers, was pacing himself and would go on to run very close to his personal best in hundreds of marathons, year after year.

A common image in Plato's writing is that of tuning the strings of a musical instrument. If the strings are too lax, then the instrument is out of tune. If they are too tight, it is out of tune. A toned body is in tune. What tones is a tonic.

In the first century A.D., Seneca, then quite near the end of his life, gave this advice to his young cousin:

> For it is silly, my dear Lucilius, and no way for an educated man to behave, to spend one's time exercising the biceps, broadening the neck and shoulders and developing the lungs. Even when the extra feeding has produced gratifying results and you've put on a lot of muscle, you'll never match the strength or the weight of a prize ox. The greater load, moreover, on the body is crushing to the spirit, and renders it less active. So keep the body within bounds as much as you can and make room for the spirit. There are short and simple exercises which will tire the body without undue delay and save what needs especially close accounting for, time.

A WALK

YIELD: FITNESS OF BODY AND MIND

Comfortable, flexible walking shoes with good arch support
A safe walking environment

Stand up straight; your ears, shoulders, hips, knees, and ankles should be aligned. Keep your head erect, your stomach in, your back straight. Relax your shoulders.

Take a full, natural stride. Let your legs walk you, walking heel to toe. Keep your arms relaxed by your side, elbows bent more or less at right angles (not hanging down straight or punching up at the sky).

Set a brisk but sustainable pace. For many people, 3 or 4 miles an hour is about right. But walk for time, not speed.

If you are out of shape, walk 10 minutes the first day. Repeat daily, gradually building up to 30 minutes or more daily.

Breathe deeply. Think good thoughts. Look ahead.

WALNUT

In 1656, William Coles's *The Art of Simpling* was published in England. In an era of superstitious, complicated, pseudo-astrological, and often useless herbals, Coles's book was a model of simplicity: one plant per remedy. (In this book our "simples" include rosemary for headaches, lavender for insomnia, and garlic for high blood pressure.)

A year later, in *Adam in Eden,* Coles drew on the ancient "doctrine of signatures": appearance as a sign of function. For example, carrots are yellow and therefore it was believed good for jaundice. Of walnuts he wrote, "The Kernel hath the very figure of the Brain, and therefore it is very profitable for the Brain, and resists poysons; for if the Kernel be bruised, and moystned with the quintessence of Wine, and laid upon the Crown of the Head, it comforts the brain and head mightily."

When I peruse contemporary medical journals, it's not immediately apparent what this brain connection might be, though walnuts and other nuts are clearly good for the heart.

In 1992, researchers at Loma Linda University in Loma Linda, California, published a report about more than 31,000 Seventh-Day Adventist men and women. Over six years, those who ate a small quantity of nuts more than four times a week were 48 percent less likely to die from a heart attack than those who ate nuts less than once a week. Those who ate whole-meal bread were 11 percent less likely to die of heart attack than those who ate white bread; in men, but not women, those who ate beef three or more times a week were more than twice as likely to die of a heart attack.

Most of the findings made sense in terms of the healthful Mediterranean diet pattern (see "Olive Oil," page 208, and "How to Eat," page 11). But the nut thing was way out of whack.

A year later, in the *New England Journal of Medicine*, Loma Linda researcher Gary Fraser and his colleagues published a small, carefully controlled metabolic study. They fed 18 healthy men a standard low-fat diet, the kind the American Heart Association prescribes to lower blood cholesterol. After a month, the men's blood cholesterol levels averaged 182 milligrams per deciliter (mg/dcl), a healthy level. For the next month, the men stayed on a low-fat diet but ate walnuts in place of other high-fat foods such as fatty meats, oils, margarine, and butter. Their blood cholesterol levels fell 22.4 mg/dcl, a very significant amount. Harmful LDL fell 18 points, while beneficial HDL, which often drops on a low-fat diet, fell only 2.3 points.

Was it the walnuts? Partly. Walnuts are low in saturated fat, yet rich in monounsaturated fat and polyunsaturated fat. Seven whole walnuts (14 halves) have 18 grams of fat, very little saturated (1.6 grams), a good part monounsaturated (4 grams), and mostly polyunsaturated (11 grams). Cutting out meats, margarine, and butter would cut out lots of saturated fat, and substituting walnuts—or nearly any nut, olive oil, avocado, or any other source of monounsaturated fat, as it turns out—would predictably lower blood cholesterol. Similar studies have found that almonds and macadamia nuts do the same thing. Says Harvard School of Public Health nutrition professor Frank Sacks, M.D., "Walnuts lower cholesterol when substituted for foods high in saturated fats. This is extremely predictable." The dramatically lower heart disease death rate in the Seventh-Day Adventist study, however, is "more provocative," Sacks says.

It turns out that just lowering cholesterol, even by 22 points, isn't enough to cut your risk of dying from a heart attack in half. Nor is nutrition much help: those seven walnuts have a small amount of folic acid (19 milligrams), calcium

(27 milligrams), and a pretty good amount of magnesium (48 milligrams), an underappreciated nutrient that helps regulate blood pressure. But the amount of magnesium in seven walnuts, about 12 percent of the U.S. RDA, isn't likely to halve heart attack rates.

In 1994, two years after the original Loma Linda study was published, researchers in the industrial northern French city of Lyons reported similarly astounding findings: in men who had already had a heart attack, adopting a standard low-fat diet cut the rate of fatal second heart attacks significantly; of 303 following the prudent diet, 16 died of a heart attack in the next 27 months. But only three of 302 men following an experimental diet died. The results were so strong that for ethical reasons, the study was stopped and all the men were advised to adopt the experimental diet.

That "experimental" diet didn't particularly emphasize walnuts—or nuts at all. It did emphasize a Mediterranean eating pattern. As described in the 1994 article in *The Lancet,* patients were counseled to eat "more bread, more root vegetables and green vegetables, more fish, less meat (beef, lamb, and pork to be replaced with poultry), no day without fruit, and butter and cream to be replaced with margarine supplied by the study."

Because the men wouldn't accept olive oil in place of butter on their bread, the researchers formulated a special margarine from unhydrogenated canola oil. It had little or no saturated or trans fats, plenty of monounsaturated fats, and a good amount of alpha-linolenic acid. (One wonders why American manufacturers, whose stick margarines contain heart-unhealthy saturated fats and trans fats, can't develop a similar spread.)

Alpha-linolenic acid is the main plant source of omega-3 fatty acids. It's also found in tofu and some green plants, such as purslane. Another food that's very rich in alpha-linolenic acid is—you guessed it—walnuts.

Until a few years ago, alpha-linolenic acid wasn't taken too seriously in nutrition circles. It's technically an omega-3 fatty acid, but it's not like the heart-protective elongated omega-3 fatty acids EPA and DHA in fish (see "Tuna," page 275). Although fish can take alpha-linolenic acid from, say, seaweed and algae and turn it into EPA and DHA, it wasn't clear how efficiently humans could do that.

Then, in 1995, Australian researchers reported a study in which they put healthy volunteers on a diet rich in alpha-linolenic acid. It turns out, the more alpha-linolenic acid (alpha-LA) you consume, the more EPA your body produces. The Australians concluded that "increasing dietary alpha-LA will elevate tissue EPA concentrations in a predictable manner." This confirmed the findings of a 1994 Australian study of 30 volunteers that "alpha-linolenic-acid-rich vegetable oils can be used in a domestic setting . . . to elevate EPA in tissues to concentrations comparable with those associated with fish-oil supplementation."

A 1993 French study found that feeding small animals alpha-linolenic acid also increased DHA levels. It's a little harder to study DHA in humans because it is stored mainly in the brain.

Once we realize that alpha-linolenic acid provides the same benefits as the special omega-3 fatty acids EPA and DHA found in fish fat, many doors open. It means that the many benefits of eating fish also accrue to eating a more plant-based diet rich in these oils. Those benefits include greatly reduced risk of cardiovascular disease, prevention of breast and other cancers, reduction of inflammatory and autoimmune processes, enhancement of immune function, and better development of the brain and eye in the fetus and the infant up to the age of two.

Alpha-linolenic acid by itself has been shown in human studies to inhibit blood clotting, and it has been linked with the prevention of breast cancer. It also benefits infants' eye and brain development.

DHA levels are extraordinarily high in the human brain and eye. If alpha-linolenic acid does increase brain levels of DHA, as animal studies suggest it might, then the good William Coles's doctrine of signatures may not have been far off: the kernel could indeed be "very profitable for the Brain."

SWEET AND SPICY WALNUTS

Blanching the walnuts first, a common practice in Chinese cooking, brings out their natural sweetness.

YIELD: 4 CUPS

½ cup honey
2 teaspoons dark sesame oil
1½ teaspoons kosher salt
1 pound (4½ cups) walnut halves
1½ teaspoons cayenne
2 teaspoons ground cumin

Bring the honey, sesame oil, 1 teaspoon of the salt, and 4 cups water to a boil in a saucepan. Add the walnuts, reduce the heat to low and simmer for 12 minutes. Drain the walnuts, spread them on a cookie sheet, and let them dry for an hour.

Place a rack in the center of the oven; heat it to 300 degrees.

Sprinkle the remaining ½ teaspoon salt and the cayenne on the walnuts, and toss to coat.

Bake for 8 minutes, turn the walnuts with a spatula, and bake for about 8 minutes more, until golden brown but not scorched. When cool, store the walnuts in an airtight container. They will keep for up to a week.

AMERICAN GRANOLA CONGEE

Use any dried fruits and nuts you like in the quantities listed. For speedier preparation, cook the rice in a pressure cooker for 45 minutes, add the remaining ingredients, and cook for 10 minutes more. Serve this aromatic, warming porridge for a cold-weather breakfast. For a variation, substitute pecans for half the walnuts before toasting.

YIELD: 5 1-CUP SERVINGS

1 cup uncooked brown rice
½ cup dried cranberries or raisins
¼ cup dried apricots, coarsely chopped
½ cup walnuts, lightly toasted
Brown sugar, honey, or molasses

Combine the rice and 6 cups water in a large soup pot. Cover and bring to a boil. Reduce the heat to a simmer, and cook until the rice has swollen and become extremely soft, 3 to 3½ hours.

Add the cranberries, apricots, walnuts, pecans, if using, and brown sugar to taste. Simmer, covered, for 30 minutes more. Serve warm.

WATER

Water doesn't contain fascinating compounds—no phenolic antioxidants, no hormonelike plant sterols, no biomodulating fatty acids. Technically, it has no nutrients. Yet water is the most essential "nutrient" we consume. You can go without food for days, weeks, even a month or more. Yet without a source of water, you would die within a few days.

Drink at least eight glasses of water a day. You've heard this advice. But what good does it do? Because the body, especially the blood, is mostly water, consuming enough water helps blood to flow freely and food to move through the gastrointestinal system more easily. Consuming enough water helps prevent constipation and prevents the blood from becoming too viscous (thick), so water can improve cardiovascular function. Sometimes, drinking too little water can give you a headache.

Water's benefits are so commonsensical that they are difficult to see. Recently, epidemiologists at the Harvard School of Public Health looked at dietary factors that contribute to, or help prevent, the formation of kidney stones. They studied 45,289 men, mostly physicians. Over six years, 753 developed kidney stones. On average, they reported in the *American Journal of Epidemiology*, for every eight ounces of water a man drinks, his risk of developing kidney stones goes down 4 percent.

By my count, this means drinking eight glasses reduces my risk 32 percent. Eight glasses may sound like a lot, but we forget how much water there is in some foods. Fruit is mostly water. So are vegetables. From a scientific standpoint, salad greens are primarily water rich in chlorophyll and antioxidants held together by fiber.

One's entire diet can be water-based. A few years ago, I heard Tsukikio Hattori, a journalist and author, talk about Japan's changing diet at a conference in Hawaii organized by the Oldways Preservation and Exchange Trust. "It is a cuisine of water," she said. "It is mostly rice cooked in water." So the quality of the water becomes particularly important. "We are blessed with good clean water in many areas. In western Japan, near Kyoto, we have very clean water—it is less heavy than the water near Tokyo. With good water, there is less need to use condiments."

Whether good water means bottled water depends on where you live. Sometimes, tap water is perfectly fine. If bottled water tastes better than tap where you live, that alone is reason to drink it. You'll drink more.

Sometimes we think we are hungry when we really are thirsty. So drinking water first thing in the morning, in the afternoon, and before dinner might help us eat a little less. "Another good way to stave off the rigors of feeling famished," M. F. K. Fisher wrote in *A Cordiall Water,* "is to drink something very thin and watery, like cold weak coffee from a bottle, or wine cut with a least five times its amount of water, or water with a little vinegar in it."

Recent studies have established that as we age, we become less sensitive to thirst, so we may need to drink water and water-based beverages out of habit rather than relying on feelings of thirst. Folk traditions tell us to drink between meals but not in large amounts during meals, because the water might dilute the stomach acids needed for good digestion.

So treat yourself to good, pure water. A little squeeze of fresh lemon will give the water some character, stimulate the liver, and according to Chinese traditions, calm the mind. It certainly quenches the thirst.

WATER WITH A SQUEEZE OF LEMON

YIELD: 1 SERVING

12 ounces pure, cold water
Slice of fresh lemon

Pour the water into a tall glass. Squeeze the lemon slice into the water. Drink first thing in the morning and in the afternoon.

WATERCRESS

Watercress saved Captain James Cook and his men.

Between 1768 and 1780, the Englishman and his crew traveled around the world three times. Mostly they ate salted fish and meat, dried vegetables, hard biscuits, rancid oils, cheese and butter, plus beer, wine, and lots of rum. What they were especially lacking was vitamin C. On a long voyage, as many as three-quarters of the crew might become sick with scurvy, caused by vitamin C deficiency.

In 1742, Scottish surgeon James Lind had shown that scurvy could be prevented and cured with orange and lemon juice. So when Cook set sail for Tahiti in 1768, his provisions included sauerkraut, carrot marmalade, and concentrated lemon and orange juice, which the British admiralty thought would prevent scurvy. As it turned out, these foods didn't; air and heat had depleted almost all their vitamin C.

Joseph Banks, a botanist on board, thought wild greens might help. When the ship reached Tierra del Fuego in South America, he had the crew pick local greens. They ate them in salads. Soon, they were doing it in every port. Although many of Cook's men would later succumb to dysentery, none died of scurvy.

I learned this from a fascinating 1995 article in *The Historian* by Francis E. Cuppage. He had studied the original ship's logs, traveled to Hawaii, Australia, and New Zealand to collect plant samples, and had them analyzed for vitamin C content. Many contained a lot. Watercress was one of them.

Watercress, one of many edible cresses, has 20 milligrams of vitamin C in a three-ounce serving (about one and a half cups raw or a half cup cooked). Only about 10 milligrams are needed to prevent scurvy. The U.S. RDA is 60 milligrams, but recent studies find that the optimal amount to provide vitamin C to all the body's tissues is 200 milligrams. Take more than 400 milligrams, and you'll excrete much of it in your urine. Take 1,000 milligrams, and you'll start to excrete oxalates, which can contribute to kidney stones. It's a good argument for a plant-based diet, without megadoses of vitamin supplements.

But vitamin C is just part of the watercress story.

In *The Energetics of Western Herbs: Integrating Western and Oriental Herbal Medical Traditions,* Peter Holmes describes watercress as "one of several superior food-remedies with a strong *cleansing* as well as *nourishing* function." Holmes tells us that Paracelsus, a sixteenth-century Swiss-German doctor who greatly influenced medicine, "provides a helpful image when he says that watercress draws all toxin to itself and transforms it, in the human body, as in nature." In England, notes Holmes, watercress is called Well Grass, while in France, it sometimes goes by the name *santé du corps,* or "health of the body."

Botanist Jim Duke gave me a lesson on watercress's virtues during a walk in the Maryland woods. Jim, one of the world's foremost authorities on plants that affect health, picked a few tiny leaves of wild cress, a relative of watercress, and handed them to me. They tasted sharp, mustardy, and delicious.

"That's cancer protective," Jim said. "It's got isothiocynate, as well as ellagi-tannins."

Isothiocyanates are a class of chemicals prevalent in members of the cabbage family such as broccoli (see page 38), cabbage, cauliflower, and, yes, watercress. Isothiocyanates appear to stimulate the detoxification of foreign compounds including carcinogens. Ellagic acid, or ellagitannins—a form of tannic acid found in strawberries, raspberries, and other aromatic fruit—have strong antitumor effects in a test tube.

One compound in watercress, phenethyl isothiocyanate (PEITC), protects lab animals from many different carcinogens. It also appears to protect smokers from the main carcinogen in cigarette smoke. In one recent study, 11 smokers were given two ounces of watercress to chew three times a day. Soon after chewing it and swallowing the PEITC-rich watercress juice, there was a significant increase in the detoxification of NNK (a nitrosamine), one of the cancer causers in cigarettes, in their urine. Another recent study established that PEITC is released when people simply eat watercress, too.

Phenethyl isothiocyanate, a sulfur compound, works in a similar way to diallyl sulfide, a sulfur compound found in garlic (see page 135). Both stimulate the liver to make more enzymes that break down potential carcinogens, turn them into harmless water-soluble chemicals, and excrete them. Both may also protect the liver from the harm that alcohol can cause. In one animal study, rats were given ethanol, pure alcohol. They started exhibiting unhealthy changes in the balance of fatty acids in their livers. When they were given the compounds found in garlic or watercress, the unhealthy changes stopped.

Watercress: great cleanser, protector of the liver, savior of sailors, gatherer of toxins!

WATERCRESS TOFU STIR-FRY WITH TOMATOES

The trick to this quick dish is to add the tomatoes just seconds before you eat.

YIELD: 2 SERVINGS

1 tablespoon canola or olive oil
1 small yellow onion, peeled and chopped
1 garlic clove, smashed, peeled, and chopped
1 bunch watercress, coarsely chopped
3 or 4 small fresh shiitake mushrooms, coarsely chopped
1 pound firm tofu, cubed
1 or 2 tablespoons low-sodium soy sauce
1 or 2 teaspoons toasted sesame oil
3 or 4 small, ripe tomatoes, chopped
2 to 3 cups hot, cooked white or brown rice

Heat the oil in a skillet over medium-high heat. Sauté the onion for a minute or two. Stir in the garlic and cook a moment. Add the watercress and shiitakes, and stir-fry briefly.

Stir in the tofu, and turn the heat down to medium low. Stir in the soy sauce and sesame oil. Bring the heat back up to warm all the ingredients through. Stir in the tomatoes, and serve immediately over the rice.

WINE

I have lived temperately, eating little animal food . . . I double, however, the doctor's glass and a half of wine and even treble it with a friend; but halve its effects by drinking the weak wines only. The ardent wines I cannot drink, nor do I use ardent spirits in any form.
— Thomas Jefferson in a letter to Dr. Benjamin Rush

Yes, red wine is better for the heart.

Much of its cardiovascular benefit does derive from alcohol. All alcoholic beverages, consumed in moderation, raise beneficial HDL, reduce the tendency of blood to form potentially artery-clogging clots, and prevent heart attacks. The general recommendation is one drink a day for women, two for men. This is partly because women tend to be smaller but more specifically because they have lower stores of an enzyme that breaks down alcohol.

Moderate alcohol consumption may even enhance immunity. In September

1994, researchers reported in the *American Journal of Public Health* that moderate drinkers—people who consumed up to two or three drinks a day—were less likely to get colds when exposed to cold viruses than abstainers. Elderly people who drank moderately were also less likely to suffer cognitive declines than either abstainers or heavy drinkers.

Even at three or more drinks a day, the arteries stay clear, but other risks start to rise: high blood pressure, cirrhosis of the liver, throat cancer, accidents. That's why epidemiologists talk of a "J-shaped curve" of mortality. It means that people who don't drink any alcohol at all are at slightly higher risk of dying in any given year. Those who drink a glass or two a day have lower mortality. After that, the risk rises like the straight line of a J. Half the car fatalities, half the homicides, a third of the suicides, and as many as two-thirds of the drownings of teenagers and adults in this country involve alcohol. So do a quarter of the burns, fires, and falls. If you have high blood pressure and drink substantially, simply going from three drinks to none for one week can lower pressure.

If only one could devise an alcoholic beverage or a cultural pattern of drinking that ensured people would stop at one drink or two. Such a pattern did exist 30 or 40 years ago, in Italy and elsewhere. It involved wine but also religion, family, social attitudes, and even architecture.

Before climbing those cultural stairs, however, let's look at wine and the body. Red wine does a better job at protecting the heart than pure alcohol. It may also keep us thin where it most matters: around the middle. It improves digestion and protects against food-borne infections.

Red wine is more than just alcohol. It is whole fruit—the grape skin, its juice, its seeds—concentrated and preserved in alcohol. The dark red pigment in those grape skins derives from polyphenols, which include tannins and flavonoids (see "Tea," page 252). Like alcohol, flavonoids inhibit platelet aggregation—that is, they thin the blood. With this second blood-thinning agent, wine may be more effective than another alcoholic beverage with the same amount of alcohol.

Polyphenols are also strong natural antioxidants; alcohol isn't. This may be the major contribution of these bitter pigments to health. They protect LDL cholesterol from being damaged by oxygen free radicals. When LDL is so damaged, it becomes capable of initiating a chain of events that can result in the formation of plaque on the artery walls. When plaque builds up, blood flow is restricted. This is called coronary heart disease. When a piece of plaque breaks free and entirely blocks blood flow in an artery, it is called a heart attack.

In addition, certain flavonoids, especially quercetin, richly represented in red wine but also in onions (see page 211), are, in the laboratory at least, strongly cancer-protective antioxidants. The very process of fermentation that produces wine, some scientists report, may make quercetin more biologically active.

Flavonoids are in grape skins. Only red wine is made with grape skins, so white wine, while it contains alcohol, contains few or no flavonoids. In the test tube, red wine, diluted to a strength of 1 part wine to 1,000 parts water, protected LDL cholesterol from oxidation more effectively than vitamin E (page 285), American researchers reported in the *Lancet* in 1993.

Israeli researchers at the Lipid Research Laboratory at Rambam Medical Center in Haifa conducted an elegant experiment that further revealed red wine's beneficial action—in people. They reported it in the March 1995 issue of the *American Journal of Clinical Nutrition*. The Israelis asked 17 healthy men to drink just under half a liter (400 milliliters) of wine a day for two weeks. (Nice work if you can get it.) Eight men got red, nine white. After two weeks, blood was drawn (party's over, guys) and tested to determine how susceptible the LDL cholesterol was to oxidation. Those who drank red wine had LDL that was 72 percent less likely to oxidize. Those who drank white wine had LDL that was 41 percent *more* likely to oxidize. English researchers at the University of Birmingham reported similar results; the increase in the antioxidant capacity of the blood after drinking red wine, they noted, was about the same as one would find after consuming 1,000 milligrams of vitamin C.

White wine's alcohol is still good for the heart, but red wine's flavonoids add extra protection. You're getting fruit—concentrated whole fruit with its protective flavonoids liberated by fermentation—along with alcohol. In 1996, Danish researchers at State University Hospital in Copenhagen examined the relationship between drinking and LDL levels in 2,800 Danish men they have been following since 1985. They looked at those who had the highest LDL levels and thus the greatest risk of having a heart attack. (That group was at extraordinary risk: blood LDL levels were on average 203 milligrams per deciliter of blood. In general, an LDL level over 130 is cause for concern, and anything over 160 entails serious risk.) Over the next six years, 16.4 percent of those who never drank had a heart attack, but among those who had up to three drinks a day, "only" 8.7 percent did. Among those who drank more, only 4.4 percent had heart attacks, although they may well have had other medical problems.

Among the men with the lowest LDL levels, alcohol made no difference. This is not surprising. If one keeps one's total cholesterol low enough—between, say, 150 and 180—the risk of getting coronary heart disease is minimal. To do so, one needs to go on a basically vegetarian diet, with very little fat from any source. If you eat a more typical higher-fat diet, then factors such as blood thinning and LDL oxidation become more important.

The public health significance of red wine's flavonoids has yet to be determined. One Danish study found that people who drank wine were less likely to die from any cause, while people who drank beer showed no benefit, and drinkers of spirits (hard liquor) were actually more likely to die than teetotalers. But other studies have reached other conclusions. Some researchers believe that any alcoholic beverage consumed in moderation can reduce mortality by helping to prevent heart attacks. Others believe that the benefits accrue primarily to wine drinkers, and to red wine drinkers, at that.

My own belief is that red wine has the edge, especially if one looks at the broader picture. For example, there has been some concern that alcohol consumption can raise the risk of breast cancer. The relationship is far from proven and is modest at worst, but it is of concern, especially for women at high risk.

One recent epidemiological study found that when one looked at women whose primary alcoholic beverage was wine, the risk disappeared. It may be those antioxidant flavonoids. One thing is clear: in Mediterranean countries, where wine is consumed as part of a plant-based diet rich in antioxidants, cancer rates (including breast) are lower than in the United States.

A recent study at the Harvard School of Public Health shines a light on these interactions. The researchers looked at folic acid (page 130)—a nutrient found in green leafy vegetables that protects DNA and is linked with lower colon cancer risk—and its relationship to rectal cancer. They found that people who consumed three drinks a day or more had a greater risk of rectal cancer. In those who drank heavily and had high blood levels of a marker for folic acid, the risk was about one-third higher than average, but in heavy drinkers who consumed the least folic acid, the risk was more than ten times higher. Without the protection afforded by a plant-rich diet, one is particularly susceptible to the toxic effects of immoderate alcohol use.

Having three or more drinks a day is a bad idea for a number of reasons. On the other hand, drinking a glass or two of red wine a day, as part of a diet rich in vegetables, seems to me to be a pretty healthful habit. The richest reds are the richest sources of polyphenolic compounds, by the way, so don't go for wimpy wines. One study found that petite syrah and merlot had the most protective polyphenols.

One of the benefits of wine as the alcoholic beverage of choice may be to the waistline. Consider a University of North Carolina study that examined the waist-to-hip ratio of 12,000 men and women. A waist-to-hip ratio of more than one for a man or 0.7 for a woman is considered a risk factor for heart disease and diabetes because excess belly fat is easily mobilized by the body into blood fats. In the North Carolina study, those who drank more than six alcoholic drinks other than wine a week were 40 percent more likely to have a high waist-to-hip ratio; those who drank six or more glasses of wine a week were 55 percent more likely to have a *low* waist-to-hip ratio. The researchers, reporting in the *American Journal of Epidemiology*, didn't offer an explanation.

It may be the wine; it may be the lifestyle of the wine drinkers. Alcohol tends to boost metabolism a bit, so the body actually burns up a few of alcohol's calories. But alcohol also takes precedence over fat in the digestive process: the liver, sensing a toxin, breaks down the alcohol first and lets the fat wait. So the combination of a high-fat diet with alcohol may lead to greater deposits of dietary fat as body fat. I'd call it the beer-nuts syndrome. It is already known that wine drinkers tend to have healthier habits than drinkers of other kinds of alcoholic beverages, and wine is often consumed with meals, rather than, say, with fish-shaped crackers.

Wine is meant to be consumed with meals. In fact, wine with meals has been considered a digestive aid since the days of ancient Greece. Wine is about as acidic as stomach acid, so this makes sense. Some research finds that wine, along with beer, increases stomach secretion of gastrin, a digestive hormone. But it wasn't until 1995 that scientists, reporting in the *British Medical Journal*, found a more compelling effect: wine, red or white, kills pathogenic bacteria as effectively as Pepto-Bismol (bismuth salicylate).

The researchers tested several bacteria responsible for traveler's diarrhea: salmonella, shigella, *E. coli*. Against these powerful foes they unleashed undiluted red or white wine, pure alcohol, tequila, bismuth salicylate, and sterilized water. Pure alcohol was no more effective than water. Tequila killed some bacteria, though not very effectively. But wine of all colors killed the nasty pathogens more effectively than even the bismuth, a known antibacterial. Dipping into history, the researchers noted that during a late-nineteenth-century cholera epidemic in Paris, wine drinkers were spared. (It happened again in 1993: Florida Department of Health officials investigating an outbreak of infectious hepatitis A from contaminated raw oysters found that those who had drunk wine or whiskey with the meal were only one-tenth as likely to succumb; beer consumption didn't help.)

What is it in wine that protects? Alcohol, yes, but also our old friends the polyphenols. Quercetin, for example, a cancer-inhibiting LDL-protecting flavonoid well supplied in wine, has established antibacterial effects. Making wine frees quercetin from the sugars that bind it. "The antimicrobial agent in wine seems to be a polyphenol that is liberated during fermentation and is active against bacteria at an acid PH," the British researchers reported. "Although polyphenol concentrations have not been measured in wine aged for different lengths of time, the antimicrobial properties of wine increase with age to a certain point, peak antimicrobial activity being observed in 10-year-old wine, and activity decreases as wine is aged further."

So, red wine, well aged, with some tannin, may protect the stomach and the heart. It may lead to a smaller belly, possibly due to the tendency of people to drink wine with meals rather than mozzarella sticks.

It turns out that wine itself can be nutritious. A 1993 study of nearly 1,000 Italians reported in the *International Journal of Epidemiology* concluded that "in Italy, wine was an important source of several nutrients, including iron and riboflavin." And because red wine's antioxidants spare vitamin E, it raises blood levels of that nutrient.

Wine makes a more subtle contribution, too: it helps us absorb nutrients from food. Several studies reported in the *American Journal of Clinical Nutrition* in 1980 demonstrate the effect. In one, six healthy young men ate a controlled diet for four 18-day periods and drank a liter a day (drunken work if you can get it) of one of the following beverages: zinfandel wine, zinfandel with the alcohol removed, pure alcohol diluted in water, or sterilized water. When the men drank zinfandel, either with or without alcohol, they absorbed significantly more zinc. Further studies revealed that wine with or without alcohol also increased absorption of calcium, phosphorus, and magnesium. The researchers weren't sure why, but suggested that wine's acidity may be a factor.

Wine's affinity with food may also contribute to its association with moderation. Canadian studies of high school students find that those who consume only wine are much less likely to drink too much than those who drink only beer, only spirits, or some combination of wine, beer, and spirits. A 1979 article in the *International Journal of the Addictions* concluded that wine is "frequently associated with mealtimes, at home and with relatives."

Which brings us, finally, to society.

I was once invited to a dinner at a well-known wine maker's estate in Napa Valley. The marketing director told me fine wine was never associated with alcoholism—it's those cheap jug wines. Meanwhile, he drank several bottles of fine red wine and became less and less coherent.

There is nothing about wine itself that ensures moderation; wine-drinking countries are complex places, to be sure. Nor does wine make for a better society. But in cultures where wine is the predominant alcoholic beverage, alcoholism is relatively rare. The greatest contribution of wine to health may be its role in a cultural pattern of moderate alcohol consumption integrated into foodways.

One current medical textbook on theories of alcoholism divides cultures into four categories: abstinent; ambivalent; permissive toward drinking but negative toward drunkenness; and finally, overpermissive, including acceptance of drunkenness.

American society is ambivalent, which, according to the text, is the attitude most likely to spawn alcoholism. France—at least France in the 1960s—might be considered overpermissive. Italy—at least the Italy of the 1950s—was permissive, while remaining negative toward drunkenness. This is the pattern least associated with alcoholism.

In 1958, a slim monograph, *Alcohol in Italian Culture,* was published by the Yale Center of Alcohol Studies. By 1965, when the companion study, *Drinking in French Culture,* arrived, the publishing group had become the Rutgers Center of Alcohol Studies. These monographs are classic studies of the cultural context of alcohol consumption. These days, when one looks for the prevention of alcoholism in the genes, these kinds of studies have fallen out of fashion. But they are instructive.

In the French study, the lowest percentage of wine users and the highest percentage of uses of other alcoholic beverages were found in the areas with the highest death rates from alcoholism and liver cirrhosis, notably Brittany and Normandy in the northwest. The highest percentage of wine users was found in the areas with the lowest death rates from alcoholism and cirrhosis, notably Languedoc and the eastern Pyrenees in the south.

Compared with the Italians, however, the French exhibited beliefs and behaviors more associated with overpermissive societies. The average "safe limit" was defined as nearly two liters a day for heavy laborers, almost a liter a day for office workers. Toleration or social acceptance of intoxication was "common among the French but rare among the Italians." (Attitudes—and consumption—have changed since then. Wine consumption has been falling in France since the 1950s and in other countries such as Spain since the 1970s.)

Perhaps the main difference between the French and the Italians was that while the French drank wine with meals, they also drank a considerable amount of alcohol in the form of hard liquor and cider outside the home, in cafés and bars. The Italians drank almost exclusively wine and almost exclusively with lunch or dinner. The French were more likely to be abstinent than the Italians but also more likely to have drunk more than a half liter during the previous day. Architecture reflected the different ways of consuming alcohol. The French had plenty of freestanding bars, the Italians few.

Among the French, the report concludes, "there is wide social acceptance of intoxication as a humorous, fashionable or otherwise tolerable phenomenon. Among the Italians, intoxication is consistently regarded as a personal and family disgrace."

The Italian researchers were particularly critical of that American phenomenon, the cocktail hour. From their description, circa 1958:

> Customarily scheduled late in the afternoon, the cocktail hour comes at a time when the individual's general resistance, and specifically the resistance of his central nervous system, are usually at their lowest ebb during the day. Fatigue is the theme of the hour. . . . During the cocktail hour itself, the individual drinks on an empty stomach. As a result, the alcohol is absorbed rapidly from the digestive tract, high blood alcohol levels are produced, and the alcohol is oxidized slowly. Finally, . . . the cocktail hour is coupled with an attitude of drinking in a deliberate attempt to secure 'sociability' or to achieve the 'effects' of alcohol. On both physiological and psychological grounds, it appears clear that the ingestion of alcoholic beverages within the frame of the cocktail hour is unhealthy. If a social institution had been consciously created to foster the development of latent alcohol-addictive traits, it is difficult to imagine how a more effective mechanism could have been devised.

So let me propose a toast to your health. With red wine. Over dinner.

RED WINE CHICKEN

Flavonoids are stable compounds. They are still there after you cook wine, even though most of the alcohol evaporates.

YIELD: 4 SERVINGS

2 whole chicken breasts
1 bottle (about 3 cups) dry red wine
2 bay leaves
6 to 8 sprigs mixed herbs such as thyme, rosemary, sage, or oregano
5 garlic cloves, smashed, peeled, and coarsely chopped
1 3-inch cinnamon stick, broken into 3 pieces
1 teaspoon whole coriander seeds
1 teaspoon black peppercorns
1 tablespoon olive oil

1 pound small onions (about 16), peeled
1 pound small, waxy potatoes (about 5)
1 pound carrots, trimmed, peeled, and cut into 2- to 3-inch lengths
8 ounces button mushrooms, wiped clean and halved
Kosher salt and freshly ground pepper
1½ teaspoons (9 grams) kudzu or cornstarch (optional)

Rinse the chicken under cool running water, and pat it dry. Using kitchen shears or a large kitchen knife, split the breasts in half lengthwise. Trim off any excess fat, but leave the skin on for cooking.

Put the chicken in a large, nonreactive container (a 13-inch-by-9-inch glass baking dish works well), and pour 2 cups of the wine over it. Scatter a bay leaf, 3 or 4 herb sprigs, the garlic, and cinnamon around the breasts. Put the coriander and peppercorns in a spice mill, and grind into coarse pieces. Sprinkle over the chicken. Cover and refrigerate for an hour, turning the pieces once or twice.

Place a rack on the lower level of the oven; heat the oven to 350 degrees.

Remove the chicken from the marinade, and pat it dry. Strain the marinade through a fine sieve. Reserve the liquid and the garlic, and discard the rest of the solids.

Heat the oil in a large Dutch oven or large pot over medium heat. Add the chicken and garlic and cook 2 to 3 minutes. Stir in the onions, potatoes, carrots, and mushrooms. Increase heat to medium high, and cook until the vegetables begin to brown, about 5 minutes.

Add the reserved marinade, and bring it to a boil over high heat. (Boiling is necessary to kill any germs the marinade picked up from the raw chicken.) Let it boil for 4 minutes. Add the remaining 1 cup wine, return the liquid to a boil, and then reduce the heat to medium low. Add the remaining bay leaf and herb sprigs, and salt and pepper to taste.

Transfer the pan to the oven, and bake, covered, for about 45 minutes, until the potatoes are tender when pricked with the tip of a knife.

If you like, thicken the sauce: return the pan to a burner (leaving in all the ingredients, including the chicken), whisk the kudzu into ⅓ cup of water, and add it to the cooking liquid. Simmer over medium heat until thickened, about 5 minutes.

Remove and discard the chicken skin, if desired. Arrange the chicken and vegetables on a platter, cover with sauce, and serve.

RED WINE SORBET

The type and quality of wine affect the flavor of this sophisticated dessert. I like merlot but also zinfandel.

YIELD: 1 QUART

1 cup light corn syrup
1 cup sugar
Zest of 1 lemon
4 peppercorns
1 3-inch Chinese cinnamon stick
2 cups red wine

Combine the corn syrup, sugar, and 2 cups water in a saucepan. Stir to partially dissolve sugar. Add the lemon zest, peppercorns, and cinnamon. Cook over medium heat until all the sugar has dissolved, stirring occasionally. Cover and bring just to a boil.

Remove the pan from the heat, and let the liquid steep, covered, for 1 hour. Strain it, and discard the solids. Add the red wine, and chill.

Process the mixture in an ice cream maker according to manufacturer's directions. The sorbet will keep, tightly covered, in the freezer for 3 or 4 days.

YOGURT

Yogurt is the angel of health.
> —Maya Tiwari, *A Life of Balance: The Complete Guide to Ayurvedic Nutrition*

I am having an afternoon snack, a small bowl of French vanilla nonfat yogurt from Stonyfield Farm. A jaunty brown cow with a blue French cap looks out at me from the carton. On the label it says, "Fruit juice sweetened," which merely means they use a politically correct form of sugar. It also says, "Acidophilus and bifidus cultures." That may be important.

The fermentation of foods is one of the oldest human culinary activities. It dates back to the domestication of animals, which, perhaps incidentally, produced milk, a highly perishable commodity. Nearly every society that ever encountered fresh milk discovered that letting it ferment and turn into sour milk, yogurt, or any of hundreds of variations on that theme made it keep.

Yet we know almost nothing about the effects of fermentation on human health. There are some clues. Miso, fermented soybeans, inhibits mutations and cancer in animals. Wine (page 301), another ancient fermented product, has healthful properties. Sauerkraut, fermented cabbage, is good for a cold, according to a German proverb. Fermenting vegetables in vinegar or wine may release antioxidant flavonoids that are bound with sugar molecules, thus making them more effective (see "Onion," page 211). There is so much more to learn.

About yogurt, we know just a little. It's made by acquainting milk with beneficial bacteria that live on milk sugars. Two kinds of bacteria, *Streptococcus thermophilus* and *Lactobacillus bulgaricus,* are generally used because they make the best-tasting yogurt. These days, yogurt makers often add *Lactobacillus acidophilus* after the yogurt is made; a few add bifidobacterium as well. While largely irrelevant to yogurt making, they may benefit health in other ways, as we'll see.

One nice result of friendly bacteria devouring milk sugar is that yogurt has much less lactose than milk. So yogurt is one of the first dairy foods recommended to people who have low levels of the enzyme lactase, which digests milk sugar. For the lactose intolerant, yogurt is lovely; its efficacy has been established in well-controlled clinical studies of children and adults. The bacteria produce an enzyme, beta-galactosidase, that digests lactose. It does so in the making of the yogurt, but the bacteria are inhibited by refrigeration. Once you eat yogurt, though, these bacteria warm up in the stomach and start replicating, digesting even more lactose. Soon enough, though, the highly acidic environment of the stomach kills off most of them. *Streptococcus thermophilus* and *Lactobacillus bulgaricus* don't survive into the lower intestines.

If you believe you are lactose, or milk, intolerant, it's a good idea not only to get your dairy in the form of yogurt as well as cheese (another fermented product with lower lactose levels) but to consume your dairy in a consistent manner. A small amount daily is easier for your body to handle than eating no dairy and then splurging on, say, a pizza. That's because much of the "digestion" of lactose in people with low levels of the lactase enzyme occurs not in the stomach but in the colon, where bacteria break down milk sugars. If you consume a consistent, moderate amount of dairy foods daily, you encourage the growth of beneficial bacteria in the colon that can handle that milk sugar. Consume dairy on a "feast-

or-famine" basis, on the other hand, and you create the conditions for digestive problems, especially in the colon. Need I go on?

Another nice thing about this ecological paradise for beneficial bacteria in yogurt is that the symbiosis with milk's carbohydrates (including lactose) is so strong that hardly any other bacteria can survive. *Lactobacillus* bacteria in general secrete lactic acid, which makes yogurt acidic—sour to our taste. Few bacteria do well in an acidic medium. This makes yogurt one of the safest foods to eat if you are traveling to a developing country. Yogurt, even unrefrigerated yogurt, kills just about every pathogen known to cause traveler's diarrhea, including *E. coli, Salmonella enteritidis, Listeria monocytogenes,* and *Shigella sonnei.* One 1995 study found that the *Lactobacillus acidophilus* in yogurt killed 16 strains of six species of bacteria that cause human food poisoning.

"It's very difficult for pathogens to grow in yogurt," says Purdue University professor Dennis Savaiano. "You put them in, and they die." That's the case only with yogurt that has active live cultures, of course, not the pasteurized kind you may find in American supermarkets, or frozen yogurt. (Other fermented dairy products such as kefir, buttermilk, and sour cream have the same effect if they contain active live cultures.) What keeps yogurt safe, says Dr. Savaiano, is a combination of acidity (including lactic acid), small amounts of naturally produced hydrogen peroxide, and one more thing: the antibiotics that yogurt bacteria produce.

Some of those antibiotic-producing bacteria may survive the gastrointestinal tract. This is true for many strains of *Lactobacillus acidophilus.* This bacteria is found not only in yogurts that add it but in acidophilus milk. Drinking about two glasses a day of acidophilus milk, for example, has been shown greatly to reduce the ability of the *Salmonella* bacteria to survive in humans. Abroad or at home, consuming dairy foods with acidophilus may act as a protector against pathogens not only in the yogurt itself but in anything we eat. This doesn't mean you should eat undercooked meat and raw salads in Turkey or Egypt and wash it down with yogurt, of course. Be sensible, but eat yogurt, too.

The ability of certain strains of yogurt bacteria, such as acidophilus, to survive the digestive process and make it all the way through the colon allows for another beneficial possibility: improving the ecology of bacteria in the lower intestines and colon. With enough friendly bacteria, pathogens can't take hold. The most immediate clinical application for this is to prevent the diarrhea that often accompanies the administration of antibiotics in a hospital setting. This happens at home sometimes, too, but it's more common among sicker people in hospitals. At Tufts University, researchers Barry Goldin, M.D., and Sherwood Gorbach have developed a specific strain of acidophilus bacteria that not only survives into the intestines and colon but kills the most common cause of recurrent severe diarrhea in children given antibiotics, called *C. difficile*. It may also be effective in treating traveler's diarrhea (I guess for those travelers who didn't eat yogurt while abroad). Their strain is called GG, which stands for Goldin and Gorbach. It is now used clinically, although not yet widely, both in Europe and the United States; doctors have to request the strain from Goldin and Gorbach.

Will eating commercial yogurt that contains everyday strains of *Lactobacillus acidophilus*—or adding the acidophilus cultures you can buy in health food stores to your milk—prevent GI distress in normal, unhospitalized people? It may; many of the acidophilus bacteria do survive and colonize in the colon, making it theoretically less likely for pathogenic bacteria to take hold. But this hasn't been studied well enough to be sure.

If you have been taking antibiotics and want to try yogurt, or acidophilus cultures, it certainly make sense. Be sure to check with your doctor or pharmacist about one thing, though: some antibiotics shouldn't be taken with yogurt. If you take yogurt with ciprofloxacin, for example, it will inactivate the ciprofloxacin.

The other part of the human body that is colonized by beneficial bacteria in healthy women is the vagina. There is now some evidence that yogurt, both as a food and a douche, may prevent infection with the yeast that causes vaginitis. A 1992 study of 33 women with recurrent vaginal candida infections looked at the effects of eight ounces a day of yogurt that contains acidophilus. The women ate the yogurt for six months, then no yogurt for six months. When they were eating yogurt, the incidence of yeast infections went down more than substantially, from an average of nearly two and a half per month to one every three months. Eight of the women who had been eating yogurt for the first six months were so pleased with the results that they refused to participate in the second half of the study. A 1995 Japanese study found that a single "intravaginal application" of about a teaspoon of yogurt containing acidophilus bacteria not only killed all strains of the bacteria that cause vaginal infections but cured six of the 11 women. These are small studies, but they are promising. "It makes sense to me," says Tufts researcher Dr. Barry Goldin. "When you have normal flora in the vagina, the yeast can't take over."

Those bacteria that survive the digestive process—both acidophilus and bifidus—and help create the conditions for friendly flora may also help prevent colon cancer. "Our original theory was that the bacteria in the intestines can activate or deactivate carcinogens," explains Dr. Goldin. When volunteers are fed a low-fat, high-fiber, more plant-based diet, they tend to produce more bacteria that turn potential carcinogens into harmless compounds. When they are fed a high-fat, low-fiber, more meat-centered diet, they produce more carcinogen-activating bacteria.

Acidophilus yogurt does the same thing. It promotes the growth of colon bacteria that deactivate carcinogens. The problem is, the link between this bacterial activation or deactivation of potential carcinogens and the actual development of colon cancer has never been established. "The data support our theory, but we don't know how important these bacteria are," says Dr. Goldin. "We don't know yet what agent or agents cause colon cancer, so it's not easy to prove that bacteria are important."

We already know that eating a more plant-based diet, with plenty of fresh fruits and vegetables and less meat, helps prevent colon cancer. The cup of vanilla-flavored acidophilus-containing yogurt I have finished in the course of writing this chapter may provide additional benefits. It also contains calcium, which itself may reduce the risk of colon cancer (see "Calcium," page 45).

And bifidus? It's in the intestines of breast-fed babies. It may protect them from pathogenic bacteria—may indeed be one reason why breast-fed infants have less diarrhea and intestinal infections than bottle-fed babies. Like acidophilus, it also survives the digestive process, making it into the intestines and colon. In some studies, it also helps prevent bacteria from turning potential carcinogens into real ones.

"People say it's good for you because infants have it," says Dr. Goldin. "Breast-fed infants have very simple flora—these are the first organisms that come up." Whether this means it's also good for adults, though, is unclear. "People think because it's good for infants it's good for adults, but I don't buy it," Dr. Goldin says.

We will almost certainly learn more. Some strains of yogurt bacteria have been found to affect cholesterol metabolism in a beneficial way, while others may lower high blood pressure. Bifidus may prove to be as beneficial as acidophilus, or may turn out to be a reason to breast-feed infants and be irrelevant to adults.

We've been eating cultured dairy foods for tens of thousands of years, our traditional health texts have esteemed them for thousands of years, but we've only begun to study them scientifically in the last few decades. A decade ago, few yogurt manufacturers added acidophilus cultures to their products; now many, perhaps most, do. A few years from now, who knows what wonders might be waiting for me in my vanilla yogurt?

HOMEMADE YOGURT

Homemade yogurt tastes milder and fresher than commercial yogurt, whether you make it low fat or full fat or from goat's or sheep's milk. Use the type of yogurt you prefer as the starter, and make sure it contains active live cultures, preferably including acidophilus.

Many yogurt recipes are misleadingly simple. If you have a pilot light in your oven—I don't—it may be simple; a warm oven interior (110 degrees) is the ideal breeding ground for yogurt cultures. Don't be dismayed if your first batch doesn't succeed; it may take some experimentation to find the spot in your home with the perfect temperature. Once you do, you can make yogurt consistently and easily.

Make sure all the utensils are clean and grease free, and get an instant-read thermometer if you don't have one.

YIELD: 4 CUPS

¼ cup yogurt of your choice
4 cups skim milk, or milk of your choice
2 tablespoons nonfat dried milk (optional)

Put the yogurt in a medium bowl, and let it sit out until it comes to room temperature (about 70 degrees).

Heat the milk in a saucepan over medium-high heat to just below boiling, about 190 degrees. Reduce the heat to medium-low and simmer, uncovered, for 5 to 10 minutes. Stir often so the milk doesn't scorch. Remove the pan from the heat and let the milk cool to 115 degrees; this will take about 20 minutes.

While the milk is cooling, bring 4 cups water to a boil, and pour the water into the container you're using for yogurt making. I have had the best luck with a thermos, which retains the heat very well; a Mason jar or other glass jar with a tight-fitting lid or a porcelain or glass bowl covered tightly with plastic wrap will work, too. Just before you're ready to proceed with the yogurt making, pour the hot water out of the container, and invert the container on a clean kitchen towel to drain.

When the milk has reached 115 degrees, stir about ½ cup of it into the yogurt. Stir in the powdered milk if using; it will help to thicken the yogurt. Stir this tempered yogurt into the remaining milk, pour it all into the warm container, and cover it.

Immediately transfer the container to a warm, draft-free spot. If you're not using the oven, cover the container with an old, heavy blanket. Don't move the yogurt while it's fermenting. Check the yogurt after 4 to 5 hours; if it hasn't begun to thicken, leave it for 3 or 4 more hours, and check again. The longer the yogurt ferments at room temperature, the more acidic the flavor will be.

Transfer the yogurt to a clean container, and refrigerate it; it will firm up when chilled. Save ¼ cup as the starter for your next batch.

YOGURT CHEESE (LABNE)

Fresh yogurt cheese is a delicious alternative to high-fat cream cheese. Because it is never heated, it retains its beneficial active cultures.

YIELD: 14 OUNCES (ABOUT 1 CUP)

4 cups Homemade Yogurt (page 315) or commercial nonfat or low-fat plain yogurt with live active cultures

Line a colander with a double layer of cheesecloth. Pour the yogurt into the colander, gather up the ends of the cheesecloth, and secure them tightly with a rubber band.

Thread the handle of a long wooden spoon under the rubber band, and use it to suspend the yogurt over a soup pot or other deep container. Leave it for at least 8 hours; the liquid will drip out, and the yogurt will compress and thicken. If your kitchen is very warm, do this in the refrigerator. Scrape the yogurt cheese into a container, cover tightly, and refrigerate.

COOL YOGURT SOUP

Don't chop the dill sprigs too finely or they'll become gritty. You can make the soup up to a day ahead, but wait to add the lemon juice just before serving.

YIELD: 4 OR 5 SERVINGS

1¼ pound cucumbers (2 small), peeled and cut into ½-inch slices
     (about 3 cups)
3 garlic cloves, smashed, peeled, and chopped (1 heaping tablespoon)
1 bunch fresh parsley, leaves and stems chopped
1 small jalapeño pepper, seeded and chopped
4 scallions, trimmed and thinly sliced (white and green parts)
3½ cups Homemade Yogurt (page 315) or commercial nonfat or low-fat
     plain yogurt with active live cultures
½ cup coarsely chopped fresh dill
3 radishes, trimmed, halved, and thinly sliced
Juice of half a lemon

Combine the cucumber, garlic, parsley, jalapeño, and all but 2 tablespoons
of the scallions in a food processor. Puree, stopping once to scrape down the
sides of the bowl. Add the yogurt, and process until combined.

Scrape the soup into a large glass bowl, and stir in the dill, radishes, and
lemon juice. Cover tightly with plastic wrap, and chill for 2 or 3 hours. Garnish
with the reserved scallions, and serve.

SPICED LASSI

You can make a double or triple batch of the spice mixture and store it in an airtight container for several months.

YIELD: 6 SERVINGS

FOR THE SPICE MIXTURE:
½ teaspoon whole cumin seeds
1 teaspoon whole cardamom seeds
¼ teaspoon black peppercorns
1 teaspoon whole fennel seeds
2 teaspoons ground ginger

FOR THE LASSI:

3 cups Homemade Yogurt (page 315) or commercial nonfat or low-fat
    yogurt with live, active cultures
3 cups skim milk
1 tablespoon honey, or to taste

Heat a small, dry skillet over high heat. Add the cumin, cardamom, pep-percorns, and fennel seeds. Roast them until aromatic, about 3 minutes, shaking the pan to keep them from scorching.

When the seeds are cool enough to handle, lightly crush the cardamom pods, remove the seeds, and discard pods. Transfer all the seeds and the ginger to a spice grinder, and process into a fine powder.

Combine the spices, yogurt, milk, and honey in a blender. Process until foamy. Pour into 6 tall glasses filled with shaved ice, and serve.

POSTSCRIPT

"Nature loves to hide," wrote the Greek pre-Socratic philosopher Heraclitus. So it is: the more we learn about how the foods we eat affect our health, the deeper the mystery. If there is any truth, it lies in the logic of a whole diet.

We can rejoice in the new scientific discoveries of the beneficial effects from natural compounds. We can learn to use that knowledge. But it would be a mistake to believe that we have conquered Nature, that we can manipulate our bodies with tinctures and tablets, without paying attention to the way we eat, move, feel, think, breathe, and relate to one another. That is the way of Galen, not Hippocrates.

If we are smart, we will be humble. "Phytochemicals" have been part of the human diet since we evolved from primates—we just didn't know their names. In our search for the best way to use our new scientific knowledge, we may do better than to look to the creations of industry motivated by commerce. We can look back to ancient traditions of health and culinary custom, and ahead to an earth-friendly, human-centered dietary pattern.

If we are lucky, what we learn will illuminate the wisdom inherent in a good diet, rather than turn our food into medicine. Industrial food reduces everything to chemicals. Human food takes Nature's bounty and transforms it with skills passed down through generations into dishes that delight the senses as they nourish the body. We are learning much, but we have forgotten much, too. As Plato, another Greek, wrote, "All knowledge is recollection."

SOURCES

Here are some reputable sources for culinary ingredients, kitchen equipment, and medicinal herbs.

Asian Food Ingredients
Katagiri. All kinds of Japanese groceries, including mirin, tamari, sea vegetables. 226 East 59th Street, New York, NY 10022. Telephone: 212-755-3566. Fax: 212-752-4197. Catalogue.
Oriental Food Market and Cooking School, 2801 West Howard Street, Chicago, IL 60645. Telephone: 312-274-2826.

Culinary Herbs
Kalustyan. For dried spices and beans. 123 Lexington Avenue, New York, NY 10016. Telephone: 212-685-3451. Fax: 212-683-8458. Catalogue.
Penzeys, Ltd. They bill themselves as "merchants of quality spices." P.O. Box 1448, Waukesha, WI 53187. Telephone: 414-574-0277. Fax: 414-574-0278. Catalogue.
Sultan's Delight. For flour, grains, beans, sesame seeds, nuts, spices, and Middle Eastern ingredients. P.O. Box 090302, Brooklyn, NY 11209. Telephone: 800-852-5046. Fax: 718-745-2563. Catalogue.

Chilis and Other Mexican Ingredients
The Chili Shop. 109 East Water Street, Santa Fe, NM 87501. Telephone: 505-983-6080. Catalogue.
The Old Southwest Trading Company. P.O. Box 7545, Albuquerque, NM 87194. Telephone: 505-836-0168. Catalogue.

Grains, Flours, and Baking Supplies
King Arthur Flour Baker's Catalogue, P.O. Box 876, Norwich, VT 05055-0876. For whole-wheat and other flours, grains, bread making equipment, flame tamer, parchment paper, scales. P.O. Box 876, Norwich, VT 05055. Telephone: 800-827-6836. Catalogue.

Kitchen Equipment
Bridge Kitchenware, 214 East 52nd Street, New York, NY 10022. Telephone: 212-688-4220. Fax: 212-758-5387. Catalogue ($3).

Lamalle Kitchenware. Food mill, strainers, stove-top grill pan, flame tamer, 36 West 25th Street, New York, NY 10010. Telephone: 800-660-0750. Catalogue.

Organic Fresh Fruits and Vegetables

Diamond Organics. They ship organic fresh fruits and vegetables overnight via Federal Express. P.O. 2159, Freedom, CA 95019. Telephone: 800-922-2396. Catalogue.

Medicinal Herbs, Chinese and Western

East Earth Trade Winds. Chinese tonic formulas and bulk Chinese herbs, including astragalus, ganoderma (reishi), ginseng, poria, and Chinese angelica root (dong quai.) P.O. Box 493151, Redding, CA 96049-3151. Telephone: 800-258-6878. Fax: 916-223-0944. Catalogue.

Institute Herb Company. Bulk herbs, both culinary and medicinal, Eastern and Western; also, a line of tonic formulas developed by Harriet Beinfield, L.Ac., and Efrem Korngold, L.Ac., O.M.D., authors of *Between Heaven and Earth: A Guide to Chinese Medicine.* 1190 Northeast 125th Street, North Miami, FL 33161. Telephone: 305-899-8704. Catalogue.

Roots and Legends. Tonic herbs as teas and as soup mixes. 38 Miller Avenue, Mill Valley, CA 94941. Telephone: 415-381-5631. Catalogue.

The Tea Garden Herbal Emporium. Chinese tonic formulas and some bulk Chinese herbs, such as ginseng. 903 Colorado Avenue, Suite 120, Santa Monica, CA 90401. Telephone: 1-800-288-HERB. Fax: 301-458-6447. Catalogue.

NOTE: If you are interested in finding not only a source of Chinese medicinal herbs but a knowledgeable guide, the best place to start your search for a health care practitioner trained in traditional Chinese medicine is the American Association of Acupuncture and Oriental Medicine (AAAOM). Founded in 1981, it is the nation's largest professional association organized to further the development of acupuncture and Oriental medicine. If you are just looking for a single reference near you, they will give you a name and number over the telephone for free. Telephone: 610-266-1433. Fax: 610-264-2768. For a statewide listing through the mail, send $5 to AAAOM, 433 Front Street, Catasauqua, PA 18032.

SELECTED BIBLIOGRAPHY

In the course of writing this book, I found a few books particularly useful, and refer to them often in the text.

Ayurvedic Herbal Medicine
Frawley, D. *Ayurvedic Healing: A Comprehensive Guide.* Salt Lake City, Utah: Passage Press, 1989. A thorough introduction to principles and techniques for the layman.

Frawley, D., and V. Lad. *The Yoga of Herbs.* Twin Lakes, Wis.: Lotus Press, 1986. An herbal.

Kapoor, L. D. *CRC Handbook of Ayurvedic Medicinal Plants.* Boca Raton, Fla.: CRC Press, 1990. An academic text, citing traditional uses and scientific research.

Tiwari, M. *A Life of Balance: The Complete Guide to Ayurvedic Nutrition & Body Types with Recipes.* Rochester, Vt.: Healing Arts Press, 1995. One woman's personal guide, with recipes.

History
Duke, J. *Medicinal Plants of the Bible.* New York: Trado-Medic Books, 1983.

Grieve, M. *A Modern Herbal.* New York: Dover Publications, 1931, 1971, 1982. A classic; most useful now for old herbals she quotes, and the description of then-contemporary uses.

Griggs, B. *Green Pharmacy: The History and Evolution of Herbal Western Medicine.* Rochester, Vt.: Healing Arts Press, 1981, 1991. A fascinating, erudite history.

Moldenke, H. N., and A. L. Moldenke. *Plants of the Bible.* New York: Dover Publications, 1952, 1986.

Rohde, E. S. *The Old English Herbals.* New York: Dover Publications, 1922, 1971. A wonderful romp through English herbal history.

Western Herbalism
Castleman, M. *The Healing Herbs.* Emmaus, Pa.: Rodale Press, 1991. An accurate, entertaining description of science and lore behind 100 herbs.

Duke, J. *Handbook of Medicinal Herbs.* Boca Raton, Fla.: CRC Press, 1985. An academic text, combining traditional use with scientific studies.

Elliot, R., and C. de Paoli. *Kitchen Pharmacy.* London: Tiger Books International, 1991. Published in England, this book combines food and herbs in a holistic approach; with recipes.

Gladstar, R. *Herbal Healing for Women.* New York: Fireside, 1993. Gladstar has been practicing herbalism for nearly 30 years, and her experience and common sense show.

Hobbs, C. *Handbook for Herbal Healing.* Capitola, Calif.: Botanica Press, 1994. A concise description of herbal combinations for different health concerns.

Mowrey, D. B. *Herbal Tonic Therapies.* New Canaan, Conn.: Keats Publishing, 1993. A new approach to herbal medicine, from a prominent American researcher in the field.

Tyler, V. *Herbs of Choice,* 3d ed. New York: Haworth Press, 1993. A science-based book for practioners of herbal medicine.

Tyler, V. *The Honest Herbal,* 3d ed. New York: Haworth Press, 1993. A science-based account of the practical significance of dozens of herbs.

Holistic Medicine

Weil, A. *Spontaneous Healing.* New York: Alfred A. Knopf, 1995. A serious attempt to explore what a medical system based on the body's innate ability to heal itself could be like.

East/West Herbalism

Holmes, P. *The Energetics of Western Herbs: Integrating Western and Oriental Herbal Medicine Traditions,* vol. 1. Boulder, Colo.: Artemis Press, 1989. An exhilarating attempt to combine ancient Greek and Asian systems of herbal medicine.

Pitchford, P. *Healing with Whole Foods: Oriental Traditions and Modern Nutrition.* Berkeley, Calif.: North Atlantic Books, 1993. A practical, food-based approach to prevention and treatment.

Tierra, M. *Planetary Herbology.* Twin Lakes, Wis.: Lotus Press, 1988. A comprehensive, accessible book that combines Western and Eastern descriptions of hundreds of herbs.

Traditional Chinese Medicine (TCM)

Beinfield, H., and E. Korngold. *Between Heaven and Earth: A Guide to Chinese Medicine.* New York: Ballantine Books, 1991. A beautifully written book by two practitioners of acupuncture that describes traditional Chinese medicine in contemporary, practical terms.

Bensky, D., and R. L. Barolet. *Chinese Herbal Medicine Formulas and Strategies.* Seattle, Wash.: Eastland Press, 1990. A book of traditional formulas, of particular interest to practitioners.

Bensky, D., and A. Gamble. *Chinese Herbal Medicine: Materia Medica.* Seattle, Wash.: Eastland Press, 1993. The best scientific resource in English.

Flaws, B., and H. L. Wolfe. *Prince Wen Hui's Cook: Chinese Dietary Therapy.* Brookline, Mass.: Paradigm Publications, 1983. An eclectic account of Chinese food theories.

Reid, D. *A Handbook of Chinese Healing Herbs.* Boston: Shambhala Publications, 1995. A handy reference guide by a practitioner of TCM.

Nutrition

Barnett, R., ed. *The American Health Food Book.* New York: Dutton, 1991. An earlier work by the author, which combines nutrition reporting and recipes.

Keys, A., and M. Keys. *Eat Well and Stay Well.* Garden City, N.Y.: Doubleday & Company, Inc., 1959. A classic, reprinted in 1975, that is worth revisiting.

Pennington, J. A. T. *Bowes & Church's Food Values of Portions Commonly Used,* 16th ed. Philadelphia: J.B. Lippincott Company, 1994. A practical source of nutritional data.

Miscellaneous

Fisher, M. F. K. *A Cordiall Water.* New York: North Point Press, 1961, 1981. A beautiful book about food and folk cures.

INDEX

Chinese angelica root, 71–75; Blood-Building Lamb Stew, 75

Chinese Herbal Medicine: Formulas and Strategies (Bensky and Barolet), 31–32, 73–74, 187

Chinese Herbal Medicine: Materia Medica (Bensky and Gamble), 26, 30–31, 71, 76, 99, 164, 186, 201

Chinese Yam and Jujube Congee, 107–8

chrysanthemum, 76–78; Chrysanthemum-Honeysuckle Tea, 77–78

cinnamon, 78–80; Mexican Rice Milk with Rice Bran Oil and Cinnamon, 80; Tea, 79–80

circulation, 72, 78–79, 138, 139

clams, 81–82, 184

codonopsis, 25, 83–87; Energy-Boosting Asian Fish Stew, 85–86

coffee, 79, 87–92, 175, 252

cold, common, 136, 137, 150, 215, 240, 272, 282, 290, 302, 311

Coles, William, 113, 292, 295

colic, 113

Commonplace Book of Cookery, A, 108

Concentrate, Cranberry, 95–96

congee(s), 30; American Granola, 296; Chinese Yam and Jujube, 107–8; Fennel and Ginger Congee, 152; Leafy Greens, 251; Scallion, Ginger and Cinnamon, 152

Conney, Allan H., 233, 282

Connors, William E., 278

constipation, 224, 297

Cooling Steaming Soup, 58–59

Cool Yogurt Soup, 316–17

Cordiall Water, A (Fisher), 215, 298

coronary heart disease, 17, 26, 29, 277, 285–88; increasing risk of, 181–82; predicting risk of, 130; prevention of, 121, 133, 290; risk of, 46, 53, 54, 84, 88, 89, 106, 110; treatment of, 25, 178–79

Cost, Bruce, 146

coughing, 150, 199–200

coumarins, 222–23

cranberries, 93–98; Concentrate, 95–96;

Dessert Soup, 96–97; Jam, 97–98; Real Juice, 94–95; Sorbet, 98

CRC Handbook of Ayurvedic Medicinal Plants (Kapoor), 99, 280

Crunchy Pickled Garlic, 144–45

Culpeper, Nicholas, 99–100

Cuppage, Francis E., 299

Curry Powder, 283–84

Custard, Banana, 228

cynarin, 20

cynaropicrin, 20

cysteine, 272–73

daidzein, 190–91

daidzin, 190–91

dairy products, 46, 47–49. *See also* yogurt.

dandelion, 99–105; Dandelion Root Tea, 101; Fresh Dandelion-Leaf Salad, 103–4; Spring Tonic, 101–3

decoctions, 30, 84–85, 187. *See also* tea(s).

dementia, 157, 233

depression, 130–31, 157, 158, 187–88

DHEA, 105–6

diabetes, 30, 79, 100, 121–22, 163, 208, 215, 226–27, 291

diarrhea, 16, 256, 305, 312–13

diet, 11–12

digestion, 30–32, 83, 99–100, 107

dioscorea, 105–8; Chinese Yam and Jujube Congee, 107–8

Dioscorides, 120, 138, 229

diosgenin, 105, 120, 229

diuretics, 30, 99–100

Divine Husbandman's Classic of the Materia Medica, The, 189

Dr. Brown's Cel-Ray Tonic, 5, 60

Dorsch, Walter, 212

Duke, James A., 51–53, 120, 174, 200, 233, 257, 299–300

Dumplings, Spicy Shiitake, 243–44

ear infections, 136–37

Earthy Garlic Soup, 141

Eat Well and Stay Well (Keys and Keys), 12, 19

Keys, Margaret, 12, 19, 210
kidney stones, 297
kitchen equipment, 13, 320
Kitchen Pharmacy (Elliot and Paoli), 43–44, 212
Kitcheri, 111, 112
Korngold, Efrem, 27, 71, 83, 105, 238, 268
kudzu, 189–94; Chicken Breast with Fresh Ginseng, 171–72; Peachy-Orange Kudzu Fruity, 194; Strawberry Kudzu Fruity, 192–93; Strawberry-Mango Kudzu Smoothie, 193; Vegetable Stir-Fry with Kudzu and Green Tea, 192
Kushi, Lawrence H., 137

Labne (Yogurt Cheese), 316
lactose, 311–12
Lad, Vasant, 105, 280, 283
Lassi, Spiced, 317–18
lavender, 194–99; Bath, 198; Pillow, 198; Sweet Dreams Tea, 199
lead poisoning, 138
Leafy Greens Congee, 251
Leighton, Terrance, 110, 213–15
Lemonade, Bancha, 256
lentinan, 240–41
Leyel, C. F., 232
Li, Chiang J., 282–83
licorice, 199–204; Astragalus Tea, 27; Baked Licorice Apples, 18–19; Chrysanthemum-Honeysuckle Tea, 77–78; Dandelion Root Tea, 101; Fenugreek Tea, 122–23; Five-Flavor Tea, 239; Four-Gentlemen Soup, 32, 33–34; Ginseng Tea, 169; Heartbreak Hotel Porridge with Jujube-Licorice Tea, 188–89; Honey-Roasted Licorice Sticks, 203–4; Honey-Roasted Licorice Tea, 204
liferoot, 120
lignans, 126–27
ligustrum, 26, 29; Vegetarian Wei Qi Soup, 27–29
Lin, Robert I., 138
Lind, James, 299

Linnaeus, 274
liqueurs: American Ginseng, 172–73; Artichoke and Milk Thistle, 21–23; Fenugreek, 123–24; Ginger Brandy, 155; Memory, 160–61
liver, 20, 23, 64, 83, 84, 99–100, 105, 107, 197, 205, 233, 238, 280, 300, 307
longevity, 86–87, 110, 167–68
long pepper, 204–7
Loosli, Alvin R., 181
low back pain, 89
Lucky-Heart Soup, 275
lungs, 52, 64, 140, 222, 233, 249
lupus, 25, 106, 277, 278
lutein, 249
Lycium berries, 86–87; Energy-Boosting Asian Fish Stew, 85–86
lycopene, 265–67
Lydia Pinkham's Vegetable Compound, 6, 118–20, 122, 183

malaria, 5
Marcella's Italian Cooking (Hazan), 137
Marriage Present, A (Hacket), 232
Martarano, Joseph, 158
Mastering the Art of French Cooking (Child), 18
Materia Medica (Dioscorides), 138
Materia Medica (Linnaeus), 274
McCaleb, Rob, 180
McClesky, Edwin W., 163–64
Medicinal Mushrooms (Hobbs), 229
Mediterranean diet, 12, 19, 40–41, 111, 149, 208–9, 293, 294
melanoma, 222
memory, 158, 166–67, 231–32, 233
Memory Liqueur, 160–61
meningitis, 136
menopause, 106–7, 120, 127, 187, 261
menstrual problems, 45–46, 49, 72–74, 113, 120, 257
Messina, Mark, 260–61
methionine, 131–32
Mexican Rice Milk with Rice Bran Oil and Cinnamon, 80

AUTHOR'S NOTE

The author welcomes correspondence, including comments, experiences with recipes, and requests for scientific citations. He may be contacted by mail: Robert A. Barnett, P.O. Box 1674, NY, NY 10025 or e-mail: rbarnett@interport.net.